EXCAVATING the BIBLE

EXCAVATING the BIBLE

New Archaeological Evidence for the Historical Reliability of Scripture

YITZHAK MEITLIS, Ph.D.

Eshel Books

Baltimore • Washington

Manufactured in the United States of America

Published by:

Eshel Books
8600 Foundry Street
Mill Box 2043
Savage, Maryland 20763
800-953-9929
www.EshelBooks.com

In Cooperation with:

David Dov Foundation
603 Twin Oaks Drive
Lakewood, New Jersey 08701
www.DavidDov.org

Library of Congress Cataloging-in-Publication Data

Meitlis, Yitzhak.
  Excavating the Bible : new archaeological evidence for the historical re-liability of Scripture / Yitzhak Meitlis.
    p. cm.
  Includes bibliographical references (p.   ) and index.
  ISBN 978-0-935437-41-6
  1. Bible--Antiquities. 2. Palestine--Antiquities. 3. Excavations (Archaeology)--Palestine. 4. Bible--Evidences, authority, etc. I. Title.
  BS621.M45 2012
  221.9′3--dc23
                              2012000258

In memory of my father, Abraham (Adam) Meitlis, who planted within me a love of the Bible and of the Land.

———————————

The David Dov Foundation wishes to thank the following individuals for their assistance:
Dr. Irving and Cherna Moskowitz
Dr. Bernard Lander z"l
Leonard A. Wein, Jr.
Lee C. and Anne Samson

CONTENTS

FOREWORD

It is with the greatest of hope that we bring this long anticipated study of Biblical Archaeology by Professor Yizhak Meitlis to the minds of religious leaders, interested readers and open-minded archaeologists.

It is of great significance that those of us who believe in the reliability and sanctity of Scripture finally view the many findings of Biblical archaeologists, which demonstrate that much of what has been unearthed under Israel's soil, is also found in the Biblical text.

The world may be divided into those who believe that God is the Author of the Bible and Creator of the world, those who think otherwise and those who are just not sure.

For those for whom the Bible is a matter of faith, no convincing is necessary and for people who reject its truth, perhaps no convincing is possible. *Excavating the Bible* is meant to encourage readers to discover that many of the events described in the Bible not only happened, but that they can be scientifically corroborated, an indication that the entire scriptural text is accurate as well. This is a simple thought with profound consequences.

Many people who are unsure will find assurance. Some will feel more comfortable in their beliefs. Others will just enjoy the excellent scholarship. It has been said that our role as human beings is to help "perfect the world." By demonstrating the reliability of the Biblical narrative, perhaps we can cast new light on the foundation of much of civilization.

Along with Rabbi Pinchas Stolper, President of the David Dov Foundation, I am optimistic that *Excavating the Bible* will mark a turning point in Biblical Archaeology,. We hope it will encourage more people to find their heritage in the excavations taking place in Israel and recognize their origins in the Bible itself.

Leonard A. Wien, Jr.
Vice President
David Dov Foundation

ACKNOWLEDGMENTS

I wish to thank the following who were of significant assistance in bringing this book about: Mr. Shlomo Musaiif, a lover of Israel and archaeology. Professor Israel Rosenson and Dr. Gabi Barkai who read the manuscript and made brilliant suggestions. Dr. Orli Albak who was helpful with vocabulary. Rabbi Pinchas Stolper was supportive in every possible way. Finally, I wish to thank the Israeli Department of Education for awarding me the 2005 Prize for Innovation in Israel Studies.

WHY THIS BOOK HAD TO BE WRITTEN

Defusing the Tension between the Bible and Archaeology

Until the 1970s, Biblical archaeologists viewed the historical sections of the Bible as reflecting some degree of historical authenticity, even though not everyone accepted all of the details at face value. No serious arguments raged over the existence of the Patriarchs; no stormy sessions were held over the reliability of the Exodus account. Though some scholars looked for natural reasons to explain the plagues in Egypt and the splitting of the Re(e)d Sea, it was clear that the Israelites entered the land of Israel from the Sinai Desert.

The major argument of the 1960s was over the path the

Israelites followed in the desert and the way they entered the Holy Land. Did the Israelites mount a comprehensive military operation when they entered the land, as described in the Book of Joshua, or was the Israelite entry slower and more gradual? In contrast, there was no argument at all about the era of David and Solomon.

Yet winds of Bible-criticism blowing from various European universities began to fascinate and influence Israeli scholars. During the '70s, and the early '80s, the first generation of archaeological researchers in Israel passed away. They were replaced by a new generation of scholars, some of whom tried to cut a new path. The new approach led to an impasse. During the past few decades, tension between the new archaeology and the Bible has grown more palpable.

The scholars of the new school dismiss the authenticity of most of the Bible out-of-hand. In their view, the books of the Pentateuch, Joshua, Judges, Samuel, and parts of Kings are nothing more than folklore, without any historical basis. The new rules of the game are: (1) the more ancient the period, the less the Bible reflects historical truth, and (2) some degree of historical truth could be ascribed only to events confirmed by external sources, i.e., Assyrian, Babylonian or Egyptian documents.

Our challenge in this volume will be to put the approach adopted by these later scholars to the test. Is there a contradiction between archaeological findings and the Biblical text? The question has become a wedge between Bible scholars and archaeologists. Though it intrigues many Bible scholars, they tend to ignore archaeology altogether, due largely to the dogmatic attitude of today's archaeologists. At the same time, many archaeologists refrain from referencing verses in the Bible when evaluating archaeological finds, even when to do so seems obvious and logical.

The gap has been steadily widening. The group known as "the Bible deniers" is to all intents and purposes cutting the ground away from under their own feet, for most general interest in Biblical archaeology is generated by people's desire to understand the Bible. It is the Bible that links Judaism and Christianity with the archaeological sites of the Holy Land. Biblical archaeology without the Bible becomes a dry study of yet another branch of human culture that interests only the very few.

Need this gap exist? This work examines, using archaeological instruments, whether there is indeed a clash between archaeology and the Bible. Having earned a doctorate in archaeology from Tel Aviv University, with many years of service as a teacher of geography and Bible studies, this writer believes that no substantive contradiction exists between the two fields.

No significant discovery has been made that indicates any contradiction. On the contrary, recent studies have confirmed the links between the Bible and the material findings of the last few years. The present crisis stems from a passing fad which has given rise to a mistaken interpretation of archaeological findings. I am sorry to report that these interpretations are often based on a lack of objectivity on the part of the researcher who, on occasion, is even tempted to distort archaeological data in order to strengthen his own weak arguments.

This book will center on the history of the Judean Hills– the epicenter of the Jewish people for many generations, from the Period of the Patriarchs until the destruction of Solomon's Temple.

Chapter 7 is devoted to geography and pure archaeology. It reviews archaeological finds in the Judean Hills, and is based largely on my extensive research. In general, the material in this book relies on the work I carried out throughout the Judean Hills as well as on my analysis of other studies in this field. I have attempted not to go into too much detail with regard to pottery and architecture–details important for research purposes, but unnecessarily tiresome for the lay reader. Nevertheless, the archaeological and geographical data may well prove useful to anyone interested in a more profound study of the elements of the archaeological survey carried out in the Judean Hills that provide firm grounds for my arguments on the topics presented throughout this book. It is for the benefit of these readers that this material is included.

Chapter 8 is a succinct summary and a list of conclusions. This will allow the more casual reader to glean the significance of the archaeological data presented.

The reader may well ask why I have chosen to focus on the Judean Hills for the purpose of legitimizing the Biblical account. One may further ask if the Bible needs to be "defended" on scientific grounds.

Why Explore the Judean Hills?

The unique nature of the Judean Hills is expressed in their simplicity and isolation. They extend over a region that reaches an altitude of some 1,000 meters above sea level, they border on the deserts in the south (the Negev) and the east (the Judean Desert).

Hundreds of millions of people view this region as their spiritual homeland and have willingly sacrificed their lives for it, generation after generation. The area includes three cities, only some 20 or 30 kilometers from one another, on which the interest of the entire world focuses: Hebron, Bethlehem, and Jerusalem.

Hebron was where the Patriarchs and Matriarchs of the Jewish people–Abraham, Isaac and Jacob; Sarah, Rebecca and Leah–lived and were buried. It was from Hebron that Joseph was sent to see how his brothers were faring, an action which led to the period of Israelite servitude in Egypt. Hebron served as King David's first royal capital. The fourth Matriarch, Rachel, was buried near Bethlehem, to the north of Hebron, where Ruth and the Moabitess later lived. David, the founder of the Israelite kingdom, was born there, as was Jesus, according to Christian sources. Further north, there are another three sites of interest: Bet-El, Shiloh and Shechem.

High above them all, reigns Jerusalem, the city ruled by "Melchizedek, King of Shalem, Priest of the Supreme Deity" (Gen. 14). Isaac was bound upon the altar by Abraham on the mount where the political capital and spiritual center of the Israelite nation was later established. It was in Jerusalem that the prophet Isaiah spoke out; in nearby Anatot where the prophet Jeremiah lived; while somewhat to the south, in Tekoa, lived the prophet Amos. It was to Jerusalem that the Babylonian exiles returned, which led to the building of the Second Holy Temple by Zerubavel and it was there that Ezra and Nehemiah rallied the people to revive Judaism.

Ever since those times, it was to Jerusalem that the Jewish people lifted its eyes in prayer. For over 2,500 years, Jerusalem has served as the Jewish national center, despite its repeated destructions and the exile of its people time and again. Christianity and Islam each look to Jerusalem as a spiritual center. Because of the centuries-old desire to rule over this holy city, bloody battles have been fought at its walls and in its streets.

But this is not merely past history, for today Jerusalem once again is the focal point of struggle. This city, which has become the largest metropolis in Israel, functions today as a site holy to each of the main monotheistic faiths.

Some four kilometers to the north of the Old City of Jerusalem, we find Givat Shaul (Tel-el-Ful), the capital city of the very first king of Israel–Saul. Nearby is Ramah, the birthplace and home of the last of the Judges, the prophet Samuel, whose task it was to anoint the first two kings of Israel.

In the northern part of this region is Bet-El (Bittin), we find the place where Jacob had his dream of the angels ascending and descending the heavens, and where Jeroboam erected a golden calf to counter the monotheistic influence of the city of Jerusalem. We can state with certainty, therefore, that the geographical background of the Bible extends in the main from Shechem to Be'er-Sheva and centers on the Judean hill country.

It is interesting that the region is rocky and its agricultural potential is limited and sparse. The great Bible commentator Rabbi Shlomo Yitzhaki (Rashi) noted, (in the Babylanian Talmud Sotah 34B) "There is no rockier spot in the entire land of Israel than Hebron" (in his commentary on Numbers 13:22). Yet surprisingly enough, it was those 1,600 square kilometers of rocky hills that shaped the nature of the Hebrew nation and of the faiths that derived from it.

The Uniqueness of the Bible

Is there a rational explanation for the fact that the Bible, the masterpiece which underwent the final stages of its formulation[1] in the Judean Hills, broke out of the narrow confines of its local origin and permeated the entire world? What is there in this work that intrigues millions of people from Australia to Scandinavia and from Japan to America?

What is it that tempts so many people to seek in this ancient text an historical framework, a book of advice and inspiration, and a wellspring of consolation? For that matter, what prompts the strict criticism and microscopic examination of its texts by academic institutions?

Why *has* the Bible recently become a toreador's red cape that arouses so many people to try to debunk its historical authenticity? The explanation for this development is probably not in the realm of the rational, for the Bible touches hidden sensitivities in the human soul, preventing indifference. Some study it from an historical or a geographical point of view, while others focus on its literary aspects, and still others deal with its legal and philosophical facets. For each of these pursuits there is an appropriate niche.

Yet there are also scholars who tear the Biblical text apart in the same way a pathologist works over a cadaver. They dig into its very innards, as it were, and interpret it as if it was nothing but a collection of assorted pieces randomly assembled. They have succeeded, by design or otherwise, in detaching themselves and others from the Bible and from Biblical values.[2] These scholars devote their very existences to negating the Bible and denying its beauty and its relevance.

Before turning to archeology as a key to understanding the Bible (and the Bible as a key to archaeology), we must stress that the purpose of the Bible is spiritual, moral and ethical, and that it comprises various levels of comprehension accordingly. The Bible is definitely not a history book nor does it strive to be one.

This fact was noted by Jewish sages many centuries ago when they formulated the rule that "chronology is of no significance in the Torah [Bible]" (Babylonian Talmud, *Pesachim* 6b). So it is not surprising to find that not all the travails of the Jewish nation are recorded in the Bible. The omission of various events does not testify in any manner to a lack of knowledge of the compilers of the Bible. To paraphrase the well-known adage of the sages regarding prophecy, "a prophecy needed for all time was recorded [in the Bible]; that which was not needed was omitted" (Babylonian Talmud, *Megillah* 14a), we may state that details of an event needed for the purposes of guiding future generations was recorded in the Bible, while one that was not needed was left out. To achieve its ethical ends, the Bible employed various scattered events taken from the historical past of the nation, yet the events and the reality they describe faithfully reflect historical truth.[3]

The Uses and Limits of Archaeology

Several points must be made at the outset so that a reader not specializing in the archaeology of the Biblical period will be able to understand both the approach taken and the basis of my conclusions.

First: Archaeology, which is based mainly on the study of the traces of the past that are found *in situ*--i.e., in the location where the event took place--is not and *cannot* be the entire story of the past. Archaeology does indeed have an important role to play in the reconstruction of the past, but it cannot stand alone, as the school of "new archaeology" would have us believe.[4] Without available additional testimony that has survived, e.g., the Assyrian and Egyptian written historical records, the ceramic vessels by themselves cannot provide even a single absolute date.[5]

The pottery on which archaeologists build their chronology in Israel can provide, at best, relative dating. Absolute dating is possible only when there are archaeological findings unmistakably linked with some Assyrian, Egyptian, or biblical finding dated by means of historical sources.

For example, the dating of the Early Bronze Age II (approximately 2800-2600 BCE) is based on Egyptian findings in Israel and on Canaanite vessels found in graves in Egypt which were dated on the basis of inscriptions, such as those known as "Abydos Vessels." These vessels were discovered in the grave of an Egyptian king at Abydos in Egypt. Since the written Egyptian sources enable us to date the death of this king, we are also able to date the Canaanite vessels found in his grave.[6]

The chronology of Iron Age II (the period of the Israelite Monarchy) is based on an attempt to correlate various strata of destruction with the wars documented in historical sources, such as the expedition undertaken by the Egyptian king, Shishak, at the end of the 10th century BCE, the expeditions of Assyrian kings Tiglat-Pileser and Sennacherib towards the end of the 8th century BCE, and those of the Babylonian king Nebuchadnezzar at the beginning of the 6th century BCE.[7] Any second thoughts on the significance and nature of an historical source of this type must inexorably result in a revision of the dating of the various strata in different archaeological sites in Israel.

Second: We must yet be aware that, in certain cases, the archaeological findings in Israel do not match Egyptian sources. For example: an Egyptian source tells of an expedition by Egyptian King Thutmose III to the land of Canaan at the beginning of the 15th century BCE, including the episode of a seven-month siege of Megiddo,[8] but archaeological research reveals that Megiddo was not surrounded by a wall at this time.[9] In the tablets of Merneptah, an Egyptian king who reigned in Egypt at the close of the 13th century BCE, Ashkelon is described as a fortified city; archaeological research, however, has found no sign of any fortifications dating from this period.[10] The common denominator of these two archaeological sites is the fact that Middle Bronze Age fortifications do indeed exist there, though there is no evidence of any fortifications dating from the Late Bronze Age, when these two Egyptian monarchs ruled.

A similar problem exists with regard to 14th century BCE Megiddo. We learn from the Egyptian El-Amarna letters that Megiddo was an important city at the time.[11] However, archaeological findings indicate that Megiddo was a small, unfortified town during this period.[12] One must proceed with caution, therefore, in making chronological determinations based on archaeological findings or, alternately, on the Egyptian sources, for these do not always correspond with one another. Yet, as we have seen, they are very strongly intertwined.

Third: Most of the archaeological findings in inhabited strata are merely "informative fragments" relating mainly to the end of the period, rather than to its beginning. It is very difficult for archaeologists to draw an accurate picture that also includes the early history of a settlement that existed continuously over a long period of time. For instance, archaeology is unable to portray Jerusalem during the period of the Jewish return from the Babylonian exile, or during the Hellenistic period because walls from these periods have not been found. Without written historical sources, almost nothing would be known of the history of Jerusalem between the 6th and 1st centuries BCE.

Fourth: A clear distinction should be made between various parts of the country and especially between the hilly regions and the plains. The hill country--and mainly the Judean Hills--was quite isolated and historical processes took place there more slowly than elsewhere.[13] Settlement patterns, burial customs, and pottery styles varied considerably from one area to another as well. Imported implements were less common in the hilly regions. Political changes that occurred in the coastal plain did not necessarily have any effect on what transpired in the hills. The inhabitants of the plains were afraid to traverse the mountainous regions,[14] and this fact undoubtedly influenced the relations between the populations of the hill country and those of the plains.

Because of these differences, no analogies may be drawn automatically from the historical processes in progress on the plains to those of the mountainous areas. It is quite possible that pottery considered characteristic of a certain period and common in the plains was not to be found at all in the hills. There were periods when a new ceramic era began in the plains, while in the hill country the pottery characteristic of the previous era was still in use.[15] The significance of this factor in the dating of archaeological sites is discussed later in this volume.

Fifth: Arguments in the fields of the humanities and social sciences, though apparently scientific in nature, are largely shaped by the cultural backgrounds and *weltanschauung* of the scholars wording them. In this regard, for example, Henri Pirenne writes, "It is thus possible to say that even in its purist and most substantive expression, *history is a science based upon hypotheses,* or–in other words–a subjective science."[16][emphasis added] However, so long as the facts presented in each argument are correct, complete and accepted, and the debate concerns their interpretation, the discussion is a legitimate one. Only when "scientific" arguments are based upon partial data only--or in extreme cases upon distorted data--the debate loses its scientific character altogether and consequently ceases to be a legitimate one.

One of the "new" historians, Benny Morris, has written against the "old" historians: "History is made up of an infrastructure of facts which the historian has to uncover and combine with one another to make up a logical and acceptable description of events, personalities and processes. A 'good' historian will reveal the facts and put them together in such a way as to create a logical, persuasive narrative; an historian who is less 'good' reveals only part of the facts (ignores others or even conceals them) and creates a narrative which is not as good, not as logical, not as credible, and not as convincing."[17] On this, Professor Oded Shermer says: "This is not a question of distorting the facts or problems of that nature–*such actions would lead to the expulsion of the historian from the research community*"[18] [emphasis added].

Morris' description applies unfortunately to some of the "new" archaeologists and historians, those who are prepared to ignore scientific facts that disprove their claims. For example, the elimination of the term "Patriarchal Period" by some archaeologists is based on a number of false claims, as we shall demonstrate in this book. As a result of my own familiarity with some of these scholars (some were my own teachers in the past, to whom I am deeply indebted) and my acknowledgement of their considerable professional abilities, I feel that it is not a case of ignorance of the facts, but rather of a clear lack of objectivity. They are striving to present a pre-determined thesis, depending upon their assumption that *the average reader is unaware of the present state of modern archaeology, which actually debunks the picture they present.*

My goal, therefore, is to propose an alternative—well grounded in empirical findings and in my familiarity with the geographical arena—which relates respectfully to the Bible, the book that provides us *inter alia* with many historical and geographical facts.

The objective is to restore the Bible to its former stature as a reliable historical record, while at the same time legitimating the study of archaeology for Bible scholars as an adjunct which will greatly enlighten their understanding of the Biblical Era.

UNDERSTANDING
TIME AND PLACE

lbrecht Alt, a German scholar who dealt with the historical geography of Israel during the Biblical period, realized that biblical studies are best when they view extended periods of time; in that way, they can register continuity, on the one hand, and dynamic change, on the other.[19] The present work draws its inspiration from Alt, in accordance with the principle of "longue durée,"[20] which was developed by the French historian Fernand Braudel. He concluded that one must observe historical processes over extended periods of time and that such processes operate in accordance with a kind of "natural law."

The beginnings of the settlement processes taking place in Israel during the Biblical periods were already discernible in the Intermediate Bronze Age (2200-1950 BCE). Archeological research shows that activity in all the central sites of the Jerusalem Hills and those of Bet-El, as well as in many burial sites, commenced in the Intermediate Bronze Age, and that many material characteristics of the prevalent economy and culture originated in this period. This book will therefore begin with the Intermediate Bronze Age, of which more is unknown than known.[21]

Chronology

In the study of Israel, archaeological periods are known by various names, reflecting varying dating systems. The periods referred to in this book are:

♦ **2200 – 1950 BCE** – Intermediate Bronze Age

♦ **1950 – 1800 BCE** – Middle Bronze Age I

♦ **1800 – 1550 BCE** – Middle Bronze Age II
(1800-1400 BCE, according to an alternative system outlined below.)

♦ **1550 – 1200 BCE** – Late Bronze Age

♦ **1200 – 1000 BCE** – Iron Age I
(the period of Israelite settlement)

♦ **1000 – 586 BCE – Iron Age II**

(the period of the Israelite monarchies)

In the case of several of these periods, my opinion differs somewhat from accepted convention. See the Chronological Table on which my dating system is listed under "Alternate Dating System." (page 16)

The Geographical Structure of the Judean Hills

The Judean Hills rise above the lower regions surrounding them on all sides. To the south and east, they border desert areas, while to the west they adjoin lower regions that form an interim buffer zone between the coastal plain and the hill

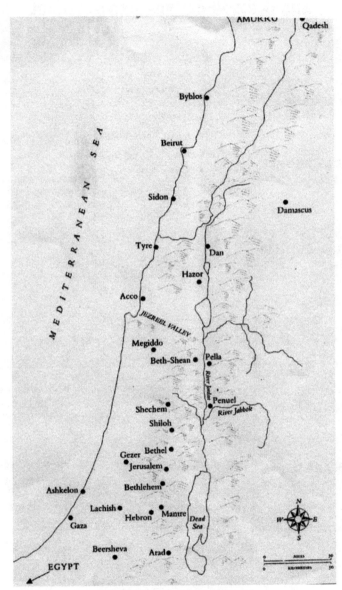

Ancient Palestine, Eretz Israel

CHRONOLOGICAL TABLE OF BIBLICAL ARCHAEOLOGICAL PERIODS OF ISRAEL

PERIOD	ACCEPTED DATING SYSTEM	CHARACTERISTICS
INTERMEDIATE BRONZE AGE	2200 - 1950 BCE	Initial use of bronze, small villages, population mostly nomadic
MIDDLE BRONZE AGE I	1950 - 1800 BCE	Renewed urbanization in Israel; In the Judean Hills, continuation of nomadic life; on the plains – renewed urbanization
MIDDLE BRONZE AGE II	1800 - 1550 BCE	Development of urbanization and fortifications; Violent destruction at the close of the period
LATE BRONZE AGE	1550 - 1150 BCE	Renewed urbanization; Egyptian rule of Israel; Large number of imported vessels in the country
IRON AGE I	1150 - 1000 BCE	Spread of use of iron; Israelite settlement in the hill country and Philistines on coastal plain
IRON AGE II	1000 - 586 BCE	Renewed urbanization; Central planning throughout the country; Spread of Hebrew script.

ALTERNATE DATING SYSTEM	AS REFLECTED IN THE BIBLE
2200 - 1950 BCE in the plains, to 1800 BCE in the Judean hill country	
1950 - 1800 BCE Urbanization only in the plain	Beginning of Patriarchal Period
1800 - 1400 BCE Renewed urbanization in the plain and throughout the country; Violent destruction at the close of the period	Patriarchal Period Exile in Egypt, exodus, desert encampments
1400 - 1150 BCE from here Canaanite culture and some Egyptian control, mainly in the valleys and on the coastal strip; Israelite culture in the hill country	Israelite Conquest of Canaan under Joshua Period of the Judges until the penetration of the Philistines
1150 - 1000 BCE Israelites concentrated in the hills, Philistines in the plains from 1150 BCE	Period of the Judges until the conquest of Jerusalem in the time of David
1000 - 586 BCE Renewed urbanization all over the country	Period of Israelite Monarchy and the first Temple

country. An understanding of the geography of this heartland, in which the Israelites lived for centuries, is important.

To understand the history of a region, it is critical to be familiar with its geography. The Judean Hills and surrounding areas are no different in this respect, for its geography played a key role in peace and war, through famine and prosperity. Before delving into details about the excavations that penetrated the surface of the land and exposed layers of history, we must first look at the land itself.

Much has been written about the geographical and geological structure of the Judean Hills,[22] and this knowledge is vital for an understanding of the patterns adopted by settlements and settlement processes.

The Judean Hills[23] are a fairly uniform hilly region approximately 80 kilometers (km) long and 15 - 25 km. wide. On three sides, its boundaries are quite clear: in the east, the eastern bend of the Hebron ridge and the Ramallah ridge; in the west, the escarpment of the bend towards the coastal plain; and in the south, the Be'er-Sheva gorge. The definition of its northern boundary is more problematic, since there is no clear break between the Judean Hills and the hills of Samaria. The Shiloh Valley, the southernmost of that series of internal gorges, is part of the hills of Samaria region, and not of the Judean Hills.[24] This division is simply a geographical-physical one, but in our discussion, we shall see that these boundaries have cultural and material significance.

An anticline,[25] the Judean Hills extend along the axis of the major ridge of Israel. The peak of this ridge is characterized by a high, plateau-like region, whose margins are also the eastern and western margins of the entire mountain range. The axis of this curve is not continuous, as there is a discontinuity between the (southern) Hebron ridge and the (northern) Ramallah one, which is somewhat to the west of the Hebron ridge. The two meet southwest of Jerusalem.

East-to-west land shifts in the Jerusalem area caused division of the area in the direction of the shift. As a result, the ridge in this area is very narrow and somewhat lower than the rest of the Judean Hills. To the south of Hebron, the axis of the ridge descends. The plateau broadens, and splits into two secondary ridges–the western Dahariya ridge and the eastern Ma'on ridge. A basin is between them, and the Hebron Stream flows through it toward the south. This tectonic activity created four geographical sub-units in the Judean Hills, upon which this work is based (see map on page 20).

The Northern Sub-Unit: The Bet-El Hills

This is a broad mountainous plateau where the average altitude is over 850 meters above sea level. The rocky base comprising this sub-unit is made up of hard chalk rock and dolomite, on which there is *terra rosa*–a reddish brown residual soil suitable for agriculture. Some well-developed karsting activity (dissolution of limestone rocks by water) took place in this area, resulting in the formation of shallow valleys, rocky surfaces, and shallow holes. Because of this activity, only a small portion of the available area is suitable for agriculture. A special feature in this region is the Gibeon Valley which is composed of a number of small depressions. The rich, deep agricultural soil in this valley and the broad stream that flows there made it possible for concentrated settlements over a relatively limited area.

The Central Sub-Unit: The Hills of Jerusalem

This is the low section of the Judean Hills with an average altitude of some 650 meters above sea level. The mountain ridge in Jerusalem is limited in certain regions to a breadth of a mere score or two meters (the areas of the Yemin Moshe neighborhood and the railway station). The streams flowing to the west and to the east create a system of tributaries making it difficult to create a settlement continuum; however, in the valleys through which the streams flowed, fertile agricultural areas came into existence, as well as a rich system of springs based

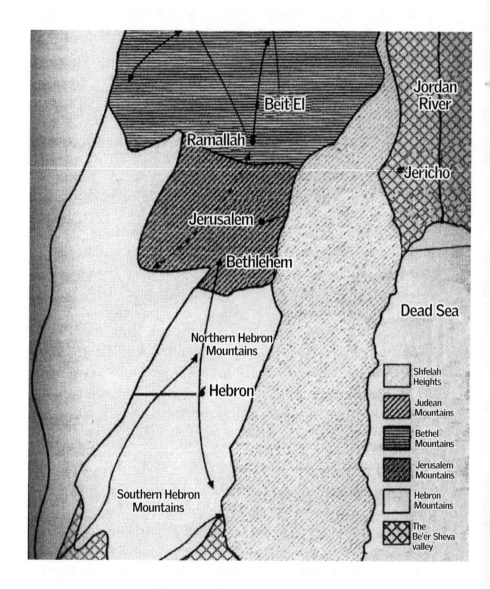

The Mountains of Judah by Karmon

upon strata of *hawar*—a soft, crumbly chalk rock with elements of clay in it. In the hills of Jerusalem, there are two central drainage systems: the Soreq Stream basin which drains a set of tributaries to the Mediterranean Sea, and the Kidron Stream basin which drains to the Dead Sea.

The Southern Sub-Unit: The Hills of Hebron

This unit has two sub-units within it: the Northern Hebron Hills sub-unit, extending northward from the town of Hebron, and the Southern Hebron Hills sub-unit, stretching to the south from the town of Hebron toward the northern Negev.

The Northern Hebron Hills sub-unit is a high, mountainous plateau, generally more than 900 meters above sea level. The highest point in the Judean Hills is within the boundaries of the township of Halhul, near Hebron, where the altitude reaches 1,020 meters above sea level. The highest town in Israel is Hebron. The bedrock of the area is mainly made up of hard chalk rocks and dolomite. The region has a number of fertile valleys with *terra rosa* soil as well as water-eroded soil, in which plantations (mostly vineyards) flourish at the present time as in times of old.

The Southern Hebron Hills sub-unit is a region gradually descending southward, which splits into two ridges: the Dahariya Ridge to the southwest, and the Yata or Ma'on Ridge to the southeast. Between these two ridges is a geological depression along which the Hebron Stream flows towards the Be'er-Sheva Stream. The drop in altitude and the proximity to the desert in the south are the direct causes of the minimal precipitation in this area. The bedrock is mainly soft white chalk; it is not penetrated by water, but it is easily quarried. On this bedrock, there is *rendzina* topsoil, which is of poorer quality than the *terra rosa* soil that develops over the hard chalk rock. The soft chalk rock results in the lack of springs in the area because of the impenetrability of the bedrock, yet it facilitates the digging of water cisterns. The climate and the poor quality of the soil are reflected in the sparse settlement of this region typical of all historical periods.

Neighboring Regions

Shfelah: The Judean Lowland

To the west of the Judean Hills, lies the Shfelah, a low-lying region. Its maximal altitude reaches about 450 meters (in contrast to the altitude of the Judean Hills, which reaches some 1,000 meters) above sea level. The bedrock of this area is also soft chalk. Over this is a stratum of harder rock known as *nari*, which is easy to quarry but water-impermeable. Man has exploited the properties of this rock to dig caves for various purposes: caves for dwelling, water cisterns, sites for various industries such as olive pressing and pigeon breeding, burial caves (columbaria) and hiding places in times of war.

Four broad valleys exist between the hills and the low lands. The valley furthest to the north is the Ayalon Valley; the second is the Soreg Valley; the third is the Elah Valley; and the southernmost–the Tarkumiya Valley. Important routes extend through these valleys from the plain to the hills.

Bitter battles were fought in the two northern valleys: in the Ayalon Valley, significant battles took place in the days of Joshua and in the Hasmonean Period, as well as during the Israeli War of Independence in 1948. The famous confrontation between David and Goliath occurred in the Elah Valley. Later, the armies of the Assyrian king Sennacherib and the Babylonian King Nebuchadnezzar marched through the valley on their way from Lachish to Jerusalem.

Some well-known Biblical sites in the Shfelah:
- Bet-Shemesh, where the Ark of the Covenant was brought after being sent from one Philistine town to the next (I Samuel 6) and where Amatziah, king of Judah, was defeated by Yoash, king of Israel (II Chronicles 25)
- Timna: the home town of Samson's wife (Judges 14)

• Gat (Tel Tsafit), the birthplace of the Philistine giant, Goliath (I Samuel 17:4);

• Lachish, the city conquered by Joshua (Joshua 10:31-32)

• Mareshah, the site of the war between Asa, King of Judah and Zerah the Cushite (II Chronicles 14:8)

• Socho and Azekah, near the Elah Valley, site of the Philistine camp prior to the battle between David and Goliath (I Samuel 17:1).

The geographical location of the Shfelah influenced the people of the region culturally: the people there represented a "transit culture between the people of the hills and those of the plain."

The Judean Desert

The Judean Desert lies to the east of the Judean Hills. This desert is not another link in the worldwide chain of deserts like the Negev, but is rather a local desert that came into being as the result of its topographical features. The lofty Judean Hills block the advance of the rain clouds coming from the Mediterranean Sea to the west. These clouds, forced to rise to an altitude of over 1,000 meters above sea level, release their rain over the hills, so that when they continue on to the east and lose altitude (because of the low topography of the Judean Desert) they grow warmer and are unable to release whatever moisture they still contain.

This desert may be divided up into longitudinal strips, according to its topography and its bedrock. The first strip is that of the desert edge – the western region where little rain falls. In this region, the bedrock is made up of hard chalk and soft, crumbly chalk, and so is able to support limited agriculture and grazing land.

The second strip extends over the desert plateau; it is made up of soft chalk rock and hard silicate rocks, and rainfall there is very rare indeed. There are no permanent settlements in this region.

To the east of the desert, lies the slope of rock shifts, a region bordering on the Syro-African Rift in the Dead Sea area. A number of springs flow at the foot of this rock shift slope, including the Ein Gedi Spring, the Boqeq Spring, the Feshha Spring and the Zohar Spring. These springs make it possible for life to survive there and they attracted settlers during various periods of history.

The most important oasis there is Ein Gedi. The proximity of the Judean Desert to the center of the settled area in the Judean Hills made it possible for people who needed to distance themselves from government or from the restless center in Jerusalem to find a place to live in the desert, just a few hours' walk away. David fled there from Saul, the Hasmonean monarchs established fortresses and palaces there, and Christian monks in search of solitude moved there during the Byzantine Era.

Samaria

Bordering on the Judean Hills to the north, Samaria is part of Israel's central mountain range. Unlike the Judean Hills, this area is split up by geological breaks, with broad valleys in the central part of the region that are lower than the Judean Hills and more fertile as well. The southern part of Samaria, the area inherited by the tribe of Ephraim, is a rocky region where living conditions are quite severe. However, the northern part of Samaria, the area once inhabited by half the tribe of Menashe, is more fertile and so was relatively densely populated in early periods as well. The western slopes of Samaria are less steep, the movement from the plain area to the mountains of Samaria thus made simpler.

Most of Samaria is composed of sea sedimentary rock: hard chalk (limestone), soft chalk, and *hawar*. Upon the limestone rock base is fertile *terra rosa* soil. In the basin-like areas where soft chalk rock is common is *rendzina* topsoil, similar to that of the Judean plain. Both the relatively dense population of Northern Samaria and the convenient accessibility of the plain resulted in the establishment of fairly good ties with the culture of the plain, a fact that all through history resulted in the population of Samaria being more influenced by events in the coastal plain than were the inhabitants of the Judean Hills.

The Be'er-Sheva Valley

South from the Judea Mountains, the Be'er-Sheva and Arad Valleys link the Judean Hills with the Central Negev. These valleys are located on the border between areas of vegetation and wilderness. The Hebron Stream flows through the Be'er-Sheva Valley, where it joins up with the Be'er-Sheva Stream flowing from the east. Tel Sheba, a central point in this area dating from the First Temple Period, is located at the spot where the two streams come together.

These valleys are lined with loess soil, a fine-grained buff to gray colored soil which facilitates the growth of wheat and barley in rainy seasons, as well as pastureland. This region is extremely important as a link between the Hebron Hills and Egypt, for one of the main routes between them used to pass through Be'er-Sheva. (See Genesis 46, 1-5).

We may now consider the archaeological findings and historical data concerning these regions and the important facts they reveal.

A Review of Past Studies

Based on major field studies carried out in the Judean Hills and adjoining areas, as well as a number of comprehensive works based upon these, our review will follow a geographical sequence, from north to south.

Excavations

The Bet-El Hills

At the site of **Bittin**, identified with Bet-El, significant findings have been unearthed, dating from the Intermediate Bronze, Middle Bronze, and Iron Ages. The excavation was administered by James L. Kelso in the 1930s and then again in the'50s.[26]

The Jerusalem Hills

Gibeon: An archaeological excavation was carried out by James B. Pritchard at Gibeon, identified with the village of el-Jib, in the 1960s.[27] Numerous gravesites dating from the Intermediate Bronze, Middle Bronze, and the Late Bronze Ages -- as well as Iron Age II -- were discovered in this excavation. At the tell itself, a stratum of burnt material, dating from the Middle Bronze Age was discovered, and fortifications and a water system dating from Iron Age II were uncovered as well.

Givat Shaul, identified with Tel-el-Ful in the north of today's Jerusalem, has been excavated a number of times, twice by William F. Albright in the 1920s[28] and the second time, in the '60s by Paul Lapp.[29]

Most of the findings date from Iron Ages I and II. A few pottery fragments dating from the Middle Bronze Age were discovered there as well.

The City of David: This site has been excavated by many archaeologists, but only Kathleen Kenyon,[30] Yigal Shiloh[31] and Ronny Reich[32] uncovered meaningful finds dating from the Middle Bronze Age II and Iron Age II.

Ramat Rahel: This site, located within the boundaries of Kibbutz Ramat Rahel to the south of Jerusalem, was excavated in the 1960s by Yochanan Aharoni. The excavation revealed a settlement and a royal fortress dating from the 8th or 7th centuries BCE.[33] An additional excavation was carried out at this site by Gabriel Barkay, but its results have not been published. While we do not have a precise identification for this site, Barkay suggests identifying it with a settlement named Mameshet, a name appearing on seals found on handles of *LaMelech* "[belonging to] the king" jars dating from the 8th century BCE.

The Unfortified Sites: two large sites from the Intermediate Bronze and Middle Bronze Ages were excavated in the Refaim River Valley. One is Manahat, excavated in the 1980s by Gershon Edelstein,[34] while the other, near the Refaim River, was

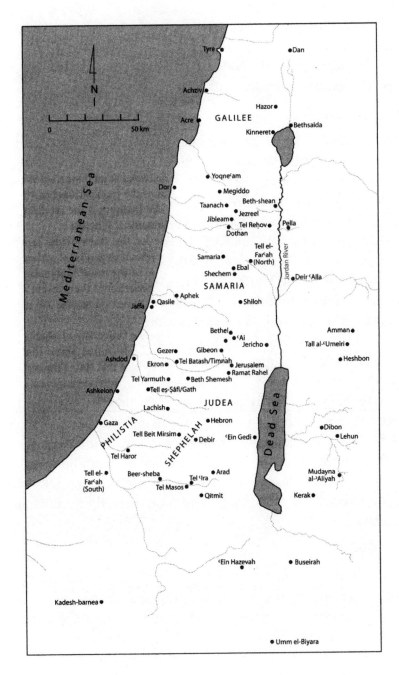

Map of Iron Age sites

excavated during the 1980s and '90s by Edelstein and Emanuel Eisenberg.[35]

The third site is the **Nahal Zimri** site to the northeast of Jerusalem, excavated by this author in 1990.[36]

The Hebron Hills

Bet-Zur: a small site that was apparently once a citadel during the Middle Bronze Age, the Iron Age, the Persian Period, and the Hellenistic Period. The site was excavated by Ovid R. Sellers in 1931 and again in 1957.[37]

The Cave in Wadi Et-Tin: Not far from Bethlehem, this site is rich in findings from the Early Bronze Age II and the Middle Bronze Age. The findings were published by Hugues Vincent.[38]

Khirbet Kufin: North of Hebron, a number of graves from the Intermediate Bronze Age and the Middle Bronze Age were found and excavated by Robert H. Smith.[39]

Efrat: a cemetery rich in findings, dating from the Intermediate and Middle Bronze Ages was excavated by Rivka Gonen[40] in 1979.

Tel-Hebron (Tel-Rumeida): an Early Bronze Age, Middle Bronze Age and Iron Age site that was excavated in the 1960s by an American expedition, headed by Philip Hammond. A report of the findings of the excavation was submitted by his student, Jeffrey Chadwick.[41] In the early 1980s, the site was excavated again by Avi Ofer,[42] and more recently by Emanuel Eisenberg.

Surveys

A survey is an examination of the site without digging, only collecting pieces of pottery from the surface. (It is less trustworthy than an excavation.) A number of surveys conducted in the Judean Hills must be added to the above excavations. We shall mention only the major surveys in which Middle Bronze Age and Iron Age sites were discovered.

The first comprehensive survey carried out in the Judean Hills was the "Emergency Survey" conducted by Moshe Kochavi in 1968, shortly after the Six Day War.[43] Another survey was carried out by Avi Ofer in the Hebron Hills.[44] A partial report stressing the Iron Age in the Jerusalem region, based on surveys carried out in Jerusalem, can be found in Meitlis (1988-9).[45]

Surveys of other parts of the Jerusalem Hills and the Bet-El Hills were carried out by teams acting on behalf of the Archaeological Staff Officer in Judea and Samaria.[46] A comprehensive list of all the sites from the Intermediate and Middle Bronze Ages in the Judean Hills can be found in Meitlis (1997).[47]

Reviews

A vast number of reviews, all based on intensive field studies, have been written about the Middle Bronze Age. We shall include here only those dealing with the central mountainous region that serve as a basis for this book.

Pioneering studies in the regions adjoining the Judean Hills in the north have been carried out in the Land of Ephraim* by Israel Finkelstein,[48] in the Hills of Menashe** by Adam Zertal[49] and in the Hills of Hebron by Avi Ofer. Most of these studies stress the Iron Age. The present author conducted a field study in the Judean Hills, stressing the Middle Bronze Age for his doctoral dissertation.

Attempts to understand the settlement and political arrangement in the Middle and Late Bronze Age in the central hill region were made by Shlomo Bunimovitz[50] and Finkelstein.[51] These attempts were based in the main on field studies in the regions of Ephraim and Menashe, as well as on geographical-settlement models.

For a deeper and more detailed description of the geographical importance of the Judean Hills and archaeological data, see Chapter 7.

ARCHAEOLOGY
AND THE BIBLE

The Patriarchal Period
Settlements and Culture

The first archaeologists to concentrate on Israel, such as William F. Albright[52] and Kathleen Kenyon,[53] made good use of the term "Patriarchal Period." Under Albright's influence, this term came to be seen as the equivalent of the Middle Bronze Age, and it has been familiar to all ever since.

In recent years, however, there are scholars who object to this equation, claiming that the objects mentioned in the Book of Genesis do not fit neatly into any particular historical period, and if they reflect to some extent a time period at all, it is later

PERIOD	ACCEPTED DATING SYSTEM	CHARACTER- ISTICS	ALTERNATE DATING SYSTEM	AS REFLECTED IN THE BIBLE
MIDDLE BRONZE AGE I	1950 - 1800 BCE	Renewed urbanization in Israel; In the Judean Hills, continuation of nomadic life; on the plains – renewed urbanization		Beginning of Patriarchal Period

than the Middle Bronze Age. This, for instance, is the argument made by Nadav Na'aman:

"The collection of patriarchal tales does not relate to any early reality, such as that of the Middle and Late Bronze Ages [the 20th-13th centuries BCE]. It actually seems that the earliest memories... reflect, at best, the transition stage from the Late Bronze Age to Iron Age I [end of the 13th and all of the 12th centuries BCE]. From an historian's point of view, one cannot refer to the Age of the Patriarchs as an historical period, and presenting it as a separate period in the history of Israel is a theological-literary attempt to sketch the beginnings of the Jewish people; an attempt which began in the period subsequent to Israel's becoming a distinct political category and ethnic entity, when people began to ask questions about their origin and about the stages in the development that led to their becoming a nation."[54]

The above statement is problematic, contrary to the intentions of its author, as we shall see below. Specific items mentioned in Genesis actually meet the requirements of the Middle Bronze Age to an amazing degree, and are reflected in the archaeological findings dating from that period. Yet, there have been questions raised in scholarly literature relating to the Bible and archaeology, and I will respond to them one by one.

Settlements Mentioned in the Bible
Reflect the Era of the Patriarchs

No one can ignore the similarity between the settlement picture in the central hill country in the Middle Bronze Age and the stories of the Patriarchs. All of the settlements mentioned in the Book of Genesis in connection with the travels of the Patriarchs along the main highway (known as the "road of the Patriarchs"), located on the watershed in the central hill country, existed during the Middle Bronze Age (MBA).[55] These include Shechem, Bet-El, Jerusalem (Shalem) and Hebron. (There were also additional settlements which are not mentioned, such as Shiloh, Gibeon and Bet-Zur, but all of them, except for Ai, were indeed sites along the road of the Patriarchs.)

The exception is the town of Be'er-Sheva, which is mentioned in the Bible as a town in the Patriarchal period, however its precise position as yet has not been located. To strengthen his argument, Na'aman claims that no traces of MBA settlement have been found in Be'er-Sheva. While it is true that in the extensive excavations carried out at Tel Sheba (in Arabic, Tel-Saba') nothing preceding the Iron Age has been uncovered as yet, but it was Na'aman himself who once claimed that Tel Sheba is not Biblical Be'er-Sheva in the first place! He argued that Biblical Be'er-Sheva should be sought at Bir a-Saba', (within the confines of the city built there by the Turks during the past century) near the Bedouin market, some five kilometers to the west of Tel Be'er-Sheva.[56] This site has never been excavated except for several test shafts, in which potsherds were found from the Roman period and from Iron Age II (the period of the Israelite kingdoms).[57] Therefore it is as yet uncertain if Bir a-Saba' was the site of Biblical Be'er-Sheva or not.

It is quite possible that the Patriarchs' Be'er-Sheva mentioned in Genesis was not a well-established town which could be located in archaeological excavations, for it is largely described in the Bible as a cluster of wells—as proposed by Israel Rosenson.[58] (See Gen. 21: 30-31; 26:32-33) Indeed, if the correspondence between the settlement picture described in the Bible and the archaeological picture is evidence of authenticity, we have solid evidence of the authenticity of the descriptions found in the Book of Genesis.

Moreover, if one accepts the claim that the Book of Genesis was compiled by later authors at the close of the period of the Israelite kingdoms, one must ask why those authors refrained from adding to the list of settlements other central sites that were already in existence in Iron Age I, such as Mizpah—which functioned as a sanctified site—or Ramah, the hometown of the prophet Samuel, both of which are located on the main highway. If the Book of Genesis is indeed to be considered a late literary work, whose authors had only "a vague notion of the distant past,"[59] it would be logical that they would have included Mizpah in the "tales of the Patriarchs," for it was an important site with religious significance during the Iron Age.

We see that the Bible reflects *precisely* the settlement picture during the Middle Bronze Age, when the Patriarchs lived, and not a later period of the supposed "later" authors.

How Do Biblical Lifestyle Descriptions Square with Archaeological Findings?

One of the unique MBA features characteristic of the Judean Hills is the societal and settlement complexity of the region. Archaeological findings indicate that both fortified and unfortified settlements existed in the Judean Hills and that they differed prominently from one another. Nomads moved between the settlements, leaving behind pottery fragments and burial sites without adjoining settlements.

In the wake of his study of the Hebron Hills, Avi Ofer stated that, "Another settlement process took place in the Middle Bronze Age, contemporary with the continued existence of a strong, partially nomadic, sheep-breeding element." He describes the Late Bronze Age as a period in which "the significance of the nomads grew stronger," while he says of Iron Age I, "the settlement process has become total, and leaves no nomads whatever contemporary with it in the Judean Hills."[60]

Archaeological findings show that the more densely populated areas were those of Jerusalem and Bet-El, while the Hebron region contained only a few permanent settlements, with the nomadic population more numerous there. Another conclusion to be drawn from the findings is that the nomads maintained good relations with the permanent residents of the region, since their burial sites were located at some distance from the permanent settlements, but not adjacent to them. This phenomenon is unique since, generally speaking, the permanent residents of an area are suspicious of the intentions of nomads, because of the nomads' tendency to shepherd their flocks in agricultural areas and to rob the permanent residents of their agricultural produce.

Furthermore, various elements, such as the Hurrites and the Amorites, made their way from the north to the Judean Hills, as testified to by a tablet inscribed in cuneiform script uncovered in the excavations at Tel Hebron. This tablet, in addition to listing animals brought for sacrificial purposes or in payment of taxes, contains the names of the donors.[61] Evidence of the presence of Hittite elements was found at Shiloh (see below).

During all the Biblical archaeological periods, there was never any similar integration of populations, other than during the MBA, the Era of the Patriarchs.

The picture just described is reflected clearly in the Book of Genesis and matches to an amazing degree the description of the complex relationships between the dwellers of towns--such as Hebron and Shechem--and the nomadic groups, including the Patriarchs of the Jewish nation. Esau married Hittite women (Gen. 26:34), and the residents of Shechem were to intermarry with the sons of Jacob (Gen. 34) and even form a single tribal unit with them ("...to live with us, to be a single people," as stated in Gen. 34:22).

Abraham, who led a nomadic life and dwelt in a tent, purchases land from Ephron, and his grandson, Jacob, buys land near Shechem. The permanent population in the hill country was made up, according to the Book of Genesis, of Canaanites and Prizzites (Gen. 13:7), Amorites ("the oaks of Mamre, the Amorite" Gen. 14:13), Hittites (Gen. 23) and Hivites (Gen. 34), while the Philistines lived in the northern Negev (Gen. 21:32-33). This mosaic, which was a rare occurrence in the history of this region, is reflected both in the Bible and in the archaeological findings, testifying to the authenticity of the Biblical description.

The Bible's Precise Descriptions of Cultural Life in the Patriarchal Era Prove Authenticity

Literacy and Illiteracy

At the end of the First Temple period, the Jewish nation was undoubtedly literate. The considerable evidence amassed throughout the country dating from the close of this period shows that broad sections of the people were familiar with reading and writing. Note the prophet Jeremiah's purchase of land from Hanamel, his cousin, at Anatot, on the eve of the destruction of the First Temple: "Then I purchased the field from Hanamel my cousin who lives in Anatot, and I weighed him out the seventeen shekels of silver coins, *and then I wrote in the book and sealed it* and I brought witnesses and weighed out the silver on the scales." (Jer. 32:10-11) This procedure was in no way unusual during the First Temple period, for one of the most basic ways to prove ownership over land is by means of a deed of sale.

Against this background, it is glaringly apparent that no mention of writing is made throughout the Book of Genesis. The Hebrew words *katav* -- "he wrote," or *sefer* – "a book" or "a document" -- do not occur in this book, and the verb "to write" is found for the first time only in the middle of the Book of Exodus (Exod. 17:14).[62]

The absence of the root *k-t-v* is especially noticeable in the narrative of the purchase of the Cave of Machpelah by Abraham from Ephron the Hittite. The bargaining process and purchase are related in great detail in chapter 23 of Genesis, but no mention is made there of the signing of any contract between Abraham and Ephron. Negotiations were carried out publicly in the presence of many people: "in full view of the Hittites, amongst all those congregating at the city gates" (Gen. 23:18) – i.e., in public, this being the confirmation of ownership over land in an illiterate society.

We may conclude that in the Patriarchal Period, writing was limited to a stratum of scribes who functioned in the administrative centers, and was not widespread among the general public. In those days (Middle Bronze Age), script was either cuneiform or Egyptian hieroglyphics, both of which were complex systems made up of hundreds of signs, which only a limited number of experts could master. We may surmise that the inhabitants of Hebron, a small, isolated town in the Judean Hills, were not familiar with this art. Indeed, in none of the numerous excavations have written documents from the onset of the Middle Bronze Age (18th century BCE) been found there.

Furthermore, only a small number of documents inscribed in cuneiform script and dating from the 17th and 16th centuries BCE have been uncovered. In the Judean Hill country, one single document has been discovered – in the Tel Rumeida excavations in Hebron,[63] and it is ascribed to the 17th century BCE, more than 100 years after the onset of the Patriarchal Period.

In this light, it is apparent that the arts of reading and writing were not widespread in Israel in the period of the Patriarchs, and certainly not in a region so isolated as the Judean Hills.[64] A description so precise undoubtedly indicates the authenticity of the Bible: a scribe living a thousand years later, without any archaeological knowledge we enjoy in our times, would not be able to describe Middle Bronze Age society in the Judean Hills -- and the means of transactions -- in a credible and exact a manner.

Abraham's Purchase According to Hittite Law

The process whereby the Cave of Machpelah was acquired is even better understood in light of Hittite law as revealed in the documents found in Hattushash, the Hittite capital city (in present-day Turkey) that were written during the 15th century BCE. Manfred Lehman notes that according to sections 46 and 47 of the Hittite law, the royal taxes from tasks imposed on landowners as obligations apply only to those who purchase the land in its entirety. If the buyer acquires only part of the land, the obligations—services to the king—remain the responsibility of the seller. It is quite possible that Ephron the Hittite wanted to rid himself of his obligations to the king which he had incurred by virtue of his ownership of the land, and insisted on selling the *entire* field, though Abraham was interested only in purchasing "the cave... at the end of his field." (Gen. 23:9)

Lehman adds that according to Hittite law, the existence of trees growing on the land was always registered at the time of sale. This information makes it easier to understand the verse: "So the field of Ephron which was in Machpelah, which was before Mamre, the field and the cave therein, *and all the trees that were in the field*, that were within all its surrounding boundaries, were confirmed..." (Gen. 23:17).[65] Lehman's study attests to the fact that the transaction between Abraham and Ephron conformed perfectly to Hittite law, and thus the authenticity of the background provided by the Bible is thorough and accurate.

To sum up, the description of the acquisition of the Cave of the Machpelah provides us with invaluable information concerning the process of purchasing land in an illiterate society, according to Hittite law which, presumably, the inhabitants of Hebron followed.

Sale of Joseph into Slavery Bears Out Exact Knowledge of Middle Bronze Age Prices

Regarding the bargaining process during Patriarchal Period, it should be noted that there is an interesting Biblical detail which can be explained *only* in a Middle Bronze Age context or, more precisely, against the backdrop of the 18th-17th centuries BCE. In the narrative of the sale of Joseph, mention is made of Joseph being sold for twenty pieces of silver (Gen. 37:28). British scholar Kenneth A. Kitchen discovered (in documents from Mesopotamia) that in the third millennium BCE the price of a slave was ten shekels (silver); *in the 18th and 17th centuries BCE, the price of a slave was twenty shekels;* while in the 14th and 13th centuries it was thirty shekels. By the onset of the first millennium, the price of a slave had gone up to 50–60 shekels, while during the period of Persian rule the price was 90–120 shekels. The price paid for Joseph as described in the Bible fits perfectly with the economic reality of the Middle Bronze Age;[66] he was sold for twenty shekels, the going price at the time. Surely, no one writing centuries later would have known the market value of slaves in that era!

Denial of the Historical Authenticity of Genesis

In light of the evidence at hand, why do some archaeological researchers argue that the description in the Bible does not reflect any specific archaeological period? Their main arguments against the historical reliability of the Book of Genesis revolve around populations and developments that they claim did not exist during the Patriarchal epoch. According to this school of thought:[67]

The **Philistines, Hivites** and **Hittites** appeared only at the onset of the Iron Age (the end of the second millennium BCE), and not earlier.

The **Aramaeans** appeared for the first time on the stage of history at the end of the 12th century, and not earlier.

The **Chaldeans** appear for the first time in external documents only in the first millennium BCE.

The description of **the camel** as a domesticated beast of burden in the stories of the Patriarchs does not fit what we know of the domestication of the camel, which it is claimed took place only at the end of the second millennium BCE, long after the Middle Bronze Age of the Patriarchal Period.

These arguments are not new and at one time, they may have been daunting. But the latest conclusions of archaeological research confirm the descriptions in the Bible rather than disprove them. Let's examine some of these claims in light of modern research.

Ethnic Groups

What of the claim by some archaeologists that there is no evidence of the Aramaeans, Hittites, Hivites, Philistines or Chaldeans during the Patriarchal Era? These ethnic groups are mentioned in the Book of Genesis, but not all of them are mentioned in external sources of the era. This absence of data is not "proof," for the discovery of ancient documents is a matter of chance. The fact that they are not found in other sources does not automatically negate that they existed at that time.

Nevertheless, Nadav Na'aman even denies the existence of some ethnic groups in the Middle Bronze Age for whom there *is* historical and archaeological evidence! He argues that the **Aramaeans** first appear on the historical stage in the 12th century BCE, yet elsewhere he states that "the name 'Aram' is mentioned in a very few documents from all over the ancient East ever since the close of the third century BCE... "[68] i.e. well before the Biblical Period. It is true that Aram *as a political state* appears only at the close of the second millennium, but nowhere in the Book of Genesis is mention made of an Aramaean state. The Bible speaks only of Aramaean families from which the Patriarchs sprang.

The **Hittites**, too, already existed at the close of the third millennium BCE.[69] An indication of their existence was found in the central hill country in the excavations of Tel Shiloh, in the form of a large silver ornament on which a Cappadocian symbol, a Hittite symbol of divinity, was engraved. According to Baruch Brandl who studied the finds, this ornament originated in Anatolia (Asia Minor, the ancient home of the Hittites). The excavator of the site believes that during the Middle and Late Bronze Ages, a sanctuary stood at Shiloh,[70] and it would be reasonable to assume that the Hittite god was worshiped by Hittites who had brought the ornament to Shiloh from their place of origin. In the opinion of the publishers of the findings, this ornament should be linked with northern groups (such as Hittites) present in Canaan at that time. Here, too, Na'aman contradicts himself regarding the non-existence of the Hittites during that period, and uses this ornament as evidence of the penetration of Hittite, northern groups into Canaan.[71]

In addition to this find, vessels originating in Anatolia were found in Israel from the MBA I (c. 1950-1800 BCE). Such a connection is unknown in other time periods.[72] These details match data gleaned from tests carried out on skeletons of those buried in the MBA in Ephrata (in the Gush Etzion area) suggesting that the origin of those buried there may indeed be from Anatolia,[73] further proof of Hittites in the region.

In general, one cannot expect to identify various ethnic groups merely on the basis of potsherds and architecture. There are a number of examples of this difficulty in archaeological research, as noted by Na'aman in his article.[74]

The **Hivites** was one of the nations in Canaan. In the story of Dina, the daughter of Jacob, Shechem ben Hamor is called "the Hivite" (Gen. 34:2). In other words, during the Patriarchal Period, the ruling family in Shechem, perhaps the founders of Shechem, were Hivites. The Gibeonites who reached an alliance with Joshua were also Hivites (Josh. 9:7). Despite these explicit references in the Bible, archaeologists have not succeeded in identifying the Hivites in external documents. This would seem to be an example of an "imaginary" people that, from an archaeological standpoint, never existed.

Unlike the Hivites, the Hurrites are known from various sources. They originated in northern Mesopotamia. Documents that include Hurrite names have been found in Hebron, Gezer, Taanakh and Shechem.[75]

The Bible itself quite possibly identifies Hivites with the Hurrites or perhaps with a specific Hurrite tribe: in Gen. 36:2 Esau's wife, Oholibama is identified as the daughter of Anah, daughter of Tsiv'on the Hivite, while in Gen 36:20 both Tsiv'on and Anah are said to be Hurrites, descendants of Se'ir.[76] Furthermore, in the Hivite center in the Shechem region, Mount Ebal rises north of the town of Shechem (Deut. 11:29). The name 'Ebal' is the same as the name of one of the Hurrite chieftains in Se'ir (Gen. 36:23).

A similar "problem" involves the **Philistines**, who are mentioned in the Book of Genesis as living in the northwestern part of the Negev, on the banks of the Gerar Stream, and led by a king. These are certainly not the Philistines mentioned in the Book of Judges and known also from various Egyptian documents. The latter lived in the coastal plain, and were headed by leaders called *seranim*.[77] The name "Philistine" shared by these two groups may have stemmed from the possibility that both arrived from the Aegean Sea and Anatolia region. In fact, their unique burial sites were uncovered in the archaeological excavations conducted in the northwestern Negev. Nothing parallel to them has been found in Israel. However, certain parallels exist in Greece, Cyprus and Anatolia. These gravesites date from the close of the Middle Bronze Age and the onset of the LBA.[78]

In her study of burial customs in the Late Bronze Age, Rivka Gonen notes a unique burial method in coffins made of clay. This kind of burial, where the bones of children were found in a clay coffin, occurred in Gezer (on the low lands) and in the Persian Garden of Acre. This method was commonplace in the Minoan culture of Crete, and it is thus "indicative of ties of some kind with the Minoan world." These graves, however, are dated from the close of the period under discussion, yet the archaeological findings indicate that *people from the Aegean Sea area were present in Canaan in the northwestern part of the Negev* (the region of the Gerar Stream) *centuries before* the Philistines familiar to us from Egyptian sources were there.[79]

Attempts to trace those Aegean groups have almost failed in the excavations of settlement sites in this region. Only the excavations of burial sites have made it possible to discern them. (This fact alone underscores the difficulty in identifying ethnic elements on the sole basis of archaeological findings.)

Nevertheless, to this data we must add the findings recently published: In the excavations of Tel-Harur in the northwestern Negev, a fragment of a large container inscribed in Minoan characters has been discovered. Examinations made of the material of which this container was made (petrographic tests) show that the vessel was made in Crete. Researcher Eliezer Oren notes that other evidence from Egypt and Canaan shows something of the ties of Egypt and Canaan with Crete, as does the palace from the MBA found at Kabri in the western part of Galilee, with its Minoan-style fresco.[80] Once again, it is interesting to stress that this obvious find is found mainly *in the northwest Negev* and fits in well with the burial sites mentioned above.

The Biblical verse (Deut. 2:23) may have been referring to these Philistine elements in saying: "[As for] the 'Avim' dwelling between Hatzerim and Gaza – Caphtorites from Caphtor destroyed them and dwelled in their place." Caphtor is the Hebrew word for Crete, and the "Caphtorites" may well be a branch on the Philistine family tree. The confusion over the presence of Philistines is dispelled when we consider the strong evidence that there were different groups called by the common name "Philistine" settling in Canaan at different times.

Then there is the issue of **Ur of the Chaldees**, mentioned in Genesis. The problem has not yet been resolved, because we are familiar only with the Chaldeans of later periods. Yehoshua Grinetz[81] argues that in the historical sources available to us, all of which are later than the MBA, the name is Chaldees (with an "l") rather than *Kasdim* (the Biblical Hebrew term, spelled with the Hebrew letter *sin* indicating an "s" sound and no "l" sound). This means that the Biblical term *Kasdim* is an ancient one, reflecting an ancient entity, very likely not the "Chaldeans" known in later periods.

Camels [82]

In scholarly circles, there is a well-known argument that the camel was not used as a beast of burden prior to the close of the second millennium BCE,[83] i.e. not until long after the era of the Patriarchs. This argument, which was based at the time on the knowledge available in the 1960s, has not been mentioned for over thirty years! In his book, *The Camel and the Wheel* (published in 1975) Richard W. Bulliet refers to a fragment from a document from Alalakh in northern Syria (stratum VII, dated from the 17th century BCE)[84] in which mention is made of "one portion of food for the camel."[85] We therefore know that by that time, the camel was domesticated, and it is possible that it began even earlier.

Ofer Bar-Yosef writes that the use of the camel goes as far back as the fourth millennium BCE, well before the Biblical Era, and that evidence of this has been found in Iran.[86] Furthermore, in the excavation headed by Rudolph Cohen and William G. Dever at a site in the Negev highlands (Be'er Resisim) from the close of the third millennium, the bones of a camel were found together with goats' bones,[87] clearly indicating domestication.

It is interesting that the camel is mentioned in the Book of Genesis primarily in connection with the arid areas to the east of Israel: concerning the journey of Abraham's servant to Haran, about Jacob's return from Aram, and in the story of the sale of Joseph, where an Ishmaelite caravan of camels is mentioned coming from Gilead. Therefore, it would seem that the use of the camel was in fact limited, as evidenced by the story of the sons of Jacob traveling to Egypt and making use of donkeys, rather than camels. It is quite possible that the use of donkeys when traveling eastward reflects the fact that the camel at this time was commonplace mainly to the east of Israel. Bulliet surmises[88] that camels were not common in this period, and were used primarily for transporting burdens and valuable items. It is his opinion that Abraham's servant was dispatched with camels specifically to demonstrate Abraham's wealth, and thus convince Laban and Bethuel to send Rebecca across the Syrian Desert to Canaan to marry his son.

To Which Population Group did the Patriarchs Belong?

Now that we have confirmed the dating of the Patriarchal Period in the Middle Bronze Age, let us explore the place of the Patriarchs in the overall society of the land of Canaan.

Glimpses of a Nomadic Lifestyle

The life of Abraham reflects to a considerable extent the knowledge we have of nomadic life in the Judean hill country during the Intermediate and Middle Bronze Ages. Abraham traveled the route from Shechem to Be'er-Sheva, and his primary place of residence and that of his sons was near Hebron. Their homes were of a temporary nature; they were tent-dwellers, and did not build houses. This lifestyle was theirs by choice, and was certainly not forced on them by economic straits, for according to the Bible the Patriarchs were fairly wealthy people.[89] Abraham makes sure to bury his wife, Sarah, in a specific spot in a cave at the edge of the field he bought from Ephron the Hittite, and that cave continued to serve as a family burial-site.

Judging from archaeological findings, it seems likely that the people of the Intermediate Bronze Age culture came from

Mesopotamia, Abraham's own land of origin.[90] This description of Abraham's lifestyle matches the description of the lifestyles of the hill country's Intermediate Bronze Age inhabitants.

The similarity between the lifestyle of Abraham and the people of the Intermediate Bronze Age finds expression in nomadic routes used throughout the year. William G. Dever argues that the settlements of the Negev highlands and the hills of Yeruham should be linked with the burial-sites discovered in the Hebron hills. In his opinion--in comparison with the semi-nomadic societies in various parts of the world and on the basis of archaeological findings--the people of this nomadic culture at the close of the third millennium and the onset of the second millennium BCE wandered in fixed routes. In the winter, they sojourned to seasonal settlements in the Negev, while in the hot, dry summer they would move northward and enable their flocks to graze in the hill country of Hebron. The many shaft graves found in the Judean Hills belong, in his opinion, to the inhabitants of the Negev who let their flocks graze there during the summer, when they lived in caves and tents.[91]

Dever's opinion is reinforced by Yuval Goren's study, in which a petrographic test was made of the clay vessels found in the Negev highlands sites. These showed that the source of a good portion of the raw material from which these vessels were made was from across the Jordan River and in the Judean Hills.[92] It may be concluded that the inhabitants of the Negev highlands did indeed reach the Judean Hills in their travels, and made vessels or purchased them in these regions.

This description indeed matches the pattern of Abraham's life, insofar as he divided his time between the Negev and the Judean Hills: "And he [Abraham] went on his travels from the Negev to Bet-El, to the place where he had pitched his tent earlier, between Bet-El and the Ai." (Gen. 13:3)

Nelson Glueck noted the similarity between the description of Abraham's life and the lifestyle of the people of the Intermediate Bronze Age in a series of articles and in his book

Rivers in the Desert: A History of the Negev.[93] Moshe Kochavi, however, does not accept Glueck's approach, largely because in the Book of Genesis, Shechem and Bet-El are mentioned, and no archaeological evidence has been found for the existence of settlement in those places during the Intermediate Bronze Age.[94]

Kochavi's opinion is reasonable if we view Israel as a uniform geographical unit in which historical processes apply everywhere in an identical fashion. It is generally accepted that the Intermediate Bronze Age (2200-1950 BCE) ends at the onset of the second millennium and at this time Shechem, Bet-El and Hebron did not exist. However, the transition from the Intermediate Bronze Age to the Middle Bronze Age was not uniform; it was gradual. While towns existed in the hill country, the nomadic population continued to live nearby, at least until the 18th century BCE. (See Part VIII for archaeological data.)

This archaeological picture fits in well with the lifestyle descriptions of the Book of Genesis. Abraham's period is thus to be dated to the 19th and 18th centuries BCE —the transition period between MBA I and MBA II, the period when the towns of the hill country were first built and fortified.[95]

Hebrews and Canaanites

Now that we have pointed out the ties between Middle Bronze Age and the Patriarchal Period, as well as the nomadic population group to which the Patriarchs may belong, the next step is to clarify--by means of archaeological findings --the significance of the terms "Hebrews" and "Land of the Hebrews" that appear in the Book of Genesis.

Abram is called *ha'Ivri* "the Hebrew" (Gen. 14:13), and Joseph is called by the Egyptians *ish Ivri* -- "a Hebrew man" (Gen. 39:14), and *na'ar Ivri*—"a Hebrew youth" (Gen. 41:12). The Egyptians do not break bread with the Hebrews "for this is an abomination for Egyptians" (Gen. 43:32). Moreover, in speaking with one of Pharaoh's ministers, Joseph uses a striking geographical term: *eretz ha'Ivrim* "the land of the Hebrews" (Gen. 40:15).

Of all the above, it would seem that the term *Ivrim* —"Hebrews"—is a common noun denoting a large population group named, perhaps, after *Ever*, the patriarch of the group (according to Seforno's commentary), or because they originated *"ever ha-nahar,"* on the "other side of the river" (according to the commentary of Rashbam). These *Ivrim*, Hebrews, were held in contempt by the Egyptians.

However, this term appears not only in the Book of Genesis, but also in the Book of Exodus, where it seems to be synonymous with the Israelites, rather than being a general term as seen above. Early confirmation of this change is recorded in *Targum Onkelos*, who translates the term *Ivri* appearing in Genesis *ivra'a* (a "Hebrew"), whereas he translates the same term appearing in Exodus *Yehuda'a* (a "Jew"). It thus appears that the term *Ivri*--"Hebrew," once a general term referring to a broad ethnic group, became in time a specific term referring only to the Jewish people.

It is therefore very likely that the people of the Intermediate Bronze Age are the ancient Hebrews. (See chapter 7) Keeping in mind that ages overlap depending on local development, we find that the urbanization process of the Middle Bronze Age began later in the Judean Hills than it did in the coastal plain and this process was apparently a gradual one. Burials in shaft-graves (such as those seen in earlier periods) continued far into the Middle Bronze Age. This seems to indicate that at the beginning of Middle Bronze Age II the urban population that had entered the coastal plain and the veteran nomadic population coexisted side by side, the nomads gradually being replaced.

It is very likely that this nomadic population was known in Egyptian sources as *'prw*. These sources use this term from the onset of the second millennium BCE, mainly in the El-Amarna letters from the 14th century BCE. They indicate that the *'prw* were nomads and that they were held in contempt by the Egyptians, just as the Hebrews were, as stated in the Book of Genesis.

What then, was meant by the geographical term *eretz ha'Ivrim* (Gen. 40:15), "the land of the Hebrews," an expression appearing in the entire Bible only once? It may be assumed that this term was well known in Egypt, for otherwise Joseph would have made use of a better-known geographical term. Yehoshua Grinetz has proposed that the area of greater Israel and Syria was generally known as *eretz ha'Ivrim* "the land of the Hebrews,"[96] while Yoel Bin-Nun has suggested that the specific area of Shechem was that land.[97]

Neither of these suggestions is likely, for the following reasons: Israel and Syria had other names by which they were known in Egypt, such as Canaan and Rethnu. The term "land of the Hebrews" does not exist in Egyptian sources, while Shechem, on the other hand, is mentioned by name in Egyptian sources.[98] If Shechem was known in the Egypt of his day, why would Joseph choose to refer to the "land of the Hebrews" instead? Did he, in fact, mean Shechem?

No. When we examine the settlement array in the Middle Bronze Age, we are led to the conclusion that *eretz ha'Ivrim* is the region of Hebron. The areas to the north of the Hebron Hills, the Jerusalem Hills, the Bet-El Hills and the region of Shechem were all settled with an urban and a suburban population; while the cold, rocky hills of Hebron were only sparsely settled by a permanent population. It was possible to pasture one's sheep there without confronting the permanent residents of the area. And accordingly, a large concentration of shaft-graves characteristic of the nomads (such as the Patriarchs) is located in the hill country of Hebron.

In support of this opinion, one may add that Nahmanides argued that "the land of the Hebrews," *eretz ha'Ivrim*, was indeed Hebron (in his commentary to Gen. 40:14). His reason: Abraham's family was so well known in this region that its fame had reached Egypt.

It is interesting to note that there is no reference in Egyptian sources to the region of Hebron. This omission may stem from the area being considered of marginal importance since it was inhabited only by the inferior Hebrews.

Summary

There is no way, nor is there any need, to confirm archaeologically every detail of the stories of the Patriarchs. (We might say that no one really expects to find either Abraham's tent or the ram he sacrificed in place of Isaac.) Yet at present, not only do archaeological findings not contradict the historical and geographical background of the Book of Genesis, they actually complement it and clarify certain Biblical episodes.[99]

Despite the fact that Genesis is not a historical book in the modern sense of the term, the historical information it contains-- and especially the settlement picture it reflects--+make it possible for us to establish the stories of the Patriarchs on solid historical ground. The combination of Biblical and archaeological research makes it possible to reach broader insights regarding the period and the events recounted in Genesis.

Archaeological research deals with the study of "silent" findings made up of many details that appear, at first glance, to be a mere collection of insignificant rocks and potsherds. But archaeology imbues these rocks with the breath of life. It creates an exciting account of the past, a story of variegated population movements and of lifestyles, of the building of towns and of their destruction, of economics and of trade, of life and of death. All of this provides the Biblical narrative of the lives of the Patriarchs – the founders of the Israelite nation – with a realistic and highly credible background.

5

CHAPTER

THE CONQUEST OF
THE LAND OF ISRAEL

The Conquest as Recounted in the Book of Joshua

The Book of Joshua may be divided into two parts: Chapters 1–14 describe the conquest of the land and notes the regions which were not conquered, concluding with the words, "then the land had a rest from war." (Josh. 14:15) The second part, which includes Chapters 15-24, delineates the land appropriations of the tribes, lists the Levite cities and describes the transition to a quiet period of settling in, during which Joshua copes with questions of religious and social significance. The conquest is portrayed in the first part of

53

the book as a short military campaign made up of a number of
stages:

- The first stage includes the crossing of the Jordan River and
  the conquest of Jericho, described as a fortified city surrounded by a wall.

- The second stage narrates two attempts to conquer Ai and
  the razing of that city to the ground.

- The third stage describes the construction of an altar on Mt.
  Ebal and a ceremony on both Mt. Gerizim and Mt. Ebal.

- The fourth stage tells of concluding an alliance with Gibeon
  and of the attack on Gibeon made by the Emorite kings (the
  rulers of Jerusalem, Hebron, Yarmouth, Lachish, and Eglon.)
  This assault concludes with the defeat of these kings by
  Joshua on the slope of Bet Horon which, in ancient times,
  was the main route from the plains to the Jerusalem Hills.
  Following the battle on the Bet Horon slope, Joshua carried
  out a military campaign on the piedmont and conquered its
  towns.

- The last stage of the campaign is a battle at Mei Marom
  against the kings of the north who were led by the king of
  Hatzor, as well as the conquest of the northern part of the
  country.

In addition to these battles, others also were fought. These
are mentioned briefly in the list of 31 kings defeated by Joshua
(Chapter 12), where kings appear who were not mentioned else-

PERIOD	ACCEPTED DATING SYSTEM	CHARACTER-ISTICS	ALTERNATE DATING SYSTEM	AS REFLECTED IN THE BIBLE
LATE BRONZE AGE	1550 - 1150 BCE	Renewed urbanization; Egyptian rule of Israel; Large number of imported vessels in the country	1400 - 1150 BCE Canaanite culture and some Egyptian control, mainly in the valleys and on the coastal strip; Israelite culture in the hill country	Israelite Conquest of Canaan under Joshua Period of the Judges until the penetration of the Philistines

where in the various stages of the war. We may conclude from this that not all the battles actually fought are mentioned in the description of the military campaign.

The narrative in the Book of Joshua has led Bible scholars and archaeologists to seek out the cities mentioned and to try to locate signs of battle. The focal points of this search were two important sites conquered by Joshua; Jericho, and Ai. Archaeological research has identified Jericho with Tel-el-Sultan, near the Arab town of A-riha, which apparently preserves the name of Jericho. Ai is identified as a site called E-Tel, not far from the Arab village of Dir Dibwan. (The name *Ai* means "a ruin," and this is also the meaning of the Hebrew and Arabic word *tell*.)

According to accepted opinion, the Israelites entered the country at the end of the Late Bronze Age, i.e., at the end of the 13th century BCE. The excavations at both sites presented the researchers with a dilemma: in Jericho, no wall was found from the Late Bronze Age, and at E-Tel, no signs of a settlement dating from this period were found at all. The fact that no signs of that war were found raised doubts concerning the accuracy of the Biblical description.

A further problem cropped up when excavating the sites of Lachish and Hatzor. Both of these sites indeed existed during the Late Bronze Age, and they were both razed to the ground as described in the Book of Joshua, but there is a gap of some 100 years between the dates of the destruction of the two sites. Hatzor was destroyed in the 13th century, while Lachish was destroyed in the second half of the 12th century BCE.[100] Because of this discrepancy, it was impossible to attribute the destruction of the two cities to one and the same cause, i.e. the invasion of the Israelites.

We cannot minimize the significance of these problems, yet in order to deal with them—and with additional questions arising in the wake of this confrontation between the Bible and scientific research—we must first become familiar with the relevant archaeological research and to understand it in depth. To this end, we shall note the archaeological characteristics of the Late Bronze Age and Iron Age I periods.

The Late Bronze Age, 1550-1150 BCE
(in generally accepted chronology)

The Late Bronze Age is described in research literature as a period in which the population throughout the country thinned out considerably. Some of the towns that were destroyed at the close of the Middle Bronze Age (MBA) were not resettled, and those that were resettled were smaller than they had been previously. In most of the settlements, no wall was found dating from this period, for the settlements generally relied on walls that had survived from the MBA.

During the Late Bronze Age, there was clearly continuity in pottery from the Middle Bronze Age, but there was also an innovation—the presence of vessels imported from Mycenae (Greece) and Cyprus.

This period parallels that of the New Kingdom in Egypt, mainly the 18th and 19th dynasties, and these dynasties were directly involved in a good deal of what transpired in Canaan. The clearest evidence of this link is found in the El-Amarna letters discovered in Egypt, including many letters from various Canaanite kings sent to the king of Egypt. Numerous Egyptian artifacts found in the land of Canaan from this period fit in well with the impression given by those letters that the rulers of Canaan were subordinate to the king of Egypt, and that internal struggles characterized relations between the various local kings.

The Late Bronze Age was a period of sparse settlement in the hill country, with heavier settlement on the coastal plain. It is difficult to speak of the Late Bronze Age in the Judean Hills because of the rarity of archaeological findings from this period in that area.

Settlements dating from the Late Bronze Age have been found at Bet-El,[101] Manahat,[102] and Khirbet Rabud (identified with Biblical D'vir).[103] A few potsherds were found at Bet-Zur, but these do not connect well to the structures at the site. Similarly, potsherds have been found at Tel Rumeida (identified, according to some, with Biblical Hebron.) On the map published by Avi Ofer concerning his studies in the Hebron Hills, only a single site appears to date from the Late Bronze Age: Khirbet Rabud, near which a number of graves were found. At Tel Hebron, he believes that only graves were found, while in the Gush Etzion region, a single grave was found (at Khirbet Jadur.[104]) If there was settlement at Tel Hebron during this period, its area was extremely small. The settlement at Khirbet Rabud is exceptional in comparison to other settlements of the time in that its area was apparently about 60 dunams. (A dunam is equal to 1,000 square meters.)

One survey conducted in the Benjamin region argues[105] that between Bet-El and Jerusalem only two sites were found. (As noted in the Introduction, a survey is an examination of the site without digging, only collecting pieces of pottery from the surface. It is less trustworthy than an excavation.) One of these is Bittin (Bet-El) and the other is *"apparently* also Beit Ghor e-Tahta"* (emphasis added). Only five or six sites dating to the Late Bronze Age (LBA) were located in the area of Ephraim, as compared to 81 sites settled earlier, during the MBA. It should be noted that the only excavated site in the area of Ephraim is Tel h, where only potsherds from the LBA were uncovered, but not even a single segment of a wall.

In the Hills of Menashe, 33 sites were found dating from the Late Bronze Age, as compared to 135 sites from the MBA.[106] It is only proper to stress the fact that most of the findings dating from this period in the Hills of Menashe come from surveys rather than from excavated sites, so it is not possible to learn details of the settlements. On the basis of the archaeological data, it may be concluded that the overall settled area in the mountains of Judea and Ephraim (from Shechem southwards) was no greater than 100 dunams in the LBA II (14th and 13th centuries BCE), as compared to some 730 dunams of settled area during the previous MBA II (480 dunams in the Judean Hills and some

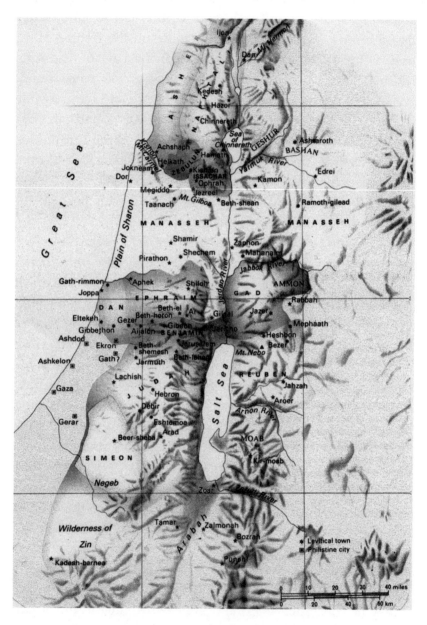

Map of Eretz Israel at the time of Joshua

250 dunams in the Hills of Ephraim).[107] The settlement density in the Hills of Menashe is greater, though no more than a quarter of its value in the MBA and a little less than a third of the settlement density in Iron Age I.[108]

Were it not for the discovery of the El-Amarna letters, one might never have imagined that Jerusalem was settled in this period, and certainly not as an independent kingdom (for Jerusalem and El-Amarna see below).

Such a vacuum is most unlikely, and the question is whether or not the archaeological findings reflect a true picture of this period. How are we to explain the scarcity of archaeological findings from the Late Bronze Age in the hill country sites, in general, and those of the Judean Hills, in particular? An attempt must be made to deal once again with the question of the nature of the Late Bronze Age by re-examining another important topic: the onset of the era that followed it, Iron Age I.

The Onset of the Iron Age in the Hill Country—a New Look

What are the initial signs of the existence of a new culture or of a new era? When drastic changes in pottery shapes are found and the new pottery style becomes the main style used in the following period (accompanied by additional changes such as the form of settlement, the style of burial, or eating habits that express significant cultural changes), scholars view it as a sign that there was a stage of chronological co-existence between the old culture and the new one. Let's look at evidence of such co-existence. It will show an overlapping of the Late Bronze Age culture with that of Iron Age I, very likely indicating the simultaneous coexistence of two cultures–the Israelite and Canaanite.

Evidence from the 13th Century BCE

At various sites, collared-rim jars characteristic of Iron Age I appear in groups of vessels typical of the Late Bronze Age. At Aphek, near Rosh Ha-Ayin, a collared-rim jar was found together with Canaanite vessels dated to the 13th century BCE.[109] At Tel Nami, a collared-rim jar used for burial purposes in the 13th century BCE[110] was found, while at Manahat, in western Jerusalem, collared-rim jars with reed imprints on the lip were found at the site together with Canaanite vessels and Egyptian 19th Dynasty scarabs. (Similar jars were found in Iron Age I sites in Samaria.) At the same time, Mycenaean and Cypriot vessels characteristic of the Late Bronze Age were found in sites defined as Iron Age I sites in the highlands of Judea and Samaria. The following are the relevant sites:

Mt. Ebal: one of the most prominent Iron Age I sites. Without entering into the debate raging over the nature of this site, it is generally agreed that the site dates from one period only, Iron Age I. In the single-period assemblage dated to Iron Age I, two Mycenaean sherds were found. These sherds were defined by the excavator as Myc III B-C vessels. At the same site, a bi-conical jar found mainly in 14th century BCE sites and two scarabs attributed to the days of Ramses II[111] were also discovered.

Tel Nasbeh: Vessels dating from the Late Bronze Age were found in this site, which is dated to the Iron Age. C.C. McCown notes that fragments of Cypriot vessels were found at the site.[112] Unfortunately, they are not noted in the ceramic report. Nevertheless, this report does include local vessels characteristic of the Late Bronze Age, such as a dipper juglet (Plate 40: 756), a cooking pot (Plate 46: 979) and angular bowls (Plate 53: 1156, 1163).[113]

Giloh: This site, excavated by Amichai Mazar, serves as a key site from Iron Age I in the hill country; it is the most prominent site from this period in the Judean Hills.[114] Located on a mountain ridge southwest of Jerusalem within the boundaries of the modern neighborhood of Giloh, it is a single-period site that has been preserved relatively well. A residential building made of rough, unprocessed stone, reminiscent of a four-space building was uncovered there. (Also known as "buildings on columns," the typical plan of a four-space building includes three parallel living spaces built lengthwise, and a fourth space found in the back, at right angles to the three lengthwise spaces. The length of this fourth space is approximately that of the width of the other three spaces. The division into spaces was often carried out by means of rows of four-sided columns. It is generally assumed that the middle space was attached.)

In addition, sections of walls encompassing the site that apparently served as a defensive wall were found, as well as walls dividing the site into secondary units. In the northern part of the site, the foundations of a four-sided tower built of large, rough stones were found. On the floor of this tower, a bronze dagger characteristic of the Canaanite sites of the Late Bronze Age was discovered. According to the excavator, the families that resided at this site apparently divided up its area, each family living in a building with a large adjacent yard in which sheep were kept. Since the surface is rocky and not suitable for agriculture, the excavator concluded that the residents of the village engaged in shepherding flocks. He suggested identifying the site with Ba'al Peratzim, mentioned in the context of David's

Four space buildings

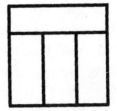

Now let us add the doorways.

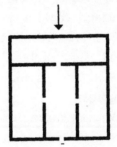

Often, there were no solid walls separating the three parallel rooms. Instead, there were columns. Now, the configuration would appear like this.

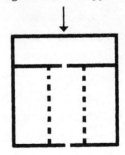

Side bar: Diagram of four space houses

war against the Philistines in the Refaim Valley (II Sam 5:20), especially because of its proximity to the Refaim River and because it is the only site in the vicinity dating from this period.

Objections have been raised concerning the classification of the Giloh site as Israelite, primarily because nearby Jerusalem was not conquered by the Israelites until the rule of David. Some suggest that Jebusites inhabited the site, just as they inhabited Jerusalem. Yet the plan of the building and the local pottery, without any evidence of imported vessels, lead to the conclusion that the site was part of the settlement array of Iron Age I, despite the existence of a defensive wall and a tower, which were uncommon in the hill country during this period.

Some of the vessels found at this site, including in the main jars and cooking pots, resemble vessels from the Late Bronze Age. As a result, the excavator dated the founding of the site to the end of the 13th century or the beginning of the 12th century BCE; and its abandonment was dated to sometime in the 12th century.

Bet Zur: In various excavated areas, in assemblages of vessels from Iron Age I, Mycenaean vessels, Cypriot vessels, local sherds and a Ramses II scarab were found. The excavator, Ovid R. Sellers, has repeatedly stressed that there had been no settlement in the places excavated dated to the Late Bronze Age, and that the findings characteristic of the 13th century BCE were found in "good Iron Age loci."[115]

Sasa: Canaanite pottery was found together with collared-rim jars in the destruction stratum of an Iron Age I at this site in Upper Galilee. The dating resulting from carbon 14 tests conducted on organic remains found at the site range chronologically from the end of the 13th century to the onset of the 12th century BCE.[116] The carbon 14 tests are consistent with the existence of Canaanite vessels at the site and point to the existence of an Iron Age I site of the 13th century BCE.

The data amassed up until now points clearly to the existence of a new culture concentrated mainly in the central highlands and in the Upper Galilee as early as the 13th century BCE.

Evidence from the 14th Century BCE

Archaeological data from the 1980s made it possible to conclude that the appearance of new settlements might be moved back to the 14th century BCE. Interesting evidence of this was found at Shiloh, the Israelite center during the period of the Judges.

Yochanan Aharoni, Aharon Kempinski and Volkmar Fritz noted that in the excavations carried out at Shiloh (by the Danish team between 1920 and 1930) vessels were found that belonged to the Late Bronze Age, within Iron Age I assemblages. For this reason, Aharoni and his colleagues argued that these vessels belong to the Iron Age I stratum, and so the penetration of the Israelites must be dated to the 14th century BCE.[117] In later excavations carried out by a team sponsored by Bar-Ilan University and headed by Israel Finkelstein, a stratum was found from the Late Bronze Age, according to the excavator, and so Finkelstein argued that the pottery found at the site was to be ascribed to a separate stratum from the Late Bronze Age, rather than to the Iron Age settlement.[118]

According to the excavation report of the Bar-Ilan team,[119] the findings from the LBA are concentrated in area D. A large number of local pottery fragments and imported vessels were found in this area, buried deliberately in that place together with ashes and animal bones. No structures dating to this period were found at the site. In the excavator's opinion, there was a sanctuary at the site, but it has not been located because of the later construction covering the central portion of the tell.

An exact examination of the detailed loci where imported pottery was found shows that about 30 of some 90 Mycenaean and Cypriot sherds found at the site were actually found mixed in loci, or in loci clearly dating from Iron Age I, in areas C, D and J.[120] Assuming that the excavation was carried out properly, it may be concluded that Mycenaean and Cypriot sherds typical of the 14th century BCE were found in clean, Iron Age loci. The excavators of the Danish team, too, note that LBA sherds were found together with vessels from Iron Age I.[121]

An examination of the ceramic data presented by Shlomo Bunimovitz reveals a problematic situation. The local pottery, most of which was found in area D, is described as pottery preserving Middle Bronze Age tradition and is dated to LBA I (15th century), while some of the imported Cypriot ware, as well as the Mycenaean vessels, are even later, yet are dated to LBA II (i.e., the 14th century BCE). The use of imported vessels found at the site, consisted of an earlier vintage, extends into LBA II as well. No typical imported ware belonging to LBA I, such as vessels called "white slip I ware," were found. This would indicate that the imported Mycenaean and Cypriot vessels are later than the local ones. It appears that the imported ware found at the site in loci where Iron Age pottery was found are of the same period of time, and the appearance of the Iron Age pottery is to be advanced to the 14th century BCE. The argument can indeed be made that a few LBA vessels found their way into later strata, but the excavations at Tel Qiri in the Jezreel Valley indicate that finding imported vessels dating from the 14th century BCE in Iron Age I loci is not an exceptional phenomenon. At Tel Qiri, no LBA stratum was found to testify to the existence of a settlement, yet LBA vessels dating from the end of the 15th century and the first half of the 14th century BCE were found in various loci in strata (VIII-IX), attributed to Iron Age I.[122]

The excavator wondered how to explain the phenomenon of imported ware at the Tel Qiri, especially since it included luxury vessels such as Mycenaean and Cypriot vessels, as well as alabaster and faience. He suggested two possible explanations: 1) the architectural traces of the LBA stratum had disappeared; 2) the vessels had been brought over from a nearby site.

However he does admit that, "it is difficult to come up with a convincing explanation for this feature."[123]

In a limited excavation carried out at a nearby site, Tel Abu Qudeis (Tel Kedesh), a similar phenomenon was discovered. In stratum VIII, the stratum in which Mycenaean and local ware dated to the 14th and 13th centuries BCE, no architecture at all was found. Above these vessels, there was a floor with pottery belonging to Iron Age I.[124] While one can say that the Mycenaean vessels belong to a settlement stratum earlier than the Iron Age floors, but since no LBA architecture was found at the site, it is reasonable to assume that these vessels belong to the period when the Iron Age floors were laid, while the Iron Age pottery found above that floor, in a stratum characterized by fire, belongs to the period when this stratum was destroyed.

The data from Mount Ebal, Tel-en-Nasbeh, Bet-Zur and Sasa shows that the data from Shiloh are in no way exceptional. In light of the fact that Mycenaean and Cypriot vessels were found in Iron Age assemblages in a number of excavated areas in the site (in the Danish excavations of Building A and in areas C, D and J), rather than in a single isolated locus, it is reasonable to assume that the phenomenon is widespread. Since no architecture from the LBA was found at Mt. Ebal, Bet-Zur, Tel-en-Nasbeh, Shiloh Tel Qiri and Tel Kedesh, one may conclude that the Canaanite vessels from the 14th and the 13th centuries BCE belonged to Iron Age I settlements.[125] The logical conclusion is that the pottery characteristic of the Iron Age began to appear in the central hill country as early as the 14th century BCE.

This conclusion matches the results of the Tel Dan excavations in the north. Despite the remoteness of this site from the central highlands, the findings from strata VI and V closely resemble the findings typical of the highland sites from Iron Age I. Characteristic collared-lip jars and silos for the storage of grain were discovered at this site, too, and neither pig bones nor graves were found from this period. (Pig bones are common in most of the sites, but absent from Israelite sites.) Carbon 14 tests of carbonized wood samples found in strata VI and V at Tel Dan, dated by the excavator to Iron Age I, provided interesting results: of the 28 samples examined, four are dated with a high degree of probability to the 14th century BCE and eight others to the first half of the 13th century BCE.[126]

It should be noted that according to the Book of Judges the settling of the descendants of Dan at this site took place at a relatively late stage, so that according to Biblical evidence the results at Tel Dan do not reflect the beginning of this period.

This explanation may also serve to clarify an interesting feature of the excavations at Tel-Taanakh, according to which it seems that the settlement from the LBA was destroyed in the 15th century BCE and was renewed only at the onset of Iron Age I. The excavators note that Mycenaean wares dated to the Mycenaean period IIIA2 (the 14th century BCE) were discovered at this site. The excavators did not suggest any explanation for the existence of imported pottery at a place that, in their opinion, was deserted at this time.[127] If we accept the thesis that Iron Age I vessels appear as early as the 14th century BCE, then these Mycenaean wares belong to an Iron Age I stratum.

An Alternate Suggestion

The above data indicate that during the 14th century BCE new sites were found, especially in the central hill country, where a new style of pottery was used that was characteristic of Iron Age I. It appears that in the 14th century BCE, two cultures co-existed there side by side: that of the Canaanites and that of the Israelites. While the Canaanite culture survived for many more years, at the same time a new population (Israelite) settled the hill country, so that there came to be an overlapping of the LBA culture with that of Iron Age I.

In this light, it seems that some of the settlements defined as Iron Age I settlements that actually came into existence as early as the 14th century BCE must be added to the list of settlements dated to the earlier Late Bronze Age. Proving that the highlands were not uninhabited, is a claim referred to at the beginning of this chapter.

We do not have the means to differentiate between Iron Age I settlements from the 14th and 13th centuries and those of the 12th century BCE, and so we cannot know which of these settlements co-existed with the LBA settlements and which were established at a later date.

The following table sums up the historical situation:

Date	Hill Country	Plains
18th --end of the 15th century BCE	MBA II culture	MBA II culture
14th -- 12th century BCE	Iron Age I culture in the central highlands and in the hills of Galilee (except for such centers as Shechem and Bet-El)	LBA culture
From the 12th century BCE	Iron Age I culture (Israelite)	Philistine/Canaanite culture

The chronological pattern discussed above solves a number of questions which arose from broad-based surveys carried out in the north of Samaria by Adam Zertal. A unique assemblage of vessels was discovered in Khirbet Einun, in the north of Samaria, and were dated by Zertal to Iron Age I. The uniqueness of the "Einun vessels" stems from their strong resemblance to vessels of an earlier era, the MBA II. Jars with lips descending outwards in two or three stages as well as bowl bases or high-based flasks resembling trumpets characteristic of the close of the Middle Bronze Age are prominent in this group.[128]

The dating of the Einun vessels is based in the main on the fact that well-known potsherds from Iron Age I were found at the same sites, and that they are made from clay material similar to that of other Iron Age I vessels. Finding these jars in this region of Samaria matches the distribution of the stepped lip jars, that are common in the Middle Bronze Age, mainly in Samaria towards the conclusion of this era.[129] In other words, this group was characteristic of Samaria in the MBA as well.

Israel Finkelstein noted the relationship between MBA and Iron Age I in his book on the period of settlement and Judges. He writes, "One must not overlook the considerable resemblance between the collared-rim jars and the jars of the highland sites in Middle Bronze Age II. In this period, too, large jars of similar size to the collared-lip jars appear in the central hill country."[130] Finkelstein solves this riddle with the following words: "It is important to mention that many of the settlement sites in the central highlands came into being in places that had been settled in the Middle Bronze Age... One cannot thus deny the possibility that the new settlers imitated the jars of the early period, the fragments of which were strewn all about, and it is even possible that there were cases where entire vessels found in these sites were re-used."[131]

Such an argument, according to which the people of a certain period imitated the vessels of an era that had ended some 300 years earlier, and even made use of whole vessels some 400 years old or more, is one that clashes with one of the principles of archaeology: periods of time are divided on the basis of vessels typical of the period and it is assumed that these vessels had a short life-span. For example, according to Finkelstein, one can argue that perhaps people living in the Second Temple period made use of or imitated vessels from the First Temple period. Such an argument flies against logic and the accepted principles of archaeology.

Finkelstein's argument concerning the re-use of MBA pottery as late as Iron Age I is based on the finding of a jar characteristic of the MBA, with Hyksos seals on its handles and a corded ornament on its neck, in the middle of a row of collared-lip jars. This row was found inside a warehouse destroyed in the destruction of Shiloh, apparently in the 11th century BCE.[132] And, in fact, Shlomo Bunimovitz writes, "It is not impossible that the people of Iron Age I found a Middle Bronze Age jar and re-used it."

It seems that the similarity between the groups of vessels from each of the two periods which, at first glance, are far from one another in time shows that the potters of the MBA influenced those of the later Iron Age in Samaria. It is quite possible that there was direct contact between the potters of the two periods, and it might even well be the very same family of potters.

Furthermore, the petrographic examination of vessels from the two periods taken from the Shiloh excavation shows that one of the three types of raw material used in the manufacture of these vessels was taken from strata from the lowest exposed cretaceous period in the Wadi Farah, Wadi Malih in northeastern Samaria[133] The appearance of these strata is restricted to defined regions not far from the area where the Einun vessels were found, and it may just be that the potters of the Einun vessels made use of the raw material from this region.[134]

How is this unique phenomenon to be explained? It would seem that if we alter our grasp of the accepted conventions regarding the sequence of archaeological periods in Israel, our problems will be solved. This means that we have to change our conception of the Late Bronze Age: i.e., *this period was not an independent era separating the Middle Bronze Age from the Iron Age, but rather a period partly paralleling Iron Age I.* During this time, Canaanite culture continued to exist in the plains, the valleys and in a number of central sites in the highlands, while in the central hill country and in Galilee another culture existed, with different characteristics. (For the characteristics of this culture, see below.)

In this period, just as in other periods, greater Israel is not to be viewed as a single unit, but rather as two different units with differing cultures: the highland culture and the culture of the plains.[135] This new viewpoint indicates a direct link between the onset of Iron Age I and the end of the Middle Bronze Age, and provides us with a logical explanation of the connection between the vessels of the MBA and those of Iron Age I in Samaria.[136]

In the wake of the surveys conducted by Zertal in northern Samaria, he realized that about 50% of the Iron Age I sites were built on MBA sites. His opinion is that "This is a unique connection, repeated only in serial families: in the transition from Iron Age I to Iron Age II, from the early Roman period to its later counterpart and from the Byzantine Era to the Muslim Era."[137]

Different interpretations of this phenomenon can be offered, but it is difficult to ignore the fact that in all the examples provided by Zertal, the periods under discussion were chronologically consecutive. This analysis is what points to the direct link between Middle Bronze Age II and Iron Age I.

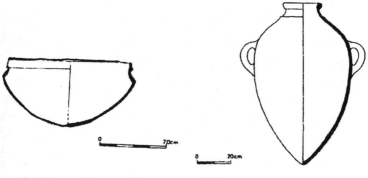

Cooking pot Iron age I   Collared rim jar with small neck

In light of the table on page 67, it can be seen that the Iron Age *in the hill country* is directly linked with the MBA, and so the Einun vessels are a direct continuation of MBA pottery. Furthermore, the existence of the MBA jars together with the collared-lip jars at Shiloh, while being exceptional, can itself be explained.

What Characteristics Distinguish the New Population?

According to the picture described above, a new population penetrated into Canaan at the onset of the 14th century BCE. This population set up over 300 sites all over the highlands, mostly on virgin soil. The settlements built by them had unique characteristics. The buildings were built simply, but with originality. They were constructed as "four-space" buildings or "buildings on columns" described above.

The pottery found in these new settlements is simple, with new elements alongside evidence of the influence of the local Canaanite pottery (the two typical vessels were 'collared-rim' jars[138] and 'axe-lip' cooking pots). Finkelstein has noted correctly that even if it is possible, in certain cases, to point out a certain similarity to Canaanite pottery, in general the pottery of the new population found at these settlement sites is the diametric opposite of the Canaanite centers: single, roughly made vessels with many sub-types, as opposed to excellent, variegated pottery.[139] The ritual sites in the highlands (the altar at Mt. Ebal and the "bull" site in Samaria) were open sites, different from the ones which operated inside structures found in the lowlands,[140] such as the Philistine Temple at Tel Kesila in North Tel Aviv. A system of agricultural stepped terraces was built next to the settlements, an unprecedented phenomenon. (No agricultural terrace from the Bronze Age has been found to this day.)

The New Population Were Israelites

The inhabitants of these settlements used an alphabetical writing system, even for everyday needs. Documents written in earlier periods in greater Israel are official documents written in cuneiform script and located in central sites. Now, for the first time in history, there appears a new script, the ancient Hebrew script, even in small sites of marginal significance. The most renowned and complete of these is the ostracon from the Izbet Sartah site on the western edge of Samaria,[141] on which all the ancient Hebrew letters (except for the *mem*) were inscribed in alphabetical order. This ostracon was probably intended as a writing exercise for a young student. Most of the (rare) inscriptions found up until now from the 14th and 13th centuries BCE were found in the Judean Hills, in southern Samaria and on the inland plain.[142] In contrast, almost no examples of this script before the 8th century BCE have been found in the coastal plain and in the valleys where large, important sites were located, except for vessels on which single words or letters were inscribed.[143]

Despite the intensive excavation of many sites throughout the central highlands, only one gravesite has been made public until now, where Iron Age I potsherds were found.[144] In contrast, many burial sites of different kinds were found on the coastal plain. It would appear that the burial system in the highlands was in simple ditch graves located outside the settlements. This type of grave is generally not preserved, and so no evidence of their existence has survived.

It appears that the most interesting fact for our purposes is the study made of the animal bones found in the hill country sites of this period. In all previous periods throughout the country, these bones included those of sheep, goats, cattle, and pigs. (Some 5%, and as much as 20%, of the bones found were those of pigs). In contrast, in the sites with the architectural and ceramic characteristics noted above, almost no pig bones have been found,[145] probably because of the well-known Jewish prohibition on the eating of swine (Lev 11:7).

We may conclude that the element that settled in the highlands had a number of unique characteristics, different to a considerable degree from the Canaanite culture that preceded it. It is reasonable to assume that the new settlers were Israelites.

Marnepath Stele

External Sources

No inscriptions have been found in the hill country settlement sites to enable us to learn something of the new population and its culture. Yet it seems that the name of this new element was noted in an Egyptian inscription known as the Merneptah Stele.[146]

In this inscription, Pharaoh Merneptah, the king of Egypt who reigned at the close of the 13th century, describes a military campaign and mentions a new element called "Israel" defined as a people (unlike Ashkelon, which is mentioned in the inscription as a city). There is no way to know for sure what the scribe had in mind, but it is clear that when the inscription was written, the Egyptians were familiar with a certain population living in Canaan known as "Israel."

In this connection, Nadav Na'aman writes, "Regarding the identification of 'Israel', there is an unresolved disagreement."[147] Is the inscription speaking of the element that appeared in the central highlands during the 14th century and consolidated its position during the 13th century? In Na'aman's opinion, the consolidation of the tribes of Israel as a unique group came after the 13th century. Therefore, he is not prepared to identify the "Israel" of the inscription with the "Israel" mentioned in the Bible.

On the other hand, if we accept the argument that at the end of the 13th century a new highland element was already entrenched in the hill country, it is difficult to assume that Merneptah completely ignored it. If he did not mean the Israelites, to whom was he referring? To some other element called "Israel" that left no traces of its existence?

Egyptian sources from the 14th and 13th centuries BCE mention an element by the name of 'Asher', located in the Galilee.[148] Is it merely by chance that the Book of Joshua also fixes the location of this Israelite tribe in the Galilee?

Mesha, king of Moab, who lived in the 9th century BCE, writes in his famous inscription, "And men of Gad have lived in the land of Atarot from time immemorial." (line 10) And indeed, in the book of Numbers, we find, "And men of [the Israelite tribe of] Gad built Dibon and Atarot and Aro'er" (Josh. 32:34). Is this not perfect correspondence? (In addition, there are Iron Age findings corroborating this claim from the excavations carried out at Diban i.e., Biblical Dibon.)

To sum up: external sources are indeed rare, yet the mention of Israel in the 13th century BCE, the tribe of Asher in the 14th century BCE, and the evidence provided by Mesha, king of Moab, of the 9th century, of the antiquity of the men of Gad in the region of Atarot on the eastern bank of the Jordan River, all support the ceramic analysis and the carbon 14 testimony: we are witness to the beginnings of the sojourn of the people of Israel in the land of Israel.

From Where Did the Hill Country Settlers Come?

Research literature mentions a number of opinions regarding the origins of the new culture that developed in the central hill country in Iron Age I. Yet it seems that in this matter, the abilities of archaeology are limited. It can indeed suggest reasonable and logical possibilities regarding the builders of the new settlements, but it is unable to provide a complete answer to the question of who they actually were.

The old (Canaanite) culture undoubtedly had some influence on the new (Israelite) culture, especially as it regards the shape of the pottery. Ceramic styles surely passed from one potter to another, yet the difference between the two cultures is so vast that it is very difficult to assume that the highland culture sprang up out of its Canaanite predecessor. (Not a single researcher argues that the Philistine culture originated in Canaanite civilization, despite the considerable influence exerted by Canaanite culture on various elements of Philistine culture in the fields of pottery and architecture. The substantive difference in the design of housing, in the foods, religious ritual and burial customs testifies to the population being of different origin.

The Merneptah Stele, which mentions a people named Is-

The Moabite Mesha stele (ca. mid-9th century BCE)
Ancient-Hebrew script (Paris, Louvre)

rael at the close of the 13th century also indicates that Israel was a uniquely distinguishable element that both foreign rulers and local inhabitants recognized.

In the 1960s, it was argued that the builders of the new settlements and the manufacturers of the new pottery were in fact Canaanites who were fed up with the social order in the Canaanite cities and set up separate settlements for themselves.[149] This view has been called the "sociological approach," since its proponents assume that the changes that took place occurred against an internal social background within Canaanite society, rather than resulting from a foreign element penetrating from outside. Similarly, Israel Finkelstein claimed that the sources of the new population were elements of Canaanite society that had escaped from the Canaanite cities at the close of the Middle Bronze Age and had adopted a nomadic way of life. They lived at the edges of the deserts of Israel, and at some stage, chose to live sedentary lives once again.[150] This thesis, however, has no archaeological basis.

If indeed there were a nomadic people in the highlands, why have they left no real traces? Where are the burial sites of this nomadic population? Are the few graves that have been discovered near Gibeon, Hebron, Jerusalem, and Rabud representative of this nomadic people who built—according to Finkelstein—over 300 settlements throughout the central hill country and in the Galilee during Iron Age I? It should be noted that the graves were discovered near settlements, and apparently served the nearby settlements rather than the nomadic people who naturally enough would have buried their dead far from permanent settlements. Even if we were to assume that we are indeed dealing with a nomadic population that built these settlements, is it logical that they would have made use of pottery typical of the Late Bronze Age in their burial sites, while in their settlements they used new pottery styles such as collared-lip jars? Why, then, have we not found even a single burial site in the highlands containing a collared-lip jar, the most commonly

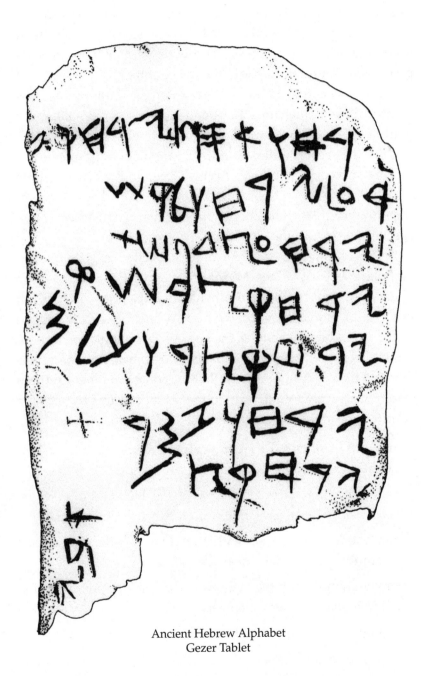

Ancient Hebrew Alphabet
Gezer Tablet

found vessel in the highland settlements? From where did that nomadic population get the prohibition on eating pigs and their unique housing style, four-space buildings, that came to be a prominent feature throughout the hill country?

Finkelstein argues that it was not possible for the new element to have come from the remote deserts since "before the domestication of the camel for grazing, probably towards the close of the second millennium BCE, population groups of significant size could not have survived deep in the deserts of the ancient East; thus the shepherd-nomads (who kept flocks of sheep rather than camels) and the sedentary settlers were two specialized parts of the very same society...."[151]

This argument is odd, for domesticated camels were commonplace as early as the Middle Bronze Age. (See the section titled "Denial of Historical Authenticity of Genesis" in Part I of this work.) Moreover, we have already mentioned the unique feature found specifically at the sites of this population, whose origins were—according to Finkelstein—Canaanite. For it was there, in the central highlands, that the most prominent written testimonials were found, written in the script called by scholars "Proto-Canaanite," that is ancient Hebrew script:

- the ostracon with the Hebrew alphabet from Izbet Sartah in western Samaria[152]

- an engraving on potsherds with the Hebrew letters *nun, mem, shin* or *shin, mem, nun* from Khirbet Tanin in Samaria[153]

- an engraving on a jar with the Hebrew letters *aleph, chet* from Khirbet Raddana near Ramallah

- an engraving with the Hebrew word *lasadeh* from the region of Manahat near Jerusalem, and

- an inscription from Bet-Shemesh on the inland plain[154]

In contrast, in the developed sites and population centers of the Canaanite culture they still made use, in the main, of cuneiform script (documents from Aphek, Hatzor, and a cylindrical stamp found in Bet-Shean.) In clearly Canaanite sites from the 14th and 13th centuries BCE, such as Hatzor, Megiddo, Bet-Shean, Aphek and Gezer, no inscriptions were found in the Proto-Canaanite script. In the south of the country, a number of engravings were found on jars in what is known as the Proto-Canaanite script, as in Lachish, at Tel Hesi, and in a few more places, though in strata dated from the 14th and 13th centuries BCE, and not in later strata.

Furthermore, the finds at Aphek reinforce the argument that the Canaanites themselves made no use of the so-called "Proto-Canaanite" script. The excavations at the site revealed two lexicon fragments, one tri-lingual: Sumerian, Akkadian and Canaanite, and the other bi-lingual, in Canaanite and Akkadian. It appears that even the words in ancient Canaanite were inscribed in cuneiform script. The excavator of the site comments: "Indeed, the scribes of Aphek whose lexicons served them well... trained themselves even to write their national tongue in cuneiform script."[155] Had the "Proto-Canaanite" script been in use in Aphek, it would have been necessary to add a column of transcription in this alphabet to enable the scribe to translate Canaanite words into foreign tongues. In contrast to Aphek, in Izbet Sartah, a small isolated village only about a mile and a half to the east of Aphek, all the letters of the Hebrerw alphabet were found, whereas at Aphek, the large town, they still wrote their own Canaanite language in cuneiform. Is this not clear evidence of two cultures completely different from one another?

Why has no development of this new script been found in Canaanite centers, while in the remote heighland sites the development of the script can clearly be discerned? Logic would have it that conservatism in writing is the central factor involved. Thus, for example, the Assyrian, Babylonian and Persian Empires continued to make use of the complex cuneiform script up until the 5th century BCE, despite the existence of simple alphabetic script that was used in neighboring areas ever since the 10th century BCE.[156]

Therefore, if the Canaanite people were the creators of the alphabetic script known in scholarly circles as "Proto-Canaanite" script, which is still pictorial and shows the influence of Egyptian hieroglyphics (this has not been unambiguously demonstrated, as it depends on chance findings), it was not commonplace in their places of abode. Those who used this script the most in Iron Age I were the highland settlers, unlike the Canaanite settlements that survived until the 10th century BCE (the time of King David), such as Megiddo and Gezer, where no trace of this alphabetic writing has been found.

The best opponent of this view known, as noted above, as "the sociological approach" appears to be Israel Finkelstein himself, for he once wrote that "the sociological approach has risen and fallen, to the best of our understanding, because of the twofold gap between its progenitors and the reality in *Eretz* [the land of]-Israel."[157] This seems to be the truth to this very day.

The bottom line: the highland settlements were constructed by a population whose culture was not of local origin, but rather a people that came to Israel from outside. Analysis of their buildings and the arrangement of the houses testify that they lived in tents in the past, and that their origin was the desert. It is reasonable to assume that parts of that new population mixed with the older population and adopted some of its customs and culture. This means that even a site that seems to show signs of Canaanite culture may well be Israelite. An example of this is Bet-Shemesh, which, according to the Book of Samuel, was populated by Israelites; yet archaeological findings indicate the existence of a Canaanite/Philistine culture.

Is there, then, a contradiction between the Bible and archaeological findings? No. The excavators of Bet-Shemesh noted the fact that the bone finds were similar to those in the highland settlements, i.e., they are characterized by an almost complete absence of pig bones.[158] In light of this, they concluded that despite the Canaanite and Philistine pottery found at the site, the settlement was an Israelite one.[159]

The assumption that the new population on occasion took on the practices of the old population is supported by the testimony of the Bible itself, which tells of some Israelite adoption of paganism, particularly the worship of Baal and Asherah, cleansed periodically by God-fearing Israelite kings, only to backslide into the religious/cultural influences surrounding them. For example, the story of Gideon's destruction of his father's altar for Baal worship and the Asherah tree, and the anger of the townspeople over it, in Judges 6:25-32. Another clear rendition of the assimilation by some Israelites into the cultures that preceded them in the land of Israel may be found in II Kings 17:7-18.

Evidence of Israelite Settlement East of the Jordan

Biblical tradition tells of the passage of the Israelites along the eastern bank of the Jordan River on their way to western Israel. Portions of these regions were conquered by the Israelites, to become the inheritance of the tribes of Gad, Reuben and half the tribe of Menashe. Other parts of the eastern bank of the Jordan remained under the control of various nations: the Moabites, the Ammonites and the descendants of Esau. These three groups are described in the Bible as belonging to the family of Abraham, the patriarch of the Israelite nation.

Ancient Hebrew Script

As archaeological research east of the Jordan lags behind the studies conducted west of the river, most of our knowledge is based on partial surveys and only a few excavations. It is difficult to evaluate the reliability of the surveys, and even the identification of potsherds is riddled with doubt. Nevertheless, we may unequivocally state that a unique ceramic style developed there, the details of which will be appreciated only after more intensive study. (Today, we are aware of "Midianite" pottery dating from the 14th to 12th centuries BCE, as well as "Edomite" pottery from the 7th and 6th centuries BCE).

The Rise of Edom

Israel Finkelstein[160] conducted a survey of the research done in this field. He argues that there is a need for additional surveys in order to reconstruct the history of the area. This is very true; only recently have archaeologists become aware of the traces of the kingdom of Edom from the 11th century BCE. Until just a few years ago, archaeologists claimed that the kingdom of Edom was not founded until the 8th century BCE, contrary to the Biblical description that lists, for example, eight kings who ruled in Edom prior to "the installation of a king over the Israelites" (Gen 36:31-43), and mentions wars conducted by David against Edom (II Sam 8:14).

With the aid of carbon 14 testing, archaeologist Tom Levy and his team have dated copper mines and a fortress they excavated at a place called Khirbet en-Nahas (*nehoshet*, copper, in Hebrew) to the 11th century BCE, and perhaps even earlier than that. The palatial fortress, about 220 square feet with a four–roomed entrance gate, was found. The palace predated the previously held beginnings of the kingdom of Edom by several centuries. It was the missing proof of an independent political entity settled permanently south of the Dead Sea as early as Iron Age I.[161] The dating was determined mainly on the basis of carbon 14 tests, and not by means of pottery, as is generally done.

It can be said with certainty, however, that the Iron Age

I settlement characteristics east of the Jordan are very similar to those west of it. In both regions, researchers have noted an extremely impressive wave of settlement at the onset of the Iron Age. In both regions, similar characteristic pottery has been found, including collared rim jars and cooking pots. Architectural and ceramic features typical of the hilly regions of the central highlands in Iron Age I have been discovered in important sites of this period (Sahab, Khirbet el-Medayna, Lahon and el-Umayri).[162] Larry G. Herr, the excavator of the el-Umayri site in Transjordan, notes that the absence of aesthetic and imported vessels emphasizes the isolation of el-Umayri from the coastal sphere of influence, contrary to its strong links with the central hill country west of the Jordan. He stresses the similarity of the pottery at the site to that found at Mt. Ebal, Giloh, Khirbet Radna (highland sites) and the absence of links with Jericho, Bet-Shean and Peleh, typical Canaanite sites.[163] Herr also suggests that this site should be identified with Biblical Heshbon, the city of Sihon, king of the Amorites (Num 21:21).

So the strong cultural ties between the highland regions on both sides of the Jordan point to the settlement wave that began at the onset of the Iron Age, and it is reasonable to conclude that the settlers were all of a common origin. As in the hilly region on the west bank of the Jordan, so too on its east bank, only a few sites were found that date from the Late Bronze Age. In other words, the beginning of Iron Age culture should be dated the 14th century BCE. Thus, the Late Bronze Age and Iron Age I sites existed side by side.

From where did the new inhabitants appear? It is logical to connect the settlement wave with people arriving from outside the area, i.e., from the desert which is the most likely area for the arrival of a new population, as in western Israel a similar, unprecedented wave of settlement was taking place at the same time.[164] The source of the new population could only have come from the desert.[165]

Are there Contradictions between the Bible and Archaeology concerning Israelite Settlement?

We have noted that the theory that this new population was indigenous to Israel is unacceptable in light of archaeological findings. If so, it is only proper to view the source of the Iron Age I culture as originating outside of western greater Israel. However, in this regard, too, there are two approaches: the first claims that this was a quiet penetration of a nomadic population that lasted a long time,[166] unlike the description appearing in the Book of Joshua, a narrative not accepted by the proponents of this approach as historical. The second relies on the Bible and accepts its general descriptions of Joshua's military campaign.[167] In the following paragraphs, we examine these two views.

According to the Book of Joshua, the Israelites wandered in the desert after the exodus from Egypt and entered the territory of Israel from the eastern bank of the Jordan, conquering the land in a short-lived military campaign. They settled mainly in the highlands, while considerable sections of the country, primarily the plains and valleys, remained settled by Canaanite inhabitants. A distinction must be made between the conquest of the country and settling it. The Israelites conquered most of the land, but established their control only over the hill country in Judea, Samaria and the Galilee.

For many years, this narrative was accepted by scholars as generally reliable. As the years went by, more and more doubt was cast *on the assumption that the entry of the Israelites into the country took place in the 12th century BCE.* This assumption led to the conclusion that the Biblical descriptions of the conquest of Jericho and of Ai were not historical, because the wall of Jericho–which was dated to the Late Bronze Age–was not found in the excavations. Furthermore, no findings from the Late Bronze Age were found in e-Tel, which was identified with Ai, the second city conquered by Joshua.

The battle of Arad, appearing in the Book of Numbers, has

had no archaeological support either, because no Late Bronze Age stratum was found at the site, generally identified as Tel Arad. Yochanan Aharoni proposed, on the basis of the Shishak Inscription, which mentions two settlements in the Negev that were both called Arad. One settlement is indeed Tel Arad and the other is Tel Malhata, which has been identified as the Arad of the Books of Numbers and Joshua. However, in the excavations conducted at Tel Malhata nothing was found from the Late Bronze Age, only from the earlier Middle Bronze Age.

The contradiction between the Biblical account and archaeological findings at Jericho and Ai has strengthened the argument advocating a quiet penetration of the land rather than a military conquest.

In our approach, however, the Iron Age I population entered Israel not during the 12th century, but at the onset of the 14th century BCE! They brought new customs to the region in the fields of construction, food, ritual, and burial. Archaeological findings are unable to identify the destroyers of the settlements in the territory of Israel at the end of the Middle Bronze Age (according to our chronological system, at the end of the 15th century BCE.) *It is, however, most reasonable to assume that this was the very same population that settled the land at the onset of the 14th century BCE, i.e., the tribes of Israel.*

If the entry of the Israelites into Israel occurred during this period, most of the archaeological problems concerning the conquest of the country are resolved:

- Jericho was indeed a fortified city at the close of the Middle Bronze Age.

- In an examination of the pottery found in the excavations conducted by Yehudit Marka-Krause at e-Tel-(Ai), pottery was found that dated from the Middle Bronze Age.[168]

- At el-Jib (Gibeon), a settlement stratum from this period was found, and at Tel Malhata, the site preferred in the past by Aharoni as Arad, a settlement was found dating from the

Middle Bronze Age. This is true of Tel Masos, located in the same area.

• Both in Hatzor and in Lachish (that were burnt to the ground by the Israelites, according to the testimony of the Book of Joshua) there is a stratum of destruction dating from the end of the MBA. Since the Israelites did not take control of the larger part of Israel, the Canaanites returned and settled anew on the site, where they built up a new culture known scientifically as the Late Bronze Age.

In the words of the Book of Judges (3:1-5): "Now these are the nations which the Lord allowed to remain, to test Israel through them – all those who had not known all the Canaanite wars; only that the generations of the Israelites might know, to teach them war, at least those who before did not know these things: the five lords of the Philistines and all the Canaanites... and the Israelites dwelt amongst the Canaanites, the Hittites and the Amorites and the Perizzites and the Hivites and the Jebusites."

The wars with the Canaanites, who grew gradually stronger, lasted a long time. The Canaanite culture continued to survive, as the Bible relates, until the reign of King Solomon. For example, we are told of Gezer that maintained its independence until the days of Solomon: "Pharaoh, the king of Egypt, went up and captured Gezer and burnt it to the ground with fire, and killed all its Canaanite inhabitants, and gave it as a wedding present to his daughter, the wife of Solomon." (I Kings 9:16)

Conquests Recorded in the Book of Judges

The first chapter of the Book of Judges tells of conquests made by the Israelite tribes after the death of Joshua. In this list, we read of the conquests made by the tribes of Judah and Simeon: Bezek (not yet identified with any certainty), Jerusalem, Hebron, D'vir and Zepat (location unknown). The tribe of Judah captured Gaza, Ashkelon and Ekron as well, though the Biblical text says of this: "And the Lord was with Judah, who drove out the inhabitants of the hill country, but they were unable to drive out the inhabitants of the valleys, for they had chariots of iron" (Judges 1:19). In other words, Judah effectively controlled only the highlands, and not the plains. Another conquest mentioned in this chapter is that of Bet-El by the tribes of Joseph. In the second part of the chapter is a list of the cities the Israelites were unable to capture, in contrast to the cities taken by the tribes of Judah and Joseph.

Archaeological findings in the hill country sites that were conquered, according to the Book of Judges, reveal artifacts from both the MBA and from the LBA. Such artifacts were found in Jerusalem, Hebron, D'vir and Bet-El. Shechem (Nablus)--where LBA settlement strata were found as well--is mentioned in the Book of Judges as a place inhabited by Canaanites who allied themselves with Avimelech, the son of Gideon.

In the narrative of the Book of Judges, Canaanite enclaves remained in the highlands, at least at the beginning of the era of Judges. This description fits well with the archaeological evidence. As noted above, these sites are the main highland sites where artifacts were found dating from the Late Bronze Age.[169]

Therefore, the archaeological findings in no way clash with the historical narratives of the Book of Judges. A major question of Biblical scholarship is resolved: The Book of Judges (Chapter 4) describes a battle between the Israelites (whose leader at the time was Deborah) with Sisera, military commander for Yevin, king of Hatzor.

The generally accepted question has been, if Joshua conquered and burnt down Hatzor *in the 13th century BCE*, how did Hatzor become such a major city, governed by the powerful Yevin? According to the archaeological evidence, subsequent to the destruction at the close of the Late Bronze Age, the city was never rebuilt, and only a poorly attested Iron Age I site was found there. However, if what we are discussing is actually the destruction of the city by Joshua *at the close of the Middle Bronze Age, i.e., the end of the 15th century BCE (as we calculate it) and not the 13th century,* Hatzor was restored gradually during the LBA, as the archaeological excavations indeed testify (strata III and IV in the lower city of Hatzor, and the palace in the upper city). The destruction of the city of Hazor during the 13th century BCE was indeed caused by the war waged by the Israelite leader, Deborah, and her general, Barak, against Yevin, king of Hatzor and his military commander, Sisera. The city had ample time to rebuild after its earlier destruction by Joshua.

The Book of Judges contains yet another indication that the entry of the Israelites into the land was very early, earlier than generally believed by the new school of archaeologists. The first chapters of the book tell us of the struggle between the Israelites against the local Canaanites and later against other nations who invaded from the east: the Moabites, Aramaeans, Midianites, Amalekites and the Ammonites. Only in the stories of Samson are the Philistines mentioned at any length (in Chapter 3, a local military event is mentioned against a Philistine unit), and in the Book of Samuel, they become dominant and significant. If there is in the Bible some measure of chronological order, it seems that the Philistines became a significant element in greater Israel at a late stage in the period of the Judges.

Archaeologists date the arrival of the Philistines to the middle of the 12th century (based on documents from the period of Ramses III). Traditional archaeology also dates the consolidation of the Israelite nation in Israel to the very same period of time. This dating clashes with the descriptions in the Book of Judges.

But if the Israelites entered the country in an earlier era (the 15th century BCE), all relevant events follow a single historical sequence. According to an historical narrative rendered by the judge Jephthah (Judges 11:26) and data throughout the Book of Judges--as well as known periods of tranquility between one event and the next--some 300 years passed from the days of Joshua to those of Jephthah. This is feasible if the entry of the Israelites into Israel was c.1400 BCE.

This calculation corresponds well with other Biblical data denoting the time that passed from the Exodus from Egypt to the building of the First Temple. According to the Book of Kings, 480 years passed from the Exodus to the building of Solomon's Temple (I Kings 6:1); in other words, 440 years from the conquest of the country to the construction of the Temple. In the list of the sons of Korah, there are nineteen generations from Korah (who belonged to the generation that left Egypt) until Himan, who lived to the time of Solomon (I Chron. 6:19-22). If we calculate 25 years for each generation and multiply by 19, the sum is 475 years. In addition, historical research based on historians from Tyre and from Rome, put the building of the Temple in the '60s of the 10th century BCE.[170] This outside source--in addition to the Biblical statement--is another confirmation that the Israelites entered the country 440 years before–c. 1400 BCE.[171]

The above combination of archaeological data, Biblical information, and external sources create quite a uniform and reliable picture of the beginnings of the Israelite nation in its land during the period of the Judges.

The El-Amarna Letters and the Book of Judges

Based on the above evidence, the Israelites were already in the land of Israel in the 14th century BCE. Another foreign source helps bolster this conclusion: the El-Amarna letters, dated to the middle of the 14th century BCE, serve as the most important source for Canaanite history in that century. Most of the letters originate in the royal archives of Akhetaten, the capital city of Egypt at the time of Amenhotep IV, known later as Akhenaten. We have access to 382 documents which make up only a part of a much greater archive, most of which did not survive.[172]

The picture gleaned from this archive is undoubtedly incomplete, reflecting only a period of some 25 years, but there is valuable information in it; and the settlement and political picture derived from it reflects a longer period of time.[173] Three basic facts are apparent from the El-Amarna letters:

1. Canaan was subservient to Egypt, though anarchy reigned supreme throughout the land. Limited Egyptian expeditionary forces were stationed in various places in Canaan--such as Jerusalem and Megiddo--yet this army did not prevent the robbery of caravans on the roads, perhaps because it was powerless in the highlands.

2. Canaan was divided into various city-states that ruled their own city and its immediate environs. Canaanite kings quarreled with one another over a number of issues. Many of the letters dealt with mutual complaints.

3. In addition to the inhabitants of the cities that were subservient to some degree or other to Egypt, there was an additional element in the country known in the letters as `prw. (The possible identity of this group will be discussed below.) This group was considered a negative element and an enemy of the existing social and political order by the Egyptians and by some of the rulers of Canaan.

In this light, it is advisable to see if the settlement picture we get from these letters fits in with the information presented in the Bible in connection with this period of time, i.e., the period of the Judges.

Various city-states are mentioned in the El-Amarna letters. The following are the cities to the west of the Jordan River; arranged geographically from north to south. We shall note their situation and status as reflected in the Books of Joshua and Judges:

The Kingdom of Amuru: This kingdom is mentioned as one located in the region of Mt. Hermon and Lebanon, and covers a broad area. The Book of Judges notes that the Hivites living in the Lebanese highlands were not conquered by the Israelites (Judges 2:3; see also Josh. 13:6).

Hatzor: Hatzor is mentioned in the El-Amarna letters as a large city-state that ruled parts of the Golan and maintained contact with Tyre on the Lebanese coast. Nadav Na'aman argues that Hatzor may well have been a territorial kingdom with a capital city and peripheral towns as well, rather than a city-state like the other important cities in the country (except for Shechem).[174] This opinion appears to be reasonable in light of the fact that in one of the El-Amarna letters, the local ruler writes: "Now at present I am protecting Hatzor and its cities" (EA 228),[175] while in another letter this same ruler calls himself "the king of Hatzor" (*sarru*; EA 227), rather than "governor" (*khazanu*), as the other city rulers called themselves.

In the Book of Joshua, Hatzor is called "the head of all these kingdoms" (Josh. 11:10), while in the Book of Judges, Yevin, king of Hatzor, is called "the king of Canaan" (Judg. 4:2, 24). Hatzor was wiped out by the Israelites only after the war of Deborah: "Now the pressure of the Israelites grew greater and greater on Yevin, king of Canaan, until they wiped out Yevin, king of Canaan" (ibid.).

Megiddo and Taanakh: Both of these cities are mentioned as city-states in the El-Amarna letters, corroborating the text of the Book of Judges (Chapter 1), which states that these cities were not conquered by the Israelites. The "Song of Deborah," too, supports this point: "Then the kings of Canaan fought at Taanakh, at the waters of Megiddo" (Judg. 5:19).

Four major towns in the western Galilee are mentioned in the El-Amarna letters: Sidon, Tyre, Acre and Akhshaf. The Book of Judges (1:31) notes that the tribe of Asher did not take control of Acre or of Sidon, as well as other towns such as Akhziv, Aphek, Rehov and Halba. The Bible makes no mention of either Tyre or Akhshaf (which has been tentatively identified with Tel Kison).

There also was a city-state called Rehov in the Bet-Shean Valley. While this city is not mentioned in the Book of Judges, "Bet-Shean and its suburbs" are mentioned there (1: 27). The territory of Bet-Shean was less than that of Rehov. A "governor's mansion" built in Egyptian style was found there, as well as memorial inscriptions commemorating Seti I, king of Egypt. It seems that, from an administrative and military point-of-view, Bet-Shean was more important than Rehov, apparently because of its location on a central road junction on the banks of the Harod Brook.

Shechem: The city of Shechem (Nablus) figures prominently in many of the El-Amarna letters. The kingdom of Shechem which controlled a fairly large amount of territory was ruled by king-governors who strove to expand at the expense of Megiddo and Jerusalem. Shechem is not mentioned at all in the Book of Joshua, but in the narrative of Avimelech (Judg. 9), it appears that the city of Shechem, with its Canaanite inhabitants, survived during the period of the Judges and maintained good relations with the Israelites. We find support for this in the El-Amarna letters, where we read of one Lebaya, king of Shechem, who apparently controlled all of Samaria and parts of the Jezreel Valley, and was accused by his rivals of good relations with the `prw (quite possibly a term the Egyptians used for the Israelites, as we will see below.) From the letters, it seems that the king of Egypt was unable to harm Lebaya, king of Shechem, despite his many attempts. In the end, by means of a trick, he lured him out of his city, captured him and put him to death in the city of Ginna (identified with modern Jenin).

Jerusalem: From the letters written by Abdukhiba, king of Jerusalem, he seems to have been under pressure and was accused of betraying the king of Egypt and joining the `prw. He requests Egyptian military reinforcements against the `prw, claiming that the `prw were conquering "the cities of the king" (EA 288).

In the Book of Judges (1:8), we are informed that the tribe of Judah burnt down Jerusalem, but the very next verse tells us that the tribe of Benjamin did not drive out "the Jebusite inhabitants of Jerusalem." The question thus arises: did they or did they not conquer the city? Despite the complexity of the answer–and there seems to have been a short-lived conquest–it appears, on the basis of the Book of Judges (19:11-12) and of II Samuel (5:6-8), that the city of Jebus–i.e., Jerusalem–was not vanquished until the reign of David.

Gezer: An important city-state that was taken in the days of the Israelite King Solomon by pharaoh, king of Egypt (Judges 1:29; I Kings 9:16).

Ashkelon and Gat: city-states that were conquered by the Israelites, but not completely subdued by them (Judg. 1:18-19; Josh. 13:3).

As already noted, we are limiting ourselves to cities west of the Jordan River. Nevertheless, we shall also note the cities of the "Gari" that are mentioned in the El-Amarna letters as a group of cities located in the southern part of the Golan plateau. Benjamin Mazar suggested that "Gari" is a distortion of the Geshurites mentioned in the Book of Joshua (13:11-13). Joshua did not drive out the Geshurites, and they remained amongst the Israelites until the time of David.[176]

In short, the list of major city-states found in the El-Amarna letters matches almost exactly the cities that the Bible regards as cities that survived as Canaanite cities during the period of the Judges.

Mazar, too, writes in this vein, "The list of unconquered cities (Judg. 1:15-35) is corroborated by archaeological research. In many of the cities mentioned, especially in the Jezreel and Bet-Shean Valleys, we find continuity in the survival of Canaanite culture up until the close of the 11th century BCE."[177]

Who are the "prw" in the El-Amarna Letters?

Much has been written on this subject.[178] No Bible scholar can overlook the similarities between what is described in the El-Amarna letters and the description of the Israelites in the periods of Joshua and the Judges.

Nadav Na'aman denies the possibility of a connection between the `prw and the Israelites. Nevertheless, he notes that the Egyptians did not distinguish between the various groups of nomads because of the conservatism of the Egyptian scribes before the days of the 19th Dynasty (13th century BCE). "Even if there had been Israelite tribes in the land prior to the period of the 19th Dynasty, they would not have been mentioned specifically in the documentation; they would have been called '*shutu*' or '*shusu*,'"[179] meaning nomads.

At the same time, he notes that regarding lifestyle and social status there was a strong parallel between the `prw mentioned in the external sources and the Hebrews in the Book of Samuel.[180] In contrast, Yochanan Aharoni writes: "Though the concept of *hbyrw-hpyrw-`pyrw* itself was an ancient one, denoting in the main a certain foreign social caste in the land, a caste without any permanent rights to land or property, in this period it refers to the scions of the Semitic wave that began to penetrate into the lands of the fertile crescent, and would in time consolidate and become a Hebrew-Aramaic wave. The appearance of the `pyrw-Hebrews in the El-Amarna period is their first appearance in the country... It is certainly not to be regarded as a coincidence that their appearance seems to concentrate in the highland region."[181] With these words, Aharoni indicated a development in the term "Hebrews" from a common noun for a nomadic population without property to a proper noun denoting an ethnic element.

To all appearances, then, the settlement and political picture described in the El-Amarna letters matches that of the Book of Judges. It is likely that the very same period is referred to in both sources.

A Perplexing Question

At the same time, the question arises as to how it happened that the people who conquered Israel rapidly and forcefully, overthrew fortified cities and defeated 31 kings from the Galilee to the Negev, were unable to take control of the cities and settle in them.

The Canaanite and Amorite populations continued to inhabit the widespread, fertile regions of the country and had the power to torment the Israelites. Neighboring peoples such as the Moabites, Midianites and Ammonites entered the country at will and there was nobody to stop them. We have no clear answer to this question–neither from the Bible nor from archaeological finds.

However, there is a slight hint in the Bible: after the list of unconquered cities listed in the Book of Judges (Chapter 1), the text reads as follows: "And the angel of the Lord came up from Gilgal to Bochim, and said: 'I have brought you up out of Egypt and have brought you to the land...but you have not hearkened to My voice; what is this that you have done! Wherefore I also said: I will not drive them out from before you, but they will be unto you as snares...' And it came to pass, when the angel of the Lord spoke these words...the people lifted up their voice and wept. And they called the name of the place Bochim" [i.e. "weeping"] (Judg. 2:1-5).

Why did the Israelites weep? What was the background for this? It seems likely that this declaration followed a traumatic event in which they lost the ability to take effective control of all of Israel. The Book of Judges indicates the reason for this on a divine plane: the people failed to carry out the commandment to destroy the idols. Yet it is unclear what the historical, prosaic events were that brought about this perplexing situation: a nation that had begun so promisingly as a conquering force deteriorated into a marginal group concentrated in the hill country, attempted to survive under difficult conditions, while the best part of the land remained in the hands of the Canaanites. The weeping mentioned in the Book of Judges was undoubtedly connected to this frustrating situation, and the prospect that it would continue.

The opinion held by Alrecht Alt and others, who argue that the settlement of the population from the east was a gradual, quiet process, is well based from an archaeological point of view. However, *this opinion overlooks the fact that there were two stages:* a short-lived conquest reflected in the destruction of the Middle Bronze Age cities, and a second stage of a quiet settlement process in regions not possessed by the Canaanites.[182]

Egyptian Activity in Canaan in this Period

During the 14th and 13th centuries BCE (the period of Joshua and the Judges), Egypt was involved in the development of Canaan. Egyptian administrative centers were built at key points in the coastal plain (in Gaza, Jaffa, Aphek and Bet-Shean). We learn from the El-Amarna letters that small expeditionary forces were stationed in various places such as Jerusalem, Megiddo and others.[183] At the same time, it appears that the Egyptian military forces were not active throughout this entire period, even in the places they were garrisoned, for the king of Jerusalem complains that the expeditionary force was taken out of his city, leaving him without a military force to defend his city from the incursions of the `*prw*.

Scholars are puzzled as to why Egypt is not mentioned in the Book of Judges. Is it because the writers of the book were unaware of the Egyptian presence in Israel? This question has three possible answers:

1. The Bible is not a history book in the modern sense of the word, but rather a book of moral and religious goals. Its editors clearly selected only the events of the time that are in accordance with the aims and ideas of the book. It would seem that mentioning the fact of the Egyptian presence in the country was not sufficiently important in presenting the book's message to its readers. Tel Aviv University's Itamar Singer writes in this vein: "The Bible does not mention in any way the Egyptian rule over Canaan... This does not necessarily stem from ignorance of the geo-political reality in Canaan at the onset of the period of settlement, for the Bible presents a fairly reliable picture of the structure of the Canaanite city-states. The fact that the Bible

ignores the Egyptian rule over Canaan is rooted mainly in ideological and political considerations..."[184]

2. The Book of Judges rarely deals with the coastal plain and the valleys where the Canaanites lived, as it is mainly concerned with the hill country. The El-Amarna letters reveal that the Egyptian force in the hill country was very limited, and so did not play a central role in this region. As noted above, they failed to prevent the activities of the `prw;` trader caravans were robbed on the roads; Lebaya, king of Shechem, continued with his activities until he was murdered. From the El-Amarna letters it appears that, in general, the Egyptians were afraid to send its army against the king of Shechem.

3. There may be, in fact, an indication of an Egyptian presence in the Book of Judges. The following passage appears in Chapter 10, verses 11 and 12: "And the Lord said unto the Israelites: [Did I not save you] from the **Egyptians** and from the Amorites and from the Ammonites and from the Philistines? The Sidonians, too, and the Amalekites and the Maonites oppressed you...and I saved you out of their hand!" The Egyptians mentioned here are generally presumed to be those who enslaved the Israelites during the period of the Israelite sojourn in Egypt. However, Y. Elitzur, in his commentary in the *Da'at Mikra* series, suggests that this mention of Egypt should be ascribed to the period of the Judges, perhaps to the Merneptah campaign that took place at the close of the 13th century. This presumption appears reasonable, for all the other nations appearing in the verse are peoples that oppressed the Israelites during the period of the Judges. The list includes the Maonites and the Sidonians, neither of which is mentioned again in the Book of Judges, or in any other book, as nations that op-

pressed the Israelites.[185] Therefore, there is no evidence that the Book of Judges ignored the presence of Egypt.[186]

The Philistines as a Test Case of the Bible's Reliability

Scholars who reject the reliability of the Bible as an historical source argue that the Biblical authors, presumably writing at the close of the First Temple Period, cannot have known exactly what took place in earlier periods. They charge that the Bible is therefore historically fuzzy and imprecise.

To put this argument to the test, we must consider a topic in which Biblical sources, archaeological finds and Egyptian sources come together. We can then examine the familiarity of the compilers of the Bible with the distant past. A good case in point is the question of the origin of the Philistines.

The Bible contains statements by various prophets concerning the origin of the Philistines. The prophet Amos, who lived in the 8th century BCE, says: "...Did I not bring Israel up from the land of Egypt, and the Philistines from Caphtor and Aram from Kir?" (Amos 9:7). Jeremiah (47:4) calls the Philistines "the remnant of the island of Caphtor," while the prophet Zephaniah (2:5) writes, "Woe unto the inhabitants of the coastal strip, the nation of Kerethim! The word of the Lord is against you, O Canaan, the land of the Philistines... " It appears that the prophets, at the close of the era of the First Temple, were very much aware of the homelands from which Israel's neighbors had come.

At the close of the First Temple Period, the Philistines had largely--though not completely--lost their national identity and culture. Surviving evidence shows that in the 7th century BCE they made use of the old Hebrew alphabet seen in the dedication inscription of "Padi, lord of Ekron" that was discovered at Tel-Mikneh. The pottery characteristic of the Philistines in Iron Age I had vanished, and had come to resemble the pottery typical of the other parts of the country, with certain regional differences (coastal pottery). Nonetheless, the kings of Ekron bore Philistine names, and their religious rituals originating in Greece survived as well.[187]

Despite the passing of about 500 years from the time they departed the land of their origin, the historical knowledge of their origin remained impressed upon the consciousness of all the inhabitants of Israel.

Has an archaeological basis for the origin of the Philistines been found? Yes. The Philistines had an urban culture in their land of origin. Such cultural characteristics as pottery, religious rituals and burial practices have been discovered in excavations carried out in their lands of origin. Thus, for example, it is accepted amongst archaeologists that the shapes of Philistine vessels and their ornamentation originate in the Greek Mycenaean culture. This culture was destroyed at the close of the 13th century BCE, and groups of refugees reached the eastern shores of the Mediterranean Sea. Sanctuaries found in a Philistine settlement (Tel Kesila on the banks of the Yarkon River in the northern part of Tel-Aviv) resemble in a number of aspects sanctuaries located in the vicinity of Greece.

The well known relief of Ramses III from the Medinet Habu in Egypt, which describes the naval battle between the Egyptians and groups of warriors termed by scholars "the sea peoples"--including the Philistines--demonstrates that part of this group "from over the sea" did reach our area. Taken together, all the evidence shows that the prophets were correct regarding the origins of the Philistines. The matter is clear and not doubted by anyone, for the Philistine migrants had fortunately brought with them customs and traditions that had prevailed in the lands of their origin.

A comparison of the archaeological finds in those lands with the finds in Israel provides a fairly clear picture and, as Amihai Mazar put it, "This is a rare example of the settling of a group of migrants who brought with them cultural traditions of their own and then established, together with local people, a magnificent urban culture. This is a culture with unique features recognizable mainly in the development of pottery, of clay statuettes, of burial customs, of various types of seals and weapons..."[188]

A good example, such as this, obliges anyone who wishes to study a population and its origins to pause and ask: how does one study the origin of a group of people who had *no* traditions in the fields of pottery or construction in their land of origin? For example, various nomadic groups who settled in a new place alongside an established population with its own old urban culture, and there developed their own culture? How can archaeology, dealing mainly as it does with potsherds and stones, ascertain their origins?

The only possibility is to learn of these origins from oral or written traditions. The prophet Amos stated that the Israelites came from Egypt and the Philistines from Caphtor (which is Crete); we have seen that Amos was correct in his statement regarding the origin of his neighbors, the Philistines; why then would he err in stating the origin of his own people?

By applying this rational logic, it is impossible to deny the reliability of Amos and the other prophets, even when they refer to the distant past of their own people.

The Destruction of the Shiloh Center—the End of an Era

The religious center at Shiloh, located in the tribe of

PERIOD	ACCEPTED DATING SYSTEM	CHARACTER-ISTICS	ALTERNATE DATING SYSTEM	AS REFLECTED IN THE BIBLE
Late Bronze Age	1550 - 1150 BCE	Renewed urbanization; Egyptian rule of Israel; Large number of imported vessels in the country	1400 - 1150 BCE Canaanite culture and some Egyptian control, mainly in the valleys and on the coastal strip; Israelite culture in the hill country	Israelite Conquest of Canaan under Joshua Period of the Judges until the penetration of the Philistines

			1150 - 1000 BCE	
Iron Age I	1150 - 1000 BCE	Spread of use of iron; Israelite settlement in the hill country and Philistines on coastal plain	Israelites concentrated in the hills, Philistines in the plains from 1150 BCE	Period of the Judges until the conquest of Jerusalem in the time of David

Ephraim, served the Israelite nation for hundreds of years. From the description in the Book of Samuel, national leadership during that time was in a process of decline. Eli, the high priest, was old and his sight was failing; and his corrupt sons were not worthy of leading the Israelite people. As is generally the case, prolonged leadership results in deterioration and corruption which grows steadily more prevalent as the years go by.

Against this background, the unique figure of Samuel emerges. The lad was born after his mother, Hannah, offered an ardent prayer until God blessed her with a child. He served as the last Judge of the Israelite nation, and was the one who transferred political power to the first two Israelite kings, Saul and David.

The decisive blow which led to the destruction of Shiloh was the battle of Eben Ha'ezer (I Sam. 4). This battle found the Philistines drawn up at Aphek, near the sources of the Yarkon River, while the Israelite forces were stationed at Eben Ha'ezer, probably to be identified with the village of Izbet Sartah (within the boundaries of the present-day city of Rosh Ha'ayin), on the slopes of Samaria.

At Izbet Sartah, a single-period settlement from Iron Age I (the period of the Judges) was found with four-space buildings, silos cut into the rock, many, Iron Age I ceramic vessels, as well as an ostracon inscribed with letters of the old Hebrew alphabet.[189]

The Israelites were defeated in this battle. Hofni and Pinhas, the sons of Eli who led the Israelite forces, were killed, and the Ark of the Covenant fell into Philistine hands. As a result of the rumor of his sons' death, and the capture of the Ark

Eli fell, broke his neck, and died. The priestly leadership dynasty was extinguished in a single day.

The Book of Samuel does not relate what befell Shiloh, but the archaeological evidence indicates that the settlement was razed to the ground in a fierce fire. The memory of the destruction of Shiloh was engraved in the consciousness of the people for many years. In fact, the prophet Jeremiah--who prophesied the destruction of the First Temple, centuries later--compared this coming catastrophe with the destruction of Shiloh: "And I shall do to this House upon which My name is called... as I did to Shiloh" (Jer. 7:14). Shiloh remained in ruins for a long time until its partial restoration in Iron Age II.

Let us return to the war which led to this destruction and attempt to trace its roots. The Book of Samuel makes no mention of the cause of the struggle between the Israelites and the Philistines. The verse opening the description of the development of events notes: "And the Israelites went out to wage war against the Philistines, and encamped at Eben Ha'ezer" (I Sam. 4:1). Who began hostilities, and the aim of the aggressors are unclear. The Bible sees no point in discussing this, since the purpose of the narrative is to describe the realization of the prophecy uttered in the previous chapter about the annihilation of the House of Eli and the "exile" of the Ark of the Covenant in the hands of the Philistines. Once again, the purpose of the Biblical narrative is to underscore the message that the events occurring to the nation of Israel are the results of Divine intervention. On a more mundane level, it is clear that the war itself involved human considerations of security or economic threats.

What was the geographical arena of the episode? The historical background, understood through archaeology can provide us with an explanation for this war. A glance at a map of Israel (see map on page 103) clearly shows that Aphek was an important, central point on the international seacoast highway leading from Egypt to Mesopotamia and northern Syria. It is located at the very sources of the Yarkon River, which was, in the

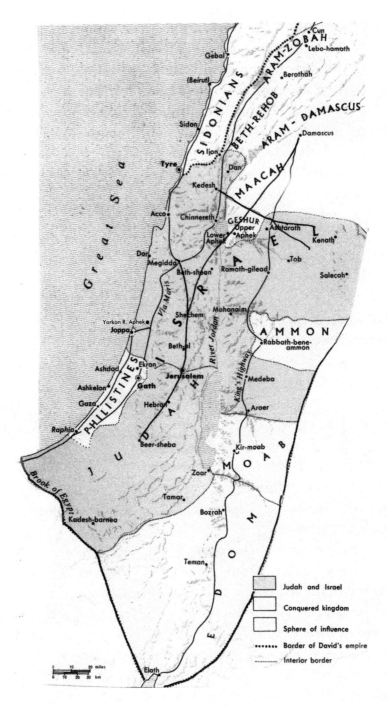

Main roads during the split monarchy

past, fairly wide. (Today most of the waters of the Yarkon are pumped to Jerusalem, so that Yarkon is no longer particularly impressive. Traces of milling stations located along the river, which were based on the exploitation of waterpower, demonstrate how powerful the flow of water in the Yarkon was in the past.) Almost a mile to the east of Aphek, are the mountains of Samaria. A caravan traveling from Egypt to Syria, Assyria or Babylonia–the world powers of the ancient period–would have had to pass Aphek, through the gap between the sources of the Yarkon and the slopes of Samaria.

In the Biblical Period, bridges were not yet existent, so crossing the Yarkon was quite a complex matter. Traveling on the slopes of Samaria was not easy either, especially for a caravan that included beasts of burden loaded with goods. The result was that whoever controlled Aphek was in actual control of the main thoroughfare and of the largest sources of water in Israel (except for the sources of the Jordan). This was indeed a good reason to take control of the spot and entrench oneself there.

Indeed, the archaeological excavations conducted there point to a large settlement of some 200 dunams that was located there from the Early Bronze Age (the third millennium BCE).[190] Is it possible to surmise the historical causes of the Israelite-Philistine confrontation, and what led to the battle of Eben Ha'ezer? Archaeology is able to provide us with an answer, or at least a partial one.

In the excavations conducted at Aphek by Professor Moshe Kochavi of Tel Aviv University between 1972 and 1985, a large city which had existed for hundreds of years was uncovered. In the upper area of the tell (the acropolis), a palace was excavated that dated from the 14th century BCE. On top of this palace, a large structure was exposed, some 500 square yards in area with extremely thick walls (some 55 inches thick). It was a two-story building, the floor plan of which was amazingly similar to that of Egyptian buildings known as "governors' mansions." Such buildings have been found in key sites in the southern part of Israel as well as in Bet-Shean, on the historical Sea Highway.

The generally accepted assumption is that in the 13th century, the Egyptians constructed stations along this important international road for purposes of control and administration. In the building at Aphek, artifacts were found which inform us of its significance: documents with benedictions to be said before Egyptian gods, documents in the Hittite language, as well as in Akkadian and in Canaanite (which we mentioned above). These finds clearly indicate an Egyptian administrative center positioned at the Aphek passage. Signs of its destruction and of a raging fire, as well as traces of arrows that were found, all indicate that the palace was destroyed in battle, and that the Egyptian presence at the site was thus brought to an end.

We know nothing of the identity of the destroyers of the governor's mansion. After the destruction of the building, the ruins of which remained above the ground for a long time afterward, housing was built nearby. Lead weights were found (apparently belonging to fishing nets), as well as sea turtle shells. The excavator surmises that the inhabitants of the area made their living from fishing in the Yarkon River. Moreover, Philistine pottery was found in this stratum, together with the heads of statuettes, the likes of which were first discovered in Philistine Ashdod–and so they are called "Ashdoda." We can assume that the Philistines took over the place from the Egyptians.[191]

In light of these findings, the battle of Eben Ha'ezer can be reconstructed: during the 13th century the Israelites were compelled to come to terms with Egyptian rule at Aphek, but in the 12th century the Egyptian hold of the area began to weaken, and they were forced to abandon the site--perhaps because of a Philistine or, alternately, an Israelite attack. One way or another, the Egyptian departure left a governmental vacuum which the Philistines quickly filled. After the destruction of the Egyptian governor's palace, the Philistines or some other group of "sea people" settled at the site, thus expanding the area of their dominion northwards to the banks of the Yarkon. This Philistine expansion enabled them to take control of the Aphek passage--that important, strategic thoroughfare on the sea highway.

The takeover seems to have disturbed the Israelite nation living nearby on the slopes of the hill country, and thus war broke out in the area of contiguity of the slopes of Samaria, where the Israelites dwelt, and the southern coastal plain, where the Philistines lived. Both the Bible and archaeological research indicate a Philistine settlement at Aphek and a stratum of destruction at Shiloh which confirm the Biblical narrative of the Philistine victory in battle. In the history of Israel, this defeat marks the onset of a new period without any central spiritual or religious replacement for the now-destroyed Shiloh.

The Spotlight Moves to the Judean Hills

The description of the Ark of the Covenant being moved from one location to another in the territory of the Philistines is provided in detail in I Samuel 6. The ark was moved from Aphek to Ashdod, from Ashdod to Gat (Tel Tsafit), and from there to Ekron (Tel Mikneh)–the northern cities of the five Philistine urban centers. Wherever the ark was placed, an epidemic struck the local inhabitants. This phenomenon led them to interpret the presence of the Ark in their midst as the cause of the epidemic, and to send it away to another place.

In order to find out if the ark really was the cause of the epidemic, the Philistines sent it off on a wagon harnessed to two cows whose suckling calves were left behind. The cows began to move along a path leading to Bet-Shemesh and, contrary to nature, ignored their calves mooing behind them. This unnatural conduct on the part of the cows convinced the Philistines that the ark was indeed to blame for the epidemic, and that they should get rid of it. The cows continued on their way "up to Bet-Shemesh," an Israelite city.

The inhabitants of Bet-Shemesh were overjoyed to see the ark, but for an obscure reason: they, too, suffered an epidemic, and the ark was dispatched to Kiryat Ye'arim, in the hills of Jerusalem (today within the municipal boundaries of the Arab town of Abu-Ghosh). There it remained until it was brought up to Jerusalem during the time of King David. The ark's route, then, was that it went down from Shiloh in the hill country of Ephraim to the flatlands, moved from place to place in the coastal plain, and then returned to the hill country, this time to Kiryat Ye'arim. This settlement, like Jerusalem, is described in the Book of Joshua as located on the border between the tribal homes of Judah and Benjamin (Josh. 14).

Archaeologists confirm the description of the cities of Ashdod, Gat and Ekron as Philistine cities in Iron Age I. At first glance, however, they do not support the description of Bet-Shemesh as an Israelite town. In the excavations carried out at Tel Rumeila near the Arab village of Ein Shams, a central, important site was found, dating from the Middle Bronze Age, the Late Bronze Age, and the Iron Age. No sign has been found there of an Israelite settlement in Iron Age I (when the episode of the ark would have occurred). In fact, a large amount of Philistine pottery was found there. Where then was the Israelite settlement described in the Book of Samuel?

As already noted, an interesting find that may answer this question was uncovered in excavations conducted in recent years by Shlomo Bunimovitz and Zvi Lederman.[192] In their study, an unusual situation was found in all the plain and shefelah (lowlands) sites: the animal bone finds covering hundreds of years included the bones of sheep, goats, cattle, and pigs. The number of pig bones was generally between 8% - 20% of the total number of animal bones. Yet in Bet-Shemesh, *no* pig bones were found, despite the fact that such a finding is characteristic of the highland settlements of that period. This finding must be considered together with a potsherd dated to the 12th century BCE, found at the same site. The potsherd was inscribed with the word "Hanan," a Hebrew name. Furthermore, this name appears in the list of Solomon's provinces close to Bet-Shemesh:

"the son of Deker, in Makaz, and in Sha'albim, and Bet-Shemesh, and Elon-bet-Hanan" (I Kings 4:9).

Bunimovitz and Lederman propose that the settlement was really an Israelite one, despite the material finds characteristic of the Philistines. In light of the stories in the Book of Judges indicating that at times the Philistines "ruled over them [the Israelites]" (Judges 15:41), it is possible that in many areas of daily life the Philistines exerted their influence on the Israelite inhabitants of the coastal plain, while in certain respects the Israelites maintained their identity–such as refraining from eating swine. At the same time, the people of Bet-Shemesh were apparently not found worthy of keeping the Ark of the Covenant within the boundaries of their town, and so the Ark was moved to Kiryat Ye'arim.

From this point on, the lead passes to the realm of Benjamin: from the period of the rule of Samuel, who lived in Ramah, (in the area given to the tribe of Benjamin), through Givat Shaul, Saul's royal capital, and ending with Jerusalem, on the border between the two tribal patrimonies of Judah and Benjamin. Historical developments led to the Judean hill country becoming the center of the Israelite nation with the establishment of the monarchy. Despite repeated attempts to undermine the status of Jerusalem as the center of the nation, the result has been an awareness of Jerusalem that continues to flourish in the heart of the Jewish people.

As time passed, the term "Jew" was added to the term "nation of Israel." "Jew" derives from the name of the tribe of Judah, the tribe of King David.

How Jerusalem became the Capital

The selection of Jerusalem as the capital, as well as the city of central sanctity, was not at all a simple matter. The unification of the religious center with the political center of the state was not self-evident, and much had to be done before it became a fact.

The first king of the Israelite nation–Saul, son of Kish, a

Benjaminite–had to make extremely significant decisions as the founder of the Israelite monarchy. One of the main decisions Saul had to make was the selection of a central town to serve as his capital city.

The Focal Point in Benjamin – Givat Shaul

Saul chose the city in which he lived, the *Giv'ah*, the town of Giv'at B'nei Binyamin, to be his capital and renamed it Givat Shaul after himself (I Sam. 11:4). The town which had been devastated by the Israelite tribes after the terrible abomination known as *Pilegesh Ba-Giv'ah* ("the concubine of Giv'ah" – Judg. 19-20) now became the central town of all the Israelite tribes. The Israelite nation had to accept a king from the excommunicated tribe with which they would not marry, and to make occasional pilgrimages to the town they had banned and razed to the ground not many years before.

This town is identified today with Tel El-Ful, located just over two miles north of Jerusalem. The excavations carried out at the site have not added much to our knowledge of the first capital city of the nation of Israel, apparently because of later construction from the close of the First Temple Period and from the Hellenistic Period.

Nevertheless, two items were found which indicate the unique nature of the site. The first is a tower dated to the period of Saul which was apparently part of a fortress built there during that period. We know of no fortresses or other fortifications from the period of the Judges (Iron Age I) in the hill country; thus its existence in the days of Saul testifies to the efforts made to fortify the place, probably as a result of its special significance. The second find is cisterns cut into the rock, some of which are dated from Iron Age I, while others are dated from Iron Age II. Similar cisterns were found at el-Jib–identified with Gibeon–and at Tel e-Nasbeh, identified with HaMitzpah. It is conjectured that these cisterns served as silos or as storage pits for jars of wine.

These two towns were of considerable religious importance during this period. The Ark (I Chron. 21:29) rested at Gibeon, while at HaMitzpah, Samuel performed a ceremonial sacrifice and water libation before the battle with the Philistines (I Sam. 7:5-6). During the period of the monarchy, HaMitzpah was a border town between Judah and Israel; after the destruction of the First Temple, it served as the town of residence of the Babylonian-appointed "commissioner" in Israel, Gedaliah ben Ahiqam. The fact that such cisterns were also found at Givat Shaul indicates the importance of the place.

Saul saw no need to unite the ritual center with his capital city. He left the religious center at Nov, to the north of Jerusalem,[193] where the Tent of Meeting was stationed, and later transferred it to Gibeon, where the "great high place," the sacrificial altar and the sanctuary were located (I Chron. 21:29). Gibeon has been

A fragment of a tablet uncovered during excacations at Tel Dan bears an inscription which includes the phrase "House of David".

identified with el-Jib, northwest of Jerusalem, with a high degree of certainty because of the discovery there of 31 jar handles with the name "Gibeon" inscribed on them. The handles were found inside pits cut into the rock. In addition to these pits, a large pool was also found there, cut into the rock, and a set of stairs descending to the bedrock. This may well be the pool mentioned in the battle at Gibeon between Joab and Abner.[194]

Why was the religious center moved from Nov to Gibeon? The likely reason stemmed from Saul's rivalry with David, who had been anointed as the new king (to replace Saul) by Samuel. It would seem that because of the assistance proffered by Ahimelech, the priest to David (I Sam. 21:2-11), and the subsequent liquidation of the priests of Nov, Saul wanted to relocate the religious center to a place whose loyalty to him was not in doubt. Gibeon was suitable for it was the city of Saul's birth (I Chron. 8:29-33), and the members of his family resided there. He evidently thought that there he would be able to keep an eye on the priests serving in the sanctuary. At the same time, while these ritual centers were active, the Ark of the Covenant was in Kiryat Ye'arim, a town in the territory of Benjamin.

All these centers were in Benjamin, and Saul entrusted all central positions in his monarchy to members of his tribe of Benjamin: "And Saul said unto his servants...Hear now, you Benjaminites, will the son of Jesse [meaning his rival, David] give every one of you fields and vineyards, will he make you all captains of thousands and captains of hundreds?" (I Sam. 22:7). Saul enjoyed great loyalty, even from David's tribe of Judah. When David fled from him, he found no refuge, largely because his own tribe was loyal to King Saul to such an extent that there were even some who wanted to hand him over to Saul. In the end, David had no alternative but to flee to the land of the Philistines.

The status of Givat Shaul as a capital city faded with the death of Saul. His heir, Ish-Boshet, moved it to Mahanayim, on the eastern bank of the Jordan. But the religious centers Gibeon and Kiryat Ye'arim continued to function until the days of David and Solomon.

The Focal Point in Judah — Hebron

After the death of Saul, David came up to Hebron, where he established his capital city. Hebron was the central city in the region south of Jerusalem and was a natural candidate to serve as the capital city of the Hebron hill country. In contrast to Saul, David did not establish his capital in the city of his birth, Bethlehem. There was a religious site in Hebron, too, as we observe from the explanation offered by Absalom to David explaining his going to Hebron: he went to fulfill his vow and to worship God at Hebron (II Sam. 15:7-9). Avi Ofer, the excavator of Tel Rumeida which has been identified with ancient Hebron, claims that the city attained the high point in its flourishing between the 11th century and the close of the 10th century BCE–the period with which we are presently dealing. He identifies a flowering of settlements throughout the region, which expresses itself first and foremost in the establishment of new settlements.[195] The verse describing the arrival of David and his men in Hebron, "and they settled in the towns of Hebron" (II Sam. 2:3), apparently refers to these settlements.

In Hebron, David reigned for seven and a half years. Throughout that period, he was embroiled in a war with Ish-Boshet, the son of Saul, and, to all intents and purposes, with Abner ben Ner, the military commander of Ish-Boshet.

The decisive battle which tipped the scales took place at Gibeon between Joab, David's military commander, and Abner ben Ner (II Sam. 2:12-32). The outcome of this battle compelled Abner to retreat to Mahanayim; and it led to Ish-Boshet relinquishing control of the religious center at Gibeon, the site of the sanctuary. The Bible tells us: "And the House of David grew stronger and stronger while the House of Saul grew weaker." (II Sam. 3:1)[196]

The city of Hebron was thus the political center for David and of the entire tribe of Judah, and David could have ruled over the nation of Israel from this city, just as Saul had ruled from his town of Givat Shaul. But this is not what David did. The fact that he became king of the entire Israelite nation at God's direction and with broad national agreement led him to take a revolutionary, far-reaching step–his choice of Jerusalem as his capital city. The Bible tells of this step, but refrains from explaining it explicitly.

The Critical Move to Jerusalem

According to the Book of Samuel, the first thing David did as king over all Israel was the conquest of Yebus, i.e., Jerusalem (II Sam. 5:6-9). This is not really surprising, for the town of Yebus created a foreign partition between the hills of Hebron and the high country of Bet-El, between the tribal territory of Judah and that of all the other tribes. He needed to take control of the area in order to create territorial continuity for his kingdom.

It is natural that a tension developed between the king's city and the needs of the monarchy: David wanted a new city that would be located in a more central geographical position than that of Hebron. Furthermore, in order to stabilize his capital city, he would have to construct various governing institutions, for which he would confiscate land (which was legal for a king of Israel in order to benefit the nation). He needed to maintain his control without having to placate the veteran inhabitants of the city who would doubtless complain should he seize land. It is therefore not surprising that he chose a new city for this purpose, a city whose inhabitants were foreigners toward whom the king had no emotional or moral obligation.

Another reason for the move speculates that David, as the new king, was mindful that the tribe of Benjamin would resent the monarchy being taken from them and given to his own tribe of Judah. David wanted to compensate the tribe of Benjamin, but could not and would not desert the people of his own tribe. Therefore, he sought and found a solution in the form of Jerusalem, a city which straddled the boundary line between the two tribes. Placing his capital there would signal to both tribes that the king empathized with them and was aware of their needs.

In contrast to Saul, David also tried to appoint to key positions people who were not of his own tribe, particularly those who were of the tribe of Benjamin. This effort stands out prominently in the list of David's property officials (I Chron. 27:25-32) as well as in the list of his mighty warriors (II Sam. 23:27-32).

Nevertheless, the tribe of Judah felt it had been slighted, and the seat of Absalom's rebellion against David was in Hebron, David's first capital city. On the other hand, there were people of the tribe of Benjamin who were not satisfied with David's rule, as illustrated by the story of Shim'i ben Gera of the family of Saul, who stoned David as he was escaping from the forces of Absalom (II Sam. 16:5-6), and by the episode of Sheva ben Bichri, the Benjaminite, who organized yet another rebellion against David (II Sam. 20).

The plethora of difficulties which David encountered at the onset of his reign indicates the profundity of the revolution David had ignited in the Israelite nation, a revolution that displeased many.

Another revolution David engineered was the unification of the seat of monarchy with the seat of religious ritual. David brought the Ark of the Covenant to the new "City of David" (Jerusalem) and prepared the way for the construction of the First Holy Temple that would replace the sanctuary at Gibeon.

From the geographical and social points of view, it seems that this was a long and complex process that began during the period in which the Israelite nation had no national center other than the religious center at Shiloh. The religious center moved from Shiloh in the patrimony of Ephraim to Benjamin, where it split into two centers, with the sanctuary at one and the Ark at the other, to which a new national center was added–Givat Shaul, the capital of the first king of Israel. After the fall of Saul, the national center itself split in two: Hebron, the center of the tribe of Judah, and Mahanayim across the Jordan River, the base of Saul's son, while the religious centers remained in the territory of Benjamin. This process came to its conclusion in Jerusalem, positioned on the border between the two tribes, where the focal points of the government and of the religion were united in a single place.

From this point on, Jerusalem became the religious and national center of Israel and, in a gradual process over hundreds of years, made its way into the heart of the nation where it has rested to this very day.

Bullae with Ancient-Hebrew script from the City of David

Recent Archeological Research from Edom

Thomas Levy's excavations at Wadi Faynan in the eastern Arava at the foot of the Edom mountains were already described in this chapter.

Excavations there are continuing and have provided interesting evidence congruent with Biblical testimony.

As early as seventy years ago, the area was explored by Nelson Glueck, archeologist and President of the Hebrew Union College (as well as CIA agent), who thought that he had found sites in Wadi Faynan dating to the tenth century BCE, including evidence of copper mining activity. He believed that he had found King Solomon's mines.[197]

In later excavations carried out at sites in the high section of the Edom mountains, findings dated to the eighth century BCE were uncovered. Nothing located on these sites came from earlier periods. Since the characteristics of the pottery differed to a great extent from vessels in western Transjordan, the Eretz Israel archeologists could not meet the challenge of identifying the pottery from this period. Owing to that, Glueck's opinion was rejected and the claim that the Edomite kingdom was established only in the eighth century BCE was accepted, meaning that the Biblical descriptions of David's conquests in Edom were not based on historical reality ("He stationed garrisons and all the Edomites became vassals of David..." II Samuel 8:14).

As a result of these arguments, the basis for the Biblical testimony of kings who ruled "before any king ruled over the Israelites" (Genesis 36:31) and about David's war with Edom was undermined, since they claimed that the Edomite kingdom had yet to come into existence. As noted above, in Thomas Levy's excavations at Hirbet enNahas in Wadi Faynan, located about 50 km (31 miles) southeast of the Dead Sea, extensive evidence was found of copper mining as early as twelfth century BCE. The results of Carbon-14 tests made on numerous organic samples discovered at the site all show that they come from between the twelfth to the ninth century BCE.[198]

In addition to the evidence of copper production, a fortress was found measuring 73x73 meters, plus a four-chamber gate. Revealed in the fortress were a number of stages of construction ranging from the tenth to the ninth centuries BCE.

In excavations carried out in 2006, two Egyptian objects were found on the floor of one of the structures.[199] One was a scarab and the other, an amulet with a ring attached. Similar scarabs typical of the eleventh and tenth centuries BCE have been found at other sites in Israel. These objects were made in Egypt.

The excavators feel that they were produced in the time of the pharaoh Siamun or the pharaoh Shoshenk who ruled in the tenth century. Regarding the amulet, made of faience, parallels have been found at other sites in Israel. The amulet seems to be connected to the goddess Mut, the most important goddess in the period of Siamun and Shoshenk.

A survey conducted in the Edomite region found dozens of other sites belonging to the same economic-settlement system. Some have been excavated and pottery similar to that uncovered in the Negev was found, such that today a correlation can be made between the Negev sites and those in Edom.

Tom Levy believes that such a system could only have been administered under a central authority, thus providing testimony to the existence of the Edomite kingdom prior to the time of David. The presence of Egyptian objects at Hirbet en-Nahas is perhaps related to Shoshenk's campaign, which reached the Negev a few years after Solomon's death in the third decade of the tenth century BCE. The Biblical description of the war against Edom and the recent information supporting the existence of a kingdom in Edom even before the Davidic period (Genesis 36) are therefore compatible with current archeological research.

We now know that the source of the error in the archeological research was that the search for the kingdom of Edom was in the high areas of the Edom mountains, not at their foot. The existence of an Edomite kingdom in the Arava region instead of in the high mountains shines a new light on the verse in I Chronicles 18:12, "Avishai son of Zeruiah defeated Edom in the Valley of Salt, he [defeated an army of] 18,000 men." The presumption is that the Valley of Salt is located in the region of the Dead Sea, a few kilometers north of Hirbet en-Nahas, and that the war was apparently waged over the control of this highly important mining site.

Perhaps the fortress, whose plan is similar to others in the Land of Israel and whose gate is typical of those found on many sites in the country, is a fortress built by David or Solomon for the purpose of putting their rule on firm footing, "He (David) stationed troops in Edom and all the Edomites became vassals of David" (II Samuel 8:14; I Chronicles 18:13).

In the time of Jehoram son of Jehoshaphat, Edom rebelled against Judah's rule (II Chronicles 21:8-10). It may be that the cessation of copper mining in the fortress at Hirbet en-Nahas is connected to this rebellion, although there is still no clear-cut answer as to why the copper mining operation was haulted.

It would seem that the Edomites moved their dwelling places to the heights of the Edom mountains, perhaps out of fear of the kingdom of Judah. It seems reasonable to think that the large fortress at Hazevah built in the ninth century (see above, the chapter on the Negev) was erected to thwart the possibility of an Edomite invasion of the Negev. At the end of the seventh century BCE, when the kingdom of Judah weakened, the Edomites spread into the Negev region.

Evidence of their presence is found at various sites in the Negev, such as Hazevah, where an Edomite shrine was discovered; in a letter found at Arad; in a shrine at Hurvat Qitmit not far from Arad; from an Edomite letter discovered at the Huvat Uza, and elsewhere. After the destruction of the First Temple, the Edomites spread northward and reached Hebron and the Hebron Mountain region known by the name Edumea.

THE ISRAELITE MONARCHY

Archaeological Finds of the Israelite Monarchy

With the close of Iron Age I (c. 1000 BCE), a new culture developed on the ruins of the Canaanite towns. This Iron Age II culture is identified with the period of the Israelite Monarchy. According to archaeological finds, a centralized regime planned and built fortified cities, defensive systems, public buildings, and arrangements for water supply in times of war–from Dan, in the north, to Eilat in the south. The construction is of high quality, and the pottery of the period reflects excellent craftsmanship as well. This is the first time in the history of this country that the influence of a strong, directed, guided governmental regime can be detected. Before

119

PERIOD	ACCEPTED DATING SYSTEM	CHARACTER-ISTICS	ALTERNATE DATING SYSTEM	AS REFLECTED IN THE BIBLE
IRON AGE II	1000 - 586 BCE	Renewed urbanization; Central planning throughout the country; Spread of Hebrew script		Period of Israelite Monarchy and the First Temple

dealing with the chronological questions involved, let us look at the era based on archaeological findings.

Cities during the Israelite Monarchy

From the 10th century on, we see a new stage in the urbanization process of Israel. New settlements of different sizes and levels of planning and construction were built. As a rule, the quality of construction in the central cities was higher than in the smaller towns. Yet despite the differences between the various settlements, they share a number of common characteristics:

1. For the first time in Israel, there is widespread use of high-quality beveled rocks in construction. Buildings using ashlars[200] have been discovered at Dan, Hatzor, Megiddo, Dor, Gezer, Samaria, Jerusalem, Ramat Rahel and other sites.

2. For the first time in Israel, public buildings are constructed with their roofs supported by rectangular columns topped by capitals called proto-Ionian or proto-Aeollian capitals (see drawing). Buildings of this sort have been found in Jerusalem, Ramat-Rahel, Samaria, Megiddo, Hatzor, Tel-Dan and Medebia on the eastern bank of the Jordan River.

3. Private homes are usually built in the four-space house plan which includes three parallel spaces and a single space in the back, perpendicular to them. Houses of this type have been discovered throughout the country from Hatzor in the north to Tel-el-Khuleifa (Etzion-Gever) near Eilat in the south, both in the settlements and as isolated

farmhouses. Stairs were found in some of these structures. It is unclear as to whether the stairs led to a roof or if some led to a second story. This is significant for understanding the size of the residence and for estimating how many people lived in such a house.

4. Scattered all over the country are public structures that are rectangular in shape and divided into three parts by two rows of square columns. They were also found in the cities

Proto-Aeolian Capitals (Source: Raich 1987)

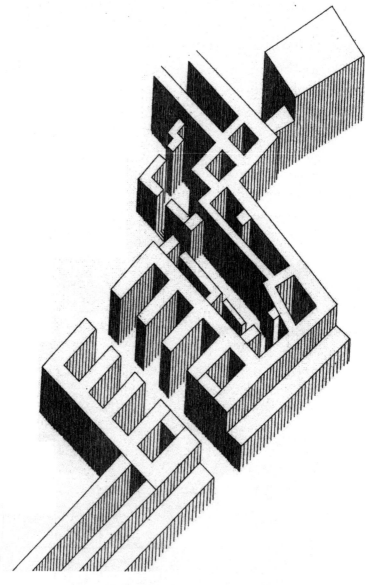

Gate with six chambers (Tel Ira) (Source: Beit Aryeh 1999)

of the monarchy period throughout the country, from Hatzor in the Galilee to Be'er-Sheva in the south. Some scholars identify these structures as horse stables, while others claim they were storehouses.

5. The city plan is generally oval, and the network of streets is peripheral with the outline of the city. The best example of the preservation of the outlines of the city is Tel Sheva.

6. Two kinds of walls are used: casement walls and offset-inset walls. A casement wall is a double wall with rooms or separate cells between them. In an offset-inset wall, a section of the wall protrudes outward and an adjacent section indents or withdraws a few decimeters inward (see illustration on page 122).

7. The design of the city gateways is standard. The function of the gates is not only military; they also serve as a place for residents to assemble. The commercial center was there, and legal disputes were handled there, as well. (See, for example, Ruth 4:1-12, where Boaz goes to the city gate to legally transact the redemption of Naomi's field and resolve the marital status of Ruth.)

The gateway had to meet two mutually contradictory requirements: on one hand, it had to be a place where people could convene or just pass through in days of peace; while, on the other hand, it had to be fortified and impenetrable if the city was attacked. The solution adopted by the people of that day was to construct gateways made up of a number of rooms on either side of the entrance, with open squares both inside and outside the gate. There was a door between the rooms on both sides of the entrance. In peacetime daylight hours, it was open, to be shut only in emergencies.

In times of war, this arrangement ensured the defense of the city: even if the enemy broke through the main external door, the army would have to break through the other doors between the rooms at the gate. The earliest of these gates were the largest, and included six rooms of this type. In Hatzor, Megiddo, Gezer, Ashdod, Lachish and Tel Ira (see page 136) the gates (known as "Gates of Solomon") had three such rooms on either side of the opening. At a later stage, the gateways were reduced to a total of four rooms as in Dan, Megiddo stratum IV (instead of the gate with the six rooms), Dor and Tel Sheva. On occasion, it was deemed sufficient to build only two rooms, as in Lachish stratum II and Dor.

8. Waterworks: Every city of significance has an underground water system cut into the rock, to provide water if and when the city is besieged. In the northern part of the country, underground channels were cut to a source of water, a fountain or an underground source, located outside the city walls (as in Megiddo, Hatzor, Gezer, Yivl'eam, Gibeon, and Jerusalem.) In the south, underground water reservoirs were cut into bedrock within the city walls and then plastered to prevent seepage. Rainwater and floodwater would be fed via channels into the reservoirs (as in Bet-Shemesh, Tel Sheva, Arad[201] and Kadesh Barnea.) Besides these complex projects, wells were dug inside the city or adjacent to it, as found in Lachish, Tel Sheva and Arad.

Brilliant Innovations Made Important Tasks Easier

It is apparent that, for the first time, innovations were developed in numerous aspects of life. These improvements were not limited to construction, but can be seen in agriculture and food preparation as well.

In Iron Age II (c. 1000-586 BCE) the processing methods employed on the agricultural terraces constructed during Iron Age I developed greatly. It appears that an increase in population resulted in a shortage of arable land. To resolve this problem, additional tracts of land were created by terracing the rocky slopes. In this way, larger areas were made available for agriculture.

Winepresses, using wooden beams to increase the pressure

Agricultural steps from the Zimri stream northeast of Jerusalem

on the grapes, were used for the first time. One end of the beam was inserted into a depression cut into the rock while a weight was fastened to the other end, which was then placed on the baskets of grapes. The pressure of the weighted beam on the remains of the grapes in the basket resulted in a greater amount of juice extracted from the grapes.

A similar and even more impressive development took place in the olive oil industry, where industrial structures were erected to facilitate the mass production of oil. Structures of this type have been found in the western Galilee, Samaria and mainly in the Judean plain (shefelah).

This technological development was accompanied by the wide dissemination of Hebrew alphabetic writing, as well as a uniform system of weights used for making payment. (Lumps of metal of various sizes were used, for coins had not yet been invented.) The number of letters found inscribed in various settlements indicates that literacy had spread throughout the country and neighboring lands.

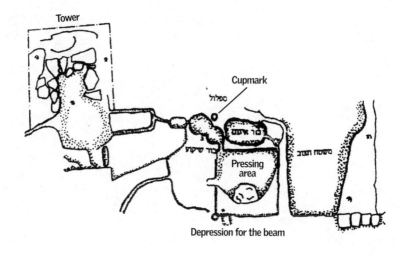

Map of the wine press and tower; from the Zimri stream

Ostraca have been found in various sites in the Negev, Lachish, Jerusalem, and in the city of Samaria. Inscriptions were engraved in rock, like the Siloam gravestone inscription in Jerusalem ...*yahu asher 'al ha-bayit*. (The first part of the name is not legible, but the name ends with "yahu." This person's impor-

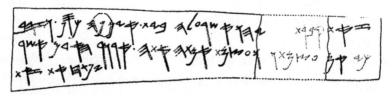

Siloam gravestone inscription in Jerusalem "*yahu asher 'al ha-bayit*"

tant title indicates that he was responsible for the royal house.) Similar inscriptions were also engraved on royal memorial monuments, such as the Mesha Inscription found on the eastern bank of the Jordan River. Pentateuch verses were written on silver slabs that served as amulets, like the one found at Ketef Hinnom in Jerusalem.

It should be noted that a relatively greater number of ostraca were found in the Negev sites than at central sites in the north, perhaps because writing was better preserved in the arid Negev than in the moist north.

Who Was Responsible for the Great Change?

Israel obviously underwent great changes during this period. The question is who brought this about and when?

As we have already seen, archaeological findings without external historical sources are unable to focus on a single absolute system of dating. Unfortunately, we have no external historical sources that document the causes of these changes. From the onset of the Iron Age, we enter a period about which the Bible is our only record. To some, this period is a kind of "Dark Ages." How did it come about?

During the 12th century BCE, the Egyptian kingdom went into decline. It sank into a morass of internal problems and lost its grip on Israel. Except for a short-lived campaign at the close of the 10th century BCE (that of Shisha[202]) Egyptian intervention in the affairs of Israel was over.

The interference of Mesopotamian powers in Israel did not begin until the middle of the 9th century BCE. So there is a period of some 300 years in which there are no records of external historical sources about Israel. As Itamar Singer wrote, "With the reduction of the number of Egyptian sources relating to Canaan and the disappearance of Egyptian artifacts in Canaan itself, the data necessary for a definitive chronology no longer exist, and even the construction of a relative chronology encounters serious difficulties."[203]

The attempt to link widespread royal construction with familiar events and personages leads naturally enough to the founders of the monarchy in Israel, i.e., David and Solomon. They were the first, but also the last central figures in Biblical Israel, whose monarchy extended over large areas in all parts of Israel. They were the first to wield the necessary political and economic power to carry out widespread projects of the sort that are revealed in excavations.

Regarding Solomon specifically, the Bible states clearly that he engaged in widespread construction at various sites in the country, as in Jerusalem, Hatzor, Megiddo, Lower Bet Horon and Gezer, and in the building of supply cities, chariot cities and cavalry cities (I Kings 9:15-19). There is no rational reason not to ascribe these construction projects to Solomon, the great builder.

Arguments For and Against Solomon as the Great Builder

Until not so many years ago, the Biblical description of the kingdom of David and Solomon was accepted universally. Archaeological research strengthened the Biblical record through various discoveries, mainly in the wake of the discovery of the "Gates of Solomon" in Hatzor, Megiddo, and Gezer. The considerable similarity between these gates matched the passage from the Book of Kings noting King Solomon's construction projects: "And he built Hatzor and Megiddo and Gezer" (I Kings 9:15). Traces of impressive construction were found in various regions of the country. These evidences of major construction include planned cities, ashlar construction, spacious houses of a high quality with proto-Iolian capitals, agricultural implements, a high standard of pottery and impressive waterworks. It was clear that only a serious power could plan and execute such impressive countrywide construction projects.

As years went by, however, it became evident that to the

"Gates of Solomon" of Megiddo, Hatzor and Gezer one must add gates from Ashdod, Lachish and Tel-Ira in the Negev, which were excavated at a later date. These new discoveries were found to be similar to the "Gates of Solomon," though some were built after the days of King Solomon. This realization led to an undermining of the assumption that the gates should be linked to King Solomon, which led in turn to erosion of the image of Solomon as the great builder. The term "Gates of Solomon" came to be less accepted.

In time, a question arose regarding the dating of the gates attributed to Solomon. Since we have no archaeological means of dating the pottery found in the strata of the gates, we have no independent chronological anchor. In the past, those strata were ascribed to the days of the King Solomon of the Book of Kings. Scholars who wish to ignore the Bible and date the strata independently are unable to do so, because the dating of the pottery wavers between the onset of the 10th century and the close of the 9th century BCE.

Identifying royal construction in Jerusalem and the Judean Hills that can be attributed to the days of David and Solomon is difficult: while the Book of Kings describes impressive construction projects throughout the country, at the very heart of the kingdom, in Jerusalem and its environs, there are almost no findings from this period.

The fact that remnants of these structures have not been found does not mean that they were never built. (They could have been destroyed during subsequent building projects, for instance.) Other possible explanations for the absence of these remains will be discussed below.

In contrast to Jerusalem, magnificent remnants testifying to great wealth were found in the acropolis of the city of Samaria, the capital of the Kingdom of Israel, at a spot where there had been no later construction. These findings match our knowledge (from the Book of Kings) of the construction of Samaria by Omri and of its becoming the capital city of the Kingdom of Israel. The inscription of the battle at Karkar, written by King Shalmaneser III of Assyria in the year 853 BCE, which mentions "Ahab the Israelite" who had the largest chariot force in that battle, dovetails neatly with the rich finds at the city of Samaria.[204] King Mesha of Moab also notes Omri's conquest of Moab in his famous inscription.

In a series of articles that appeared at the close of the 1990s, Professor Israel Finkelstein added a new argument denying the connection between the royal construction and the period of David and Solomon. A characteristic of the coastal plain sites in Iron Age I is two-color Philistine pottery found in various cities such as Ekron, Ashdod, Ashkelon and Bet-Shemesh (on the plain). The accepted date for the first entry of the Philistines is during the period of Egyptian King Ramses III, probably during the seventies of the 12th century BCE. This dating is based on documents and inscriptions found in Egypt. [205]

In contrast to the abundance of Philistine vessels found in various towns in the coastal plain, their absence is very conspicuous in two sites of central importance: Lachish in the inland plain, and Tel-Shera in the northwest Negev. According to Egyptian inscriptions found at these sites, it seems that the Canaanites survived at least until the end of the days of Ramses III and perhaps even longer, i.e., until the end of the fifties of the 12th century BCE.

Finkelstein's conclusion was that the absence of Philistine pottery stems from the fact that the Philistines arrived in the country only subsequent to the destruction of Tel-Shara and Lachish, and so those two sites would show no Philistine vessels. In this light, Finkelstein proposed to fix the entry of the Philistines into the country sometime during the forties of the 12th century BCE (after the departure of the Egyptians).

The consequence of lowering the dating of the Philistine pottery is that the Philistine archaeological strata then must be dated later by a few decades. Therefore, the strata that were built on them that had been attributed to the 10th century (i.e., to the time of Solomon) were built later than originally thought. According to Finkelstein, this means that the establishment of the cities that the Bible attributed to Solomon must be attributed to someone else, apparently Ahab. [206]

Finkelstein's argument is weak. Does the absence of any one type of pottery from a site indicate that the site was not a contemporary of a nearby site where that type of pottery was found? This is a hypothesis that requires proof, especially since we are speaking of pottery characteristic of a particular ethnic group. There are many cases where the people of a certain ethnic group did not make use of vessels they identified with a nearby, but hostile group. [207] It should be noted that the Philistines conquered portions of the coastal plain from the Canaanites. The Canaanites remaining at Lachish and other sites on the hills of the inland plain were certainly not overjoyed with the pottery characteristic of the group that had killed their brethren on the plains.

Furthermore, it is generally accepted that Lachish was probably destroyed in the middle of the 12th century BCE, i.e., some twenty years after the arrival of the Philistines. This is an insufficient period of time for economic relations to have developed between two mutually hostile ethnic groups. It should also be noted that if the Philistines did not arrive in the days of Ramses III, despite the written evidence in Egypt that such was indeed the case, it would be necessary to discover a new, third wave of Philistines that arrived on the coast of Israel. There is no evidence at all of such a third wave. [208]

Despite all the counter-arguments [209] and the inadequate basis of the new theory known as "the Low Chronology," it finds support, primarily at Tel Aviv University, where Finkelstein was the director of the Nadler Institute of Archaeology. According to their contention, the period of Iron Age I extended until the middle of the 9th century BCE. In their opinion, a northern kingdom developed in the 9th century, a strong and rich kingdom, while to the south there was a small, poor, highlands kingdom.

Finkelstein and his collegues claim that only after the destruction of Samaria in the year 721 BCE did the southern kingdom—the Kingdom of Judah—develop into the center of the Israelite nation. Only then–well after the era of David and Solomon--did Jerusalem become a large and strong city.[210]

At first glance, this theory fits well with the Braudelian concept known as "long duration."[211] As noted later in this volume, the French historian Fernand Braudel coined this term to denote that history must be studied over a period of time, because there are historical patterns that repeat themselves after hundreds of years, rendering predictability to historical processes. Braudel also claimed, on the basis of observations made in the Mediterranean Basin that "the culture of urbanization in the low-lying areas penetrated into the highland world in an incomplete fashion and at a slow pace. The men of the highlands oppose the historical trend with the blessings and the burdens that accompany it, or accept it with reservation."[212]

This approach indeed has been validated in the Judean Hills. As we will later see in connection with the Middle Bronze Age, the highlands developed at a slower rate than the plains. At the onset of the Middle Bronze Age (c. 2000 BCE), an urban culture developed in the plains while in the highlands of Judea a population typical of the Intermediate Bronze Age was still actively pursuing a nomadic lifestyle and would continue doing so for quite a long time. Only at about 1800 BCE did they begin building fortified cities in the hill country, and these were extremely small in comparison with the cities on the plains and the lowlands. In Iron Age I (1150-1000 BCE) as well, there was a considerable difference between the hill country and the plains. The Canaanite and Philistine settlements were many times more developed than the small and severely limited settlements in the hills. [213]

The material culture reflected in the Iron Age II sites (the Israelite Monarchy) in the north, on the plains and in the valleys of Samaria was undoubtedly more developed than in the

Judean Hills. Archaeological finds at Samaria, Hatzor, Megiddo, Dan, Gezer, Dor, Ashdod etc., in the strata dated to the 10th and 9th centuries BCE, are most impressive. Yet in the Judean highlands, the findings are less impressive; in fact, almost nothing was found from these centuries in this part of the country.

To make our point clearer, let us skip to the Persian Period, following the destruction of the first Temple, where we find a similar phenomenon. In this period, too, the sites on the coastal plain are more developed and impressive than the few sites that existed in the hill country. The researcher of this period, Ephraim Stern, wrote, "The boundary between these two cultural regions is often very sharp, almost like the border between two countries."[214]

It appears that we have here a fairly fixed model over a period of hundreds of years. The period of the Monarchy is not substantially different from other periods. This description, of course, contradicts the Biblical description of Solomon's kingdom. Are Solomon's vast building projects largely imaginary, in spite of everything, as various scholars, spearheaded by Finkelstein, argue?

While there is a 9th century BCE inscription found at Tel-Dan, which notes *"bet david"*—the existence of a king of "the House of David"[215]—there is little else extant attesting to this monarchy. Is the absence of contemporary external documentation concerning David and Solomon, and the lack of impressive archaeological evidence from this period in the Judean hill country, *proof* of inaccuracy of the Biblical narrative?[216]

I believe that lack of findings is not sufficient proof and I support the protest against the movement that would use the *absence* of data to strip Kings David and Solomon of their role as important rulers of the Israelite nation. As one important Bible scholar voiced: "This bitter protest stems from the fact that from the very beginning the archaeology of Israel took upon itself… a role it is unable to fill and is not supposed to fill: 'to prove history' or to disprove it… The role of archaeology is to reveal the ancient material culture and to establish as far as possible the characteristics of the various cultures... it still remains only one of the sources for the reconstruction of history."[217]

A famous veteran archaeologist and researcher of Jerusalem writes in a similar vein: "From a methodological point of view, every historical reconstruction based on the absence of findings is valueless."[218]

Archaeology is not everything when it comes to the study of the past. Nevertheless, the best thing to do is to examine all the archaeological finds, the (few) external historical sources and the words of the Bible.

In describing Solomon's construction projects, the Bible mentions a number of sites other than Jerusalem where he built: Hatzor, Megiddo, Gezer, Lower Bet-Horon, Ba'alat and Tamar

Area G in City of David

(possibly Tadmor).[219] This list contains no site whatsoever in the hill country of Judea or Samaria. Various conjectures may be made as to why Solomon did not build in the highlands, but the list is quite clear and is imbued with strategic logic. Gezer, Megiddo and Hatzor are towns straddling important key positions along the Sea Road; Bet Horon was a significant site on the central road coming up from the coastal plain to the Jerusalem region;[220] Tadmor is an important site on the convoy route from Damascus to the region of the Euphrates. (Ba'alat has not been identified.) Indeed, no royal construction in the hill country is mentioned, except for Jerusalem.

Is it possible that the tribes of the highlands in the days of Solomon were unhappy with the cost and extreme effort involved in impressive building projects initiated by King Solomon? This sentiment is expressed in the message brought by representatives of the Israelite nation to Solomon's son and heir, King Rehoboam: *"Your father made our yoke [of taxation] difficult; now, you lighten the grievous service of your father and the heavy yoke which he placed upon us, and we will serve you."* (I Kings 12:4) Indeed, in a survey conducted in the hill country of Hebron by Avi Ofer, many sites were discovered that were built in this period, though state construction has not been found until now. "The period from the close of the 11th century until the end of the 10th century BCE marks an important stage in the settlement of the region. In this period the great break-through took place in the settling of the Judean highlands, a break-through that led to the transformation of the area from an internal sparsely-settled part of Israel to a real inhabited region... Permanent settlements were thus greater by over 50% than what they had been at any previous period of time."[221]

The Ascendance of the Highland Culture

An examination of the "long duration" model casts doubt on the validity of this rule in Iron Age II (1000-586 BCE, the period of the Israelite Monarchy)for there are a number of significant differences between this period, the Middle Bronze Age and between both of these and Iron Age I.

1. In the Middle Bronze Age, we perceive a slow process of cultural penetration from the better-developed plains to the conservative highlands area, and the subsequent cultural overcoming of the hill country. Yet in the Iron Age, the highlands finally overcame the lowlands. Philistine and Canaanite cultures disappear. The Philistines adopt the Hebrew script, Philistine pottery vanishes and Judean pottery is found on the plains.

2. In the Middle Bronze Age, there is a clear connection between the highlands culture and that of the plains; in Iron Age I, there is a link between the people of the highlands and those of the eastern bank of the Jordan. During the MBA, the origin of the people is from the north, to the plains, and then to the hills, while during Iron Age I, the direction of the movement of people of the central hill country seems to be from the east.

3. From the 8th century on (Iron Age II), an anomaly exists regarding the status of Jerusalem, which, according to archaeological evidence, became the greatest city in Israel. Its walled-in area was some 650 dunams, and according to Gabriel Barkay,[222] it had neighborhoods outside the city walls, so that its real area came to approximately 1000 dunams. Considering Jerusalem's topographical problems and its lack of abundant water sources, this is exceptional, even in modern days. It is clear beyond a doubt that in this period the "longue durée" model does not apply.

4. An interesting settlement process took place in the Negev in the Iron Age. Many sites began to develop throughout the Negev, both in the Be'er-Sheva Valley and in the highlands of the Negev. While there were only two sites in the Be'er-Sheva Valley during the MBA, during Iron Age II there were scores of sites there. A large number of these

sites were dated by their excavators to the 10th century BCE. This is the period from which finds in the hill country are extremely poor. To a considerable extent, this period resembles the Intermediate Bronze Age, when there were many settlements in the Negev highlands (but not in the Be'er-Sheva Valley).

5. The final point to be noted is that throughout the earlier ages, material culture was imported from outside countries. Naturally, the inhabitants of the lowlands along the Sea Road and alongside the ports were more influenced by these outside cultures than were the people of the hill country. However, the material culture of the Iron Age--when Israelites ruled their own land--was largely of local manufacture. Similar gateways, four-space houses, water works, agricultural terraces, and installations to manufacture wine and oil, all of these are unknown in the neighboring countries in this period. Development was clearly internal, contrary to the other periods we have considered.

We simply cannot apply the "long duration" model here. Even if this model is valid in most cases, we are confronted here with an exceptional feature that can only be explained by the inner strengths of the Israelite monarchs and inhabitants of the hill area in the Iron Age. They challenged the laws of nature and succeed in establishing an extremely well developed material culture.

Shishak's Campaign and the Negev Sites

The controversy over the 10th century has not as yet been resolved, and even C-14 testing has not provided an unambiguous result. Each excavator tends to interpret the results in accordance with his understanding, and the difference between the opinions is no more than 100 years, a difference which falls within the accepted range of error in such examinations. In this light, we shall now introduce another element into this argument which has not been referred to until now, the Israelite fortresses in the Negev and Shishak's campaign. The Egyptian king's invasion of the territory took place c. 925-924 BCE, five years after the death of Solomon and the split in the Monarchy.

Shishak's campaign to Israel and his list of conquests have kept archaeologists and Bible commentators busy for a long time. This is a one-time occurrence, when an historical event in Israel is illuminated by an external source providing a detailed list of scores of settlements all over the country. [223] This military campaign undoubtedly took place, since both the Book of Kings and the Book of Chronicles mention it, and a fragment of a monument was discovered bearing the name of Shishak was found in excavations at Megiddo. (Unfortunately, this fragment was found in a dump and not in its original place). This is not the place to go into questions of the coordination between the Biblical narrative and the Egyptian description at the Temple at Karnak, nor shall we discuss the route of the campaign. For our purposes, the description of the campaign in the Negev is what interests us.

A list of 70 sites in the Negev appears in the description of the campaign appearing in Karnak, Egypt. In light of this inscription, it is certain that in the 10th century the Negev had scores of settlements. In fact, archaeologists have uncovered many of these, most being single-period sites. Various opinions have been expressed over the years regarding the substance and function of the sites in the Negev. Were they settlements established by desert nomads, or by the Israelite nation? [224] Perhaps they were royal fortresses from the days of Solomon? [225] A moderate opinion claims that they are a combination of local settlements and external initiatives. [226]

Interpretation of the findings is certainly not simple. Some of the sites have thick walls and look like military fortifications. Others have similar floor plans, but their walls are thin and not suitable for withstanding attack. The plans of some of the sites derive from their surface conditions, while in other cases there seems to be no connection between surface conditions and the plan of the site.

Whatever the solution may be, there are a number of points of agreement. All archaeologists agree that these sites should not be dated later than the 10th century BCE. They are protected by a barrier, and they contain four-spaced buildings, two widespread features of contemporary settlements in the northern part of the country. The relationship between the northern sites and those of the Negev finds expression in two parameters: architecture and pottery.

Round fortresses attributed to the 10th century are found both in the periphery of the region known as Samaria and on the Golan Heights; the plans of these fortresses resemble those of the round fortresses in the Negev.[227] It seems quite clear that these similarities of contemporary architecture reflect a concentrated effort made by a single authority, in the 10th century BCE, to build a network of fortifications in the border regions of western Israel.

Logic leads to the conclusion that these fortresses are the sites mentioned in connection with Shishak's invasion, for if these settlement/fortresses did not exist in the second half of the 10th century, what did Shishak encounter during his campaign? It must be emphasized that these were single-period sites; they existed for only a few decades and were then abandoned. It is not possible to ascribe the existence of these sites to any post-Shishak period. [228]

This fact serves as a chronological "anchor." Consequently, the pottery found in these sites is to be dated to the 10th century BCE. Rudolph Cohen, the archaeologist of the Negev who made a study of scores of sites and excavated some of these, notes that the pottery in some of them parallels the collections found in Hatzor strata X and IX, and in Megiddo stratum V, *the very strata that are attributed to the era of Solomon.*

This holds true in the excavations Cohen conducted at the Haro'e site, at Khirbet Rehava and at Khirbet Halukim.[229] Yo-

chanan Aharoni and his colleagues also note the similarity between the pottery at Ramat Matred in the Negev and that of
Hatzor stratum X and Megiddo stratum V.[230] Like Cohen and
Aharoni, Zeev Meshel argues that the pottery found in his excavation at Khirbet Ritma parallels that of Megiddo V and Hatzor
X and IX. Meshel also notes its resemblance to the pottery in
stratum II at Tel Asdar in the Be'er-Sheva Valley, where pottery
was found to parallel stratum V at Megiddo.[231]

In light of this, it is indeed impossible to date independently the strata in which the "Gates of Solomon" were found,
yet the archaeological "anchor" is in the Negev, where scores
of single-period sites have been found without any settlement
continuity. The Negev sites must be dated to the 10th century,
the time of Shishak's campaign, for at a later time, such as the
9th century, the Negev was desolate.

In the same way, the pottery found in the Negev highland
sites serves as a chronological "anchor" embedded in the 10th
century. We can use it for comparison with sites in the north.
This conclusion restores the dating of the gateways with the
six rooms to the days of Solomon. The words of I Kings 9:19,
"all of Solomon's storage cities and his chariot cities and his
cavalry cities" may well be referring to the sites of the Negev,
the periphery of Samaria, and the Golan Heights, border areas
and key sites on the main roads. It is reasonable to assume that
state-authorized construction was of a military and/or administrative nature.

On the other hand, not much was invested in the regular
settlements that were already in existence even before the days
of Solomon. Is it not possible that in some of these settlements
the pottery characteristic of Iron Age I was still in use? Since the
Israelite population of the highlands remained stable, as far as
the individual potter in a village was concerned, no substantive
changes took place that would precipitate changes in the shape
of the pottery.

In this respect, I accept the opinion of Finkelstein who

would extend the period of Iron Age I pottery until the 10th century BCE *with but a single, significant reservation:* during the 10th century, Iron Age I pottery made by local inhabitants may have been used in the small hill country sites simultaneously with the first appearance of Iron Age II pottery which were more commonplace in the new cities built under the aegis of the central government in that period.

Why has Nothing from the Days of Solomon been Found in Jerusalem and Judea?

Archaeological finds uncovered in Hatzor, Megiddo and Gezer can be interpreted as state-authorized construction from Solomon's days. In the numerous excavations conducted in Jerusalem, however, impressive findings date from a later era, the 8th and 7th centuries BCE. While potsherds from the 10th century indeed have been found on the eastern slope of the City of David, including fragments manufactured in Phoenicia that would confirm the Biblical account of the special relationship between Hiram, King of Tyre, and David and Solomon, Kings in Jerusalem, still no signs of royal structures have been found. [232]Is it possible that perhaps there were no public buildings at all in Jerusalem from this period, and that Jerusalem was a small, unpretentious town until the 8th century?

To confront this problem, we have to consider the limitations of archaeology. We noted above that most of the im-

Seal of "Shema servant of Jeroboam" from Megiddo

pressive state-authorized construction was concentrated in the northern part of the country, in cities such as Hatzor, Tel Dan, and Megiddo.

The common denominator of these sites is that they were all in ruins before the end of the 8th century BCE, and were abandoned almost completely at the end of the Iron Age (6th century BCE). Because so many sites throughout the country were abandoned at the end of Biblical periods and *remained relatively untouched*, archaeologists are able to find significant traces of the various Biblical periods.

Yet in the city of Samaria, which was rebuilt in the Hellenistic Period and afterwards in the Herodian Era, almost no Biblical traces were found, except for the impressive compound in the acropolis of the city. (This remained because there was almost no late construction there.) We do not know what the area of Samaria was and what it looked like in its early days. King Sargon of Assyria, who conquered Samaria, wrote that he rebuilt the city and made it greater than it had been previously, but his city has not survived and we have no idea whatever of what it looked like. *Later construction obliterated the record of earlier buildings.*

If the city of Samaria is problematic, though it served as the capital city of the Kingdom of Israel for about 150 years, Jerusalem is far more so. Unlike Samaria, Jerusalem has existed continuously from the Middle Bronze Age to the present day. We are hardly able to make discoveries from the Bronze and Iron Ages, especially with regard to those periods when the city stood for long periods of time.

It is relatively easy for archaeologists to unearth finds from strata characterized by destruction. In this way, for example, discoveries were made of items confirming the destruction of the Second Temple; yet we do not possess valuable finds from the onset of the Second Temple period, only testimony of its destruction. We are not able to point to any structure dated from the Persian Period (539-333 BCE) or from the Early Hellenistic

Period (333-152 BCE). Nevertheless, does anyone doubt the existence of the city during these periods?

Why should we doubt the existence of Jerusalem, a central city at the onset of Iron Age II? The El-Amarna letters indicate the existence of a central city of Jerusalem in the 14th century BCE, yet almost no artifact from this period has been found. We can formulate a rule applicable to archaeology: *the more important the site, the fewer the findings from its earliest periods.* [233]

Despite its limitations, archaeology has succeeded in uncovering artifacts from the Biblical periods in the early nucleus of the city of Jerusalem, the City of David, especially from the MBA and the close of the Iron Age. An examination of the geographical distribution of the finds dating from these periods indicates quite clearly that most of them were found on the eastern slope of the City of David. This region has been deserted from Second Temple times to the present day. The lack of subsequent construction in the area made possible the preservation of ancient relics.

It should be noted that all the excavations carried out on the ridge of the City of David resulted in no findings whatever from the earliest periods to the days of the Hasmoneans. In the area known as the Ophel (just below the Temple Mount), it is apparent that the bedrock had been cut into, and all the artifacts found date from the close of the Second Temple Period or later. The staircase leading to the Hulda Gates rests on bedrock, and it is inconceivable that the place was uninhabited before the staircase was laid. Data gleaned from the site indicate that while the area was being prepared for the construction of the Temple Mount in the Second Temple Period, it was cleared of everything but the bedrock. To the west of the Temple Mount, too, it can clearly be seen that the construction carried out in the Second Temple Period went down to bedrock.

Was there no activity at all in these areas in earlier times? Of course, under present political circumstances, the Temple Mount itself cannot be excavated, but even if it were, it is unlikely that Herod left any ancient remnants predating his own period. His demolition project in preparation for the expansion of the Temple Mount area and the Second Temple would have razed any structures built in an earlier age.

Only on the eastern edges of the Ophel, in its lower part, has a gate been found from the First Temple Period. [234] The question concerning the absence of extant structures from 10th century BCE Jerusalem fits well with two other questions relating to the very same area. The first concerns the Late Bronze Age and the second, the Hellenistic Era.

Was there a City of Jerusalem in the Late Bronze Age?

In the archives found at El-Amarna, Egypt, letters were discovered which had been sent from Canaan to the Egyptian kings Amenhotep III and Amenhotep IV (Akhnaton) who ruled Egypt in the middle of the 14th century BCE. Among the letters were a few from the king of Jerusalem. It can be deduced from these that Jerusalem was a city-state controlling a fairly wide area, [235] and it can reasonably be assumed that the area of the city itself was considerable.

The archaeological finds from this period do not meet the expectations of a city-state (in contrast to other city-states during the same period, such as Shechem, Lachish, Gezer and Hatzor, where the findings do meet the expectations of a city-state in this period). [236] Findings in Jerusalem are few and far between, and are concentrated on the eastern slope of the City of David.

PERIOD	ACCEPTED DATING SYSTEM	CHARACTER-ISTICS	ALTERNATE DATING SYSTEM	AS REFLECTED IN THE BIBLE
LATE BRONZE AGE	1550 - 1150 BCE	Renewed urbanization; Egyptian rule of Israel; Large number of imported vessels in the country	1400 - 1150 BCE Canaanite culture and some Egyptian control, mainly in the valleys and on the coastal strip; Israelite culture in the hill country	Israelite Conquest of Canaan under Joshua Period of the Judges until the penetration of the Philistines

In addition, a few burial sites were found on the Mount of Olives, in the Talpiot Mizrah neighborhood and in the Nahalat Ahim area. [237] The paucity of findings has given rise to the argument that there was actually no settlement in Jerusalem in the Late Bronze Age. [238]

Were it not for the discovery of the El-Amarna letters that undoubtedly date from the Late Bronze Age, we never would have imagined that Jerusalem was a city-state in the 14th century BCE. However, the discovery of the letters has led many researchers to grasp at the slightest traces in order to fit them into the picture painted by the letters.

Where did the Seleucid Aqra Stand?

Moving on to the Second Temple Period, hundreds of years later, we find that one of the subjects that has engaged the researchers of Jerusalem for a number of generations is the location of a fortress known (in Greek) as the Aqra.

Josephus Flavius notes that Antiochus IV (of the Seleucid Empire) built the Aqra in the Lower City, "a lofty citadel towering over the Temple" (*Antiquities of the Jews* XII, 22). The Book of Maccabees states that the Aqra was located in the City of David in Jerusalem (Maccabees I 14:36). Both of these sources note specifically that this fortress stood to the south of the Temple Mount. The problem which researchers face is that this area is topographically lower than the Temple Mount. It is difficult to understand just how it was possible to build a fortress that could overlook the Temple, which was located high above the Lower City.

Various suggestions attempted to bring the written sources into line with the conditions on the ground. [239] Some suggested that the Aqra was in another part of the city, ignoring the testimony of the written sources, all of which agreed that the Aqra was located south of the Temple Mount, in the Lower City. Moreover, at the close of the Second Temple Era, the southeastern hill was known as the Aqra (The Jewish Wars V, 4:1). It is reasonable to assume that this name indicates that in the past there had stood at that site some central structure bearing that name.

Contrary to accepted opinion, B. Bar-Kochba doubts the reliability of the historical sources regarding the Aqra overseeing the Temple. He argues that the purpose of the Aqra was merely to maintain control over the City of David. [240]

In other words, three different historical sources dealing with three different historical periods bear evidence that the region of the southeastern hill of Jerusalem was populated and that it had public buildings. However, archaeological finds do not support these sources. In the case of the Aqra, the topographical structure of the area contradicts the historical evidence as well.

Yet, if we accept an account presented in the book by Josephus Flavius, *The Wars of the Jews* at face value, all of these problems are immediately resolved. This historical source is the description of Jerusalem at the end of the Second Temple Period, but it is difficult to comprehend and has been considered by some as questionable. Let us take a closer look.

Jerusalem Described in "The Wars of the Jews"

"… the second hill is the one called [H]aqra, upon which the Lower City was located. It is misshapen in two directions. Opposite this hill there was a third hill which was originally lower than the hill of the Aqra, and a wide valley separated the two. Later on, however, when the Hasmoneans reigned, they blocked up this valley because they wanted to connect the city with the Temple *and so they demolished the top of the Aqra and reduced its height,* so that the Temple would be taller than it" (*The Wars of the Jews*, Book V, 4:1). A detailed description of the processes that led to the destruction of the Aqra and to the lowering of the hill on which it stood appears in Josephus's other book, *Antiquities of the Jews*, where he relates that the lowering of the hill took three years, day and night, without a pause, until the entire site of the fortress-hill was rendered flat (*Antiquities of the Jews* XIII, 212-215).

If we accept this account of Josephus Flavius, it may be the solution to our problem. The region we today call "the City of David" seems to have been higher than the Temple Mount until the Hasmonean Period. The present shape of "the City of David" is artificial; it came about as the result of the Hasmonean effort to glorify the Temple. If this is so, we are discussing widespread excavation that lowered the ground level, as a result of which all the relics from the ancient periods were removed. This would be the reason for the lack of pre-Hasmonean archaeological finds on the City of David ridge.

Indeed, a study of the distribution of the finds from the early periods in the City of David indicates that the early findings were on the slope of the ridge, rather than on the ridge itself. [241]

The nature of human beings in general and of archaeologists in particular is that they want to see proof, and find it difficult to trust written descriptions, no matter how reliable. Nevertheless, it appears that on this particular subject we have no choice but to settle for an historical description made by an historian who, up until the present time, has not been caught in erroneous geographical or topographical descriptions.[242] The present topographical appearance of the site, however, is very convincing; it is difficult to envision and accept Josephus's remarkable claim, and many have indeed rejected it.[243]

In contrast, Avram Kahana, in his comments on the Book of Maccabees (Maccabees I 13:53), states on the subject of the artificial lowering of the hill that, "it would seem that Josephus had a source for this."

A similar idea was raised regarding another question in the history of Jerusalem: the question of the existence of the southern Cardo in Roman Jerusalem. In the excavations led by Nahman Avigad, it became clear that the flooring of the southern Cardo, dated from the Byzantine Age, was laid

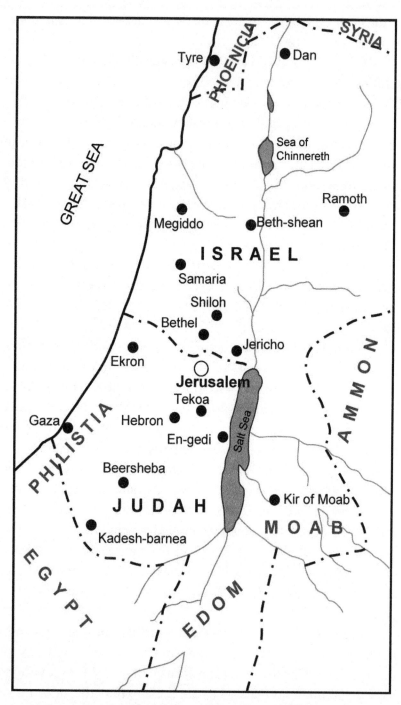

Kingdoms of Judah and Israel during the time of David and Solomon

directly upon remnants from the 1st century BCE. No findings were uncovered at this site from the Late Roman Period
(2nd and 3rd centuries BCE). This led Avigad to argue that in
the Late Roman Period the area of the southern Cardo was
unpopulated.

Yoram Tsafrir argued, on the other hand, that the southern
Cardo was already in existence in the Roman Period. To explain
the lack of findings from the Roman Period, Tsafrir claimed
that widespread excavations were conducted in the wake of the
building of the Nea Church at the southern end of the Cardo
in the Byzantine Period, "and the entire region was lowered
considerably."[244] So we see that (despite the fact that there is
no written historical testimony to the existence of the southern
Cardo in Roman Aelia Capitolina) this kind of surprising solution has already been suggested when the appearance of the site
and the testimony of other sources conflicted.

The description of the lowering of the Aqra hill also
solves the question of the Ophel in Jerusalem. What is the
"Ophel"? It is a term that appears in various Biblical sources
with regard to Jerusalem and the city of Samaria, as well as
in the Mesha Inscription .[245] Commentators and researchers
surmise that the term "Ophel" means a high place, the "Aqra,"
or acropolis of the city. [246] The Ophel in Jerusalem was apparently to the south of the Temple Mount (Neh. 3:26); in the
First Temple Period, the place was fortified with high, separate fortifications (II Chron. 33:14). A glance at the present-day
topography of the Temple Mount and the City of David provides no answer to the question of why it was built here, in a
place lower than the Temple Mount. The logical place should
have been to the north or to the west of the Temple Mount, on
higher ground.

The description provided by Josephus clarifies the matter
entirely. The area of the City of David *was* higher than the Temple, and so it was logical that the city's fortress was built there.

Summary

The archaeological finds discovered in the City of David do not match the historical data from the 14th century BCE (LBA II), from the period of the United Monarchy (Iron Age II) or from the Hellenistic Period.

Archaeological data have provided no support for existing historical descriptions, and for this reason, a fierce debate has developed over the subject.

The solution to the problems is given by Josephus Flavius, who claims that significant topographical changes took place in the City of David, the surface having been lowered deliberately and artificially.

In an excavation of the valleys of the Kidron, the excavated wastes may be found with indications of the activity described by Josephus. I must emphasize that even if one rejects Josephus's description, he cannot ignore the evidence on the ground. The ancient excavations in the region around the Temple Mount are prominent, especially to the south of the Temple Mount. The drainage channels and the many pools cut into the bedrock do not leave any chance for the survival of more ancient relics. Thus, even if the area was not higher than the Temple Mount, as Josephus claims, the excavations carried out in the Second Temple Period left no ancient remnants in this area.

Are there Iron Age Findings from the Israelite Monarchy in the Judean Hills?

To date, no findings from this period have been discovered in other Judean sites. It is not surprising that we have not found evidence of King Solomon's construction projects, for as already noted, most of his construction took place in key sites: along the border in the Negev and at central points along the Sea Road.

But why has nothing been found from later stages in the Iron Age, such as the days of Kings Rehoboam, Jehosephat, and Uzziah (9th century - beginning of the 8th century BCE), like the impressive findings in the north? Here, once again, we must consider the nature of archaeological finds.

The Kingdom of Israel (in the north) was destroyed in the year 721 BCE. The Galilee was conquered even earlier, in 732 BCE. As noted earlier, most of the sites have remained deserted or, at most, only partially rebuilt. Dan and Hatzor were abandoned almost completely; Jezreel seems to have been destroyed and abandoned as early as the second half of the 9th century BCE, when Jehu was coming to power. The acropolis of Samaria was never rebuilt either, while Megiddo was rebuilt as an Assyrian administrative center which was only sparingly reconstructed. The fact that these places remained relatively untouched explains why artifacts from the 10th to the 8th centuries BCE survived in these sites.

This was not the case in the south of the country, the Kingdom of Judea, where the veteran population continued to live continuously until the onset of the 6th century BCE. In some cases, towns were destroyed and then rebuilt. For example, the conquest and destruction of Lachish in the year 701 BCE is demonstrated by Assyrian, Biblical, and archaeological evidence, but the settlement continued until the Persian Period. A clear majority of the southern sites were inhabited continuously. In the 7th century BCE--the century in which the Kingdom of Judea came to an end--the Judean highlands flourished. Jerusalem developed and expanded, new towns were created or built, mostly on the sites of older settlements, in the Judean hills, on the plains, in the Negev and in the Judean Desert. This construction explains the absence of traces of the earlier stages in the development of these settlements.

Furthermore, the phenomenon of populations descending during the Biblical Eras from the hills to the plains (a movement with which we are familiar from the Hellenistic Period) is not prominent in the Judean highlands. There, people continued to build on the foundations of the earlier settlements, rather than move. The northern settlements were built mainly near

plains onto which they either expanded in the Hellenistic Era
(e.g., Bet Shean and Megiddo), or they ceased to exist at all (as
in Hatzor). In contrast, this geographical choice did not exist in
the Judean Hills or on the inland plain, generally speaking. This
was so, for instance, in the cases of Bet-El, Shiloh, Tel-el-Ful,
Jerusalem, Ramat Rahel and Bet-Zur, in the highlands; Gezer,
Maresha and Lachish on the plain; Tel Sheva, Arad, and Tel Ira
in the Negev. In these and many other sites, new settlements
were built directly on the Biblical settlements in the Persian,
Hellenistic and the Roman Periods, and in many cases in the
Byzantine Period as well. All these factors taken together ex-
plain the paucity of findings from the beginning of the Iron Age
Period of the Monarchy in the southern part of the country.

As we discussed briefly above, the lack of artifacts gave
rise to a distorted picture encouraging the formation of the new
"Low Chronology" school of thought. Since no traces from the
days of Solomon survived in the Judean hill country, these archaeologists claimed that if nothing was found, it was a sign
that nothing had existed. They argue that the royal construction
just described must be dated to the 9th century BCE only.

They ignore the question of how to explain vessels found
in the Negev that resemble those in Hatzor and Megiddo. Their
assumptions defy logic. How is it possible for vessels attributed to the 10th and 9th centuries to exist both in the north of the
country and in the south, but not in the central region at all?

In two 7th century sites in the Kingdom of Judea, Ramat
Rahel to the south of Jerusalem and Tel Ira in the Negev, we
find an indication that the royal construction of palaces and
six-roomed gateways attributed to the Solomonic Era did not
originate in the northern Kingdom of Israel, as argued by Israel
Finkelstein, [247] but rather in the southern Kingdom of Judea or
perhaps in the United Kingdom that preceded both. In Ramat
Rahel, a magnificent palace and fortress was found, amazingly
similar to the ivory palace found in the city of Samaria, while in
Tel Ira a six-roomed gateway was found attached to a casement

wall as in Hatzor. These buildings were constructed after the destruction of the Kingdom of Israel.

A question arises: who built these buildings in the south, in a style well known in the north of the country hundreds of years earlier? It is unreasonable to postulate that they originated in the northern Kingdom of Israel, for when Tel Ira was being built, the northern kingdom was no longer in existence. But it is logical to assume that architectural and building traditions survived in the 7th century from the days of the building of Hatzor, Megiddo, Gezer, and Samaria during the 10th and 9th centuries BCE, all the way to Tel Ira in the distant Negev and to Ramat Rahel to the south of Jerusalem. This tradition could have been preserved only in Jerusalem, which had existed continuously for some 400 years.

One can perhaps argue that the six-roomed gateway in Tel Ira and the fortress in Ramat Rahel indicate that the Kingdom of Judea was influenced by the construction methods employed in the Kingdom of Israel, yet it should be recalled that in the 8th century six-roomed gateways were no longer built in the Kingdom of Israel. In the 8th century, smaller four-roomed gateways were constructed, such as those in Megiddo, Tel Dan, Dor and Tel Sheva.

Royal Construction in the Negev

We have just considered the absence of signs of royal construction in the Judean hill country during the period of the Israelite Monarchy. In contrast, a number of indications of royal construction during the 10th and 9th centuries BCE have been found in the Negev.

Ein Hatzeva

Between 1987 and 1995, a large fortress was excavated at Hatzeva, in the northern Aravah. Six strata were uncovered, the most important of which for our purposes are the earliest strata at that site, strata V and VI. [248]

Stratum VI was built in the 10th century BCE, according to the excavators. Not many remnants of this period survived. Part of a large rectangular structure was uncovered, the walls of which remained intact up to the height of about 1 meter. Potsherds from the 10th century BCE were found on the floor of this structure.

Stratum V belongs to the 9th and 8th centuries BCE. Here stood a huge fortress, the length of each of its sides was approximately 100 meters. Its upper levels were made of hewn stone, and towers stood in the corners of the fortress. The fortress was enclosed by a unique wall–a casement wall with the external surface built of offset-inset walls. The entrance to the fortress was a four-roomed gateway, a common feature in the fortifications of that era.

The excavators noted that the floor plan of the fortress closely resembles that of the fortified compound at Tel Jezreel, which may have been Ahab's palace, dated to the 9th century BCE.

This site is extremely important for our discussion, for its fortress is evidence for the royal construction in the 9th century in a region far away from the Judean highlands. Its existence disproves the "low chronology" approach that argues that only in the 8th century did Judea become a monarchy of any consequence. Besides the existence of a site here as early as the 10th century, this is clear testimony to there having been royal construction in the Judean area as early as in the 9th century, including fortifications, gates, and hewn stone construction. It should be noted that the excavators link the building of stratum V to the kings of Judea in the framework of their struggle against Edom.[249]

There is no justification for an argument that the royal construction including building with hewn stone, complex gateways, and fortifications should be ascribed to the Kings of Israel only. Clearly, the Judean kings had the power and resources to construct such buildings as well.

Kadesh Barnea

Three fortresses were uncovered, one above the other,[250] at a site called Tel Kudirat in the southwestern part of the Negev. The outline of the floor plan of the bottommost (and earliest) fortress was oval, and its wall was a casement wall like that of other fortresses in the Negev of that period (see above). This fortress was dated by the excavator to the 10th century BCE.

The middle of the three fortresses was oblong, and was surrounded by a broad wall four meters wide. An impressive water cistern was found inside the fortress with 25 steps going down to its bottom. A water channel connected the spring outside the fortress with the cistern. Two ostraca were found inside the fortress, bearing two Hebrew names. This fortress was constructed in the middle of the 8th century BCE.

The uppermost fortress was built in the 7th century BCE. Its overall floor plan resembled that of the middle fortress, but it had a casement wall instead of a broad wall. (A similar feature has been noted in the fortress in Arad.) Hebrew ostraca were found in this stratum as well. The uppermost fortress was destroyed by fire, apparently at about the time of the destruction of the First Temple. This was undoubtedly a site of national significance, inhabited by people who wrote Hebrew and had Hebrew names. The style of building, too, is characteristic of many sites throughout the country in Iron Age II. It is reasonable to attribute the construction of this site to the Kingdom of Judea.

Tel Sheva

An important site from the First Temple Period, Tel Sheva is located at the meeting point of the Hebron Brook and the Be'er-Sheva Brook. Many articles have been written about this site, and widespread excavations have been conducted there.[251] This is the best-planned and preserved site from the First Temple Period.

Spread over an area of only eleven dunams, the site has been identified by some scholars as an urban administrative center, while others identify settlements of this type as "storehouse cities." Four settlement strata existed there from the First Temple Period. It was destroyed at the close of the 8th century BCE, well before the destruction of the Holy Temple. In this light, the settlement strata in it are dated to the 10th - 8th centuries BCE.

This settlement was unique in that it was carefully planned (at least in strata III and II), and this included a four-roomed gateway, a casement wall, three-space buildings, warehouses and an extremely impressive waterworks. There was a peripheral network of roads.

Ostraca written in the ancient Hebrew alphabet were found in the warehouses. This was undoubtedly a Judean settlement planned and organized by a central governing agency.

Tel Malhata

Tel Malhata is an important site in the Be'er-Sheva Valley, but because of a Muslim graveyard on the tell, the excavations conducted there were very limited.[252] In the Middle Bronze Age, it was fortified with a large rampart and a glacis (a downward slope in front of a fortification to make it easier to fire on attacking forces). In Iron Age II, the site reached its maximal development. In Period C, that of the United Monarchy, (according to the excavator), this site, too, was enclosed by a rampart of smooth stones, upon which stood a wall 4.5 meters wide. A typical storehouse building was uncovered here, resembling the storehouses at Tel-Sheva.

Period C began in the 10th century BCE. The excavator claims that the 10th century settlement was the largest in the Be'er-Sheva Valley and was apparently destroyed, as it stood in the way of Shishak's campaign. (Yochanan Aharoni suggests that Tel Malhata is to be identified with '*Arad leVeit Yeruham*,' which is mentioned in the Shishak Inscription.) In the 9th century, the settlement was rebuilt and survived until the destruction of the First Temple.

Tel Shera'

Tel Shera' is a 16-20-dunam site located in the northwestern part of the Negev, on the north bank of the Gerar Stream. Settlements strongly resembling the sites in the north of the country were found in stratum VII, dated by the excavator[253] to the 10th or 9th centuries BCE, and in stratum VI from the 8th century BCE. Four-space buildings, buildings made of hewn stone together with brick construction, and pottery characteristic of the period were found there. The excavator notes the similarity of the construction in Tel Shera' and other state-sponsored buildings in the north: Hatzor, Megiddo, Gezer, Samaria and Ramat Rahel, and suggests that the hewn stone construction be ascribed to Uzziah, King of Judah.

Summary

While it is true that in the central region of the Judean highlands no state construction has been found from the 10th or 9th centuries BCE, on the outskirts of the Kingdom of Judah throughout the Negev, where the finds were better preserved, archaeologists have uncovered impressive construction projects that demonstrate that a strong authority built and maintained these sites. This authority could not have originated anywhere except in the Kingdom of Judah, for in these centuries no foreign powers were involved in the southern part of the country.

Even if one argues that the strata that have been dated from the 9th century should be attributed to the 8th century, the 8th century still preceded the destruction of the northern Kingdom of Israel.

The archeological finds, therefore, *do not* corroborate the claims of the minimalists who strive to reduce the strength of the Kingdom of Judah to a small, regionally insignificant hill country kingdom, surviving in the shade of its northern counterpart. We have shown evidence that the Kingdom of Judah wielded considerable power and built impressive defense structures.

Sources of Wealth During the Reign of David and Solomon

We have seen that a flowering of settlement activity from the Negev to the Galilee took place from the 10th century on. This is borne out both by the findings on the ground and by Biblical descriptions. What made this flowering possible?

According to the Bible, this economic boom is attributed to Solomon. What was the source of his wealth? Was it merely the exploitation of the conquered lands over which he ruled? Was it the result of a successfully organized administration, as seems possible from the list of governors (I Kings 4) and from the organization of forced labor? (I Kings 5:29-31)

The tribute amassed from the conquered states, together with Israelite control of the two international routes, the "Sea Road" that passed through the coastal plain and the "King's Road" that crossed over the eastern ridge of hill country, undoubtedly contributed considerably to this wealth. Yet if we examine the information which the Bible provides regarding the economic aspects of Solomon's kingdom, it appears that another source must be sought.

In the deal concluded by Solomon and King Hiram of Tyre, Solomon delivered to Hiram two significant products, wheat and oil, in return for cedars and cypresses. "And Solomon gave Hiram 20,000 measures of wheat for food to his household, and twenty measures of beaten oil; thus gave Solomon to Hiram year after year." (I Kings 5:25) This was simply a commercial deal.

Is a deal involving such large quantities feasible? Where did Solomon obtain such large quantities of wheat and oil for export? The answer to this question is based on the historical fact that wheat was grown largely to the east of the Jordan River. A number of sources provide evidence of this: In the Book of Chronicles, we read that the Ammonites paid tribute to Yotham [in the amount of] 10,000 measures of wheat and barley (II Chron. 27:5). Ammon was east of the Jordan. The (east of the Jordan) regions of Gilead and Bashan were considered "storehouses of grain" in later periods. In the Muslim Period, there is evidence of camel caravans moving loads of wheat from the Bashan to the port of Acre.[254] Clearly, in addition to controlling the central King's Road across the Jordan, Israelite sovereignty over the eastern bank of the Jordan and of the Bashan made it possible to export wheat to Tyre.

In addition to wheat, Solomon provided Hiram with oil. In what way was Israel unique in this field? It seems that the optimal place to grow olives for oil was in Israel.

Olive oil was an extremely valuable product in the ancient world. It was used for illumination, for food, for religious rites, for medicine and for cosmetics.[255] Olive trees (which would yield rich oil) did not develop in the centers of the ancient world, Egypt and Mesopotamia, as these regions are too hot for olive plantations. Israel, in contrast, was called "a land of olives for oil" (Deut. 8:8), and was suitable for this purpose. As early as the Bronze Age, Israel supplied Egypt with oil.

In the list of King David's treasury officials (I Chron. 27:28), we find mention of Baal Hanan the Gederite, who was in charge of the olives and the sycamores in the plain, and of Yo'ash, who was in charge of the oil reserves. Other Biblical sources relate that Israel exported oil to Egypt and Lebanon: "And oil is carried to Egypt" (Hos. 12:2). See also Ezek. 27:17 and Ezra 3:7.

To this Biblical evidence, we must add archaeological research which has uncovered scores of oil presses dating from the First Temple Period, mostly in the inland plain and in southern Samaria.

According to these finds, and even later sources, the manufacture of oil on these oil presses was accomplished in three stages:
- Stage I: the olives were crushed
- Stage II: the oil was extracted
- Stage III: the oil was separated from the other liquids with which it was mixed.

For the first time in the history of Israel, such sophisticated

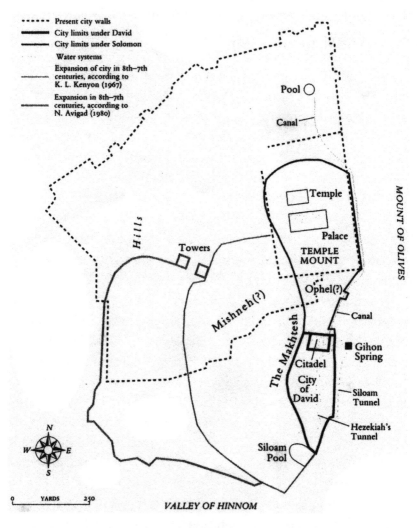

Present city walls
City limits under David
City limits under Solomon
Water systems
Expansion of city in 8th–7th centuries, according to K. L. Kenyon (1967)
Expansion in 8th–7th centuries, according to N. Avigad (1980)

Pool

Canal

Temple

Palace

TEMPLE MOUNT

MOUNT OF OLIVES

Hills

Towers

Ophel(?)

Mishneh(?)

Canal

The Makhtesh

Gihon Spring

Citadel

City of David

Siloam Tunnel

Hezekiah's Tunnel

Siloam Pool

N
W · E
S

0   YARDS   250

VALLEY OF HINNOM

Jerusalem during the First Temple period, 1000-586 BCE

olive presses were used in great numbers. No similar installations identifiable with the same degree of certainty as olive presses have been found from periods preceding that of the First Temple. It is no exaggeration to say that these discoveries reflect substantial industrial activity on an international scale.

The uniqueness of these installations is the beam of the olive press, a technological innovation that made it possible to manufacture large amounts of olive oil. In similar household methods, the olives would be crushed with a stone; the crushed mixture would be placed in a basket and a heavy stone laid upon it, as a result of which the oil would separate from the mixture and flow into a suitable receptacle. In the industrial installations, a long, heavy beam was laid on the basket. One end of the beam was inserted into a niche in the wall while stone weights were attached to the other end. The pressure generated by the weights crushed the mixture and forced the separation of the oil. In the third stage, common to both the industrial installations and the household ones, the oil was separated from the water. This separation is based on the fact that oil is less dense than water.

As already noted, the oil industry developed during the First Temple Period. Do we have any evidence of the beginnings of this industry? Most of the olive presses discovered date from the close of the First Temple Period, but there are a number of indications that olive presses already existed in the 10th century BCE, both in the lowlands and in the northern part of the country. In excavations conducted at Gezer, an olive press was discovered that is dated by the excavator to the second half of the 10th century. In Megiddo, part of an olive press was found in a stratum cut off abruptly by the stables that are ascribed to the times of Ahab, i.e., the olive press belongs to stratum V, i.e., the 10th century. In the western Galilee, at a site known as Rosh Zayit (Olive Peak), a settlement was found from the 10th century which also had an olive press. [256]

Judging from these finds, it is apparent that the invention

of the beam should be attributed to the period of Solomon. The fact that such installations are found in various parts of the country points to the importance of this industry and of the development of this export item as early as the Solomonic Period.

The fact that an industry of such sophistication developed during the Temple Period confirms the existence of a central government administration. Such a government would be necessary to facilitate the manufacture and marketing of these products which were in great demand, both inside the state and beyond it to foreign ports. This booming industry supports the description given in the Book of Kings of the Solomonic Kingdom.

The memory of this great kingdom in Jerusalem--that ruled over vast territories--survived for hundreds of years. In the letter of the King of Persia quoted in the Book of Ezra, mention is made of the kings of Jerusalem who ruled the area across the river and collected tribute from the inhabitants of that area: "There were mighty kings over Jerusalem who ruled all of the trans-river region, and various taxes were paid to them." (Ezra 4:20)

Why Have We Found No Inscriptions by Israelite Kings?

It is the ardent desire of every archaeologist to discover inscriptions. Assyrian steles, as well as inscriptions of kings of Egypt, Lebanon, and Syria, of Moabite King Mesha, and of an Aramean king have been found in Israel. From later periods, there are inscriptions of Roman prelates, such as Pontius Pilatus, and of Roman monarchs, such as Emperor Hadrian. Kings of Judah and Israel are indeed mentioned in state-sponsored inscriptions, but these are inscriptions of Assyrian, Babylonian, Aramean and Moabite rulers, not inscriptions they themselves commissioned!

There is no question about it: the discovery of an inscription of one of the kings of Israel or Judah would help prove that he actually existed. Unfortunately, despite intensive archaeological activity throughout Israel, not a single inscription belonging to one of the kings of Israel has yet turned up.

Though letters written in Hebrew have been discovered on potsherds in Arad and Lachish (and in other sites as well), not a single royal inscription has yet been found. Even the great builder, Herod, has not left behind even a single inscription eternalizing his name; were it not for the histories written by Josephus Flavius, we might not have known that Herod built Caesarea, Sebastia, Masada, and the Herodion.

Why have such inscriptions not been discovered? Or would it be better to ask, were such inscriptions ever written, but not found, merely by chance?

We may speculate that the lack of such inscriptions is not a chance occurrence, but rather reflects the *weltanschauung* of the Jewish people: they believed that the great enterprises built by human endeavor are to be ascribed not to the builder himself but to the Creator; a human being should not glorify himself by his victories or his magnificence, for "the world and all it contains is of God."

Two individuals mentioned in the Bible erected monuments to their own glory: both are connected to the inception of the monarchy, and the attitude the Bible takes towards them is a negative one. The first king of Israel, Saul, erected a monument in his own honor at Karmel in the southern Hebron hill country, after his war with Amalek (I Sam. 15:12). Though it ended with Saul's military victory, the lack of its completion is recorded in the Biblical text as a serious religious failure. The other person to erect such a monument was Absalom, the rebellious son of David, who built "the Absalom memorial" (II Sam. 18:18).

All the kings produced by the Jewish people, even the idolaters among them, seem to have taken care not to erect monuments and inscriptions of self-glorification. Such a deed would run counter to the religious climate of the nation of Israel, during both First Temple and Second Temple Periods. It may be

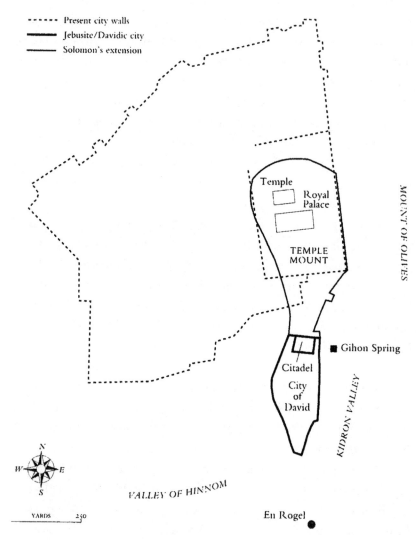

Jerusalem under David and Solomon

assumed that even if we were to excavate for another 100 years, we would not find such inscriptions originating with the kings of the Jewish people.

The Kingdom Splits

The Book of Kings tells of the magnificence of Solomon, but also of his fall. Solomon imposed a heavy burden on the Israelites, yet because of his great wisdom and his personality, his subjects did not dare rebel against him. As he grew older, social unrest arose against him. This movement was led by Jeroboam ben Nebat of the tribe of Ephraim, the tribe which strove to rival Judah and considered itself fitting to lead the Israelite nation.

However, only after Solomon's death, in the days of his son Rehoboam, did the unrest reach the boiling-point as frustration grew over the heavy taxation to which the nation had been subjected. The majority of the nation declared an independent kingdom, detached from the Davidic dynasty: "What portion have we in David, nor do we have inheritance in the son of Jesse!" (I Kings 12:16).

The new kingdom–the Kingdom of Israel–had an outlet to the sea and connections with the fertile valleys of Samaria, the coastal plain, the Jezreel Valley and Lower Galilee, as well as areas across the Jordan, which were under its control. It controlled significant sections of the Sea Road which was the main international route in that period.

The original Kingdom of Judah remained landlocked in the Judean highlands, in the shfela and in the Negev, large sections of which were either arid or rocky. Shishak's campaign, which negatively affected many parts of Israel, certainly worsened the Kingdom of Judah's situation. The Negev settlements–the fortresses–were destroyed, and most were never reconstructed (except for Kadesh Barnea, Arad and Tel-Sheva.)

Consequently, the economic and political leadership of the country shifted to the Kingdom of Israel. The important cities

built by Solomon, which were now in the territory of the Kingdom of Israel (Hatzor, Megiddo and Gezer; the ritual center at
Tel-Dan, the city of Samaria built by Omri, King of Israel as well
as other sites) all show that Israel was the richer and stronger of
the two kingdoms.

The 200 years between the close of the 10th century and the
last third of the 8th century BCE was a prosperous period in the
Kingdom of Israel and a relatively poor time in the Kingdom of
Judah. The fact that the Book of Kings deals mainly with the Kingdom of Israel and less with the Kingdom of Judah, until the exile
of the Ten Tribes, may well reflect this reality. Evidence of this may
be gleaned from the information provided about the kings of Judah (Jehosephat and Jehoram) who visited the kings of Israel as
opposed to the kings of Israel, who never came to visit Jerusalem.
Leadership had been assumed by the northern kingdom.

The Judean highlands thus recede from the pinnacle of importance they had occupied for a number of decades. Nevertheless, as we have seen, the Kingdom of Judah directed its ener-
gies towards the south, the Negev.

The Border Dispute between the Two
Kingdoms: A Triumph of Geography

The region of Judah withdrew to some degree to its natural
status, with its influence not felt beyond its own borders. Most
of the Israelite people were cut off from Jerusalem due to both
geography and attitude. It seems, however, that the kings of the
Davidic dynasty that ruled in Judah did not accept this loss of
status, and it took a long time for the border between the two
kingdoms to stabilize.

The two states feared one another and took various steps to
prevent the other from becoming too strong. King Jeroboam of
Israel took action to implement a psychological barrier between
the two kingdoms. He established his capital in Shechem, the city
that was the great rival of Jerusalem ever since the 14th century
BCE. (For obscure reasons, he later was compelled to transfer

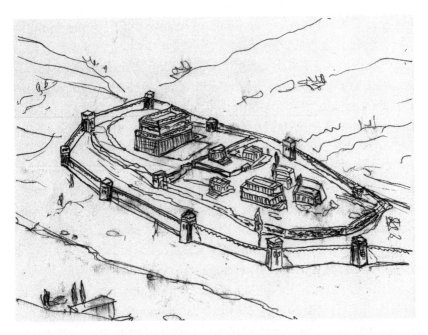

Solomon's Temple built on the summit of Mt. Moriah. Included is the palace complex of King Solomon 1000 BCE - 586 BCE (2760-3174)

his capital to Penuel, on the eastern bank of the Jordan River. The claim has been made that this move was forced on him by Shishak's campaign, but there is no proof of this.)

Moreover, he established "high places" for the worship of golden calves at the two extremes of his kingdom, at Dan and at Bet-El. These two sites had traditions of sanctity, which were intended to show up Jerusalem, a city in which the political capital and Holy Temple were united. At these two ritual sites Jeroboam appointed priests not of the tribe of Levi (I Kings 12:33), thus challenging the traditional mandate that only a single tribe was to preside over Temple worship. Furthermore, he invented a new festivity on the fifteenth day of the eighth month, called Heshvan, apparently to offset the festival of Tabernacles celebrated in Jerusalem. In fact, Jeroboam was successful in implementing his plans and as time went by there does not seem to have been any longing in the Kingdom of Israel to restore the tradition of making pilgrimages to Jerusalem.

Across the Judah-Israel border, King Rehoboam of Judah wanted to take military action and conquer the Kingdom of Israel, but he was prevented from doing so by the prophetic words of Shema'ya, "Thus said God: 'Do not go up and fight with your brethren, the Children of Israel; let each man return to his home, for this matter was brought about by Me'" (I Kings 12:22-24).

The fears of the kings of Judah were undoubtedly great, especially considering that the border between the two kingdoms passed to the south of Bet-El, just a few kilometers to the north of Jerusalem. The ambition to restore the Kingdom of Israel to Judah did not subside, and Abijah, son of Rehoboam, conquered parts of the hill country of Ephraim, including Bet-El and Jeshanah (II Chron. 13:19). Consequently, the border between the two kingdoms moved north of Bet-El, though its exact location is unclear.

This border did not last for long, for in the days of Asa, son of Abijah "… Baasha, king of Israel, went up against Judah and built Ramah [identified as E-Ram to the north of Jerusalem] in order not to allow anyone to leave or to come to Asa, king of Judah" (I Kings 15:17). At this point, the border was undoubtedly dangerously close to Jerusalem, the Judean capital.

The above verse describes control over the vital routes leading to the heart of the Kingdom of Judah, i.e., to the region of Jerusalem. The main road that connected the coastal plain with Jerusalem was the Beit Horon road. Well-known battles were fought along this route. Joshua fought there against the kings of the south (Joshua 10:10), and later the battle of Judah Maccabee against the Seleucid general Siron took place there. Whoever controls the Ramah area truly controls the upper part of this road. The phrase "not to allow anyone to leave or to come" is thus meaningful, for whoever is in control of this point prevents the inhabitants of Jerusalem from moving either to the north or to the west.

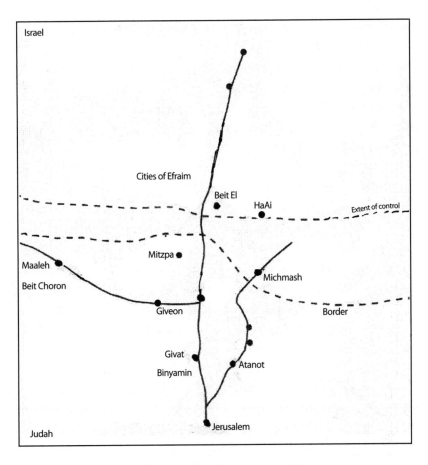

Israel-Judah borders after the invasion of King Assa

Asa was clearly unable to accept such a situation. He allied with Hadad, king of Aram, who attacked the Kingdom of Israel in the north, thus releasing the pressure on the Kingdom of Judah. Asa took advantage of this "and carried away the stones of Ramah and the timber thereof, wherewith Baasha had built, and [Asa] then built therewith Geva of Benjamin and Mitzpah" (I Kings 15:22).

Where were Geva of Benjamin and Mitzpah located? The area of the tribe of Benjamin is full of settlements bearing the name Geva: Givat Bnei Benjamin, Givat Shaul, Giv'ah, Geva, Givat E-lohim and Gibeon. It is difficult to ascertain which of them was intended by the Biblical text. (At that time, there was no government agency to ensure that the names of settlements were not repetitive.) Wherever a settlement was built on a hilltop, its residents would name it after the topography of the site. Nevertheless, it is widely accepted that this Geva in the Bible is the village of Gib'a to the northeast of Ramah.

The name Mitzpah, too, indicates that the settlement was located on a high point from which one could see (from the Hebrew, *tzofeh*) for great distances. It has been tentatively identified with Tel-en-Nasbeh, some 13 kilometers north of Jerusalem. This site has been excavated by archaeologists. Its area is approximately 32 dunams and it is located on a major road. The settlement was encompassed by two walls, one apparently built by Asa. The archaeological finds indicate that this was an important location: there were 68 seals of *la-melech*, indicating that they were meant for government or royal use. (These impressions on jar handles are of uniform form and size. It is accepted that they date from the days of King Hezekiah.) There was also a seal bearing the name *Ya'azanyahu 'eved ha-melech* ("Ya'azanyahu, servant of the king"). Ya'azanyahu is mentioned in the Bible as one of the generals who came to Mitzpah together with Gedaliah ben Ahiqam after the destruction of the First Temple, when Gedaliah established his center (II Kings 25:23). Mitzpah was an important local center in the days of the "Return to Zion" during the Persian Period (6th-5th centuries BCE) as well.

Moving the border of Judah northward meant that the threat to the main route leading from Jerusalem to the coastal plain and its harbors had been neutralized. This seems to have remained the permanent border between the two monarchies until the destruction of the Kingdom of Israel. We find no evidence from here on of struggles over it. Asa's son Jehosephat maintained friendly relations with the king of Israel, and it seems that the two parties accepted one another's existence. This is true except for a few unusual instances. During King Amatziah of Judah's rule, the wall surrounding Jerusalem was breached following his provocation of the king of Israel (II Chron. 25:23).

The area between Geba and Be'er-Sheva was considered the territory of the Kingdom of Judah from this time on (II Kings 23:8), but it also extended further to the north. We learn this from the Book of Kings: "And Jehosephat, his son, reigned in his place... and he appointed governors in the land of Judah and *in the cities of Ephraim* [emphasis added] which Asa, his father, had captured." (II Chron. 17:1-2)

Though we have no specifications of the northern border of the Kingdom of Judah, we must look at the geographical structure of the Judean hill country. The northern boundary of the Judean Hills is to the north of Bet-El. The uniformity of the Judean highlands ceases in this region, and the area is traversed by curving roads. It thus seems that while Asa reinforced Mitzpah as an internal line of fortifications on the main road, the external line was closer to Bet-El, in the region belonging to the tribe of Ephraim. In the end, geography won out in the struggle between the two kingdoms. The geographical northern border of the Judean hill country became the political border between the two kingdoms once the border between them became stable.

After the splitting of the kingdom, the Bible refocuses on the hill country of Ephraim and Menashe. The exciting events, the frequent revolutions, the wars against the Arameans and the activities of unique prophets such as Elijah and Elisha are given considerable attention. It appears that the Bible does not ascribe much significance to events taking place at this time in the Judean highlands. Nevertheless, we shall attempt to become familiar with a number of significant events that transpired in the Kingdom of Judah during this period.

Central Events in the Kingdom of Judah at the Time of the Split

The stronger and more affluent Kingdom of Israel, made up of ten tribes, was under the cultural influence of the nations to the north of it, especially Tyre and Sidon. It also tended to divide itself. The tribes engaged in a constant struggle for supremacy. Judah, on the other hand, was more isolated, more uniform in population composition (only three tribes), and the external influences affecting it were more moderate. In contrast to the Kingdom of Israel, the monarchy in the Kingdom of Judah remained in the hands of the Davidic dynasty despite various attempts to change it. The people of the kingdom remained loyal to the founding royal dynasty established by King David. The well-being of the economy and security of the Kingdom of Judah was focused mainly on the south and southeast.

King Rehoboam of Judah had failed in his attempt to prevent the stabilization of the rival Kingdom of Israel, and was unable to reunite all the tribes of Israel under his leadership. As a result, he concentrated on reorganizing and fortifying his own kingdom. To create a defensive line around Jerusalem, he fortified a series of settlements on the inland plain and in the Judean Hills: Bethlehem, Eitam, Tekoa, Bet-Zur and Hebron to the south of Jerusalem; and Socho, Adulam, Gat, Mareisha, Adorayim, Lachish, Azeka, Tsor'a and Ayalon on the Shfelah, to the west and the southwest. "Cities for defense...and made them exceedingly strong" (II Chron. 11:5-12).[257]

The search for archaeological traces of Rehoboam's fortifications has produced but few finds. At Tel Azeka on the Shfelah, a fortress with towers in its corners has been found, and the excavators attribute it to Rehoboam.[258] It should be noted, however, that the site was excavated at the end of the 19th century by Frederick J. Bliss and R.A. Stewart Macalister using methods not acceptable today in archaeological research, and there is no way to check the correctness of their dating. A fortified city dating from this period, apparently built by Rehoboam, has been excavated in Lachish as well (stratum V).[259]

Except for these two sites, we have no archaeological indication of the fortifications built by Rehoboam, though it should be stressed that most of the cities on the list have not been excavated. It is quite possible that renewed digging will result in appropriate finds.

In the Judean highlands, then, no traces have been found of state-sponsored construction, while on the inland plain two important sites, Bet Shemesh and Lachish, should be noted. These sites served as central urban settlements in their areas, where walls, gates, and public buildings have been found and identified.

In contrast, a very impressive number of indications of widespread royal construction have been found in the Negev. As noted above, these were discovered in Ein Hatzeva in the Aravah, at Tel Sheva, Tel Malhata and at Arad, all in the northern Negev; at Ein Kuderat which is identified with Kadesh Barnea in the southwest Negev; and at Tel-el-Kheleifeh which is identified with Etzion Gever, not far from Eilat in the south.

A large structure of the four-spaced house type and a ring seal bearing the engraved word *lytm* (= for Yotham) were discovered in Tel-el-Kheleifeh. Nelson Glueck, the excavator of the site, suggests that this seal belonged to Yotham, king of Judah, son of Uzziah. The Bible says that Uzziah conquered Eilat. "He built Eilat and restored it to Judah" (II Kings 14:22).[260]

These details do indeed dovetail with additional information gleaned from the Bible regarding the fact that the Kingdom of Judah at times overran Edom to the east of the Aravah (I Kings 22:48; II Chron. 25:11-13), the southern part of the coastal plain, and even overran Ammon (II Chron. 26:6-10). King Jehosephat made an attempt to renew Judean naval trade in the Gulf of Eilat, an attempt which seems to have failed (I Kings 22:49; II Chron. 20:35-37).

In the first half of the 8th century BCE King Uzziah/Azariah came to power. He is described in the Bible as a dynamic monarch who engaged in construction and agricultural development. He also extended the borders of the kingdom in the lowland areas all the way to Eilat: "And he went forth and warred against the Philistines... and he built cities in [the country of] Ashdod and among the Philistines... Moreover, Uzziah built towers in Jerusalem... and he built towers in the wilderness and hewed out many cisterns... for he was a lover of the soil." (II Chr 26:6-11)

The glorious period of the reigns of Uzziah and his son Yotham was over by the second half of the 8th century BCE. In the days of Ahaz, king of Judah (743-727 BCE), the Assyrians invaded the area of Israel. Aram was vanquished and disappeared from the stage of history, and even the Galilee became part of the Assyrian Empire.

During the time of Ahaz's son, Hezekiah, in 721 BCE, the Kingdom of Israel was conquered by the Assyrians and a large segment of its population went into exile. Some 70% of the Israelite people were lost, and the Kingdom of Judah, to the south, remained alone. The Kingdom of Judah encompassed only two tribes: Judah and Benjamin, which had merged with the tribe of Judah. In addition, some of the tribe of Levi who lived in the environs of Jerusalem survived.

From this time on, a new chapter in the history of the Israelite nation began, a chapter in which the Kingdom of Judah was the sole participant.

Population Estimates for Israel during the Period of the Two Kingdoms

One of the questions often raised in research literature is the question of the size of the population of Israel during this era. Details of the size of the population in a given geographical region at a particular period in time can cast light on various issues such as population density in the region, the lifestyle in the fortified cities and in the villages, the ability to draft laborers for public projects, as well as other social and economic aspects of life. In addition, we can compare this data with the information found in the Bible which claims that the Israelite nation was a few million strong.

For example, in the census conducted by Joab ben Tseruya,

over a million fighting men were numbered (II Sam 24), and later Sennacherib notes in his inscription (known as the Sennacherib Stele) that he had exiled over 200,000 people to Assyria from the Kingdom of Judah. Let us try to clarify whether the numbers from Biblical and non-Biblical sources are reasonable. Can they be accepted at their face value? Do archaeologists have the instruments with which to measure the size of a population in a given place and time?

In an article published in 1991, a claim was made that according to archaeological research the entire population of western Israel in the 8th century BCE was only some 400,000 strong.[261] It is clear, according to this study, that its compilers do not accept the information provided by the Sennacherib Stele, for according to their calculations, there were less than 200,000 people in all of the Kingdom of Judah.

Their approach is based on two basic assumptions:

- that archaeologists can estimate the size of the built-up area in this period
- that it is possible to learn how many people lived in that built-up area on the basis of "the population density coefficient."

Let us examine their method.

The Population Density Coefficient

As noted above, the system used in determining the size of the population at various times in the past relies on factors concerning the current population. Specifically, it is believed that:

- The intensive archaeological research that has been carried out in Israel makes it possible to estimate the dimensions of the settlements in various periods, and thus it is possible to estimate the size of the total built-up area in each period throughout the country; and
- On the basis of observations made in settlements in which the residents still live in traditional style, and which modern technology has not yet reached, the population density of

the various settlements can be determined. The definition of the concept is the number of people per dunam of built-up area. Multiplying the built-up area by the population density coefficient gives the size of the population in the country at any given period of time.

The data amassed by Magen Broshi indicate that the population density in Jerusalem in 1918 was 51 persons per dunam.[262] Data gleaned from studies conducted in such cities as Aleppo and Tripoli were similar. Yigal Shiloh, too, reached similar conclusions on the basis of his analysis of archaeological excavations in Iron Age sites.[263]

Nevertheless, the population density coefficient used by most of those dealing with the subject is 25 persons per dunam.[264] Gideon Bieger and David Grossman have questioned the fixing of a uniform density coefficient for all settlements.[265] They argue that an examination of Arab villages in Israel shows that population density varies from one settlement to another and from one period to another. In some villages, there are only 17 persons per dunam, while there is an extreme case where the population density reaches 123.7 persons per dunam!

They also point out that the number of inhabitants of ancient walled-in Jerusalem varied significantly over the 450 years of its existence, ranging from 8,000 people to 40,000. All scholars base their calculations on modern data, but it is clear to us that data from earlier periods are likely to reflect the reality of settlement in ancient times than more modern figures.

Magen Broshi amassed data from the year 1918, the year when World War I came to an end, when the Turks expelled many of the Jews from Jerusalem, while many others died of various illnesses. However, earlier data, from 1870, appear in the book by Yehoshua Ben-Arieh and indicate a higher population density. About 11,000 persons lived in the Jewish Quarter of Jerusalem, an area of some 70 dunams, during this period. [266] This means that the population density coefficient of Jerusalem's Jewish Quarter was 157 persons per dunam. On the basis of data from this period of time, Conrad Schick claimed that the population density at the close of the Second Temple Period in Jerusalem was about 113 persons per dunam.[267]

While dealing with data from the 19th and 20th centuries in our attempt to learn something of the population density in ancient times, we have been ignoring an ancient source from the period of the Jewish "Return to Zion" from Babylon in the 6th-5th centuries BCE, which may well shed light on this subject.

Population Density According to the Book of Nehemiah

In the Book of Nehemiah (11:3-24) there is a list of residents of Jerusalem in the period of the "Return to Zion." A parallel list appears in the Book of Chronicles as well (I Chron. 9), with certain differences. Various opinions have been expressed regarding the dating of this list, but most scholars accept the list as one representing a period in the 6th-5th century BCE days of Persian rule over Israel. [268]

This list contains the names of the people of Judah and Benjamin, priests and Levites, "men of valor" and "heads of fathers' [houses]", all in all 2,872 people. In addition, mention is made of Nethinim (a category of slaves) who lived in the Ophel (Neh. 11:21). Therefore, this number can probably be rounded up to about 3,000 people. The parallel list in the Book of Chronicles contains higher numbers, reaching approximately 3,600. Since the people listed were family heads, this figure should be multiplied by a family coefficient which, according to the minimalists, is an average of four people per family. [269]

It appears, then, that the number of inhabitants of Jerusalem at the time of the census was at least 12,000 people. The inhabited area of Jerusalem in the days of the "Return to Zion" was about 120 dunams.[270] If the archaeological data are correct, then the population density coefficient in Jerusalem in the period of the "Return to Zion" was 100 persons per dunam. While the data adduced from the 20th century are varied and variable, the data from Jerusalem from the 19th century CE and from the 5th century BCE indicate a density coefficient of at least 100 persons per dunam.

Such density requires that many residents live together in a single house. Indeed, the houses of the Jewish Quarter of Jerusalem examined by Thomas Chaplin, an English physician who lived in Jerusalem in the 19th century, bear witness to a high population density. Chaplin counted nineteen people in a house of about 97 square meters, while in another house, that of the Sephardi Chief Rabbi, he counted sixteen people in an area of 66 square meters.[271] A similar aspect of population density was found in a study conducted by Yizhar Hirschfeld in Arab villages in the southern Hebron hill country, a marginal region in Israel, during the '60s of the 20th century.[272]

In general, it is difficult for us in this generation to comprehend such high population density coefficients (because the average density in a modern city can reach about thirty people per dunam, and people live in more spacious homes). This should not bias our judgment. As Chaplin, who studied the population density of Jerusalem in 1878, said, "a Westerner is not familiar with Eastern customs."[273] This fact is even more correct today, in the 21st century.

The Numerical Relationship between the Population of the Cities and that of the Villages

Archaeology mainly engages in the study of large, prominent settlements, while smaller villages tend to be overlooked or, at best, reviewed superficially. If we want to estimate the size of the population at any particular period, we must first look at the numerical relationship between large urban settlements and smaller ones in periods before our own time.

Data from the Middle Ages and the Onset of the Modern Period

Studies of pre-industrial societies show that the number of inhabitants in cities with a population of 5,000 – 10,000 never made up more than 10% of the general population, (both rural and urban) and on occasion even less than 5%.[274] In his study, Davis found that in the year 1800 only 3% of the population lived in cities of over 5,000 inhabitants, and that in 1850 their percentage had risen to 6.4%.[275] On the basis of these figures, it seems that in most parts of the world the number of inhabitants of the cities was extremely low. The reason for this was their inability to generate a sufficient quantity of food, a precondition for the development of a city. The inhabitants of cities are generally not farmers, and so must be sustained by the agricultural surpluses of the surrounding rural area.

It appears, then, that in order to achieve an estimate of the population in a given area, one must multiply the population of the cities by ten or more. When considering the period of the monarchies in Israel, we must ask whether the large settlements of that period were cities in the modern sense, or whether perhaps they were merely large agricultural villages.

City Life during the Monarchies

Were the cities in the period of the two kingdoms large villages engaged mainly in agriculture, or cities in the accepted geographical meaning of the term: a settlement of a few thousand residents, with buildings erected in an organized fashion, with most of its inhabitants engaging primarily in trade and crafts, and familiar with writing and with the calendar?[276] On the basis of our knowledge of the period, it seems that the Israelite city was really a city in the modern sense: a city whose area was 50 dunams had some 5,000 inhabitants, according to a coefficient of 100 persons per dunam. The Israelite cities were organized and planned,[277] and professional specialization reached a high level.

During the period of the kingdoms, there was an organized economic set-up based on professional guilds specializing in specific crafts as well as on settlements specializing in specific branches of manufacture. This specialization is evident in I Chron. 4:23: "These were the potters (*yotserim*) and those who dwelt in Neta'im and Gedera; there they dwelt, occupied in the king's work." The verse refers to families of potters living in Neta'im and Gedera. The expression "occupied in the king's work" (Hebrew: *'im ha-melech*) may be referring to families of potters manufacturing vessels for the kingdom. Certain families specialized in writing, perhaps in the administration of official records; these were "the families of scribes, dwelling in Jabetz" (I Chron. 2:55). The position of Royal Scribe was an extremely important position in the royal court.

Previously, when we discussed the Solomonic period, mention was made of the export of olive oil. It should be noted that the processing of olive products (picking the olives and the production of oil) takes place in the autumn, when the soil is tilled for winter crops. Therefore, those who engaged in the manufacture of olive oil were unable to grow crops. The hundreds of olive presses found in the inland plains and in Samaria show that a large number of people engaged in this endeavor. Loom weights found in presses in Ekron indicate that the buildings in which they were housed were used for the textile industry during other seasons of the year. This is likely because oil was produced for only two months of the year and the buildings could be used for other industries. The Bible mentions specialized craftsmen such as weavers (I Chron. 4:21), potters (*ibid.* 23), goldsmiths (Neh. 3:8), bakers (Jer. 37:21), and wood or metal workers (I Chron. 4:14).

The Biblical account is borne out at various sites in Israel. Throughout the country, furnaces have been found for casting copper and iron, as well as molds for the casting of tools, weaponry, ornaments, and statuettes.[278] A settlement of weavers was found at Nir David (Tel-Amal) in the Bet Shean Valley, and a settlement that engaged in the perfume industry was discovered at Ein Gedi. There were trade centers (called *hutzot* [I Kings 20:34]) outside the gates of the large cities. Such an area dating from the First Temple Period has been located outside the gate of the city of Dan.

To get a true picture of city life during this era, we must include the merchants who traded with the military men, religious fuctionaries and administrative staff both in Israel and in neighboring lands. Letters and inscriptions that were found in various excavations (Jerusalem, Samaria, Lachish, Tel-Sheba and Arad) indicate the widespread use of writing skills. Similarly, the sets of weights found in various excavations throughout Judea point to organized trade making use of uniform, standard weights.

All of these facts tell us that in Israelite kingdoms the large settlements were true cities, with residents engaged in the processing of food products, trade, industry, and administration. Though we have no idea of how the education system was structured during this period, in light of the widespread use of writing it seems reasonable to assume that there was an organized education system in the various cities.

Conclusions: Population Figures
Confirm the Biblical Account

Based on the material presented above, we can conclude that the large fortified settlements (spread over 50 dunams or more) were urban settlements. A large part of their population did not engage in agriculture. Therefore, a population density coefficient of 100 persons per dunam is reasonable in ancient times.

Yigal Shiloh counted 60 settlements from the period of the Kingdoms of Israel and Judah whose areas were 50 dunams or more on the western side of the Jordan River.[279] Some were even twice that size. The area of the large settlements was over 3,000 dunams. If we multiply this number by the coefficient of 100 persons per dunam, we arrive at a figure of about 300,000 persons in the large settlements. However, since we have already found that the number of inhabitants of the large settlements in ancient times was no more than 10% of the total population of the area under discussion, to reach the total population count the number 300,000 must be multiplied by ten, if not more. Therefore, the number of inhabitants of Israel on both sides of the Jordan River, at the height of the period of the monarchies (the 9th and 8th centuries BCE) was indeed a few million!

A study of the southern part of the inland plain, the Shefelah, recently published by Yehuda Dagan[280] reinforces our calculation regarding the relationship between the large settlements and the small ones. A study carried out by this author on the data amassed by Dagan indicates that the relationship between the cities of over 50 dunams and the small settlements on the inland plain during the 9th and 8th centuries BCE was 7%. It should be noted that, in general, it is the large settlements that are discovered and excavated, while the small settlements are difficult to locate. So it is reasonable to assume that the relationship between the number of large settlements to the number of small settlements is even greater. The data from the inland plain match the worldwide data mentioned above.

Archaeological research is unable to find traces of the nomads mentioned in the Bible. These nomads must be added to the inhabitants of the permanent settlements. Thus, for example the *b'nei Rechab* who lived in tents for ideological reasons are mentioned (Jer. 35:1-12), as are *b'nei Shimon* (I Chron. 4:38-41) and *b'nei Reuben* (I Chron. 5:9-10). In light of what is known of the close of the Ottoman period, Bedouins made up some 15% of the total population of Israel at the time.[281] We may add these figures to the estimate of the general population as well.

In summary, it is difficult, or even impossible, to pinpoint unambiguous figures, for we are dealing largely with hypotheses. Nevertheless, based on the approach we have suggested, *there is no contradiction to the Biblical accounts which tell of a few million inhabitants* (in the census conducted by Joab in II Sam. 24:9, and in other places). *Nor is there any contradiction to the data supplied by Sennacherib regarding the exiling of over 200,000 people from Judah to Assyria in the year 701 BCE.* These figures are reasonable and acceptable despite the difficulty modern scholars may have in coming to terms with them.

Religion and Ritual in the First Temple Period

Worship during the Era of the Judges

The struggle to put an end to both idolatry and to the worship of the God of Israel on ritual "high places" outside of Jerusalem is apparent throughout the books of the Prophets. Sometimes successful, sometimes not, the battle went on for many generations. Because idolatry was so deeply entrenched among the people, it was won only in the Second Temple Period.

The main problem was not the fact that the Israelite nation did not worship the Creator and practice the religious life described in the Five Books of Moses, but rather the fact that they added various forms of idolatry that were common among their neighbors. Joshua's last words forewarned the danger of this happening: "Therefore be strong in keeping and doing all that is written in the book of the law of Moses, so that you do not turn aside to the right or to the left; so that you do not come among these nations that remain among you; so that you do not mention the name of their gods; so that you do not cause to swear by them, nor serve them nor bow down to them." (Joshua 23:6-7)

It is clear that this was not merely an admonition prompted by the fear that these things might take place after Joshua's death, but rather a recognition of the reality that already existed in his lifetime. This fact is demonstrated by the words of Joshua himself: "Now, then, put away the

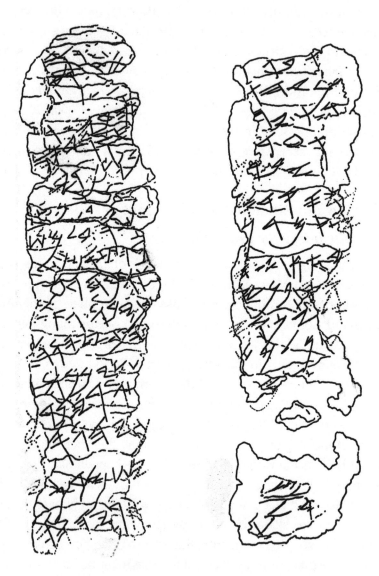

The 'Priestly Blessing' amulets from Ketef Hinnom in
Jerusalem (early 6th century BCE; enlarged)

strange gods that are among you." (Joshua 24:23) After his death, idolatry became rife among much of the Israelite nation: "And the children of Israel did that which was evil in the sight of God and worshiped the Baalim... and followed other gods, the gods of the peoples that were around them." (Judges 2:11-12)

The Book of Judges attributes the harassment of the Israelite nation and the eventual conquest of parts of Israel by neighboring peoples to the Israelites' evildoing in the sight of the Lord. Invariably, the people of Israel cry out to the Lord, and then a "judge" (who was often a military and political leader as well) rises up and saves them from the enemy.

The description in the sixth chapter of Judges of Gideon's destruction of the altar of Baal shows clearly how central a position the altar occupied at the time; it also depicts the ritual that was commonplace in various settlements throughout the country. It seems to have been customary for idolaters to plant a tree above the altar, a tree, called Asherah, that became sanctified. Gideon destroyed the Asherah of Baal's altar as well.

At the same time, the Tabernacle that traveled through the desert with the Israelites during the time of Moses resided at Shiloh. Apparently, some Israelites, such as Elkana, the father of the prophet Samuel, exclusively adhered to the worship of God alone. Many others, however, combined the worship of God with various forms of idolatry, as was customary in the pagan world, where one might appease different deities.

Sites Reveal Ancient Rites

Traces of the Israelite Tabernacle at Shiloh have not been found, despite various excavations carried out at the site. In general, it should be noted that no traces of any rituals have been found in the settlements of the period. Nevertheless, three sites from this period have been found that are interpreted as being ritual sites, two in Samaria and one in the Galilee. Two of these seem to have been used for idolatrous worship, and one for the worship of God. Both sites in Samaria are "high places," altars in the open, surrounded by a boundary wall, rather than special buildings used for ritual worship[282].

The first site is on Mount Ebal. Known in Arabic as *el-burnet*, this site is located on a ridge along its northeastern slope. Adam Zertal has conducted four seasons of excavations at this site, resulting in extremely intriguing finds.

Two stages of construction from the period of the Judges (Iron Age I) were distinguished within an area of about 14 dunams, enclosed by a stone wall. The first stage was the building of a wall defining a large central courtyard, in the center of which there was a stone circle of some two meters in diameter. In this circle and its environs was a layer of ash containing numerous animal bones. Approximately 25 meters from this, the excavator found a structure of a "four-space house," a silo, and a large number of collar-rim jars that were typical of this period.

In the second stage, which was the principal one, an oblong building was erected in the northern part of the area, measuring 9 x 7 meters. This structure is built of stone and is filled with four layers of ash, dust, stones, potsherds and animal bones. There is an additional wall which is lower than the main wall by about 50 cm and encompasses the structure on three sides and adjoins it from outside. To the southwest of it, two courtyards with stone floors were discovered, with various installations built into its floor. Ash, animal bones, and pottery were found on some of them.

Between these two courtyards is a double sloping wall which the excavator interprets as a ramp. This sloping wall rises up to the top of the central structure.

Of some 3,000 bones found at the site, some 96% are of sheep, goats, and cattle. Some are the bones of wild animals, including a fallow deer. All the bones are of animals fit for sacrifice according to Jewish law, except for the fallow deer which is fit for eating though not for sacrificial purposes. The site was abandoned at some stage in the period of the Judges and, according to the excavator of the site, was deliberately covered with stones in order to bury it.

Because of the similarity of the site to the altar described in the Book of Ezekiel and to the altar described in the tractate of *Middot* in the Mishnah (the book of Jewish law from the Second Temple Period), the excavator interprets the site as the altar built by Joshua shortly after the entry of the Israelite people into Israel (Joshua 8:30-35)[283].

The excavator does indeed seem to be right in identifying the structure as an Israelite altar from the period of the Judges. Nevertheless, it is difficult to determine if this is actually the altar built by Joshua or not. This difficulty stems, first and foremost, from the marginal location of the site, on the northeastern ridge of the mountain. This location does not match the Biblical description of the ceremony conducted between Mt. Ebal and Mt. Gerizim (Joshua 8:30-34). According to the Biblical description, the altar should have been on the southern slope of the Mt. Ebal.

For this reason, Zertal identifies Jebel Kabir, to the northeast of Mt. Ebal, as Mt. Gerizim, though his opinion is not generally accepted. His bold suggestion does not match the tale of Gideon's youngest son Yotham, who according to the Biblical narrative stood "at the summit of Mt. Gerizim... and called out, saying to them: 'Listen to me, landowners of Shechem... .'" (Judges 9:8) From this verse, it would seem that one can hear from Shechem to Mt. Gerizim. Jebel Kabir, identified by Zertal as Mt. Gerizim, is too far from the site of ancient Shechem, which is identified with Tel Balata, near Nablus. Similarly, the excavator dates the establishment of the site to the 13th century BCE, whereas the analysis of the archaeological finds described above places the date of the entry of the Israelites into Israel at the onset of the 14th century BCE.

The second ritual site is "the bull site," located in the northeastern part of Samaria, east of the village of Kabatiya. An elliptical area surrounded by a wall built of large rocks

The Altar on Mt. Ebal

has been excavated at the summit of a hill. To the east of this ellipse, a large boulder was found lying on its narrow side; the area in front of this boulder was flooring on which sacrifices were apparently made. The most important find at this site is a bronze statuette of a bull. It is 17.5 centimeters long and its maximal height 12.4 centimeters. This statuette is the largest of its type ever found; others are known from such Middle East Canaanite sites as Hazor and Ugarit.[284] One cannot ignore the connection between the location of the site in the patrimony of the tribe of Menashe, son of Joseph, whose symbol was an ox: "His firstborn bullock – majesty is his" (Deut. 33:17), and with the golden calves of Jeroboam, who was a descendant of Joseph.

The third site was found in stratum IX in Tel Hazor in Galilee. A small structure was found in Tel Hazor and interpreted by the excavator as a "high place" dated to the 11th century BCE. A small vessel was found nearby with various sacrificial implements including a bronze statuette of a seated figure with a helmet on its head, apparently the god Baal, and a few weapons. Bases of ritual artifacts were found in the vicinity of this structure.[285]

It is not clear just how this ritual collection actually functioned, but it is reasonable to assume that it represents a form of idol worship from the period of the Judges. After the destruction of the Tabernacle at Shiloh, the prophet Samuel acted to eliminate all forms of idolatry. He called an assembly of the people and demanded that all idols be obliterated. As related in the Book of Samuel (I 7:3-4): "Direct your hearts to the Lord and worship Him only... Then the Israelites put aside the idols of Baal and of Ashtoret and *worshiped the Lord alone* [emphasis added]." Samuel's campaign seems to have been fruitful, and consequently we find no reference to this subject in the days of Saul, David and the early years of Solomon.

Establishing Jerusalem as the Only Location for Sacrificial Worship

During the period between the destruction of the Shiloh sanctuary and the construction of the First Holy Temple, it was customary to offer sacrifices anywhere. For example, a sacrifice was brought before going out to war. (I Sam. 7:9; 13:8-9) On special occasions, a family sacrifice was in order: "For we have a family sacrifice in town." (I Sam. 20:19) The prophet Samuel concealed the real aim of his visit to Bethlehem by saying that he intended to offer a sacrifice there: "Peace! I have come to make sacrifice to God! Sanctify yourselves and come with me to partake of the sacrifice." (I Sam. 16:5)

In Gibeon there was a large "high place" on which Solomon brought 1,000 burnt-offerings (I Kings 3:3-4), besides the sacrifice he brought before the Ark of the Covenant in Jerusalem (I Kings 3:15). Once the construction of the Jerusalem Temple was completed, however, it was forbidden to bring sacrifices to the "high places" or anywhere outside of the Jerusalem Temple.

It appears that the people found it difficult to abide by this decree. The Book of Kings is replete with verses that testify to a reality contrary to that prohibition. We read, "yet the 'high places' were not removed; the people were still offering up sacrifices and incense at the 'high places.'" (I Kings 22:44; II Kings 12:4; 14:4; 16:4) Only the righteous kings Hezekiah and Josiah took action to rectify the situation.

Though the persistence of the "high places" for offerings to God was troublesome, more energy was directed against the outright idolatry that had spread throughout the kingdom of Israel, even tainting the Kingdom of Judah. One of the climaxes of this struggle was the ceremony on Mt. Carmel where the prophet Elijah addressed the Jewish nation: "Until when will you hesitate? If the Lord is God, then follow Him, and if Baal – then follow him!" (II Kings 18:21)

In some instances, Israelites brought all kinds of idolatrous worship, including idols, stars, constellations, from all over the ancient world and introduced them into Jerusalem. A prominent example of this situation can be discerned in the description of the elimination of idolatrous worship in Jerusalem in the days of Josiah. Chapter 23 of the Book of II Kings contains detailed descriptions of the types of idolatry that were destroyed: the Asherah, Molech (the fiery idol in the Valley of Ben Hinnom), sun worship, Ashtoret, the chief Moabite god Kemosh, the Ammonite god Milkom, and so on. In addition, the prophet Ezekiel notes the women lamenting the Tammuz, the Mesopotamian god. (Ezek. 8:14)

Archaeological finds support the existence of this complex religious situation. In almost every First Temple Era site, some type of statuette has been found in excavations (contrary to sites dating from the Period of the Judges). The most common of these are horse heads which seem have been connected with sun worship as mentioned in the Bible (II Kings 23:11): "And he took away the horses that the kings of Judah had given to the sun." Also common are the statuettes of women, mostly unclothed, which are generally referred to as statuettes of Ashtoret.[286] Egyptian and Phoenician statuettes also have been found. Yet, as already noted, all of these were used in rites performed parallel with the worship of God.

Findings at a Unique Site in the Sinai Desert

An interesting example was found in a less important, yet unique, site in northern Sinai, near today's Israel-Egypt border, at a place known in Arabic as Kuntilat Ajrud and in Hebrew as Hurvat Teiman.[287] Two structures dating from the 8th century BCE were found there, one of which was well preserved and was found to contain fascinating artifacts.

The floor plan of the structure resembles that of a small fortress with square towers in its four corners. The unique nature of the site is in the large number of drawings and partially preserved inscriptions found there on plaster as well as on containers. There were also inscriptions engraved on stone implements. Two inscriptions written in ink on plaster are especially illuminating.

The following is written in the first inscription: *berachticha la-Y-H-W-H Teiman va'asherato:* "I bless you to Y-H-W-H Teiman and his Asherah."

In the second, we find: *berachti etchem la-Y-H-W-H Shomeron vela-asherato,* "I bless you to Y-H-W-H Samaria and his Asherah."

A similar inscription was found at Khirbet el-Kom in the inland plain: *la-Y-H-W-H notseri vela-asherato,* "to Y-H-W-H my defender and his Asherah."[288] This wording, which teaches us of the worship of God to which the worship of the Asherah had been added, is reminiscent of the story of Gideon destroying the altar of Baal and the Asherah which stood upon it (see above). Anticipating the possibility of this phenomenon, the Torah forbade planting trees near an altar: "You shall not plant for yourself an Asherah, any kind of tree, other than the altar of your God, which you shall make for yourself." (Deuteronomy 16:21)

The excavator, Zeev Meshel, has suggested that the place was a religious center, though there are no findings at the site to indicate that it served as a temple. Because of the mention of the word "Samaria," (which is in the north) and because the names in inscriptions ending in *yau*, such as Ovadyau and Amary-au which are characteristic of the northern Kingdom of Israel (in contrast to the ending *yahu* which is typical of the southern Kingdom of Judah) Meshel suggests that the site belonged to the Kingdom of Israel, despite its distant location from that kingdom. Yet we cannot exclude the possibility that the inscriptions were made by a group of refugees from the Kingdom of Israel fleeing Assyrian conquest in 721 BCE.

Whoever they were, it seems that they felt no conflict between faith in God, to Whom they prayed and in Whose name they bestowed blessings, and invoking the Asherah. Their faith in God was expressed in the abundance of personal names containing His name, as reflected both in the Bible and in archaeological finds. The suffixes and sometimes the prefixes added to the base of the names were made up of the theophorous element *yahu*, an abbreviation of one of the official names of God, *Y-H-W-H*.

The kings of Judah were named in Hebrew Yeho*shaphat* (Jehosephat), Yeho*yachin* (Jehoiachin), *Yoshi*yahu (Josiah), *Hizki*-yahu (Hezekiah), *Uzzi*yahu (Uzziah), *Amaz*yah (Amaziah), Ye-ho*ram* (Jehoram), and *Zidqi*yahu (Zedekiah).

There is a similar feature in the names of the kings of Israel. We encounter such names as Kings *Zechar*yahu (Zechariah), Yeho*'ash* (Jehoash), Yeho*'ahaz* (Jehoahaz), Yoram/Yeho*ram* (Jo-ram/Jehoram), Yehu *ben Nimshi* (Jehu, son of Nimshi), *Ahazya*-hu (Ahaziah), and Ho*shea* (Hosea).

This suffix is extremely widespread in the inscriptions from the period of the Monarchy as well. The best-known inscription of this type appears on the grave of an important person whose name is obscure, though its suffix has been preserved. (Though mentioned earlier, it is worth repeating in this context.) This inscription, found in the village of Siloam to the east of the City of David, reads as follows: *Zo qevurat ...yahu asher 'al ha-bayit,* "This is the burial place of ....*yahu* who was in charge of the [royal] House."[289] We do not know the name of the man, but the suffix of his name was clearly *–yahu*. His title "*asher 'al ha-bayit*" is familiar from a Biblical context: this was one of the important positions in the royal court of Judah.

It has been suggested that he was none other than Shevanyahu (Shevna), who bore that title in the days of King Hezekiah of Judah. The possible identification is based on the verses from the Book of Isaiah which criticize Shevna for his actions, and note that he had a grave cut into the rock for himself: *Thus has... the God of Hosts spoken: "Go, approach this steward, Shevna, who is in charge of the House [and say] 'What have you here, whom do you have here, that you have cut yourself here a grave on high, and prepared for yourself a dwelling-place in the rock?'"* (Isaiah 22:15-16).

In addition to this inscription relating to the highest stratum of society in Judah, letters have been found from somewhat lower officials, mainly army officers, whose names include theophoric suffixes or prefixes too. Seals and letters addressed to the commanding officer of the fortress, whose name was El*yashiv ben Ash*yahu, have been found in Arad. Such names as *Shema'*yahu, *Tov*yahu, *Ahi*yahu, *Kon*yahu, *Hosha'*yahu, and many others, appear in the Lachish letters. Seals bearing the name of the royal scribe *Gemar*yahu *ben Shafan,* with whom we are familiar from the Book of Jeremiah, and another person named Be*na*yahu *ben Hosha'*yahu have been discovered in Jerusalem. The commanding officer of a fortress excavated near Kibbutz Palmachim near the seacoast was called *Hashav*yahu.[290]

As already noted in connection with the inscriptions found at Hurvat Teiman, the common suffix in Samaria is yau. On ostraca there, we find such names as *Yeda'yau*, *Shemaryau*, and *Gediyau*.

This feature fits in well with the style of the benediction frequently found in the Lachish letters: *Yashmia' Y-H-W-H et adoni shemu'ot tov/shalom*[291] "May God enable my lord to hear good/peaceful tidings." The oral benediction with which Boaz greeted his harvesters was *Y-H-W-H 'immachem*, "May God be with you" (Ruth 2:4).

From the prevalence of names and terms that incorporated the name of God, we can appreciate the central position of the Creator in the *weltanschauung* of the people of the Kingdom of Judah in the 8th and 7th centuries BCE.

This phenomenon is part of a regional one, where name-endings and benedictions in the name of the national god were customary among the neighboring nations as well. For example, we find that Edomite names included the Edomite god Qos, as in the Edomite king named *Qosgavar* or Edomite letters opening with the salutation "blessings of Qos." Among the Moabites, the godly name Kemosh was a component of personal names, similar to that of the king well known from the Mesha Monument, whose full name was "Meisha' son of *Kemosh*iyat or Kemosh (melech)".

It appears that while many Israelites worshipped God as their main and official deity, their custom was to combine this worship with other faiths and rituals. Nevertheless, in light of what we find in the Bible and archaeological findings, it seems that it was not customary for Israelites to name their children after pagan idols.

The Struggle against Idolatry and "High Places"

Archaeological evidence of the struggle against idolatry and worship on "high places" was found in two Negev sites, where places of worship from the First Temple Period were found, though their activities ceased during this very same period. One is in Arad, where it seems that King Hezekiah put an end to its activities; the other is in Tel Sheva (near the city of Be'er-Sheva), where such activities were apparently stopped by King Heze-kiah. Relatively large altars–apparently used for sacrificing cattle and sheep–were discovered at both of these sites.

From descriptions of each excavation, one can appreciate its unique characteristics, as well as the significance of each of the altars. During the excavation seasons carried out at Tel She-va in 1973 and 1974, hewn stones were found in the walls of the warehouses and in dirt ramparts dating from Iron Age II.[292] A shape resembling a wriggling snake was found on one of these rocks. When these rocks were fit together, it turned out that they belonged to a four-horned altar about 1.57 meters high from its bottom to the top of its horns, according to the estimate of the excavator, who also estimated that the length and breadth of the altar were approximately the same, some 1.60 centimeters x 1.60

The altar with horns from Tel Sheva

centimeters. There was but a single reservation: since most of the altar stones were not found, there was insufficient data for a complete restoration.[293]

This find aroused considerable interest at the time, since no parallel to this altar had been found anywhere in the country. The excavator of the site, the late Yochanan Aharoni, noted that this altar did not comply with the Biblical injunction regarding altar construction: "Do not build them of hewn stone" (Exodus 20:25).[294]

Later excavations carried out at Tel Dan produced similar findings. A large, well-chiseled altar horn was found there. The excavator, Avraham Biran, estimated that the height of the altar was some 3 meters, about twice the height of the Tel Sheva altar.[295] The similarity between the two altars has given rise to the thought that some connection exists between them. Dan and Be'er-Sheva are two sites located at opposite ends of the country (with Dan in the north and Be'er-Sheva in the south); it is not surprising to find the phrase "from Dan to Be'er-Sheva" commonly used in the Bible as an expression of the full territory of Israel. Biblical evidence indicates that Dan was the site of an idolatrous rite (the idol of Micah, Judges 18), and a golden calf was placed there in the days of Jeroboam (I Kings 12:30). So it may be tentatively assumed that the altar found at Tel Sheva was used for idolatrous worship, similar to the altar at Dan.

Compared to the altars at Tel Sheva and at Dan, the altar found at Arad is substantially different and shows definite signs that it was used for the worship of God alone. It was found in the courtyard of a temple built inside a royal fortress near Arad. The temple is built along an east-west axis, like the Temple in Jerusalem, and it has a courtyard in which there stood a large altar built of brick and of rough stone covered with plaster. The altar's base measured 2.20 x 2.40 square meters, and its height measured 1.5 meters.[296] These dimensions resemble those of the sacrificial altar in the Israelites' Tabernacle as described in the Book of Exodus (27:1).

Channels to gather the blood of the sacrifices were found

near the altar. From the courtyard, there is an opening leading into a broad narrow hall; the excavators found the bases of two columns, one on either side of the opening. Three steps lead to a small room which, according to the excavator, is the *d'vir*, the Holy of Holies. Two small altars made of stone stand at the entrance to the small room, while inside there was a polished stone monument with a curved top, on which traces of red coloring were found.

A number of potsherds were found in the temple, with names inscribed on them: *M'ramot* and *Pashchur*, both of which are familiar from the Bible as the names of priestly families (Ezra 8:33 and Jeremiah 20:1 respectively).

It seems, therefore, that in the northern Negev the Biblical laws of building altars were known. In Arad, these rules were strictly adhered to because the altar there was one for the worship of God, but the rules were not honored in Tel Sheva because the altar was to be used for idolatrous worship. Also at Tel Sheva, excavators found statuettes of Egyptian goddesses and of the Apis bull, which was worshipped in Egypt,[297] in addition to the statuettes that were commonplace in Judah in those days.[298] This indicates that in Be'er-Sheva, idolatry was common and the altar that was discovered was used for those rituals. We may conclude that there was an idolatrous ritual center in Tel-Sheba, as there was in Tel Dan.

We do not know precisely which gods were worshiped at Tel Sheva, or how many; in addition to the Egyptian statuettes, other idols were found that were more common in Israel. Yet a clue was found in the form of a serpent engraved on one of the stones of the altar. In the ritual compound at Tel Dan, two large jars were also found decorated with a serpent design.[299] The serpent rite was indeed known throughout the Middle East.[300] In Canaanite Arad as well (Early Bronze Age II), a jar was found with a serpent design around it;[301] this is also true, of ritual platforms in Taanakh and in Bet Shean from Iron Age I, where carved serpents were found, as well as other images.[302]

It is interesting to note that King Hezekiah of Judah, to whom Aharoni ascribes the construction of stratum II and the destruction of the altar at the site, also destroyed a copper serpent in Jerusalem as part of his eradication of idolatrous practices in the country. It is related in the Bible (II Kings 18:4) that the copper snake constructed by Moses at God's behest for noble purposes was later worshipped as a deity, "for up until those days the Israelites were burning incense before it." Hezekiah felt compelled to destroy it.

However, a number of questions remain unanswered: Apparently, the altar in Tel-Sheba was not totally destroyed. Why was it dismantled and not broken, and why were its pieces buried in the walls and in the rampart?

How was the Tel-Sheba Altar Demolished?

Aharoni argued that the altar in Tel-Sheba was buried in an organized and careful manner, like the temple in Arad, however this does not appear to be the case. A perusal of the excavation report indicates that the altar stones were found in a number of places in this site.[303] Three altar horns found secondary use in the wall that blocked one of the entrances of a warehouse structure, while the fourth was found shattered in the northwest corner of the warehouse. According to Aharoni, this stone served as a threshold stone in one of the entrances to the warehouses.

Other stones were found in the layers of stones above those in which the altar horns were found. One stone was found on a slope outside the gate, and another fragment was found in the supporting wall of the smooth slope Glacis attributed to stratum III. This fragment fit one of the stones found in the wall of a building to the west of the gate. (The warehouse structure is located to the north of the gate.)[304] Aharoni also notes that only about a half of the total number of stones has been found. It appears, then, that this is not an example of an orderly burial of altar stones. It seems far more likely that the builders of stratum II simply did not attribute any significance

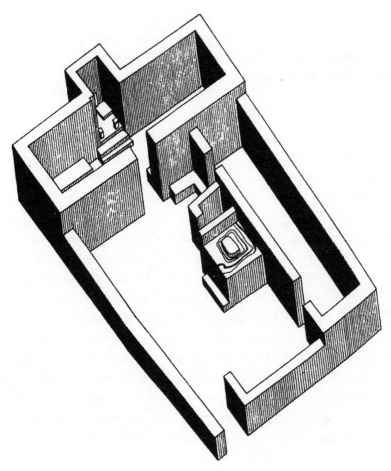

The Arad Temple; Herzog 1997

or sanctity to these stones. If that is so, we cannot assume that this was the burial of a sacred altar.

The demolishing of the altar in Be'er-Sheva was substantially different from the method adopted in Arad, where the temple was buried where it stood in its entirety. The altar in Be'er-Sheva seems to have been demolished and some of its stones shattered, as was customary when destroying an altar to idolatry in this period. Some of the altar stones that were not shattered were reused in various places throughout the site,[305] as noted above, since one was permitted to use these hewn stones for other purposes. It should be noted that the site was built largely of stones found in the nearby Be'er-Sheva and Hebron streams, as well as of mud bricks. Consequently the use of the available hewn stones was quite natural.[306]

Biblical Documentation

The finds discussed above perfectly correspond with descriptions in the Bible. Traces of this ritual center are found in Biblical writings, such as when the prophet Amos says: "They that swear by the sin of Samaria and say: 'As your god, O Dan, lives' and 'as the way of Be'er-Sheva lives' – they shall fall and never rise up again" (Amos 8:13) and (5:5): "But do not seek Bet-El nor enter into Gilgal nor pass through Be'er-Sheva, for Gilgal shall surely go into exile and Bet-El will be sorrowful."

These verses indicate that in the time of Amos (8th century BCE), the area of Be'er-Sheva was indeed an idolatrous center, just like the sanctuary at Dan. The description contained in these verses is reflected clearly in the archaeological findings,[307] and dovetails with the dating of stratum III that thrived in the 8th century.

The builders of Stratum II, which is dated to the close of the 8th century, demolished the altar that was part of stratum III, during the lifetime of Amos.

In summary, it appears that religious centers for idolatry functioned at the same time in Tel Sheva (for the inhabitants of the southern part of the country) similar to the compound at Tel Dan (in the north). In contrast, a royal fortress stood in Arad, where there was a temple for the worship of God, for the use of the local inhabitants; it therefore was constructed according to the rules laid down by Jewish law.

The Sabbath

The observance of the Sabbath was one of the unique characteristics of the people in Israel.[308] Together with the festivals and the sanctification of each new month, it is one of the most important components of the everyday life of the Jewish people. We read of these observances in the prophecies of Hosea (2:13): "I will put an end to all her rejoicing, her feasts, her New Moons and her Sabbaths, and all her appointed seasons."

From other prophetic books we learn that it was customary not to perform labor on the Sabbath day, but rather to go to the prophet for inspiration and instruction (II Kings 4:23). The study of Torah (The Five Books of Moses) on the Sabbath is also highlighted in the words of the prophet Isaiah (1:13): "New Moon and Sabbath, the holding of convocations" though this verse may actually be dealing with assemblies convening in the Temple rather than with local custom. Even dishonest merchants and exploiters of the poor did not dare open their businesses on the Sabbath. As the prophet Amos put it (8:4-5): "Hear this, you who would devour the needy and destroy the poor of the land, saying 'When will the New Moon be over that we may sell produce? And the Sabbath that we may sell grain?' Making the *ephah* [measurement] small and the shekel large, and cheating with false scales..."

Sabbath observance was not perfect in the days of the prophet Isaiah either; Sabbath observers were in need of encouragement and were praised (Isaiah 56:2): "Happy is the man that does this and he who firmly observes it: who keeps the Sabbath from being profaned, and restrains his hand from doing evil." If we follow the references to the Sabbath uttered by the prophets in their chronological order, we find that in the 9th and 8th centuries, during the days of Hosea, Amos, and Elisha, Sabbath observance was an accepted norm and so there was no need to refer to it.

Yet at the end of the 8th century, in the days of Isaiah, as at the end of the 7th century, in the days of the prophet Jeremiah on the eve of the destruction of the Temple, Sabbath observance was less widespread. Broad sectors of the population were not careful about abstaining from work on this day, consequently the prophets bewail this situation. For example, the prophet Jeremiah says (17:21-22): "Thus says God: 'Beware for [the sake of] your souls and carry no burdens on the Sabbath day, nor bring it in through the gates of Jerusalem. Do not carry burdens out of your homes on the Sabbath day and do not do any work. Rather sanctify the Sabbath day as I commanded your ancestors." Elsewhere, he lists the desecration of the Sabbath as one of the causes of the imminent destruction of the holy city (17:27): "But if you do not obey Me to sanctify the Sabbath day and not to bear burdens and enter through the gates of Jerusalem on the Sabbath day, I will kindle a fire in the gates of [the city, a fire] that will consume the palaces of Jerusalem and will not be extinguished."

It is probable that the Shabbat was mentioned in a document from the period of the First Temple. In the fortress of Hashavyahu a document was discovered in which a person complains about his clothes being taken from him despite his having paid all his debts. In lines 4-6 of this letter we find the following written: 'Let your worker reap and cease, bringing the produce into the storehouse before Shabbat.'[309]

In summary, we can say that the observance of the Sabbath was at first an accepted norm in the life of the Israelite nation, but just as matters deteriorated in connection with idolatry, so too they deteriorated with regard to Sabbath observance.

New Moon Observances

The Torah makes no special reference to the observance of the New Moon, other than specifying a special sacrificial offering. Nevertheless, during the First Temple Period the New Moon appears as a special day, second in importance, perhaps, to the Sabbath. The combination of "New Moon and Sabbath" appears in the prophetic books a number of times.

It was customary to have special feasts, as can be seen from the New Moon feast celebrated by King Saul (I Samuel 20:18-29). As observed today, then, too, there were sometimes two New Moon ceremonial days for certain months. Moreover, it seems to have been customary to study Torah and to refrain from work on this day (Amos 8:5; Isaiah 1:13-14):

"The early prophets instituted for the Israelites that the days of *Rosh Chodesh* (the New Month) should be days on which work is not done to sanctify these days to Torah study and introspection."

In the days of the Hasmoneans, the New Moon was included in the list of festive days contained in the proclamation of King Demetrius: "All the festive days and the Sabbaths and the New Moons and the appointed seasons, as well as three days before the festivity and three days after it -- all shall be days of leisure for all the Jews in my kingdom." (Maccabees I 10:24)

The Biblical commentator Radak in Hosea 2:13 comments on the verse, *I will also cause all her rejoicing to cease, her feast days, her* New Moons, *and her Sabbaths, and all her holy feasts*, "the cause for rejoicing on these days was due to the additional sacrifices (*Mussaf*) that were offered. Among the additional sacrifices was a sin-offering that was offered on behalf of the Jewish People. When the Temple was destroyed and all sacrifices were halted, the days were no longer days of rejoicing."

Interesting evidence that it was customary to abstain from certain activities on the New Moon is found in a document from the end of the First Temple Period. Found in Arad, document 7[310]indicates that Elyashiv, the commander of the Arad fortress, received an order to give the *Kittim* (apparently mercenaries serving in the army of the Kingdom of Judah) various materials on the New Moon of the tenth month (Tevet), but to record the dispatch of these materials on the second of the month. Why was he not to record this transaction on the day it was executed, i.e., on the first of the month, the New Moon? The scholar Loewenstamm has suggested that the reason was the fact that it was forbidden to write, along with other commonly forbidden tasks, on the New Moon.[311]

Festivals

In addition to the Sabbath and the New Moon, the Israelites celebrated three Biblically mandated festivals. The Book of Chronicles states that Solomon brought sacrifices to the Temple "in accordance with the commandment of Moses: for Sabbaths and New Moons and festive days, three times a year, on the Festival of Leavened Bread [Passover] and on the Festival of Weeks [Shavuot] and on the Festival of Tabernacles [Sukkot]" (II Chron. 8:13).

Mention is made in the Book of Chronicles of a mass celebration of Passover held by King Hezekiah after the destruction of the northern Kingdom of Israel (II Chron. 30) and of another mass celebration held in the days of King Josiah (II Chron. 35). It is not surprising that these two kings who celebrated mass festivals of Passover in Jerusalem had struggled against idolatrous practices and against the custom of worshiping at "high places." It seems reasonable to view the mass celebrations as part of their war against the offering of Passover sacrifices outside of Jerusalem, and part of their broader struggle for the observance of the Jewish laws in their totality.

At a later point, the people of Israel undoubtedly celebrated the festivals and brought sacrifices, but it seems that these actions were accompanied by negative features, prompting the prophet Isaiah (1:14) to assert, in behalf of God: "Your New Moons and your appointed seasons [i.e. festivals] My soul does hate; they have become a burden to Me."

Burial during the First Temple Period 312

Biblical law instructs that a person executed by court order and then hanged (as was customary), must be buried before sundown (Deut. 21:23).

In Biblical law, a corpse is spiritually impure, and any person who comes into contact with, or who enters in its immediate vicinity, becomes impure. The burial of Nadav and Avihu, two of the sons of Aaron, who were buried "outside the camp" (Lev. 10:5) reflects the care taken by the Israelites to bury the dead outside the limits of the settlement, in stark contrast to the Canaanites who on occasion buried their dead within the limits of their settlements or even under the flooring of their homes.

Some 300 burial sites have been found in Judea, all dating from the 8th-6th centuries BCE, mostly in Jerusalem and its environs. Most of the dead were buried in the ground simply, without accompanying artifacts such as clay pots or jewelry. Such burials may have been called "graves of the people" (Jer. 26:23).

Family burial caves were typical of the period. Their basic floor plan was a cave with a rectangular opening which could be closed with a stone "plug" tailored to the dimensions of the opening. In the cave, there was a central corridor surrounded by three higher shelves in the shape of the Hebrew letter, *chet* - ח. There is a strong similarity between the burial cave and the floor plan of the classical residence of the Iron Age – the four-spaced house. Accordingly, the grave is termed "an eternal home" in the Bible: "For man goes to his eternal home" (Eccl. 12:5). Like a house, it was divided into rooms. This is borne out by an inscription found in a grave at Khirbet el-Kom on the lowlands, where we read: *l'ufi ben netanyahu ha-cheder ha-zeh* "To Ufi the son of Netanyahu – this room."

These burials tended to be more elaborate than "graves of the people." The deceased were laid on their backs, on shelves. In many cases, a depression was carved into the shelf to better accommodate the head of the corpse. A large pit was cut into the rock under one of the shelves, and it was into this pit that the remains of the deceased and the artifacts placed with him were transferred when it became necessary to bury additional bodies of the same family. The deceased were buried with jewelry and various kinds of pottery.

In a cave in Jerusalem, two small silver scrolls were found with various Biblical verses inscribed on them, including a version of the priestly benediction known from the Book of

Numbers (6:24-26). In K'far Ha-Shiloh to the east of the City of David, magnificent burial caves were found, intended for the burial of either a single body or perhaps two. There, the deceased were placed in burial chests, some dug out of the rock, while others were portable. These burial caves apparently had been prepared for high-ranking government officials, for a fragmentary inscription was found on one of them, saying that a person whose name ended in –*yahu* and whose title was *asher 'al ha-bayit* (literal translation, "who is [appointed] over the [royal] house") was buried in that cave. As explained earlier, this title is that of an important prince of the Kingdom of Judah and is mentioned a number of times in the prophetic books of the Bible (such as in Isaiah 22:15). The Book of Kings mentions various kings of Judah who were buried in the City of David, but no trace of them yet has been found. (see pictures on p. 126 and 184)

Summary

Information concerning the spiritual life of the Israelite nation in the First Temple Era is not overly plentiful. The ongoing struggle to abolish idolatry, with its ups and downs, lasted from the time the Israelites entered Israel until the destruction of the First Temple. Nevertheless, the official religious ritual, at least in Judah, was the worship of God in Jerusalem. The names of the kings of Judah and of Israel, like the names of simple people of the era, testify to this.

The care taken in burying the dead outside city limits and in keeping one's distance from the dead were characteristics unique to the Israelite population. It appears that those elements of Judaism pertaining to ritual were accepted and observed in various strata by both Judean and Israelite society.

The main problem of the Israelite nation, besides idolatry, was the social corruption that accompanied their idolatrous practices. From the prophets' point of view, this way of life was in direct negation to the laws of God and was what doomed both kingdoms, Judah and Israel.

The Kingdom of Judah—the Only Kingdom

The great upsurge in the settlement history of the Judean Hills took place after the destruction of the northern Kingdom of Israel and the exile of the Ten Tribes in the year 721 BCE. The central cities in the northern part of the country were destroyed, and Jerusalem once again became the spiritual and political center of the Israelite nation. Jerusalem was developed and extended westward, and new neighborhoods were founded on the western hill (currently the Armenian Quarter, Jewish Quarter and Mt. Zion of Old Jerusalem).

Confirming the Dimensions of Jerusalem

The discovery of the "broad wall" in the Jewish Quarter of Old Jerusalem taught us something about the dimensions of the city. This was the first time that Jerusalem had attained such a large area and it likely became the largest city in all of Israel. Its area encompassed a wall measured about 650 dunams. This is most extraordinary, for in general, the large cities were located on the coastal plain.

However, the fate of the Kingdom of Judah could have been similar to that of the Kingdom of Israel. Twenty years after the destruction of the northern Kingdom, King Hezekiah of Judah rebelled against the brutal world power, Assyria. To bolster his effort, Hezekiah took a number of steps including creating alliances with the Philistines on the coastal plain, the fortification of Jerusalem, cutting a secret passage to enable the waters of the Gihon Spring to flow into the city, and the preparation of large quantities of munitions.

The manufacture of the special clay jars known specifically as the *la-melech* jars is attributed to the reign of Hezekiah. As noted elsewhere in this volume, the potters impressed on the handles of these jars a unique impression showing a winged beetle and the word *la-melech*, i.e."for the king" (or "belonging to the king") inscribed in ancient Hebrew script. In some cases, only the word *la-melech* appears, but on most of these handles, the names of four Judean settlements were added: Mameshet, Zif, Socho, and Hebron. The archaeologist Gabriel Barkay has suggested that Mameshet should be identified with Ramat Rahel. Archaeologists generally link the manufacture of these jars to the division of the kingdom into four regions, with one of the cities inscribed on the jar handles serving as the center of each region.

This activity is viewed as part of the preparations made for the impending war with Assyria. These jars may have been used by Hezekiah for wine, oil, flour or other supplies for his soldiers stationed there.

Hezekiah was a very energetic king who also acted in areas outside his kingdom. The Book of Chronicles tells of Hezekiah breaking the pagan platforms and altars "From all Judah and Binyamin and in Ephraim and Menashe" (*Chronicles II*: 31, 1). This is surprising since the area of Ephraim and Menashe was in the Kingdom which rose after the destruction of the Kingdom of Israel. It is not clear how it was possible for him to act in such a forceful way in an area that was under the direct control of Assyria without any reaction from this world super-power. Because of this astonishing fact there are various investigators who claim: 'It seems that the reform that Hezekiah instigated, according to Chronicles, outside the border of the kingdom of Judah in the area of Assyria has no possibility in reality.'[313]

In the last year it has become clear that the archaeological findings completely disprove those investigators and show that Hezekiah's reforms were real. In the rescue digs that took place in Tut Stream in the south of the Carmel, a site was discovered which the diggers defined as the administration center during the days of the First Temple. There they found an ancient Hebrew seal upon which was engraved a rare name: To Mekach (son of) Amichai. They also found two broken jars upon whose handles was written: 'LaMelech' - 'to the king' which was common during the days of Hezekiah.[314]

It therefore seems that Hezekiah used the period of disorder that existed at the beginning of Sanhariv's rule which we know from Assyrian sources. He expanded the area of his rule and built settlements beyond the northern boundary of Judah. This was perhaps one of the catalysts of the travails of Sanhariv.

However, despite Hezekiah's impressive planning for the rebellion, he was not sufficiently strong, and the Assyrian forces eventually conquered nearly all of the Kingdom of Judah, including the second-most important city of the kingdom, Lachish. We learn of both his preparations and his defeat from the books of the Bible (II Kings 18-19; Isaiah 22; II Chron. 32), and There is also proof of the Bible's accuracy in archaeological findings.

The Golden Age of the Kingdom of Judah

The Bible indicates that the Assyrian army was poised to conquer Jerusalem as well, but divine intervention altered the situation and demolished the Assyrian forces in a single night (II Kings 19:38). The enormous destruction of the cities of Judah that accompanied the campaign led by Sennacherib, King of Assyria, in 701 BCE, together with the miraculous salvation of Jerusalem, reinforced the status of the city.

The strength of the Kingdom of Judah grew swiftly in the wake of Sennacherib's campaign, during the reigns of Menashe and Josiah. Archaeologists are unable to determine to which reign to ascribe various construction projects. Yet even if certain developments took place in the days of King Menashe, who reigned 55 years in the shadow of Assyrian overlords, the development which had lasting effect, took place in the reign of Josiah.

Josiah came to power in the year 639 BCE. He took decisive advantage of the crumbling of Assyrian suzerainty to strengthen his kingdom and extend its borders. During his 31-year rule, the Kingdom of Judah entered its Golden Age, both in settlement construction and in spirituality. The Bible provides much detail of the activities of Josiah in the extermination of idolatry and in centralizing the worship of God in Jerusalem.

Josiah succeeded in unifying the worship of God in the Temple and in establishing the awareness of Jerusalem in the minds of the Israelite nation.

In addition to his spiritual achievements, Josiah undertook vast construction projects, yet the Bible tells us little about them. Archaeological research, however, together with oblique indications buried in the Biblical text, demonstrates the significant expansion of the Kingdom of Judah during the reign of this king.

Jeremiah, the prophet who was active during the closing period of the First Temple, mentions the six provinces of the Kingdom of Judah during this era:

"And they shall come from the cities of Judah, and from the environs round about Jerusalem, and from the Land of Benjamin, and from the Lowland, and from the Hill-country, and from the Negev [the South], bringing burnt-offerings and sacrifices and meal-offerings and frankincense, bringing sacrifices of thanksgiving to the House of the Lord." (Jer. 17:26)

"Men shall buy fields for money and inscribe the deeds and seal them and call witnesses in the Land of Benjamin, and in the environs of Jerusalem and in the cities of Judah, and in the cities of the Hill-country, and in the cities of the Lowland, and in the cities of the Negev for I shall cause their captives to return, says the Lord." (Jer. 32:44)

"In the cities of the Hill-country, in the cities of the Lowland, and in the cities of the Negev, and in the Land of Benjamin, and in the environs of Jerusalem, and in the cities of Judah, shall the flocks again pass under the hands of he who counts them, says the Lord." (Jer. 33:13)

These similar Biblical passages repeatedly use the terms "the cities of Judah" and "the environs of Jerusalem." These references are also used in connection with Josiah's religious reformation, as the Bible testifies: "...to offer on the high places in the cities of Judah and the environs of Jerusalem." (II Kings 23:5).

It appears that the Kingdom of Judah included six geographical regions that were administrative units as well:

1) the cities of the Lowland
2) the cities of the Negev (South)
3) the cities of the Hill-country
4) the cities of Judah
5) the land of Benjamin
6) the environs of Jerusalem

In the three aforementioned Biblical references, the regions called "the land of Benjamin", "the environs of Jerusalem", and "the cities of Judah" appear in a consistent geographical sequence: north-south or south-north. It is most probable that these six regions were the names of provinces of the Kingdom of Judah in the lifetime of Jeremiah, who began his prophetic mission during the reign of Josiah (Jer. 1:2).

This intriguing list includes regional names appearing for the first time in the Bible: "the cities of the hill-country" and "the environs of Jerusalem." The distinction between "the environs of Jerusalem" and "the cities of Judah" is an innovation, for until that period the region of Jerusalem enjoyed no special status. The list, then, teaches us of the new status of the region called "the environs of Jerusalem."

It may be assumed, then, that towards the conclusion of the First Temple Period a new situation came into being, one that made necessary a reorganization of the administrative apparatus of the Kingdom of Judah. How did this come about?

The New Administrative Division of the Country

As noted above, King Josiah came to power c. 639 BCE, when the Assyrian Empire was disintegrating. Josiah took advantage of the political vacuum, strengthening his kingdom and expanding its borders. According to II Chron. 35:6-7, he actually reached the Galilee region, though it was never annexed to his kingdom. Josiah's final battle at Megiddo (II Kings 23:29; II Chron. 35:23) indicates that he was able to move his army to Megiddo without encountering any obstacles on the way.

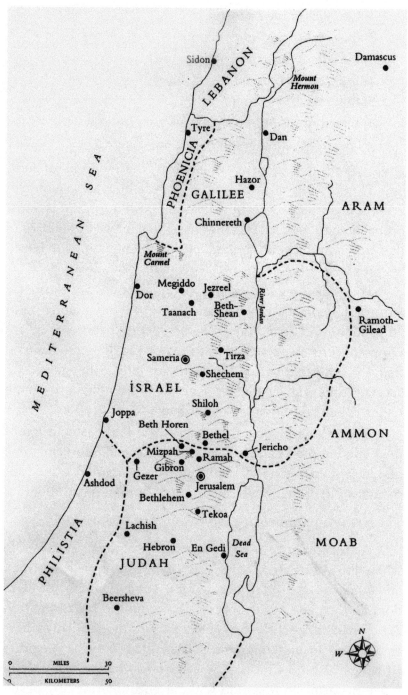

The Kingdoms of Israel and Judah

Archaeological findings indicate that numerous settlements were established in Judah during the 7th century BCE. These include:

- Lachish (stratum II)

- Tel Batash (stratum II, Biblical Timna)

- Southern sites, mainly in the Be'er-Sheva Valley

- Ein Gedi (stratum V)

- Hyrcania Valley sites in the Judean Desert

- Qumran on the Dead Sea shore, and many more small sites on the fringes of the Judean Desert

A fortress dating from this period was found near Jericho, as well. Yet there is no doubt that most of Judah's growth took place in the vicinity of Jerusalem. In various studies carried out near Jerusalem, scores of new sites were found, mainly in the northeastern part of the region. A magnificent fortress was built in the south of this area, at Ramat Rahel. This fortress points to the kingdom making efforts at construction outside the city limits of Jerusalem, while Jerusalem itself attained dimensions far beyond anything it had achieved earlier. Its walled-in area was about 650 dunams, and apparently there were parts of the city that sprang up outside the walls. The overall area of the city, according to Gabriel Barkay, was about 1,000 dunams.

Archaeological evidence indicates a densely populated area, especially in the Jerusalem region, with its orientation along a northeastern axis. Near the city and all around it there evolved a planned and organized settlement array. A settlement ring was established within 4 to 6 kilometers from the city. (This excluded territory to the east, where the Mount of Olives burial ground for the wealthy residents of Jerusalem was located.)

Various forms of agricultural settlements developed between neighboring settlements. These included "four-space" residences, water reservoirs, farming terraces, winepresses, as well as fortresses to protect the area. Archaeological studies

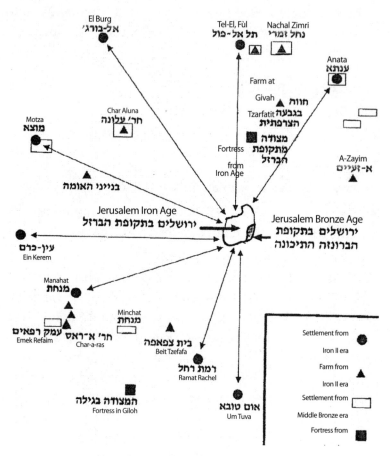

The growth of settlements around Jerusalem during
the Bronze II era and the Iron II era

therefore demonstrate the workings of a central organizer and planner striving to create highly developed settlements.

A settlement hierarchy clearly existed, which points to a typically centralized regime, a phenomenon which can be discerned through archaeological finds and also by applying a familiar geographical model. The concept of a "primate city" is known in geographical settlement research: a central town develops until it is at least twice the size of the second-largest town. It becomes the main power center, controlling the entire country. The lack of such a model, i.e., the coexistence of a number of towns of similar size, indicates the existence of a number of power centers in that country.

In Judah, the situation is clear. Jerusalem was the "chief town". With its area of some 650 dunams within its walls, it obviously outranked the second largest town in Judah, Lachish. The area of the base of Tel Lachish comes to some 150 dunams and at the top of the tell, only some 80 dunams. Another large settlement was at Tel Gezer, the area of which was a little over 100 dunams. Other towns were smaller, and their areas did not exceed 50 dunams each.

The intensive settlement activity during this period was accompanied by renewed administrative organization. This is reflected in the above verses from the Book of Jeremiah. The six geographical-administrative regions included one previously unknown, the environs of Jerusalem. What, exactly, does the term "the environs of Jerusalem" mean?

The Provinces of the Kingdom

The Province of the Lowland included the southern and northern lowlands, as well as sections of the coastal plain. A unique discovery made on the coastal plain demonstrates a Judean presence in this region. Ostraca bearing the Judean name "Hashavyahu" were found near the Palmahim coast, to the north of Ashdod, at a site known as Matzad Hashavyahu, "the fortress of Hashavyahu."[315]

In addition, a letter turned up there, written in the ancient Hebrew script, in which someone requested of the minister assurance that his garment would be returned to him, for it had been taken from him unjustly by a person named Hosha'yahu ben Shuvi. Both the names and the script leave no doubt that this was a region ruled by the Kingdom of Judah until just before the destruction of the First Temple (before the campaign of the Egyptian Pharaoh Necho and the battle at Megiddo, when Josiah was killed and Judea fell under the sway of Egypt.)

The Province of the Negev (South) seems to have included the northern Negev, mainly the Be'er-Sheva and Arad valleys, where a considerable amount of settlement and fortress construction took place in this period.

The Province of the Hills seems to have included the southern hills of Hebron, for in a number of places in the Book of Joshua, Hebron and the area south of it are referred to by means of a general term: *ha-har* "the hill-country" (Josh. 11:21; 14:12). Furthermore, the Book of Samuel (I Sam. 23:14) says of David: "And he remained in *the hill-country*, in the wilderness of Ziph."

The Cities of Judah were in the northern hills of the Hebron area.

The Land of Benjamin was the region of the hills of Bet-El. The northern border of the Kingdom of Judah was not clearly defined in this period. However, David Eitam's study of olive-presses presents evidence that the kingdom expanded northwards. Olive presses typical of Judah in the 7th century BCE were found in a number of sites in the southern part of Samaria; this may be indicative of the presence of the Kingdom of Judah as far north as the Shiloh Stream. We should note the opinion of Yochanan Aharoni that Josiah annexed to his kingdom both the districts of Samaria and of Megiddo.

With five of the six provincial regions, we are limited to educated guesses as to their borders, while in the case of the province called the *Environs of Jerusalem* we can determine the borders somewhat more precisely, based on a verse from the Book of Nehemiah.

Nehemiah Reveals "the Environs of Jerusalem"

Nehemiah tells of a dedication ceremony of the rebuilt walls of Jerusalem, a ceremony for which families of Levites gathered from the area around Jerusalem. The book relates, *"At the dedication of the wall of Jerusalem they sought out the Levites wherever they lived, to bring them to Jerusalem to joyfully celebrate the dedication with thanksgiving and song, [accompanied by] cym-*

bals, harps, and lyres. The companies of singers assembled from the plain in the region of Jerusalem, and from the Netophathite villages, Beth Hagilgal, and the fields of Geva and Azmaveth, for the singers had built themselves settlements around Jerusalem." (Neh. 12:27-29) Though this verse relates to a period later than the fall of the First Temple, it is a reasonable assumption that the name of the province remained unchanged until the "Return to Zion" from the Babylonian exile.

An examination of the sites on this list enables us to learn something of the geographical area of the "environs of Jerusalem." The first place mentioned is "the plain in the environs of Jerusalem" which, according to Michael Avi-Yonah, is the plain adjoining Jerusalem. In his scholarly dictionary, Wilhelm Gesenius explains that the Hebrew word *kikkar*, "plain," is contracted from *karkar*, meaning a circle or the circumference of a circular area. This logically would refer to a low area surrounded by hills, a description which matches that of Jerusalem as described by Yehuda Karmon: "Ancient Jerusalem was located in a kind of basin between two watersheds, and so is aptly described by the verse 'Jerusalem, surrounded by hills'" (Psalms 128:2).

These are the borders of the plain in the "environs of Jerusalem":

- To the south, Jebel Mukabbir (the Armon Hanatziv neighborhood in modern Jerusalem);
- To the east, the Mount of Olives;
- To the west, the watershed west of *Gey-ben-Hinnom* (the Sultan's Pool cleft between old and new Jerusalem);
- To the north, the Giv'at Hamivtar and French Hill neighborhoods in modern Jerusalem.

The other site mentioned in the Book of Nehemiah is "the villages of the Netophatites", i.e., the villages near the town of Natofa which has been identified by Yizhar Hirshfeld, who surveyed the area, with the village of Um Tuba, to the south of Jerusalem.

The identity of Bet-Gilgal, also mentioned in Nehemiah, is problematic. It may possibly be identified with Gilgal from the days of Joshua, in the Jericho region. Geva, also mentioned there, is identified with Jaba', and Azmavet with Hizmeh. Benjamin Mazar suggested that the fields of Geva and Azmavet should be identified with Sahil Jaba', between Hizmeh and Jaba'.

The description in the Book of Nehemiah appears to be geographically orderly. The first region mentioned is the one close to the city; then each region is listed according to its borders: in the south, the region to the south of Ramat Rahel; in the east, the territory extending as far as Jericho; and in the north, as far as Geva, the Arab village of Jaba'. No mention is made of the area to the west of Jerusalem.

The is reason to assume that during the Return from Babylon, the singers (Levites) settled in the region of Jerusalem, because of their connection with the rites in the Temple.

An examination of the archaeological data indicates that towards the close of the First Temple Period, this region was densely populated, mostly in the northeastern part of the region, as far as Geva.

The dense concentration of settlements in the Jerusalem area justified the creation of an administrative district known officially as the "Environs of Jerusalem" which was the nucleus of the Kingdom of Judah during the last stage of the First Temple Era. This settlement concentration probably served as the nucleus for the creation of the province of Yahud during the period of the Return from Babylon.

Agriculture in the Environs of Jerusalem

Scores of agricultural installations have been found in the environs of Jerusalem, indicative of the considerable activity that took place in this region. A perfect example of the agricultural installation characteristic of the period was found in the Zimri Stream site located to the northeast of Jerusalem. This installation includes a water reservoir, agricultural terraces, a central structure of the "four-spaces" variety, a winepress and a tower. This site is representative of the agricultural installations that existed in the Judean hill-country at this time. A closer look at this site will be useful in understanding the nature of the settlements established in the hill-country during this period.

The Site at the Zimri Stream

Geography
Located on a ridge between two channels of the Zimri Stream, this site is 5.5 kilometers northeast of the City of David, some 1.5 kilometers east of Tel-el-Ful which has been identified with Giv'at Shaul, and about 2 kilometers east of Anata, which has been identified with Anatot. It is therefore positioned in the .center of the tribal patrimony of Benjamin

There are no nearby natural water sources, yet there is a fertile valley at the bottom of the slope. The inhabitants of this area built a set of terraces covering the settlement which was located there in the Intermediate Bronze and Middle Bronze Ages, c. 2200-1550/1400 BCE.

The Uppermost Terrace (Area A)

In this area, there is a water cistern 280 centimeters deep. A set of channels cut into the rock led rainwater from the slope to a pool cut into the rock which was about 3 x 3 meters. and some 80 centimeters deep. A small hole was cut into the side of the pool, through which the water flowed to a small filtering pit, and from there through another hole to the water cistern. This system ensured that the water reaching the cistern was as clean as possible. This system indicates that there was considerable effort expended in the conservation of water and maintaining its quality.

The Lower Terrace (Area B)

A four-space structure of some 120 square meters stood in an east-west direction. A staircase located in the southeastern corner of the structure led to a second story. A unique feature of the structure is a small cave cut into the rock that was found in its northern space. Fragments of jars used for keeping wine were found there. Many clay vessel fragments were found inside the structure, as well a basalt millstone apparently brought from the Golan Heights, and a dome-shaped stone weight (weighing 113 grams) characteristic of the First Temple Era. From archaeological finds we know that the weight of the Biblical shekel was 11.3 grams. The value of the weight found in that building must have been ten shekels. It is not unusual that the millstone was brought from the distant Golan Heights, as these stones are of very high quality.

The Winepress and the Tower

A winepress including a trampling area, a pit in which the grape skins and pits would sink, and a collection pit into which the liquid was channeled, was discovered some 500 meters to the north of the area B structure. A step in the rock, that came about as a result of cutting the trampling area out of the rock,

Water pool and cistern in Zimri stream

had several square depressions cut out of it. These were used for placing the end of a beam which would exert additional pressure on the grapes after they were trampled under foot.

To the west of the winepress and alongside it, the foundations of a small tower built of rough fieldstones were uncovered. The dimensions of the tower were about 3 x 2.5 meters. Steps found adjoining the tower would enable one to reach its roof.

The winepress and tower were constructed towards the close of the First Temple Era. They clarify to a considerable extent the verse in the vineyard parable of Isaiah, "Then he built a tower in it, and also quarried a winery in it" (Isaiah 5:2).

The finds of this excavation reveal the nature of the agricultural arrangements in Judah at the close of the First Temple Period: they included a central structure of the four-space type, a reservoir-type system, agricultural terraces on which they grew vines and a complex installation for the manufacture of wine.

These installations, created during the First Temple Period,

Four spaces house in Zimri stream

were commonplace as late as the Mishnaic Period, reflected in the rule advanced in the Mishnah, "One who sells his field has not sold the tower... nor the cistern, nor the winepress" (Bava Batra 4:8-9).

Land Use in Light of the Bible and the Excavations at the Zimri Stream

The Bible (see Josh. 21:11-12) makes mention of three terms connected with the territory around a city which serves as the main residential area:

- "plots of land" (i.e. open spaces)
- "the city's fields"
- "hazerim farms"

The cities' plots of land (open areas) were adjacent to the city itself and belonged to it. These territories which were, according to the Biblical account, a thousand cubits around the Biblical city surrounded by a wall (Numbers 35:4-5), served as open areas on which domesticated animals, property and oth-

Remains of a wine press in Zimri stream

er city needs were stored. These areas were not used for agriculture. Therefore, it is not surprising that in various surveys carried out around First Temple sites, no agricultural installations were found within a range of about 500 meters around the cities.

The "city's fields" extended beyond this range; these were the agricultural lands of the city and contained the "hazerim" which seems to have been a kind of farmhouse intended for the owners of the agricultural land. It is unclear whether the house served the residents of the city when they went to the fields during the appropriate seasons, or if it was a permanent residence in use all year round. In the Hebron region, the wealthy inhabitants of the city would go to the vineyards in the seasons when the grapes were harvested and live there in stone houses.

Were the First Temple structures houses of this type? We have no answer to this question. Whatever the situation, archaeological research reveals a picture of a planned and organized array of settlements of various sizes and of intensive exploitation of the agricultural area in the Jerusalem region. It may be

Stairs leading to northern section of four spaces house

assumed that the Jerusalem area was more organized than other parts of the kingdom, but this does not mean that other regions were disorganized. On the contrary, all parts of the kingdom seem to have been well organized.

In this way, Jerusalem, once a site only hinted at in the early books of the Bible, became the focal point of both the settlements and the spirituality of Israel. Books composed in the Second Temple Period (Ezra and Nehemiah, Haggai, Zechariah and Malachi) discuss Jerusalem almost exclusively. The city grew after Sennacherib's destruction of the Kingdom of Israel in 721 and that of the lowlands twenty years earlier, and became the center of the life of the Israelite nation.

This growth continued and waxed stronger during the Second Temple Period, to so great an extent that a Greek historian named Fulivius, who lived in the 3rd century BCE, described the Jews as "a nation living around a Temple called Jerusalem." Such a description could only have been made after the days of Josiah.

The Last Days of Judah

The Biblical and Archaeological Record

The last glorious period of the Kingdom of Judah was short-lived. In the year 609 BCE Pharaoh Necho of Egypt went north to aid the sinking Assyria in its battle against rising Babylon. He made use of the Sea Road linking Egypt with Mesopotamia. Josiah attempted to block the Egyptian forces at Megiddo, a key spot along the Sea Road, but failed in his attempt. He was killed in this battle.

The death of Josiah marked the beginning of the decline of his kingdom. Following the battle at Megiddo, Egypt overran the Kingdom of Judah. Jehoahaz, son of Josiah, surrendered to Egypt, and Pharaoh Necho enthroned one of Jehoahaz's brothers, Jehoiakim, in his place (II Kings 23:33). Jehoiakim ruled a kingdom truncated both in its borders and in its independence, but, like all dictators who desire to glorify their rule, did not understand the seriousness of his situation. He used forced labor to begin the construction of a magnificent palace paid for with the taxes of the simple people. The prophet Jeremiah bewailed this travesty: "Woe unto he who builds his house by unrighteousness, and his chambers by injustice; who uses his neighbor's service without wages and does not give him his hire; who says: 'I will build me a large house and spacious chambers...'" (Jeremiah 22:13-14).

In the fourth year of Jehoiakim's reign (605 BCE), Nebuchadnezzar, king of Babylonia, defeated the Egyptian armies at Karkhemish, and Jehoiakim became subordinate to him. In 601 BCE Jehoiakim rebelled against the Babylonian king, whose reaction was somewhat delayed, but by 598-7 the Babylonian army reached Jerusalem. Jehoiakim died at the beginning of the campaign, and his son Jehoiachin who succeeded him surrendered. He was exiled to Babylon together with many of the political and economic ruling classes. Mattaniah, (the king of Babalonia changed his name to Tsidkiyahu,) the uncle of Jehoiachin, was installed as ruler in his stead.

In this period of subjugation to the rule of Babylonia, the army of Judah was also engaged in defending the kingdom from a former enemy: the Edomites. Taking advantage of the frailty of the Kingdom of Judah, the Edomites began to expand beyond the limits of the hills of Edom, to the south of the Dead Sea, towards the Negev.

Archaeological finds cast light on these Biblical events. A series of fortresses that served to defend the kingdom on the south were discovered in the northern Negev. The most important of these was in Arad, where interesting evidence was found of the struggle against the Edomites. A letter intended for Eliashiv ben Ashiyahu, the commander of the fortress garrison, was found in the fortress. It instructs that reinforcements are to be sent from a place called Kina to another place called Ramat Negev, lest the Edomites expand in that direction.

Numerous archaeological finds in addition to this letter

indicate that the Edomites had indeed penetrated the northern Negev at the close of the First Temple Era; these finds include Edomite temples at Hatzeva in the Aravah and at Khirbet Kitmit in the Arad Valley. At the ruins in Khirbet Uzza, letters were found that were indeed written in Hebrew characters and whose language was Hebrew, yet they include blessings to Kos, the chief Edomite deity.

The Edomites clearly took advantage of the weakness of the Kingdom of Judah, penetrated into the northern Negev, and broke through the Judean defense lines that collapsed under their pressure. After the destruction of the First Temple, they reached further north and settled in the southern Hebron Hills and the southern part of the lowlands. During the Second Temple Period, this area was named after the Edomites: Edomaea.

Cruel Babylonian repression gave rise to a renewed Judean revolt against Babylon. The revolt which was supported by Egypt (which turned out to be a "weak reed support") failed. The Babylonian army systematically conquered the cities of Judah and destroyed them. The Book of Jeremiah describes the military campaign as quite thorough: "And the forces of the King of Babylonia fought against Jerusalem and against all the remaining cities of Judah, against Lachish and against Azeka, for these alone remained of the fortified cities of Judah" (Jeremiah 34:7).

Jeremiah's description matches the archaeological evidence found at Lachish in the "Stratum of Destruction," stratum II. Here, the second-largest city in the Kingdom of Judah, 21 letters were found in one of the rooms of the garrison near the city gate. Letter no. 4 reads "We are defending with the torches of Lachish according to all the signs given by my lord, for we cannot see Azeka." These two sites, Lachish and Azeka, which appear both in the verse from Jeremiah and in the letter as two sites still withstanding the onslaught of the Babylonian army indicate their importance, as well as the considerable efforts made by the Babylonians to overcome them on their way to Jerusalem.

On the ninth day of the Hebrew month of Av in the year 586-7 BCE, Jerusalem was conquered and razed to the ground, its Temple destroyed in the great conflagration. Both the Bible (II Kings 25) and archaeological finds tell of its utter devastation. In the Jewish Quarter of today's Old City of Jerusalem, a tower was discovered. It is believed to have been part of the gateway in the northern city wall. At its base lay three Babylonian arrowheads. The excavations in the City of David have uncovered burnt buildings as well as a structure containing seal imprints on clay (with which official documents were sealed) that survived the inferno. These seals bear the names of various officials of the Kingdom of Judah, including one "Gemaryahu ben Shaphan" the royal scribe, mentioned by Jeremiah (36:12). The presence of this seal bearing his name, together with 50 other seals, indicates that in this part of the City of David (known to excavators as Area G) stood the royal archives of the Kingdom of Judah.

The Kingdom of Judah ceased to exist, and the royal line of the House of David came to an end. A long chapter of history closed, and Jewish independence in Israel no longer existed. Just as the Kingdoms of Israel, Aram, Ammon, Moab and Edom all ceased to exist, so too did the saga of the Kingdom of Judah and its people appear to come to its end.

But this was not the case, for out of the destruction and the heartbreak, Jewish life renewed itself 52 years later. A Return to Zion from Babylonia resulted in the province of Yahud, where Jewish autonomy was established once again around Jerusalem.

We may sum up and say that the focus of most of the prophetic literature of the Bible is on the process leading to the centrality of Jerusalem, from the days of Joshua when Jerusalem was not yet conquered, or at least not settled by the Israelites, through the conquest of the city by David, and culminating in its becoming the vital core of the Israelite nation.

The centrality of Jerusalem is not merely a feature of the past. On the contrary, with the passage of time Jerusalem became the most important spiritual center of the monotheistic world. The city that was once small and of only regional importance became the eternal center of the country, and today it is a spiritual magnet to which billions of people flock from all over the globe.

Recent Archeological Updates

Throughout this chapter on Jerusalem, I argued that a lack of findings in the ancient period of the City of David derived, among other things, from extensive quarrying carried out by the Hasmoneans in the area of the Akra in the City of David. Many researchers did not accept my approach and claimed that Josephus' descriptions of the cutting and lowering of the Akra, a campaign that lasted three years, had no basis in fact. They took this position despite my claim, based both on a reliable historical source from the Second Temple period, as well as findings in the field. Almost everywhere to the south of the Temple Mount there are discernible signs of the quarrying that destroyed archeological layers that existed prior to the effort to lower the height of the Akra. I am pleased that one of the respected researchers of Jerusalem, Dr. Gabriel Barkai, concurs with my opinion and has made a similar argument.

He, too, feels that the extensive quarrying work during the Hasmonean period removed many remains from earlier periods.[316]

As we know, this discussion relates to the Davidic and Solomonic period, the tenth century BCE.

The question is whether there is evidence for the existence of a significant Israelite kingdom in Eretz Israel in the tenth century BCE whose center was Jerusalem. At the same time, a new front has opened, namely, the period of Ezra and Nehemiah who initiated the Second Temple period.

An article published by Israel Finkelstein of Tel Aviv University argues that there is no archeological evidence for a sizable Jewish settlement during the Persian period, and that the detailed descriptions of the building of the Jerusalem wall in the Book of Nehemiah (3:1-32; 12:31-40), have no significant underpinning. According to his approach, these descriptions were written during the Hellenistic period and reflect the construction of the "First Wall" during the Second Temple Hasmonean period.[317] A short time after Finkelstein's article appeared, a find was discovered that contradicted Finkelstein's assertion. Based on Eilat Mazar's excavations in the City of David, it turned out that the northern tower found in Area G, which was part of the city's fortifications, belonged to the Persian period.[318]Found beneath the tower were typical pottery vessels and seal impressions that date the structure to no later than the middle of the fifth century BCE, Nehemiah's period in Jerusalem. Barkai claims that "the political reality described in the Book of Nehemiah, which incorporates the act of rebuilding Jerusalem's walls, definitely reflects the Persian period...."[319] This debate is still ongoing; we anticipate further studies that will continue to grapple with this issue.

Another subject on which opinions are divided is the massive wall uncovered by Eilat Mazar in the City of David. While she claims that the wall dates to the tenth century BCE and is perhaps a remnant of David's palace, Finkelstein and his colleagues claim that it should be dated to the Hellenistic period. [320]

In this case, I tend to favor Finkelstein's opinion and those of his colleagues over that of Eilat Mazar, since the dating of the wall has not yet been properly established. Conversely, the *mikva'ot* (ritualaria) and pools from the Second Temple period near this wall are clearly prominent.

Another impressive find has been uncovered in the area of the Western Wall Plaza. Beneath the pavement of Jerusalem's Eastern Cardo, a residential neighborhood from the close of the First Temple period has been discovered.

Structures were found that had been demolished in a sudden catastrophe, that contain many pottery vessels including jars bearing the seal "{Belonging} to the king," seals of a person called "Netanyahu ben Yaush," as well as a seal on which there appears the figure of a warrior shooting a bow with an inscription alongside it stating "[Belonging] to Hagav." All of these names are familiar to us from the Bible, as well as other inscriptions found throughout Judea. In the Jewish Quarter, too, beneath the Hurva Synagogue (the ruin of Rabbi Judah the Pious), whose restoration was recently completed, a structure was discovered from the First Temple period of which sections of wall and potsherd remained.

On the Mount of Olives in the Ras al-Amud neighborhood, during excavations which I served as consultant and field director, a settlement from the Intermediate Bronze Age and Middle Bronze Age was discovered including a few remnants from the end of the First Temple period.

The finds included a handle incised with a four letter inscription, "m/nhm." The line seperating the first letter from the others tells us that we are dealing with two different words. Apparently, the first letter, *m* is the final letter of another word that was not preserved in entirety; *nhm* is the private name of an unknown person, although the name is attested to in the Bible and external sources.

Graves from the Intermediate Bronze Age had been found much earlier in the area of the Mount of Olives and Nahal Kidron. it had previously been thought that they were the graves of nomads. In light of the uncovering of a settlement in Ras al-Amud, it now seems that the graves belong to a settlement system that existed in that period to the east of Jerusalem. This is one of the few sites found to the east of the city.

EXCAVATIONS AND FINDINGS:
INTERMEDIATE BRONZE AND MIDDLE BRONZE AGES

The Intermediate Bronze Age

At the close of the third millennium BCE, the large cities of the Early Bronze Age had been laid waste just as the Old Kingdom in Egypt collapsed, ending its involvement in events taking place outside its natural boundaries. Nomadic shepherds wandered through Israel, though here and there small agricultural towns sprang up. Researchers still dispute whether the nomadic population of the country at the time was the remnants of the population of the earlier period or a new population, which had entered the country as a result of the vacuum created by the destruction of the cities of the Early Bronze Age.

PERIOD	ACCEPTED DATING SYSTEM	CHARACTER-ISTICS	ALTERNATE DATING SYSTEM	AS REFLECTED IN THE BIBLE
INTER-MEDIATE BRONZE	2200 - 1950 BCE	Initial use of bronze, small villages, population mostly nomadic	2200 - 1950 BCE in the plains, to 1800 BCE in the Judean hill country	Beginning of Patriachal era

New information about this period came to light during the 1990s, due to the excavations conducted mainly in the area of Jerusalem. This research contributed greatly to our understanding of the nature of the period.

We shall begin our survey with a description of the various settlements excavated in recent years, after which we shall describe the settlements in the Negev, which were discovered in the 1960s.

Settlements in the Jerusalem Area

General Description: The Refaim Valley

The Refaim Valley, one of the broadest valleys in the Jerusalem area, provides a convenient transportation route from the coastal plain to the hill country. A good deal of water flows through it, there are a considerable number of springs along the route, and the underground water reservoirs in the area are full. Along the banks of the stream, there are also expansive agricultural areas. It is therefore not surprising that many settlements were constructed along the Refaim Valley over the centuries. The first settlements to be built there were those of the Intermediate Bronze Age (2200-1950 BCE).

The Manahat Excavation Site

The site is located on the southern slope of a hill leading down to the Refaim Valley, where the Jerusalem Mall stands today. There is no source of flowing water in its vicinity. The fresh water source closest to it is the Yael Spring, which is approximately 1.5 kilometers away.

This was undoubtedly an important site in the Intermediate Bronze Age, though only a few traces of it remain because it was rebuilt during the Middle Bronze Age II (1800 – 1550 BCE) due to its significance. In the Gershon Edelstein'[321] excavation, a few sections of wall and a large number of vessel fragments were uncovered, as well as the cup-mark[322] which are very typical of the period.

The Refaim Valley Site

About a kilometer to the west of the Manahat excavations, facing the Yael Spring, where the Jerusalem Biblical Zoo is located today, Emanuel Eisenberg unearthed a fairly large settlement. This early settlement was also damaged by the rebuilding of the site in Middle Bronze Age II and the surviving traces are few in number.

Some fourteen houses were found in this site. These houses were made of rectangular bricks, apparently fired lightly in an open fire. The floors were made of compressed dirt or natural bedrock, and occasionally of stone slabs. Upon these floors, ceramic vessels and stone mortars were found, as well as cup-marks cut into the rock.

The unprocessed stone slabs found at this site standing alongside the walls are unique. Eisenberg assumes that these were ritual monuments. In addition, two small ceramic statues with undefined animal-like shapes were uncovered, each about six centimeters tall.

Near the settlement a few score shaft tombs were discovered, most of which had been opened and were empty of any content.

The Zimri Stream Site

The Zimri Stream site lies on the lower part of a hill sloping down towards the Zimri Stream, which is a tributary of the Perat Stream (Wadi Kelt). The site is located today on the eastern edge of the Pisgat Zeev Mizrah neighborhood in north-ern Jerusalem. There is no fresh water source in its immediate vicinity.

Here, too, the stratum dating from the Intermediate Bronze Age was damaged by subsequent construction, so the findings there are relatively few. During my excavation of the site[323,] a number of oblong rooms were uncovered, the foundations of their thin walls built of field stones, while the upper layers were made of fired bricks. The flooring was made of stone slabs. Many potsherds and cup-marks were found on the site, as well as a few shaft tombs nearby which had been emptied in the Iron Age.

At the summit of the hill, to the west of the site, some 40 shaft tombs were discovered.

Characteristics of the Intermediate Bronze Age Settlements in the Jerusalem Region—A Summary

The three settlements described above have a number of characteristics in common:

1. They are located in the lower third of the slope forming the side of a valley.
2. The structures were right-angled and single-storied.
3. Bricks were used in building walls.
4. Cup-marks were commonplace.
5. Burial areas were located close to the settlements in areas of soft chalk rock.
6. Burials were carried out in shaft tombs.
7. Animal bones found on these sites indicate the existence of livestock, mainly goats, sheep, cattle, and pigs.

These sites, and sites in the Lower Galilee excavated later, Khirbet Kishrun (near the Golani Junction)[324] and 'Ein Hilu (in Migdal Ha-'Emek)[325], are considerably similar. This is evident both in the type of construction and in the location of the settlements. For example, monolithic columns were discovered at 'Ein Hilu, which served, in excavator Kubiliyo Paran's opinion, as monuments, like the finding at Refaim Valley.

Sites in the Negev

Surveys and excavations conducted all over the Negev have brought to light hundreds of settlements dating from this period. Rudolph Cohen,[326] who carried out a comprehensive study of the subject, divides these settlements into different types, in accordance with their size. In his opinion, the small settlements were seasonal ones, while the larger ones, attaining an area of some 20 dunams, served as permanent settlements.

The settlements in the Negev differ from their northern counterparts in a number of ways. Architecturally speaking, the Negev settlements differ from those of the northern hill country in two ways, shape and construction: 1) A considerable number of the structures are round, while others are oblong. In contrast, in the northern regions no round rooms at all were found. 2) The walls of the Negev buildings were made of stone only, while in the northern areas, walls of brick were not uncommon.

From an economic point of view, the inhabitants of the Negev seem to have eked out their livelihood from pastureland and apparently from the transportation of copper from Sinai and the Aravah to the other parts of the country, as well. This hypothesis is based on the fact that copper ingots were found in various sites in the Negev.

Furthermore, the burial customs in both regions were different. In the Negev, no shaft tombs were found. The initial burial was apparently carried out in graves made of stone slabs, which were occasionally covered with heaps of stones. (Burial customs are discussed below.)

In a site near Yeruham, two small statues were found that resembled those found in the Refaim Valley; in addition, a flat rocky surface was found at the summit of a hill, surrounded by a stone wall. Moshe Kochavi, who directed the excavation, is of the opinion that the site served as a "high place" for ritual worship.

Other Sites

The largest concentration of permanent settlements in the central hill country appears to have been in the Jerusalem area, though there is evidence that settlements existed in other regions as well. In the excavations at Bittin (Bet-El), a structure was unearthed with flooring of stone slabs, built on bedrock. In James Kelso's opinion, this structure, too, served as a "high place" for ritual worship. Fragments of cooking pots, flint knives and animal bones were found nearby [327] findings which lead to the conjecture that there was a small settlement there.

At Khirbet Rabud in the south Hebron Hills, potsherds from the Intermediate Bronze Age were found in an excavation carried out by Kochavi, findings which point to the existence of a small settlement at the site.[328]

In the region of the highlands, some twelve kilometers west of Hebron, at a site known as Jebal Ka'kir, caves were found that served as dwellings, apparently substituting for built houses.

Additional settlements have come to light through archaeological surveys. There seem to have been about fifteen such settlements in the Judean Hills, several of them exceeding small, their built-up areas of approximately only 2 dunams each.

Conclusions

The permanent settlements around the country were simple and shared a common plan. There was no complex settlement system, but rather small settlements that lived off pastureland and agriculture. On the other hand, many graves have been discovered at some distance from inhabited places. This would seem to indicate that they served a sizeable and unique population that invested heavily in burials. It thus seems that these graves served a nomadic population that did not leave behind any permanent settlements because of their nomadic nature, yet the graves testify to their existence.

Graves and Burial

The nomadic population invested very little in the construction of settlements. The small and unsophisticated houses and the lack of public structures typical of the era testify to this. On the other hand, this population made considerable efforts in burying its dead.

Their graves can be divided into two main types: burial under heaps of stones, typical of the Negev hills; and burial in shaft tombs, characteristic of the areas further to the north, mainly in the Judean Hills.

Stone Heaps

In the Negev Hills, and in the hills of Yeruham, graves were found above ground level. The method of burial was that the body was laid on bedrock and a coffin built of stone slabs was constructed around it. This coffin was covered with stones, so that at first glance the grave resembled a simple heap of stones. Skeletons were not found in all the heaps of stones, so it may be surmised that at some stage the skeletons were removed for secondary burial.

Shaft Tombs

The type of grave characteristic of this period is the shaft tomb, composed of a vertical shaft dug in the rock, with an average diameter of 60 - 100 centimeters and a depth of 150 - 200 centimeters. At the bottom of the pit, there was a small burial chamber with a diameter of about 150 centimeters. The bones of the deceased were placed inside the burial chamber, together with various objects, such as ceramic jars or weapons. Most of the burial was a secondary burial. There is no evidence as to where the dead were buried initially.

The bones of one or two corpses were placed in each burial chamber, and it would seem that this type of burial required considerable effort. The shaft tombs were dug in defined areas, generally in regions of easy-to-quarry soft rock. A common phenomenon in the Jerusalem area is that the settlements were built in the lower third of the slope, close to the fertile valley, while the graves were concentrated at the top of the hill, in places that were generally covered with layers of soft chalk rock.

Most of the shaft tombs found in Israel are in the Judean Hills and in the southern part of Samaria. Over 800 shaft tombs were found in Khirbet Karmil in the southern Hebron Hills; over 60 graves in the Etzion Bloc; and about 80 graves were uncovered in Jabel Ka'kir, west of Hebron. In the hills of Jerusalem, approximately 300 shaft tombs were found and about 290 more at Jabel Ta'amur near the settlement of Ma'ale Michmas. Near 'Ein Samia, on the edge of the desert, roughly 300 graves were found.[329] In no other period was there so large a concentration of graves in a relatively limited geographical area in the west of the Israel.

Most of the graves were discovered in surveys, and grave robbers had already ravaged most of them in ancient times. Of the graves found intact, some had served as graves in the Intermediate Bronze Age only; but in a considerable number, pottery from later periods was found as well, mainly from the Middle Bronze Age. All this may lead us to the conclusion that the people of the Middle Bronze Age also made use of shaft tombs for purposes of burial. Indeed, in a few places, only vessels from the Middle Bronze Age were found in these graves.

The Origin of the Intermediate Bronze Age People

From where did the people of this period come? Is there any evidence of migration? Unfortunately, there is no written testimony concerning their origin or culture. However, we may be able to extract information from the silent testimony available. One such kind of silent testimony is provided by the pottery found *in situ* (on site).

The pottery dating from this period is simple and pretty

much one of a kind. Vessels unique to this period are kettles and small, deep bowls (known in professional literature as "goblets.") If we examine the various cultures in the Middle East, we find that in the region of Mesopotamia (between the Euphrates and Tigris Rivers) there were settlements in that period that made use of similar vessels. For this reason, Ruth Amiran has suggested that the origin of the Intermediate Bronze Age people in the land of Israel was from the area near the Euphrates.[330] A little more evidence must be added to strengthen this hypothesis.

The fact that coppersmiths were active in Israel is noticeable. Hoards of copper vessels and copper ingots have been discovered in Jericho, in Lachish, in the Yeruham hill country (in the Negev), as well as other places. The copper ingots are uniform in shape and size. Scholars believe that these hoards testify to the existence of nomadic coppersmiths who made various kinds of weapons (such as daggers, spears, and hatchets) similar to those that have been found in graves in various parts of the country. Similar ingots and weapons have also been found in Syria and Mesopotamia. This is undoubtedly a further indication of ties having existed between these two areas.[331]

Additional unique evidence was discovered in a grave at 'Ein Samia in the southeastern part of Samaria. In excavations conducted in a burial field containing over 300 shaft tombs, a silver goblet was discovered, adorned with an engraving of two different figures clothed in skirts. Each figure was holding in one hand a kind of ribbon decorated with an image of snakes and two circles, resembling suns, divided into twelve sections, with a human face in the middle of each circle. In Yigael Yadin's opinion, these motifs represent scenes from the Mesopotamian epic poem of creation.[332] If this is indeed the case, then it is further evidence of the origins of the people of the Intermediate Bronze Age in Israel.

In fact, it would seem that while information gathered from under the ground provides a fairly distinct picture of the origin of the people of this period, no evidence is as yet available concerning their language and culture. No trace of writing from this period has been found anywhere in the country.

Summary

The Intermediate Bronze Age is one of the most intriguing periods in the history of the Israel. We have no written historical records of this period, yet archaeological research has succeeded in casting light on a number of characteristics of the period:

A. The population was mainly nomadic, and inhabited the hills of the Negev, the Judean Hills and the eastern bank of the Jordan River. (Small groups lived in the Galilee as well.)

B. Alongside this nomadic population, small, unfortified permanent settlements existed; their inhabitants engaged mainly in agriculture. They were concentrated mainly in the highlands of the Negev and in the Jerusalem area.

C. No public buildings such as temples or palaces have been found in these settlements.

D. There are no indications of the nature of the religious rituals of this population, since almost no artifacts have been found, in neither the settlements nor in graves, that seem to be of a religious character. In a number of places, upright stone slabs have been discovered, which may have served as monuments. It seems likely that they served a religious purpose.

E. This population exerted considerable effort in the burial of its dead, but not in the construction of their settlements.

F. Burial in shaft tombs was a secondary burial. A large concentration of such graves was discovered in the Judean Hills. In the highlands of the Negev, heaps of stones were found, which seem to have served as initial burial sites. Most of these heaps were empty when discovered. The nature of these burial sites is the basis for Dever's claim that the population of the Negev hill country was the same as that which lived in the Judean Hills. According to them, the people of the Negev Hills had a fixed route for their wandering.

In the winter, they lived in the Negev highlands, which are quite comfortable during this season; while in the hot, dry summers, they wandered further north to the Judean Hills, where they would bury their dead in shaft tombs, which served as their final resting place. Those that died while they were sojourning in the Negev were buried initially under heaps of stones, and when the people moved north, they would take the bones of their dead and re-inter them in the fixed burial sites of the Judean Hills.[333] Dever's opinion is supported by a petrographic study made by Yuval Goren of the pottery from the Negev highlands. This study shows that most of the vessels examined were manufactured on the east bank of the Jordan or in the Judean Hills, especially in the Refaim Valley.[334] This indicates that the people of the Negev hill country maintained close contact with the Judean Hills and the eastern bank of the Jordan.[335]

G. An examination of animal bones found in the Zimri Stream site and in the Refaim Valley indicates that the livestock raised by the inhabitants of the settlements included mainly sheep, cattle and pigs. In the Zimri Stream, processed bone fragments that seem to have served as needles or pins were found.[336]

H. The people of this era seem to have originated in the Mesopotamia region.

I. There are no clear findings regarding the factors leading to the disappearance of this population. It appears that they were displaced by a new population of an urban nature. This process took place gradually over many scores of years. The population of the Intermediate Bronze Age may even have been absorbed into the new population which seems to have penetrated from the low-lying regions of Israel.

Our opinion regarding the gradual disappearance of these people is based on the existence of shaft tombs, in which pottery dating from the Middle Bronze Age only was found.[337] This indicates that at the onset of the Middle Bronze Age, some of the people continued to rebury their dead in shaft tombs, while during the same period, the new, urban population (mainly around the new settlements they built) buried their dead in other ways. They apparently used simple ditch graves and mass graves in caves as a first burial only.[338]

The Middle Bronze Age in Israel

The Onset of the Middle Bronze Age

At the beginning of the second millennium BCE, changes took place in the settlement array. Construction began of new towns, which were extraordinary in both their dimensions and their fortifications. Palaces and temples were built, and more beautiful and more delicate pottery was manufactured. What was it that brought about these changes? Did new population groups arrive in the region, or was it perhaps an internal development for which the inhabitants of the country were responsible, without any external intervention?

This question has interested many researchers. In the opinion of many,[339] the people of the Middle Bronze Age I (hereafter: MBA I) were clearly different from their predecessors of the Intermediate Bronze Age.

William Dever[340] links the beginning of this period with the waves of "Amorite" peoples that penetrated into the country. The first wave was a semi-nomadic influx occurring in the Intermediate Bronze Age; and the second, a wave of people of an urban culture, at the onset of the Middle Bronze Age. Following Kathleen Kenyon's lead, Dever identifies the source location

PERIOD	ACCEPTED DATING SYSTEM	CHARACTER-ISTICS	ALTERNATE DATING SYSTEM	AS REFLECTED IN THE BIBLE
MIDDLE BRONZE AGE I	1950 - 1800 BCE	Renewed urbanization in Israel; In the Judean Hills, continuation of nomadic life; on the plains – renewed urbanization		Patriarchal Period
MIDDLE BRONZE AGE II	1800 - 1550 BCE	Development of urbanization and fortifications; Violent destruction at the close of the period	1800 - 1400 BCE Renewed urbanization in the hills and throughout the country; Violent destruction at the close of the period	Exile in Egypt, exodus, desert encampments

of this people as the Lebanese coast and the Orontes region in northern Syria.

By means of a comparative pottery chart, Patty Gerstenblith[341] provides support for the opinion that a new population was involved. She claims that there is a substantive difference between Intermediate Bronze Age pottery and that of Middle Bronze Age I, indicating demographic discontinuity.

In addition, Gerstenblith stresses the differences between the settlements of the populations of the two periods: while during the Intermediate Bronze Age the settlements were small and had no public buildings, during the Middle Bronze Age I there were buildings such as the palace found in Afek, alongside the sources of the Yarkon River. In her opinion, a lack of public buildings indicates an unstratified society, while their existence would indicate the existence of a societal hierarchy.

Aharon Kempinski is of a similar, though more moderate, opinion. He also claims that a new population entered Israel from the north built the Middle Bronze Age I settlements. Nevertheless, he feels that some of the Intermediate Bronze Age people were assimilated into the new population. He finds evidence of this in a few ceramic pots from that period which survived in use in the Middle Bronze Age I.[342]

Pottery is a first-class aid in the study of an era. Israel Prize winner Ruth Amiran, an expert in pottery and potsherds, wrote, "The spirit of an era, too, is reflected in its pottery, so a student of the era should also look at its potsherds."[343]

The ability of pottery to withstand the tribulations of thousands of years, the variegated uses to which these earthenware vessels were put in everyday life, as well as the changes which took place in the shapes of the vessels over the various periods of time, all made pottery a central indicator from which the nature of the period can be learned. Archaeology has realized that potters are basically conservative and that the style of the vessels is passed down in potters' families from father to son, from one generation to the next, so that changes in earthenware teach us of cultural, ethnic or political change.

Concerning the speculation that there was a new population wave at the onset of the Middle Bronze Age (based on pottery changes), Amiran[344] and Jonathan Tubb[345] have a different opinion altogether. They claim the pottery changes in the Middle Bronze Age are the result of internal development. Amiran points to the ceramic development between the IBA and MBA I (which she calls MBA I and MBIIa). She feels that this technical development and the refining of shape should be attributed to the fact that the people began to use millstones to manufacture pottery, so they succeeded in creating new pots of a higher quality.[346]

While Tubb does not perceive any ceramic continuity between the IBA and MBA I, he feels that such differences do not necessarily indicate a complete population change. Settlement continuity can be reflected in other, clearer variables, such as burial patterns, which tend to remain unchanged over long periods of time.

Like Amiran, Tubb claims that a rise in the standard of living brought in its wake an improvement in the quality of the vessels, so this change need not be ascribed to the entry of a new population in the region. Furthermore, he discerns continuity from the Early Bronze to the Middle Bronze Age in the development of weaponry, a fact he feels indicates a link between these periods.

We shall now see whether the archaeological research carried out in the hill country has anything to contribute to this debate.

The data amassed from the central hill region during the 1980s and at the onset of the 1990s revitalized the discussion of this topic from an additional viewpoint, the settlement viewpoint, as noted by Israel Finkelstein.[347] The surveys made in the Hills of Menashe, the Hills of Ephraim and the hill country of Bet-El, together with the survey of Jerusalem and that of Judea, all indicate that the answer to the question of the origin of the population at the onset of the Middle Bronze Age is not a simple one; for one thing, this is clearly a case of discontinuity, for the settlement leap from the Intermediate Bronze Age to the Middle Bronze Age is unprecedented.

According to data provided by Finkelstein (mainly with regard to regions to the north of Jerusalem), only 49 small, unfortified sites in the hill country from the Intermediate Bronze Age have been counted, while from the Middle Bronze Age 248 settlement sites have been identified, some of which were large and well fortified. During the Intermediate Bronze Age, the settlements were concentrated in the eastern part of the highlands, whereas in the Middle Bronze Age, the center of settlement gravity moved to the west. Moreover, in sixteen of the thirty-four Intermediate Bronze Age sites in the northern part of Samaria (and in four sites out of seven in the southern part of that region) there was undoubtedly continuity between the Intermediate Bronze

Age and the Middle Bronze Age. (This applies also to the unfortified settlements in the Jerusalem area.) In addition, Finkelstein notes the continued use of shaft tombs and this, I believe, is of great significance.

The new data from the excavations and surveys collected and published in this book add important details, which may well cast new light on the overall picture, indicating that the same population remained, though the ceramics did undergo change. The basis for the opinion presented herein is a regional one; accordingly, distinction must be made between the development of settlements and of pottery in the Judean Hills and those of the coastal plain.

The Settlement Pattern in Middle Bronze Age I

It should be remembered that when we refer to the Intermediate Bronze Age and the Middle Bronze Age, we are not referring exclusively to chronological timeframes. Because these terms also denote cultures, the IBA and the MBA could be going on simultaneously in different regions.

We have already seen that some scholars claim that there is no connection between the population of the Middle Bronze Age and that which preceded it. This opinion is based, *inter alia*, on the fact that towns existed on the coastal plain during the MBA I, a form of settlement unknown in the Intermediate Bronze Age. Recent research data indicate that the picture crystallizing in the coastal plain does not reflect what was going on in the central hill country, in general, and in the Judean Hills in particular. This is so because the central highlands were still a border region, where mainly groups of shepherds lived, while urban centers existed in the plain.

Just as this was the case in the Hills of Ephraim and Menashe, this was also the case in the Judean Hills. In the surveys and excavations carried out in about 120 sites in the Judean Hills in which Middle Bronze Age pottery was found, no traces were uncovered of walls or flooring, features which can be dated to MBA I.[348]

In fact, at the onset of MBA I, the settlements along the Refaim and Zimri Streams had been abandoned and the agricultural component had vanished from the Judean Hills. At that time, there was clearly a great settlement gap between hill country and plain, and from this point of view it may be said that in the MBA I a settlement recession in the hills took place simultaneously with the development in the coastal plain. The settlement wave in the Judean Hills began only in the Middle Bronze Age II (MBA II), circa 1800 BCE.

If it is true that the process of urbanization that took place in the coastal plain during Middle Bronze Age I occurred as a result of the arrival of a new population, this population certainly did not penetrate into the central hill country. Moreover, in the central hill country, the opposite process took place, in which the limited agricultural arrangements already existing there during the Intermediate Bronze Age collapsed and the process of nomadization became total. Thus, there seems to be no sign of any substantive change in the settlement pattern in the mountains, and existing data would indicate continuity there rather than a gap between the two periods.

Pottery

The other basis for the opinion stressing the break between the two periods is the significant difference between the pottery of the Intermediate Bronze Age and that of the Middle Bronze Age. It is indeed difficult to find any common denominator between the pottery found in the MBA I settlement centers along the coastal plain and that of the IBA graves and settlements. However, from the data gathered from the internal regions of the country (the central highlands and the Jordan Valley) it appears that in these areas these two periods were linked, which indicates continuity.

It seems likely that in the coastal plain a tradition devel-

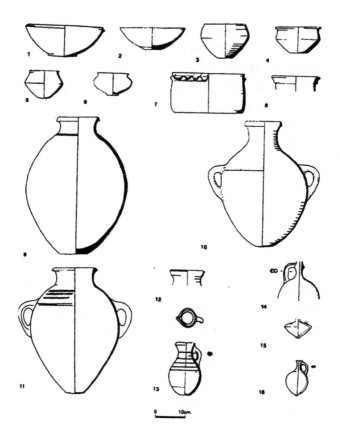

Pottery from the Judean mountains Middle Bronze I era
1. Plate from Elazar 2. Plate from site 50 Meitlis 1997
3. Vase from Aminadav 4. Vase from Maaleh Hachamisha
5. Vase from Elazar 6. Vase from Elazar 7. Cooking Pot from Elazar
8. Jar from Elazar 9. Container from Giveon 10. Jar from Efrat
11. Jar from Elazar 12. Jar from Giveon 13. Small jug from
Aminadav 14. Small jug from Elazar 15. Small jug from
Ma'aleh Hachamisha 16. Small jug from Aminadav

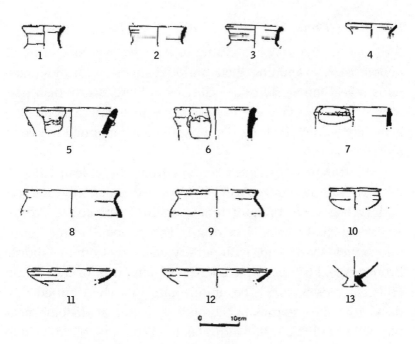

Pottery from the Judean mountains Middle Bronze II era

oped of burnishing (polishing to a luster) the pottery (which began with the "Megiddo group"[349]), but in the hill country, the "southern group" tradition was maintained, characteristic of the southern part of Israel. The burnishing and covering technique, one of the prominent signs of MBA I, was unknown in the highlands.

From the study of the pottery of the hill country, it seems that not only did the Intermediate Bronze Age pottery characteristic still exist at the onset of the Middle Bronze Age, but also that pottery shapes characteristic of the Middle Bronze Age, such as oil lamps and flasks, already existed in the Intermediate Bronze Age.[350] Certain pottery shapes did indeed reach the hill country, apparently from the coastal plain, but the burnishing that developed in the coastal plain was almost non-existent in the Judean Hills. Therefore, we see an overlapping of culture of the IBA and the new culture of the MBA.

Burial Customs

One of the ways to distinguish between two groups of people is by examining their burial customs, since these customs reveal the world of a society even more clearly than pottery shapes. When there is no change in burial customs, we generally assume that the same population continued to live in a particular area.

Shaft tombs were used continually in the Judean Hills all through Middle Bronze Age I. It appears that not only was secondary use made of shaft tombs in the Intermediate Bronze Age, new shaft tombs were dug in this period.[351] In the Benjamin survey, shaft tombs with pottery date only from the Middle Bronze Age, but this applies to the region north of the Judean Hills, such as Sinjil.[352] The unique case of a child buried in a flask from the Intermediate Bronze Age in a shaft tomb near Elazar in the Etzion Bloc indicates the beginning of a tradition common in the low areas of the Israel during the Middle Bronze Age, but not in the hill country. The withered ledge handles[353] and rounded body of the flask indicate that this vessel dates from the end of the IBA.

Summary

Burial in shaft tombs continued into the beginning of the Middle Bronze Age. Burial customs typical of this period in the coastal plain, such as burial under flooring or in ditch graves, reached the Judean Hills only in the second Middle Bronze Age.

Burial in flasks the hill country began as early as the Intermediate Bronze Age (in shaft tombs), and continued into the Middle Bronze Age, though this feature was not widespread.

Though the data relating to the Judean Hills grows progressively more plentiful, there is still no evidence of the entry of a new population into the hill country at the onset of the second millennium BCE (2000 BCE and beyond).

The characteristics of the new period, widespread urbanization and the beginning of fortification, new pottery shapes differing from those of the previous period, and new burial customs, were not found in the Judean Hills or in the other mountainous regions until later.

While an array of urban settlements developed on the coastal plain in the 20th century BCE, the corresponding process going on in the central hill country was one of settlement disintegration.

In contrast, the settlement and urbanization processes in the highlands were slow and gradual, taking some 200 years to develop fully. There were undoubtedly limited mutual relations between the inhabitants of the hills and those of the coastal plain, and some burnished pottery did actually reach the hill country (as seen at Khirbet Kufin and Wadi et-Tin). Though the pottery manufactured in the mountains was influenced in shape by the pottery of the coastal plain, the mountain pottery itself remained unadorned and unburnished.

A settlement reversal in the Judean Hills took place only in Middle Bronze Age II, from c. 1800 BCE, when fortified towns and unfortified settlements were founded in the hill country. There are no data capable of indicating unambiguously what the cause of this reversal was. It is difficult to determine convincingly whether it was a new population entering the hill country or the indigenous population adopting a life-style resembling that of the coastal plain. It does, however, seem that the extreme change in burial customs noted in the previous chapter, burying individuals in graves, the digging of which required considerable effort, in defined burial areas outside the settlement (Intermediate Bronze Age), contrasting with multiple burials in simple graves, sometimes under houses (MBA II), indicates changes in the population composition in the hill country. Additional evidence for this is found in the Refaim Valley sites southwest of Jerusalem and in the cemetery in in the Etzion Bloc, south of Jerusalem.

An examination of the bones of those buried in the graves of the Intermediate Bronze Age population and those of the Middle Bronze Age graves shows distinct differences between the two populations. In light of this, scholars have concluded that the origin of the Middle Bronze Age population was different from that of the people of the previous period.[354] It is thus reasonable to assume that a new population entered the central hill country at the beginning of the 18th century BCE (roughly at the beginning of the Patriarchal Period) and supplanted the indigenous population.[355]

The Settlement Array in the Middle Bronze Age II

The Middle Bronze Age, as distinguished from the Intermediate Bronze Age, is characterized by a developed array of settlements, unprecedented in earlier periods. The settlements of the MBA undoubtedly contributed considerably to the settlement pattern in Israel for many generations to come.

All the central settlements survived until the very end of the Biblical period (the destruction of the First Temple), and some exist even today. The largest of these settlements were concentrated on the plains and in the valleys, and the list of these is long. We shall note, for example: Laish (Dan), Hatzor ("the chief of all these kingdoms" [Joshua 10]), Tel-Rehov, Megiddo, Acre, Tel-Asraer, Aphek (Rosh Ha'Ayin), Ashdod, Ashkelon, Tel-Hasi, Tel-Far'ah South and also Tel-el-'Ajul to the south of Gaza. In the hills of the Shfelah, Lachish, Tel Gezer and Bet-Shemesh must be mentioned. These were settlements surrounded by vast earth ramparts scores of meters wide that towered over their surroundings. The area of most of these ramparts was over 100 dunams; the largest settlement, Hatzor, was over 800 dunams, an area greater than that of Jerusalem at its largest in the First Temple era. Besides those already mentioned, scores of settlements have been unearthed, the areas of which range from a few dunams to 20 or 30 dunams. Some of these, too, were surrounded by impressive earth ramparts.

In contrast, the Negev region was not settled at all in the Middle Bronze Age, except for Tel Malhata and Tel Mashosh, both in the Be'er-Sheva Valley.

During this period, settlements in Israel are mentioned for the first time in historical documents outside of the country. The first collection of such documents includes three groups found in Egypt known as the Execration Texts. The second collection includes documents found in the archives uncovered in the palace of Zimrilim, king of Mari, on the bank of the Euphrates in northern Syria, known as the "Mari Letters."[356]

The "Execration Texts" are occult writings with the names of various rulers in the land of Canaan inscribed on them, together with curses which were to befall them if they rebelled against the king of Egypt. In this way, the Egyptian kings tried to instill fear in their subjects. The names of various settlements throughout the country, such as Ashkelon, Aphek, Acre, Hatzor, Laish and other sites, appear in these lists. From the central hill country, only Shechem and Jerusalem are mentioned, indicating their central status as long ago as the onset of the second millennium BCE.

Hatzor is mentioned in a number of the "Mari Letters" as a city with strong trade ties with Mari. This evidence fits well with the size of the city and the rich findings discovered there.

The settlements mentioned above have been the subject of many studies because of their prominence, which naturally attracted the attention of various researchers of Israel as early as in 19th century. In the present review, we have no intention of once again describing settlements that have been amply described in a number of publications. (Anyone desiring to get an overall picture of these sites is referred to *The New Encyclopedia of Archaeological Excavations in the Holy Land*, edited by Stern, Lewinson-Gilboa and Aviram, published by Carta in 1993.)

We shall now examine the central hill country, where the urbanization process began in the 18th century BCE.

A review of the fortified settlements excavated in the archaeological excavations carried out in the hill country, from north to south, produces a list of only a few settlements, which are well known and meaningful. The northernmost is Shechem.

To its south lies Shiloh, followed by Bet-El, Gibeon, Jerusalem, Bet-Zur and Hebron in the Judean Hills. They are all on the central mountain range.

These settlements differ from those of the plains in that their area is strictly limited between 60 to 70 dunams in Jerusalem, down to 12 dunams in Bet-Zur). In addition to these fortified settlements, unfortified settlements of similar area were discovered on the mountain slopes.

Let us now visit the sites in the central highlands, first the fortified settlements and then the unfortified ones.

Urbanization in the Hill Country in Middle Bronze Age II

In about 1800 BCE, a new era dawned on the Judean Hills. The process of urbanization began to accelerate, and new settlements were founded. The settlements can be classified into two groups: fortified settlements and unfortified ones.

The fortified settlements in the Judean Hills are Bet-El, Gibeon, (We know that this site was fortified during the Iron Age, but we do not know if it was fortified as far back as the Middle Bronze Age.) Jerusalem, Bet-Zur and Hebron. In addition, the following unfortified settlements were built: the site at Manahat (now the Jerusalem shopping mall) and the Refaim Valley site (the Biblical Zoo) southwest of Jerusalem; the Nahal Zimri site to the north of Jerusalem; and the sites known as Alona and Motza to the west of Jerusalem.

Currently, all the unfortified settlements excavated are in the Jerusalem area. A number of graves have been found as well, which are discussed in the following paragraphs. The following list is fairly detailed, but is well worth publishing, for some of this information is being presented for the first time.

Fortified Settlements

Bet-El

The site of Bet-El was sparsely populated in the Intermediate Bronze Age (see note 26) and a significant change occurred in the Middle Bronze Age II; a fortified settlement was built here, covering an area of some 15 dunams. Several sections of its northern, western, and southern walls have been excavated. The wall is about 3.5 meters thick, and is built of large rocks, like the fortifications found at other hill country sites such as Bet-Zur and Shechem. In one place, indications have been found of what the excavator interprets as traces of a rampart. The city had a number of gates, one in the northeastern corner, one in the northwestern corner (above the ritual "high place" of the Intermediate Bronze Age), and apparently two more, in the west and in the south. Next to the northwestern gate, inside the wall, the excavators uncovered the corner of a structure built of processed stones, in which animal bones were found, as well as a few vessels used for ritual purposes.

Two stages of construction were identified at this site, according to the stratum of ash separating the two levels from one another. Evidence was found of reconstruction activities in a section of the western wall. The excavator is of the opinion that the site was destroyed in the mid-16th century BCE, remaining in ruins until the 14th century BCE. (During much of this time, the fledgling Israelite nation was in Egyptian bondage.) In his opinion, the settlement was renewed in the 14th century, the Late Bronze Age. It was again destroyed towards the end of the Late Bronze Age, in the 13th century BCE, and was rebuilt once again at the onset of Iron Age I, approximately 1150 BCE.

Summary

The pottery found in Bet-El belongs largely to the end of the Middle Bronze Age. Signs of burning and destruction were uncovered on the site, the reasons for which are unknown. It seems likely that the rise of Bet-El is linked with the decline of the settlement at nearby Et-Tel, which has been identified with Ai. After the destruction of the center at Ai at the end of the Early Bronze Age (approximately 2200 BCE), activity picked up at Bet-El, and it may well be that at the same time some activity persisted at Ai as well.

At the onset of the Middle Bronze Age circa 1950 BCE, some activity was in progress at the site, but there is evidence that there was a permanent settlement. Towards the close of this period, a system of fortifications was built, as in the other hill country sites, and continuity was maintained until the close of the Iron Age, corresponding to the era of the Kings, until the destruction of the first Holy Temple in Jerusalem in 586 BCE.

Tel Gibeon

The village of el-Jib, identified with Biblical Gibeon, is located next to a large spring, 'Ein el-Balad, which is surrounded by fertile, cultivated fields. James B. Pritchard directed a number of seasons of archaeological excavation there between 1956 and 1962. Most of the architectural findings date from the Iron Age, but the diggers also found potsherds and many graves in the tell from the Intermediate and Middle Bronze Ages. These findings were published in two reports, summarized below.[357]

The Excavations

Pritchard sank two square exploratory shafts at the summit of the tell. In one, the diggers encountered traces of a room (possibly a storeroom) which had been destroyed by fire (stratum IV). Pritchard dated the pottery to the 17th century BCE, and concluded that the structure was destroyed long before the end of the Middle Bronze Age.

This claim is unfounded. While all the vessels found in those exploratory shafts do indeed date from the middle of the period, such vessels were used until its end.[358] In addition, one must not ignore the graves at Gibeon in which the vessels found were typical of the end of the period. While we have no findings *in situ* from the Late Bronze Age, a few graves did contain vessels from this period. The settlement was revived in Iron Age I (c. 1150-1000), and continued to exist until the end of Iron Age II (586 BCE). From this period, there survived a wall, a system of pits which seems to have served as wine cellars, and two impressive water works, water systems designed to bring water to the city during a siege.

The Grave Site

At the foot of the tell, on the west, there lay a burial field of shaft tombs (forty-six such graves were excavated), which seem to have been dug during the Intermediate Bronze Age. Most of these were re-used in the Middle and Late Bronze Ages. The graves were all uniformly designed, they have a round shaft with a diameter of about 1.10 meters; their depth varies from 1 to 4 meters; and at their bottom there is an opening about 75 centimeters high and some 60 centimeters wide. This opening led to a round burial chamber about 1 meter high. The entrance to the grave was sealed by a single large boulder or by a number of rocks. In the burial chamber itself there were depressions dug out in which to place candles.

Vessels were found dating from the Intermediate Bronze Age in twenty-six graves; there were vessels from Middle Bronze Age II in twenty-nine graves, and vessels from the Late Bronze Age in nine graves. (Pottery was found dating from two, or even three, periods in most of these graves.)

Pritchard identified a single grave (grave no. 58) containing pottery from Middle Bronze Age I; whereas Patty Gerstenblith[359] identifies two additional graves with flat-bottomed vessels dating from MBA I (graves 31 and 31a). In addition, a hatchet typical of MBA I was found.

The question of whether this site existed in the Late Bronze Age remains open. While vessels dating from the Late Bronze Age were found in the graveyard of the site, no vessels were found from this period in the settlement itself. Some claim that this settlement had been abandoned by the Late Bronze Age, and the nomads who dwelt in the area were those who buried their dead in the graveyard. There is, however, another possibility as well. It is feasable that the site was populated, but that because of the digging of the large water works and the complex wine cellar arrangement in the Iron Age, traces of the Late Bronze Age were obliterated.

Evidence of Jerusalem

The Gihon Spring, flowing at the foot of the southwestern hill of Jerusalem, was the source of the city's life-giving water. Remains from the Chalcolithic Era through to the Mameluke Period were found on the hill. Findings from the Middle and Late Bronze Ages are quite scarce, apparently because of the building carried out on the steep slope in later times, especially in Iron Age II, which led to the destruction of the ancient remnants. Furthermore, the site attracted researchers to Israel as early as the end of the 19th century. While no doubt is to be cast on the initial contribution they made, their work actually caused irreparable damage.

Jerusalem during the Intermediate Bronze Age

No traces from this period were found on the "City of David" ridge, yet a number of graves were discovered east of the site, such as on the Mount of Olives and the Kidron slope. It is impossible to determine with any certainty whether these graves belonged to a nomadic population or to a permanent settlement located on the banks of the Gihon. It is unlikely, however, that there was no permanent settlement in the immediate vicinity of the spring, at a time when there were settlements of some considerable size in the region. It is thus almost certain that the widespread building activity carried out *in situ* in Iron Age II obliterated the remains of the earlier settlements located on this ridge.

During the Middle Bronze Age I (1950-1800 BCE)

No traces of this period have been found on the site, nonetheless two graves were found not far to the east of the City of David.[360]

Another find from this period attributed to the Jerusalem area is a scarab. Taken from a grave in Jerusalem and found in a private collection, its precise source is unknown. On this scarab there appears the title of an Egyptian scribe, though the meaning of this title is unclear.[361]

In the excavations carried out by R.A. Stewart Macalister and J. Duncan,[362] a grave from this period was discovered, as well as a handle with an impression of a scarab dating from the days of the 12th Egyptian dynasty (the beginning of the second millenium BCE).

It may be said in summary that just as in the picture arising from the other sites in the Judean Hills, there is evidence of a certain amount of activity in the Jerusalem region during the MBA I, but not of the existence of a settlement. It appears, then, that the findings in Jerusalem reflect the activity of a nomadic population, as seen in the nearby sites to the west of Jerusalem, such as the graves found near the village of Aminadav and the kibbutz Ma'ale Ha-Hamisha.

During the Middle Bronze Age II

Evidence of the existence of a settlement at the site in this period was first uncovered by the Macalister–Duncan expedition.[363] They record having found potsherds from this period, including part of an oil lamp, two impressions of scarabs on pot handles, and a cylindrical seal impression. They also discovered handmade cooking-pots with an upright side.

The excavations by Kathleen Kenyon[364] and Yigal Shiloh yield the following picture:[365] a town surrounded by a stone wall was built at the onset of the 18th century BCE. Its estimated area was, according to Shiloh, about 60 dunams. The town wall, which was some 3 meters thick, was built of large rocks that were placed above structures dating from the Early Bronze Age, on the steep slope above the Gihon Spring. Over 42 meters of this wall were uncovered in the excavations of Kenyon and Shiloh.

Both Kenyon and Shiloh dated the wall from the 18th century BCE, yet a section of it was incorporated in a later wall dated from Iron Age II. This wall fits into the overall pictures of town walls in the Judean Hills, and the way it was built is quite similar to what is found in Bet-El, Hebron and Bet-Zur.

All the uncovered sections of the wall are located on the eastern slope. No traces were found to the north and west. The reconstruction of the perimeter of the town was based in the main on the assumption that the wall surrounded the hill at the same height on its western side as well. In areas E1 and E3, located on the southeastern part of the ridge, Shiloh discovered sections of structures and of flooring upon which there were vessels with bone ornamentation, as well as a fragment of flattened gold.

The discovery of the system of fortifications adjacent to the Gihon Spring is indicative of the activity there; it likely extended to the very bottom of the slope, even beyond the boundary marked by Kenyon's wall.

To the findings of the excavations carried out by Kenyon and Shiloh on the southwestern hill must be added the potsherds found in the Ophel excavations to the north of the City of David. These are the northernmost finds in Jerusalem dating from this period, and it is possible that they mark the northern boundary of the town.

Summary

At the beginning of the Middle Bronze Age II (c.1800, corresponding to the Patriarchal Period), the town of Jerusalem, located on an elongated, narrow ridge, was rebuilt and fortified. It may be assumed that it was built on this site because the proximity of the Gihon Spring provided an abundance of water. This town was apparently the largest of the towns of the Judean Hills, and played an important role during this period. The material finds from this sight are sparse, and their publication has been delayed, but the fact that vessels with bone inlays and flattened pieces of gold were found there, together with the existence of formidable fortifications and water works, would indicate the importance of the place at the time. We may conjecture that this town is referred to in the Bible as Shalem, of which Malchitzedek was king.

The Mount of Olives apparently served as the graveyard of the town, because of the soft chalk bedrock of the site. In the graves, especially those uncovered in the Dominus Flevit church and in other places, a very large number of pots were found, indicating a relative level of wealth.

The excavations on the City of David ridge have not provided any evidence of the fate of the town at the end of this period. Yet it would seem that the activity there continued after the close of the era, for the ceramic findings from a grave in the Dominus Flevit church indicate a state of continuity into the Late Bronze Age.

Bet-Zur

In the northern part of the Hebron hill country, located on a conical hill, rising to a height of 1,007 meters above sea level, is Khirbet Tabika, which has been identified with the Biblical Bet-Zur. Mentioned in the book of Joshua as one of the towns within the borders of the tribe of Judah, it was later fortified by Rehoboam and was of great importance during the Maccabean wars.

Due to its high altitude, it maintains strategic control of its immediate surroundings. At the foot of the hill, to the east, is the 'Ain ed-Dirwa spring, the settlement's main source of water.

The site was excavated in 1931 and in 1957 by archaeological expeditions headed by Ovid R. Sellers.[366] The results of these excavations show that the fortified site, the area of which is estimated to have been between 8 and 15 dunams was built during the later stages of Middle Bronze Age II, apparently in the 17th or 16th century BCE. (The northern section has not been excavated, and consequently the northern boundary of the site is unknown.) Since the excavation focused on the area of the wall, the information available mainly concerns the fortifications and not the structures within the site.

The wall is some 2.5 meters thick, and in the southeastern

part of the site, there is a tower whose dimensions are 5 x 10 meters. It seems to have been intended to reinforce the wall. In the northeastern part of the site, the excavation revealed a row of rooms adjoining the wall. The rooms were built of large polygonal stones resembling the walls found in Bet-El and in Shechem. The tables of findings published show pottery characteristic of MBA II, "Hyksos-style" scarabs, and pins with simple heads no thicker than the rest of the pin, characteristic of the later stages of the Middle Bronze Age.

Pottery from the Late Bronze Age was found in this excavation too, as was a scarab dating from the 19th Egyptian Dynasty, though no structures were uncovered to which the potsherds might be ascribed.

Shlomo Bunimovits[367] suggests two interpretations of the MBA II (1800-1400 BCE) findings on the site. According to his first interpretation, the pottery relates to chance activity during the latter part of the period, whereas his second explanation links these vessels with the renewed settlement that took place in the 12th century BCE.

It is possible that the few potsherds dating from the Late Bronze Age (1400-1150 BCE) found in this site indicate the existence of a small settlement that was completely obliterated in the wake of the massive Iron Age and Hellenistic period constructions. Furthermore, it must be remembered that the northern part of the site has never been excavated.

The area of the site is small (about half the size of the other sites in the hill country, if we adopt a restrictive approach), and so it can be viewed as a fortress rather than as a settlement. The purpose of the site could have been mainly defensive, unlike those of the sites in Hebron or in Bet-El.

Tel Hebron

The site of ancient Hebron is located on a ridge descending from Jabel Rumeida to the southeast. At the foot of the ridge there is a spring known as 'Ein el-Jedida. In 1926, a grave cut into the rock dating from MBA II was excavated in nearby Wadi Tufah, adjacent to the Es-Salta Hill. According to Benjamin Mazar,[368] variegated findings were discovered in this grave, including bowls, small Tel el-Yahudiya flasks with a button base, a larger flask, and a very large one. They also include an alabaster vessel of Egyptian origin with a lid. There is no sign on the site of any settlement from the Intermediate Bronze Age.

Hammond's Excavation

Between the years 1964 and 1967, a large-scale excavation was carried out by Philip Hammond at the site and in its vicinity, in a total of eight excavation areas (I1-8). In his doctoral thesis, based on Hammond's excavation, Jeffrey Chadwick[369] mentions that sections of stone walls and flooring made of yellowish *hawar* stone, dating from the first Middle Bronze Age, were found in the various excavated areas. The results of the excavation indicate that quite a large, unfortified settlement existed at the site, extending all the way to the 'Ein el-Jedida spring to the east of the tell.

The transition from MBA I to MBA II was a gradual one, and no evidence exists of any crisis. In the second Middle Bronze Age, a thick wall was constructed of large rocks with bulges and recesses (found in area I3). Structures remaining outside the wall were abandoned.

Natural caves serving as burial sites were found near the tell. A two-phased grave from MBA I and MBA II was found in one of these caves. Four skulls were found in the grave, as well as pins, a dagger, 104 vessels including angular bowls, open simple bowls, large jars, Tel-Yahudiya flasks, and a scarab made of limestone with a decorative spiral pattern (a "Hyksos-style" scarab). Two additional burial sites were discovered in the floor of one of the rooms.

In Chadwick's opinion, the town continued to function into the Late Bronze Age, though the settled area was reduced in size. Artifacts were discovered from the Late Bronze Age in four of the eight excavated areas (areas I1, I3, I5, and I6), including a number of fragments of Mycenaean and Cyprian pottery, as well as a Ramses II scarab. The source of these imported vessels is unclear. Did they originate together with local vessels from Iron Age I, or were they part of a collection of local vessels dating from the Late Bronze Age?

Ofer's Excavation

The excavation at Tel Hebron was renewed from 1984 to1987 by an archaeological expedition headed by Avi Ofer on behalf of the Institute of Archaeology of Tel-Aviv University, the Society for the Study of Eretz-Israel and its Antiquities and the Archaeological Staff Officer of Judea and Samaria. The final report of this excavation has not yet been published, but fairly detailed reports have been brought out. [370]

Conversations held with the excavator have also contributed to the clarity of the picture.

General Description

Findings uncovered in the Tel Hebron excavation date from various periods, though we shall review only those of the Middle Bronze Age.

The main excavated area is Section S, which penetrates the summit of the tell from the very top to its bottom. Eight strata were found in this section, the section itself not going deep enough to reach the Early Bronze Age.

Ofer's excavation widened the area excavated by Hammond, where the wall was found. Moreover, a small portion of another wall (a smooth, sloped one) was uncovered.

Besides the sections of the wall, a part of a residential structure (Structure 230) was revealed next to the wall. In one room of the structure, there was filler in place of a floor, in which the excavator found potsherds dating from the Middle and Early Bronze Ages, many animal bones and a document inscribed in cuneiform symbols. In an adjacent room, a section of flooring was uncovered with a few jar fragments on it, dating from the Middle Bronze Age, as well as an axe of a type common in MBA II.

In Ofer's excavation, no traces were found of the Late Bronze Age, and, in his opinion, the settlement had ceased to exist by the end of the Middle Bronze Age.

The Findings

Potsherds: A study of the pottery has not as yet been made, yet in light of a conversation with the excavator and a perusal of some of the ceramic findings, it seems that the pottery on the site dates from MBA I and MBA II.[371]

Bones: Over 1,800 animal bones were found in Structure 230. An analysis of these indicates that about 95% of the bones are of sheep or goats, and some 5% of cattle.

Document TH1: In the filler found in room 265, a fragment of a clay tablet, inscribed on both sides in cuneiform symbols, was unearthed. The deciphered document reveals[372] that it is a list of sheep, rams and goats, as well as a number of first names, four Amorite names and a single Hurrian name. The significance of this document, the only one of its period in the Judean Hills and one of very few throughout Israel, is unclear, but those who deciphered it raise the possibility that it is a list of tithes from the flocks for ritual purposes. One can learn from it that the local scribes made use of cuneiform script in the Akkadian language for everyday purposes, and that a mixed Amorite and Hurrian population resided in Hebron during this period. The decipherers date the document from the 17th or 16th century BCE.

Seals: A potsherd was found not far from the document bearing the impressions of two Egyptian scarabs. There is no additional data at this stage regarding the dating of the scarabs.

Weapons: Two weapons were discovered in the excavation: a broad hatchet (in room 262) and a dagger that was found on the surface. While the dagger was not found in a clear context, in the opinion of the excavator it belongs to the period under discussion.

Summary

The Hebron excavations revealed a number of sections of peripheral wall approximately 3 to 3.5 meters wide, which was apparently a wall of prominences and recesses. A smooth, sloping section adjoined this wall, made partly of pressed earth and partly of flat stones (Glacis). The excavator is uncertain as to whether the smooth section was original, or whether it was erected at some later stage.

According to the reconstruction of the excavator, the wall encompassed an area of between 24 and 30 dunams. In contrast, Israel Finkelstein puts the walled-in area at about 15 dunams.[373] Since Hebron was the southernmost fortified town in the hill country, it is probable that its sphere of influence was widespread, though this is not reflected in the size of the town. The unique findings at this site, like the document and the seals, are indicative of its importance.

Hammond and Ofer disagree regarding the existence of a settlement at this site in the Late Bronze Age. While Hammond claims to have found pottery from the Late Bronze Age, Ofer states that in his excavation no pottery was found from this period, and it would seem that until final reports are published of both excavations, no decision on the subject is possible.

Emanuel Eisenberg's new excavation has not contributed substantively to the resolution of this question either. However, a burial cave dating from the Late Bronze Age was discovered in a cave found by chance on the slope of the tell. The remains of fifty-three corpses were found in this cave, mostly children, as well as a large number of potsherds, the most ancient of which belong to the end of the Middle Bronze Age and the most recent to the 13th century BCE.[374] It would thus appear that the grave was in use for over 200 years. Its very existence supports Hammond's opinion, though it does not provide outright proof of it, since it is possible that the grave belonged to a nomadic tribe living in the general area.

Unfortified Settlements in the Middle Bronze Age

We can learn the characteristics of a society and its culture by studying the layouts of its settlements. In general, the settlement pattern reflects a society's needs; it indicates the challenges its planners had to face and it testifies to both its technological standard and its social structure.

Our fundamental assumption is that groups sharing a social situation, though living in various regions at different periods of time, may well share similar architecture. Whereas groups of different social situations living simultaneously in the very same region may develop different forms of building.[375] When there is a lack of relevant historical sources, we extract as much information as possible from these silent findings, mainly by studying the findings from the *unfortified* settlements where extremely valuable data has accumulated.

Surprisingly, in the fortified settlements the findings are relatively scarce, for two reasons. First, the preservation of private structures was only partial, because of later strata which were built on that of the Middle Bronze Age, unlike the situation in the unfortified settlements in the hill country, which are of only a single stratum and so are better preserved. Second, the excavators of large sites such as Hatzor, Megiddo, Kabri, Lachish and so on, concentrated on trying to uncover public buildings such as temples and palaces, and consequently devoted considerable effort to excavating gateways and walls. These naturally attracted their attention more than simple residential neighborhoods. Only a few studies carried out in the fortified towns reveal planned settlements with housing units and organized streets.

During the MBA, a style of construction developed typical of buildings called "courtyard houses." Such houses were composed of a central courtyard enclosed by rooms. This plan existed in both small private homes and large, magnificent mansions. Similar house plans, gates, and walls have been uncovered in towns excavated in Syria and Mesopotamia as well, and testify to the influence of these northern regions on Canaan and to the close relations that existed between them.[376] Their municipal layout indicates the existence of an organized, urban population with a definite social hierarchy that felt the need to protect itself with fortifications made up of vast earthen ramparts. (The base of a rampart was up to 60 meters wide in some places.) This was undoubtedly done deliberately, for there was great similarity among all the settlements throughout the country from Dan in the Upper Galilee to the northern Negev.

While in the lower regions of the country the fortifications were composed of earthen ramparts, in the Judean Hills they were made up of stone walls. This was so in Bet-El, in Jerusalem, in Beth Zur and in Hebron. At Shiloh and at Shechem in Samaria, an interesting combination was used of stone walls, earthen ramparts and slippery slopes. It is reasonable to assume that this was connected with the geographical structure of the region. On the plains, there is no lack of earth, while in the rocky Judean Hills, earth is scarce and rocks are plentiful.

Furthermore, in the fortified mountain settlements, almost no homes have been found, nor is it possible to draft a map of the settlement. On the other hand, in the unfortified settlements in the Jerusalem area, the Refaim Valley, Manahat and the Zimri Stream, many different kinds of homes were found, a fact that expands our knowledge in this field and indicates that the population of the unfortified settlements was apparently heterogeneous in its composition. The analysis of the structure of these settlements is based on their description at the level of the single structure and at their overall planning level, as well as on observations made of traditional societies in our own day.

Topography and Construction Materials
Characteristic of the Unfortified Settlements

A comparison of the architecture of the Intermediate Bronze Age with that of Middle Bronze Age II indicates both continuity and a strong tendency towards development. In each of these two periods, settlements were found built on slopes, and so it was to a great extent the topographical structure that dictated the plans of the buildings.

In both periods, similar construction materials were used: natural rock, field stones of various degrees of processing, bricks, and wooden beams. In the Middle Bronze Age, however, the beams were thicker and straighter, and it seems that some of them were even plastered.

During the Intermediate Bronze Age, rock, stone tablets, and compressed earth were used as flooring. In the Middle Bronze Age, flooring was made of plaster and a layer of soft, pulverized chalk rock. Structures were roofed by means of wooden beams resting on wooden columns in both periods, but during the MBA stone stairs and a second floor were added to this roofing.

The inhabitants of the unfortified settlements in the Judean Hills during MBA II learned to make use of local building materials, to exploit them efficiently and to build stable, economical structures. It is reasonable to assume that the architectural innovation of these settlements was the attempt to adapt the accepted building style of courtyard-houses to the mountainous topography of the region. This attempt produced a model of a hill country settlement in Israel, the form of which was quite widespread in later periods.

The use of local building materials of rough field stones and of bricks indicates that the standard of construction was not high, for the ability of bricks to withstand the occasionally rainy and stormy climate of the hill country for any length of time is not great. Nevertheless, it appears that the difficulty of finding

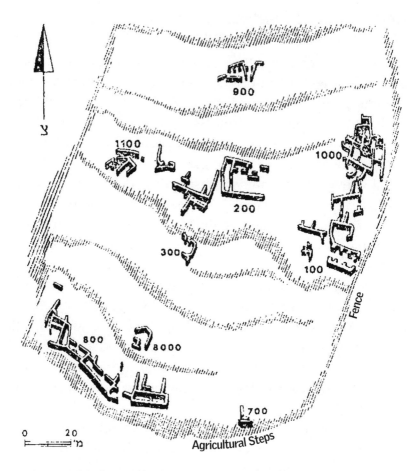

Manhat: Archaological digs revealed building map
from the Bronze period (Eisenberg)

stones ready for use forced the inhabitants to compromise on the quality of their construction.

The Settlement Plan and its Meaning

Manahat

According to the reconstruction proposal made by the excavator, the Manahat site is surrounded by adjacent structures, with the external walls of their residential rooms serving as a line of fortifications (areas 700, 800, and 1,000). The plan of some of these houses is that of a "courtyard-house," the house plan, common in that period. In addition, in area 1,000 in the east, a gateway with six cubicles can be restored. The preservation of this gateway was only partial, and so it is impossible to study its original plan in its entirety. The graphic on page 272 is a map of Manaht's original plan.

At the southern and eastern edges of the site, one can identify planned structures adjoining one another, but in their center, no planning is evident. The entire area has not been excavated, especially not the northern part. The impression gained by the excavator is that there were additional structures in the middle of the area, but it was mostly sparsely built.

The map of the settlement indicates a gateway planned in a way typical of the period in the Levant (known as "the Syrian gateway") and a planned line of defense made up of a row of adjoining structures.

The plan of the peripheral structures at Manahat is uniform, and the area of each building ranges from 100 to 200 square meters. This fact points to a society in which the basic unit is the nuclear family. In contrast, in the Refaim Valley site, the plan of the homes is not uniform and the area of a few of them reaches some 600 meters. The basic unit at Refaim Valley was the extended family. It would thus seem that the settlement at Manahat was more suited to a highly organized society of an urban background that planned its homes so that they would also serve as a line of defense for the settlement.

The Refaim Valley

Unlike the Manahat site, where the level of planning clearly indicated the existence of a relatively organized society, the settlement at Refaim Valley stands out because of its lack of planning. It consists of building clusters scattered over hundreds of meters along altitude contours, parallel to the direction of water flow in the Refaim Valley. As noted above, the area of each structure is very large, and the structure itself is made up many rooms, that seem to have been occupied by members of a single extended clan. This settlement is apparently the result of a spontaneous settlement process during a relatively secure period of time. It has no line of defense, nor does it seem to have a definite center. According to its structure and size, it would appear that the ties between members of the extended family were extremely strong.

An estimate of the relationship between the built-up area and the empty space in this settlement and a comparison of this datum with traditional settlements in our own day can only stress that this settlement was very sparsely settled.

The built-up area that has been excavated in this settlement comes to less than 7 dunams (including built-up areas, but not areas that were roofed over). Assuming that not all the buildings have been discovered, we can estimate the built-up area as about 10 dunams out of approximately 50 to 55 dunams, the overall area of the site. The significance of this is the conclusion that the built-up area was less than 20 percent of the total area of the site.

This fact points to the uniqueness of this site in comparison to traditional villages. For example, observations of villages in Iran and in Turkey carried out by Carol Kramer show a greater density (32 to 55 percent) of built-up area.[377] This site, on the other hand, was very sparingly built up and has no parallels in the Bronze or the Iron Ages. Who, then, were the inhabitants of the Refaim Valley?

To provide an answer to that question, we will make use of a settlement pattern surprisingly similar to that of this settlement. This is a type of settlement that developed at the onset of the 20th century in the hills surrounding Jerusalem; it is known as a "Bedouin village settlement."[378]

In Avshalom Shmueli's study of nomad settlements in the Jerusalem area in the 20th century, there appears a description of the penetration of nomadic tribes from the south and from the east of Jerusalem between the permanent villages (between Abu Dis and Bet Sahour) and of their settling-in process. The Bedouin village settlement is described as a settlement of a dispersed pattern, lacking a definite center and only having a few utilities buildings. The clusters of houses that it has are scattered over the area, with no geographical continuity between them. Furthermore, the structures serve family groupings in such a way that when a son married, it was customary to add another room to the existing structure.[379] This solitary structure has certain characteristics that reflect traces of the tent plan. The structures are divided into secondary units, with no internal connection between the various spaces in each structure. Shmueli claims elsewhere[380] that the nomadic Bedouin settlement pattern is visible wherever this process transpired, with no connection to topography, yet it is of course concentrated alongside the roads. A study of the plans of the structures reveals that they develop and increase in size, but the basic unit of two or three rooms is common to them all, with rooms of varied shapes being added to each unit.

A comparison of the plan of the Refaim Valley site with that of the Bedouin village settlements shows considerable resemblance both in the distribution of the buildings and in the plans of some of the residential buildings.

Just as in Bedouin village settlements, subsidiary frameworks are found in Refaim Valley. In the western group, including areas 200, 300, 400, 500, 1,300, 1,500 and 1,700, there are structures composed of rows of rooms, structures built in the "house-and-courtyard" pattern (area 400) and other buildings with different plans in areas 300 and 500. It is possible that the pottery industry was concentrated in this group, for most of the pottery wheel sections were found in this area.

The central group is found some distance away from the western group, and it contains areas 700, 800, 1,100 and 1,200. The distance between the western group and the nearest structure in the central group (1,200) is about 110 meters. Similar distances have been measured between the groups of structures in Bedouin villages.

All the structures in the central group are made up of rows of rooms, characteristic of structures of Bedouin villages. It is

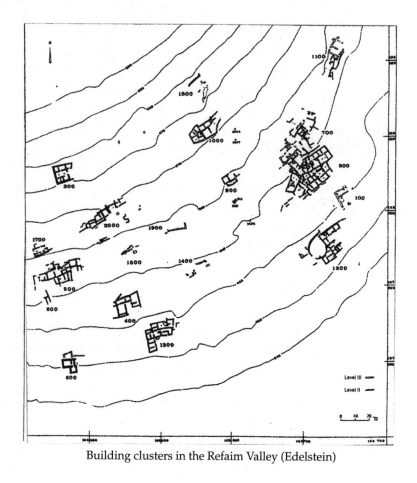

Building clusters in the Refaim Valley (Edelstein)

possible that so long as the need arose to set up an additional housing unit, new rooms were built adjoining the existing structure. A round stone enclosure, also characteristic of the Bedouin settlement stage,[381] was found adjacent to a house in area 1,200.

The eastern group is found in area 1,600, on the other side of the Manahat Stream, some 250 meters away from the central group. Because we lack data, it is not possible to determine if the structure in this area was an isolated one or whether there were other structures around it. However, the house plan resembles the plans of the house in the central group, where the rooms are situated along lines demarcating equal heights.

Shmueli's examination of the distribution of the secondary structures in the Bedouin villages reveals a prominent lack of uniformity. The number of structures in the secondary units ranges from ten to almost fifty structures, and their density is between one structure per dunam of land and one structure per 4 dunams. A similar density has also been noted in the Refaim Valley as well, where a single structure per 3 or 4 dunams was found in the western unit.

It is almost certain that this settlement is an example of the type of settlement that existed in other regions in the Middle East, and has been called a "Hatzeirim." Avraham Malamat notes that in the Mari documents found in northern Syria this term is mentioned in connection with the tribes of B'nei Yamin that camped alongside the Belikh River in northern Syria.[382] Malamat says further that the Bible denotes this type of settlement in connection with the dwelling-places of nomadic or semi-nomadic tribes (Genesis 25:16; Deuteronomy 2:23; Isaiah 42:11), and that the element *hatser* (Hebrew) "courtyard" is commonplace in the names of settlements in the northern Negev, such as *Hatzar Shu'al* and *Hatzar Susa* (Joshua 19:3,4).

If this identification is correct, it is possible to define the term *hatser* as a collective noun denoting clusters of structures scattered in a area, whether as a settlement or as individual farm buildings adjacent to towns. The latter are more characteristic of the First Temple era in the Jerusalem region.[383]

The Zimri Stream

The settlement on the bank of the Zimri Stream has been excavated only partly, so it is difficult to appreciate its overall plan. Nevertheless, this settlement seems to have been concentrated on a number of terraces. The upper part of the town was found on the excavated terrace: it includes three housing units adjoining one another: a large unit which reflects a fairly high standard of construction (area 3) and two smaller housing units (in areas 3 and 4) of unclear plan and low building standard. All of this indicates that the social structure of the population at this site was similar more to that of Manahat than to that of the Refaim Valley.

Summary

During the second part of Middle Bronze Age II, various groups settled around Jerusalem, some of them nomadic and others with what seems to be an urban or suburban background. They settled in places enjoying a surfeit of water and agricultural land. Unlike the Refaim Valley site, which serves as a prominent example of unplanned, spontaneous settlement, at the Manahat site planning is apparent with regard to the external contour lines of the settlement. There are also significant components that are lacking, such as the internal arrangement of streets and a drainage system. The planning of the settlements at Manahat and the Zimri Stream indicates a fairly structured population with organizational ability, while from the form of the site at the Refaim Valley we may conclude that its inhabitants lived in clan-like frameworks, with relatively loose links between one clan and another.

We cannot tell what the ethnic origins of the inhabitants of these settlements were, but it is clear that they were two different populations. The security apparently prevalent in this region during this period made it possible for various groups to settle in the area without taking special steps to defend themselves.[384]

The Settlement Pattern in the Judean Hills

Criteria for Estimating the Area of a Settlement

In order to properly analyze any settlement pattern, it is necessary to estimate the size of the settlements involved, individually and relative to other settlements. It is reasonable to assume that the importance of the settlement is expressed *inter alia* in the size of the area it occupies. Thus, the larger the area of a settlement, the more important it was.

It is not difficult to define the size of a settlement which has been excavated in an orderly fashion. Yet, only few settlements have been carefully excavated. In most cases, an archaeological survey is all that has been done, i.e., a team of archaeologists has collected from the site potsherds from the appropriate period and examined the dimensions of the surface area in which those potsherds were found. Though the potsherds inform us of the existence of a settlement in the period concerned, they are not sufficient to enable us to estimate the size of the areas of ancient settlements, especially when dealing with sites that existed in more than one period of time that have as yet not been excavated.

Defining a settlement's size is especially difficult when a site contains ancient traces covered up by many remnants from later periods. It is quite certain that in such cases the number of potsherds from the later periods will be greater than those dating from earlier times, even if the dimensions of the earlier settlement were no smaller than those of the later one. Various researchers have attempted to cope with this problem, such as Zertal,[385] Finkelstein[386] and Ofer.[387] Based on their work, I can establish several rules regarding the estimation of the area of the settlements in the sites of the survey.

The relative amount of pottery from a certain period present at a site serves as a gauge for the relative size of the site. For example, at a site which served several periods, in which more than 40 percent of the ceramics are from the Middle Bronze Age, its maximum area also dates to the Middle Bronze Age.

Also, when the amount of Middle Bronze Age pottery is less than 40 percent, but is no less than the amount of pottery from any other individual period, the area of the site is calculated according to the number of potsherds from the MBA relative to the site's main period or periods. For example, if the estimate of the surveyors is 20 dunams and the number of potsherds collected from the MBA is 10 percent of the number of potsherds from the Iron Age (90 percent), we assume that the area of the site in the MBA was approximately two dunams.

On the basis of this rule, the sites have been classified into six categories of size, so that even if an error in number of dunams has been made, the error will not affect the site's classification degree. The larger the site, the less significant any deviation will be.

Class A – up to 1 dunam

Class B – over 1 dunam and up to 5 dunams

Class C – over 5 dunams and up to 10 dunams

Class D – over 10 dunams and up to 20 dunams

Class E – over 20 dunams and up to 30 dunams

Class F – over 30 dunams and up to 60 dunams

Judean Hills Settlement Distribution

On the following page is a table of the distribution of some of the settlements in the secondary regions of the Judean Hills, according to size. The full list of sites can be found in my doctoral thesis.[388]

Middle Bronze Age I

Our knowledge of this period stems mainly from burial sites. A few potsherds were found at the sites of settlements such as Bet-El and the Zimri Stream, and apparently also in Jerusalem and Tel Rumeida (Hebron). In the northern Hebron Hills, at numbers 123 and 127 in the list of sites, only a few potsherds from this period were found. Therefore, we are speaking of six small settlement sites and a single cave used for housing in Wadi et-Tin. Furthermore, it is almost certain that in this period the population dwelt mainly in tents. Graves from this period have been found in Efrat, in Eleazar, in Khirbet Kufin, in Khirbet Karmil and in other places as well.[390]

Intermediate Bronze Age
Size Class[389]

Region	Class A	Class B	Class C	Class D	Class E	Class F	Total No. of Settle-Ments	Built-up Area in dunams[380]
Bet-El Hills	2	1	1	1	-	-	5	26
Jerusalem Hills	-	2	2	2	-	2	8	103
Hebron Hills	2	-	-	-	-	-	2	2
Total	4	3	3	3	-	2	15	131

Middle Bronze Age II
Size Class[3]

Region	Class A	Class B	Class C	Class D	Class E	Class F	Total No. of Settle-Ments	Built-up Area in dunams[382]
Bet-El Hills	17	10	4	2	-	1	34	164
Jerusalem Hills	5	9	2	1	-	4	21	245
Hebron Hills	6	10	1	2	-	-	19	69
Total	28	29	7	5	-	5	74	478

Data Analysis

Based on the data gleaned from the above tables, a number of prominent features are evident:

1. The number of settlements in Middle Bronze Age II was five times as large as their number in the Intermediate Bronze Age,

and the size of the settled area was almost four times as great.

2. In both periods, areas further south had progessively fewer settlements than the northern regions.

3. The large majority of the settlements were of Classes A and B. Class E settlements were non-existent. Class F settlements were mainly in the Jerusalem area.

4. While the number of settlements in the Bet-El region was the largest in both periods, the overall area of the settlements in the Jerusalem hills was the largest.

5. Settlement in the hill country of Hebron was extremely limited, despite the large area of this region.

The Settlement Pattern in the Judean Hills — MBA

Familiarity with the settlement pattern, i.e., the geographical arrangement of the sites with respect to the central town and the distances between one site and another, make it possible to appreciate the system of economic and political forces active in the region. It is assumed that the sites are indeed located in accordance with geographical-economic logic, unless external security or political forces are active in this area.

Adam Zertal became aware of just such a geographical-economic logic; he claims that the settlement pattern in the Menashe Hills was a large central fortified area surrounded by between ten and twenty villages.[391] These villages appear to have been subordinate to the central site, serving as its agricultural basis.

Moshe Kochavi perceived a similar pattern at Afek. In a survey carried out there three sites were found within 7 kilometers of Afek, and Kochavi assumed that Afek served as a center for those settlements.[392] It is probable that this was the pattern at Shiloh, where nine settlements were found within a range of 6 kilometers around that fortified site.[393]

An examination of the settlement pattern in the Judean

Hills reveals a similar phenomenon. The following geographical analysis of this feature relates only to clusters of settlements and not to small sites scattered over the area, whose geographical context is obscure.

The Bet-El Hill Country

Eleven settlements have been found clustered around Bet-El. A detailed examination of this settlement pattern shows that to the south and west of Bet-El there are five sites between 3 and 5.5 kilometers away, measured in a straight line. The two sites furthest away in the south are large. The other sites located to the east and to the northeast of Bet-El are between 1 and 2 kilometers away. (For the significance of this distribution, see Regional Analysis below.)

The Gibeon Region

Six sites are clustered in the Gibeon Region, five of which are spread out on the edges of the Gibeon Valley. Three of the five have been identified as large sites (two of them are Class D, and Gibeon itself was probably no smaller). The fertile agricultural land attracted settlers. It is very likely that the settlement at Gibeon was the central one, around which the others were spread. This conclusion is based on geographical data and not on archaeological findings, since the findings at the site itself are extremely sparse.

The Jerusalem Region

In the broad valleys of the Soreq, Refaim and Zimri Streams in the Jerusalem hill country, there are natural resources, which were quite appealing to settlers, and they undoubtedly led to the establishment of many settlements both in the Intermediate Bronze Age and in the Middle Bronze Age.

Around the City of David site, which was the largest and most central, a number of sites have been found, some of which have been excavated. To the north, the site at the Zimri Stream;

to the north-west, (site 69) that covered about 30 dunams; to the west, the settlement recently uncovered in Motza; to the southwest, the sites of Manahat; and to the northeast, the site at Refaim Stream, as well as additional sites.

The settlements to the north and west of Jerusalem were amongst the largest in the Judean Hills (Class F) and were located 4 to 6 kilometers away from the City of David.

Graves were found to the east of the Mount of Olives, the El-Azariyya and Abu-Dis area without nearby settlements, indicating that this region was populated by a nomadic population. To the northeast, a few isolated sites were found, which seem to have been quite small.

The settlement pattern around Jerusalem was quite similar to that around Bet-El, though it was more substantial.

Regional Analysis of the Geographical Pattern in the Jerusalem Hills and in the Bet-El Hills

The above description indicates the existence of rings of settlements around Bet-El, Gibeon and Jerusalem. The settlements were clustered mainly in the western part of the region, while in the border strip to the east there were only a few small settlements. Around Jerusalem and Bet-El, the settlements were between 4 and 6 kilometers away from the fortified central town, while around Gibeon they were only about 2 kilometers from the center.

From a study carried out in the Judean Hills by Tzvi Ron, it seems[394] that the distance between a settlement and its fields is never greater than 4.5 kilometers (except for Hebron, where it is 9 kilometers.) Similar results were reached in a study carried out in parts of Europe, cultivated in the traditional fashion. According to this study, at a distance between 3 and 4 kilometers from the settlement, a switch was made from intensive to extensive agriculture.[395] Furthermore, the distance of this ring coincided with the limits of one's daily commuting in ancient times.[396]

In this light, it seems that the settlements around Bet-El and Jerusalem were established beyond the agricultural territories of the central town. The agricultural territories of Bet-El and Jerusalem extended in all probability mainly to the north, the west, and the south, with the land to the east probably serving as pastureland.

Intermediate Regions

A few sites have been found in the areas between Bet-El, Gibeon, and Jerusalem and in the region to the south of Jerusalem. In these areas, a number of graves have been found (as in Kalandia and Bet-Sahour), as well as signs of the activity of a nomadic population (potsherds have been found at Tel El-Ful and in Giloh, but no architecture) and several small settlements. These regions may have served as pastureland or seed fields for the inhabitants of the settlement clusters, or perhaps as pastureland for the nomadic people who had entered the hill country and subsisted between the settlement clusters.

The Hebron Hill Country

The Settlement Distribution Table (330) shows that the area of the Hebron Hills was rather sparsely settled. No settlement pattern has been discovered around the two fortified sites found. Most of the sites are located along the mountain ridge and its offshoots.

The one small noteworthy cluster is the Gush Etzion region in the northern Hebron Hills, where several small settlement sites have been discovered.

The absence of Middle Bronze Age sites around the fortified sites of Beth-Zur and Hebron is surprising, especially if this situation is compared to that of the hill country of Jerusalem or Bet-El where the pattern found was different, composed of a ring of settlements around the central town.

It seems that the settlement pattern was different from that of the regions more to the north around the fortified settlements of Jerusalem and Beitel. Israel Finkelstein,[397] in the wake of M. B. Rowton, who examined other mountainous regions in the Euphrates River region,[398] thinks that sites such as Shiloh (and probably other fortified sites in the hills, including Hebron) were strongholds of the political authority of "local strong men", who ruled over wide expanses with small villages and a large nomadic population. It is possible that the approach adopted by Finkelstein does indeed suit the situation prevalent in the Hebron hill country.

According to this approach, these towns are not major built-up towns of a kingdom, as there seem to have been in other parts of the country (mainly in the coastal plain), but display a different pattern, a pattern characteristic of the hill country in the Middle East, as in Iran and in Turkey.

The proximity of the Hebron Hills to the desert and the scarcity of large agricultural areas even in their northern, rainy regions[399] may have prevented more widespread settlement in the area.

Summary

On the assumption that the settlement found in the Judean Hills in surveys and in excavations belong to the same period of time, three settlement blocs can be distinguished in the hill country of Jerusalem and of Bet-El, arranged according to geographical and economic logic around urban centers. This is not true of the hill country of Hebron, where settlements are scattered, sparsely populated, spread along the roads and suited to the agricultural lands and water sources.

In Jerusalem and in Bet-El there was a settlement hierarchy headed by the fortified town. The unfortified settlements were secondary, the area of which was in many cases no smaller than that of the fortified urban center and on occasion even larger. Their inhabitants engaged mainly in agriculture and shepherding. The tent or cave dwellers were teritary. This third-degree population seems to have engaged mainly in shepherding, and perhaps also a little in farming.[400]

A Population Estimate in the Judean Hills

The most popular questions asked by students of archaeology visiting sites throughout Israel concern the estimated population of the various towns and districts of the land at one time or another.

We have no knowledge of population censuses taken in the Biblical period, other than the few actually mentioned in the Bible. When attempting to estimate the number of people living in a certain area, there are many variables and uncertainties, such as the possible existence of a nomadic populace in a given region. Yet several articles have been published on the subject relating to different periods. The significance of these arithmetic exercises appears to be able to make comparisons between different periods, yet it is self-evident that citing precise numbers is rather pretentious and actually groundless.

Magen Broshi and Ram Gophna have attempted[401] to estimate the size of the population of Israel during the Middle Bronze Age. From the data they published, it would seem that the settlement in the Judean Hills was so small that it was not deemed worthy of separate mention in their article, being included, rather, together with the region of the coastal plain. An examination of the data they adduced reveals that the area settled in the Judean Hills during that period came to about 200 dunams.

The data in this book presents a different picture. If we assume that all the settlements under consideration existed simultaneously, the area settled on an extended basis, according to the size classes described above, totaled about 480 dunams, about 140 percent larger than Broshi and Gophna's estimate.

If we calculate the size of the population according to the system presented in the article by Broshi and Gophna, i.e., by multiplying the settled area by a coefficient of 25 persons per dunam,[402] we will find that the number of people who lived in the permanent settlement in the Judean Hills was some 12,000.

There is no way we are able to estimate the size of the nomadic population in the region, but since the Judean Hills border on the desert, the size of this populace in this region must have been significant. Graves that have been excavated which are not connected with the settlements, such as the graves in Kalandia,

Abu-Dis, El-Azariyya, Bitaniya and on the lands of Kibbutz Zova, prove the existence of a nomadic population of considerable size in the Judean Hills during the Middle Bronze Age. Some of the excavated sites in which potsherds have been found with no trace of architecture, such as Giloh and Tel El-Ful, may well have been shepherding sites, too.

To this list may be added the burial sites, with no settlement adjoining them, that have been discovered in the surveys.[403]Data dating from the end of the Ottoman period showing that the Bedouins made up some 15 percent of the entire population of all of Israel shed light on the situation in the MBA.[404]

A population estimate based solely on an assessment of the built-up areas does not reflect the full picture, for it is reasonable to assume that the population of the Judean Hills was actually considerably greater than it is generally said to have been. At this stage, however, we do not have the tools to form an appraisal of its true size.

Judean Sites in Comparison with the Samaria Region

Seventy-two sites[405] were listed in the survey of the Land of Ephraim (southern Samaria),[406] with only five of these extending over an area of over 10 dunams. All the others took up a more limited area including no more than 5 dunams, to which four graveyards were added.

This data indicates a lack of settlements belonging to size class E or F and a paucity of sites belonging to class D. It seems that the overall area of the settlements did not exceed 300 dunams, and were spread over a wide area of some 900 square kilometers.

Comparing these with surveys of the Hills of Menashe further to the north shows how the latter differ from those of the Judean Hills. In the Hills of Menashe (the area of which is estimated around 1600 square kilometers) 116 settlements were located; the suveyor estimates their overall area to be about

1120 dunams.[407] It appears, therefore, that the Hills of Menashe settlement was extremely strong, both in regard to the number of individual settlements, and to the area they occupy.

According to the facts available, in the Hills of Menashe there were thirty-one settlements of Classes D-F,[408] with fifteen of them identifiable as tells or as fortified sites. In the Hills of Judea, there were ten settlements of these classes, with only four of them identified as tells or as fortified sites.

The Judean Hills and the Hills of Menashe also differ from one another in the importance of their nomadic population. As previously discussed, the nomadic population of the Judean Hills was extremely significant; in contrast, almost no traces (such as graves with no adjacent settlement, scattered potsherds with no architecture nearby) of such a population were found in the northern part of the central hill country of Menashe. While in the Judean Hills the nomadic population lived within and amongst the sedentary population (apparently because there were interim areas only sparsely settled and because of the proximity of the region to the Judean Desert) the Hills of Menashe were more fertile and more remote from the desert, and were thus populated with a sedentary farming population.

Two settlement patterns have been identified in the northern Hills of Menashe: the first is concentrated in the internal valleys and is comprised of a large fortified city, surrounded by between ten and twenty rural settlements; while the second is located more towards the eastern margin of this region and is made up of groups of small settlements, with no fortified tells.

The nature of the first group appears to be quite similar to that of the settlement in the Jerusalem hill country, while the second group has much in common with the settlement pattern in the northern Hebron hills.

This suggests that it is possible that the settlement pattern made up of groups of small settlements without a central fortified town was characteristic of peripheral areas.

Summary

The surveys and excavations in the central hill country have revealed two centers of settlement gravity. The larger one was focused on the Hills of Menashe, mainly in the area of the "Shechem Basin," the area of which was some 400 square kilometers, and contained some seventy-two sites including some large ones.[409] The second focal point was in the hill country of Jerusalem. In this area (which encompassed approximately 250 square kilometers, i.e., less than a sixth of the area of the Judean Hills), the built-up area in the Jerusalem Hills occupied more than half of the settled area in the Judean Hills.

Between these two centers, there were other sites, generally smaller ones, mainly around fortified sites like Shiloh, Bet-El and Gibeon.

The central status of Jerusalem is thus reflected in the settlement density of the Jerusalem region as early as this period. It is therefore not surprising that only Jerusalem and Shechem were mentioned in a contemporary Egyptian source known as the Execration Texts.

Economy and Survival in the Middle Bronze Age

Livestock

The study of animal bones by Liora Horwitz in the areas of the Refaim[410] and Zimri Streams indicates that no noticeable difference in livestock existed among these unfortified sites. In the two sites studied, as well as in Manahat, the livestock included mainly sheep, goats, and cattle. In addition, the bones of pigs were found, as well as donkeys in the Refaim Valley settlement.

The table on page 292 demonstrates differences between the Zimri Stream site and the one in the Refaim Valley, in both the Middle and the Intermediate Bronze Ages. The data below relate only to bones found in loci that have been dated with a reasonable degree of certainty.

Animal Bones Found in the Zimri and Refaim Valleys

The increased number of cattle in the later period is evident, particularly in the Refaim Valley (from about 3 percent in the IBA to about 18 percent in the MBA). In contrast, the presence of pigs in the Refaim Valley decreased in the Middle Bronze Age. Similarly, the presence of donkeys in the Refaim Valley as opposed to its absence in the Zimri Stream site is most intriguing. At the same time, it should be noted that the number of bones found and identified in the Zimri Stream (278 bones) is small when compared with the corresponding number of bones found and identified in the Refaim Valley (515 bones). It is possible that the scope of the samples had an effect on the results of the comparison.

An examination of the age of the animals in the Refaim Valley shows that all the cattle and the donkeys were over 42 months of age at their death. This indicates that the cattle served to transport burdens and to plow fields, and were not used only for food. According to Horwitz, the sheep and goats were bred not only for their flesh but also for wool and milk, as only about 35 percent of these animals were slaughtered when still young.[411]

It may thus be concluded that the cattle and the donkeys were used for plowing and for transporting burdens, the sheep and the goats mainly for wool and for milk, and the pigs only for food.

A similar study of animal bones was carried out at Tel Hebron. In room 230 (the room where the document in cuneiform symbols was discovered) a large number of bones were found. Upon examination, they revealed that 94.6 percent were of sheep and goats, while only 5.4 percent of the bones were of cattle.[412] The findings from the excavation at Shiloh resemble those of the sites in the Jerusalem hill country: in stratum VIII, bones found were 85 percent sheep and goats, 11.5 percent cattle and 3.5 percent pigs. In stratum VII, no pigs were found; the part played by cattle was somewhat higher, reaching 12 percent, while that of the sheep and goats rose to 88 percent.[413]

Animal Bones from Refaim and Zimri Valleys

	Intermediate Bronze Age		Middle Bronze Age	
	Zimri Stream	Refaim Valley	Zimri Stream	Refaim Valley
Sheep/ goats	76%	80.57%	75%	63.50%
Cattle	11%	3.1%	14%	18.50%
Pigs	8%	15.19%	10%	8.27%
Donkeys	-	1.00%	-	7.48%
Deer	Less than 1% (a single bone)	-	Less than 1% (a single bone)	-

Significant changes in the numbers of sheep, goats and cattle are found when comparing the hill country sites with those of the coastal and inland plains.

The table on page 294 shows data of animal bones found in various sites from the MBA.[414]

This table stresses the significance of cattle in Aphek and at Tel Michal. It is probable that the various data can be explained against a geographical background. The flat areas in the coastal plain were apparently convenient for both plowing crops and raising cattle. As a result the number of cattle in such places is high in comparison to the hill country.

Under similar climatic conditions, the ability to plow the land is the main factor dictating the degree to which cattle appear in the livestock bred, whereas a drop in cattle-breeding stems from topographical limitations and rocky land.

Adam Zertal[415] also realized the importance of the geographical element as a factor in the difference in the cattle: sheep/goats ratio. The comparison he drew between the Mt. Ebal site and that of 'Izbet Sartah shows that cattle made up 31 percent of animal life at 'Izbet Sartah while at Mt. Ebal they

Remains of a house from the Middle Bronze age in Zimri stream

made up only 21 percent. Zertal credits this difference as due to the proximity of the 'Izbet Sartah site to the coastal plain, which was more convenient for the breeding of cattle. Nevertheless, this comparison is valueless in this case, for the site on Mt. Ebal was a religious site, while that at 'Izbet Sartah was a settlement.

Finally, if a large number of cattle is a type of index signifying high economic capability (because of the high price of cattle), the standard of living in the MBA was higher than that of a contemporary Arab village. Data amassed regarding the Arab village in the hill country in the middle of the 20th century CE indicate a lower ratio of cattle to sheep and goats, a mere 3 - 9 percent in contrast with the Canaanite village in the same region, where the percentage of cattle was over 12%.

The Sheep / Goats to Cattle Ratio according to the Bible

As Jacob was making his way home from Haran to Israel, he had to send a gift to his brother, Esau. The Bible lists the number of animals Jacob sent (Gen. 32:15-16): 220 goats, 220 sheep, and 50 head of cattle (plus 30 nursing camels with their colts and 30 donkeys). Here, too, an examination of the ratio of sheep and goats to cattle shows that the percentage of the cattle was 11.4 percent, a fact which may well indicate the fact that cattle were more expensive and were an important economic asset. This sheds new light on Abraham's generous hospitality in welcoming uninvited and unfamiliar visitors with a "good, succulent calf" (Gen. 18:7).

The Phenomenon of Hebron and Shiloh: the Absence of Pigs and only a Small Number of Cattle

As discussed earlier, pigs were part of the menu of the inhabitants of Israel during the MBA. Against this background,

Animal Bones in Various Sites in Israel

	Refaim Valley	Zimri Stream	Shiloh (Stra-tum VIII)	Hebron	Lachish	Aphek	Tel Michal
Sheep, goats	63.5%	75%	85%	94.6%	86.8%	49.4%	44.5%
Cattle	18.5%	14%	11.5%	5.4%	13.2%	29.6%	40.9%
Pigs	8.27%	10%	3.5%	-	?	7.7%	7.7%
Dogs	-	-	-	-	-	5.6%	-

the absence of pigs from two sites, Hebron and Shiloh, stands out prominently.

The explanation of this phenomenon lies in the character of the sites. Both researchers claim on the basis of various findings that both sites were devoted to worship. In other words, there was some kind of sanctuary at each site, where it was customary to offer sacrifices. These bones, then, were the bones of sacrifices that were offered, and not the bones of simple livestock used for food.

It seems reasonable to assume that the Canaanites them-

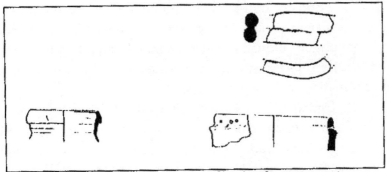

Broken earthwave vessles from E-Tel-(Middle Bronze era)

selves refrained from offering pigs on their altars, and that they, too, distinguished between pigs and sheep, goats or cattle. El-kana Billik and S.A. Loewenstam note: "Though many indications have been found in archaeological excavations that it was customary to breed pigs in Canaanite towns, no evidence has yet reached us—not in writing, not in Ugaritic, nor in Phoenician—of a sacrificial pig; and even in the descriptions of divine feasts brought down in the writings of Ugarit, the pig was never mentioned amongst the foodstuffs consumed by the gods."[416]

They also note that the pig was an abomination in the eyes of the gods of Egypt, and that anyone touching a pig and not intending to perform a divine commandment by doing so would become impure and have to undergo ritual immersion. Now if Shiloh and Hebron were indeed sites of worship, it becomes clear why the number of cattle bones is so small, in comparison with the corresponding numbers in other sites. The bones at these two sites are the bones of sacrifices. Since cattle were relatively expensive, it may be assumed that those offering the sacrifices preferred to offer goats and sheep, and of course refrained entirely from offering pigs.

Donkeys

At the Refaim Valley site a considerable amount of donkey bones were found. The donkey was occasionally used for plowing, though the ox was preferred for this purpose. The main task of the donkey, on the other hand, was to carry burdens.[417] There may be a connection between the donkeys at this site with the pottery industry, which operated here; it would seem that the donkeys transported the vessels manufactured here to the population centers in the region.

This combination of industry and animals for transportation testifies to the existence of an economy at a relatively high level, based on regional trade -- unlike a closed, autarchic economy which subsists on what it itself manages to produce.

Vegetables and their Preparation

It is possible to learn something about the vegetation consumed by human beings from vegetable remains in the settlement studied, as well as from a study of the agricultural implements and structures there.

Vegetable Remains

Botanic studies carried out at the Manahat site and at the Refaim Valley indicate a similar composition of foodstuffs. At the Refaim Valley site, in a square, stone-walled and plastered pit, the seeds of legumes, olive and grape pits were found.[418] At the Manahat site, Mordechai Kislev identified olive, grape and lentil seeds.

Similarly, at the Shiloh excavations grains of wheat, barley, vetch (a plant with feather-like leaves ending in tendrils and flowers), figs, olives, and grapes were found.[419]

Besides the findings from the hill country sites, there are the findings from Tel Jericho, which adjoins the region we are discussing. By virtue of the dry climate there, carbonized corn grains were preserved in a number of rooms, while in one of the graves pomegranates and grapes were found.[420]

Implements

Excavations of the three unfortified sites uncovered many stone implements. A study of the stone implements made at the Zimri Stream revealed that the scythe-blade is the most common of these. On five of the twenty-eight scythe-blades (besides the five Canaanite scythe-blades that seem to belong to the Intermediate Bronze Age) a white, plaster-like material was found, which may have served to attach the blade to its wooden handle. The clods of bitumen found in the area may have been used for this purpose. (The closest bituminous rock is found a few kilometers to the east, near Ma'ale Adumim, but on the site numerous clods of bitumen were found scattered all over the area).

Hammers

Thirty-one stone hammers and hammer fragments were found in the Zimri Stream site, most of them in Area D. It is extremely probable that the hammers were used to pound vegetable substances for the processing of foodstuffs.

Millstones

A number of millstones were found at the Zimri Stream site, some made of local stone and others of basalt. Two of these (neither millstones) were found in locus 352 in area C, and their location may indicate that this space served as a workroom. What was the function of these stones? It is customary to interpret them as implements used for the grinding of flour, yet they may have had an additional function, the manufacturing of oil.

The existence of oil and wine industries in the Middle Bronze Age remains an unsolved puzzle, for no installations clearly used for the manufacture of oil have yet been found. Nevertheless, oil was a central export product at various times, just as wine served as a central component of the inhabitants' menu.

Much has been written of the export of oil from Canaan to Egypt in the Early Bronze Age,[421] and it is known that this continued into the Late Bronze Age.[422] There is no doubt that in the Middle Bronze Age, oil was produced in Canaan in considerable quantities. Yet the silence of the Egyptian sources and the lack of archaeological evidence on this topic is surprising. Even if there were no well-developed commercial ties between Egypt and Canaan in this era, it may still be assumed that the manufacture of oil and wine made up an important component of the economy of Canaan, as has been the case in every period. If so, a question arises as to just how they made the wine and the oil in the Bronze Age.

Archaeologist Claire Epstein surmises that the millstones found in the Chalcolithic sites on the Golan Heights also served to manufacture oil.[423] The great similarity between the Chalcolithic millstones in the Golan and those found in the Zimri Stream site raise the possibility that these millstones were also used to manufacture wine or oil.

Processed Bones

Fragments of processed bone found on the floors in Area C in the Zimri Stream area served as raw material in this site. The complete lack of metal implements raises the possibility that the bone fragments served as needles or as pins.

Summary

The diet of the Middle Bronze Age population in the Judean Hills was fairly diverse. The large number of scythe-blades, millstones (at the Zimri Stream and Manahat) and animal bones indicates that growing and processing wheat and breeding goats, sheep and cattle were the economic mainstays of this region. The status of oil and wine in the contemporary regional economy is obscure, but olives, grapes, and legumes were part of the menu of the inhabitants of the region. The fact that basalt implements were found in the three unfortified sites indicates a trade in stone implements of considerable range, apparently towards Transjordan or Syria.

Is it possible to demonstrate any economic ties between the unfortified settlements and the fortified towns? In the section of this chapter dealing with the analysis of the distribution of settlement sites, we have seen that Jerusalem was the largest town in the hill country, and that the settlements were located in accordance with geographical and economic logic. In this light, it would seem that these unfortified settlements served as the agricultural periphery of Jerusalem, the central town. This conclusion is supported by the findings in the Refaim Valley site, which point to economic specialization with the exploitation of local advantages.

Findings from later periods in the central hill country indicate the high economic standards achieved by the hill region until Iron Age II, when the economic structure improved substantially due to the invention of industrial installations for the processing of foodstuffs (presses for oil, grape presses and wine cellars), and because of the governmental and economic centralization, which dictated both the settlement pattern and its economics to a large extent.

Pottery — Chronological and Regional Aspects

The regional aspect of pottery has almost never been considered. Despite the fact that in any given period the pottery was similar throughout the country, as if all the potters had conspired to produce identical vessels, there are still certain differences between the vessels of different parts of the country. This is true especially in regions which are less accessible, such as the Judean Hills. In this section, we shall attempt to appreciate the regional component in our study of pottery, becoming familiar with the cultural characteristics of each region as well.

Middle Bronze Age I

The earthenware findings from Middle Bronze Age I in the Judean Hills are extremely few in comparison with the coastal plain in the same period and in comparison with the central hill country in the Intermediate Bronze Age and the Middle Bronze Age II. (There is an overlap between IBA and MBA.) Findings from this period were only unearthed at three settlement sites: Bet-El, the Zimri Stream and Hebron. In the first two sites, findings were extremely rare, while the material found at Hebron has not yet been made public.

MBA I findings gleaned from the excavation of gravesites are richer, but in most of the graves, these findings are mixed with vessels from the IBA and/or from MBA II.

Since a considerable portion of the ceramic repertoire of MBA I survives into the next era as well, it is difficult to know definitely whether certain vessels actually belong to this period. Nonetheless, one can view a collection of pottery as characteristic of the Judean Hills according to the findings from Khirbet Karmil in the southern part of the Hebron hill country, from the E-Tin Cave and from the gravesites of Khirbet Kufin, in Ephrata, in Eleazar in the northern Hebron hills, in Aminadav, and in Ma'ale Ha-Hamisha to the west of Jerusalem and from Gibeon, northwest of Jerusalem.[424]

The chart on page 250 shows a representative collection of vessels from this period, including all the main types known in other regions (though the collection is not extremely variegated). The pottery found in the graves was mainly cooking pots and flasks, which were vital to one's everyday life in ancient times. Findings indicate that the pottery of the Judean hill country differed from that of the coastal region in one main aspect: burnishing, which was characteristic of this period in the coastal plain. Burnished vessels are almost non-existent in Judea except for two sites: Khirbet Kufin and the E-Tin Cave.

Petrographic examinations carried out by Yuval Goren of the Antiquities Authority on vessels of the period from the Zimri Stream site and from graves in Ephrat indicate that the vessels were made of local clay (*hawar* of Motza and dolemite sand). The results of the petrographic examinations carried out on two of the three vessels found at Aminadav are the same.

Middle Bronze Age II

Archaeologist Kathleen Kenyon considered all the pottery of MBA II found in the southern part of the country, after her excavations of graves in Jericho, though she did not refer to the

PERIOD	ACCEPTED DATING SYSTEM	CHARACTER-ISTICS	ALTERNATE DATING SYSTEM	AS REFLECTED IN THE BIBLE
MIDDLE BRONZE AGE I	1950 - 1800 BCE	Renewed urbanization in Israel; In the Judean Hills, continuation of nomadic life; on the plains - renewed urbanization		Beginning Patriarchal Period
MIDDLE BRONZE AGE II	1800 - 1550 BCE	Development of urbanization and ;fortifications Violent destruction at the close of the period	1400 - 1800 BCE Renewed urbanization in the hills and throughout the ;country Violent destruction at the close of the period	Exile in Egypt, exodus, desert encampments

differences between the northern part of the country and the south.[425] Professor Aharon Kempinski broadened the scope of the subject by referring to the end of the Middle Bronze Age; he studied groups of settlements and made the distinction between the south of the country and the north.[426]

The work done by archaeologists Dan P. Cole in Shechem[427] and William G. Dever in Gezer,[428] the publication of the excavations at Shiloh,[429] and the excavations at the Zimri Stream, at Manahat, at the gravesites in Ma'aleh-Ha-Hamisha, at Eleazar and at Zova, as well as the examination of the pottery found at the sites covered by the survey, all render possible a renewed examination of the chronological and regional dimensions of the Judean Hills pottery.

Another means employed in recent years is the statistical examination of the pottery. These examinations, carried out at the sites in Shiloh, the Zimri Stream, and in some of the sites of the survey, make it possible to learn not only of the existence or the absence of certain ceramic shapes, but also of their frequency.

This book does not discuss all the vessels, but instead only those that present new facts either from the chronological or from the regional standpoints. In general, most of the characteristics of the southern group, as defined by Kempinski, are still valid, while most of the changes affect only a small number of characteristics.

The pottery of the Judean Hills is not burnished and does not include imported vessels. The petrographic examinations of the Zimri Stream, Ma'aleh Ha-Hamisha and Zova vessels made by Yuval Goren show that the vessels were made of locally-found material. The pottery industry discovered in the Refaim Valley may have been the source of the pottery in the region, and it is possible that certain ceramic shapes common in other regions never penetrated to this center.

The uniqueness of the pottery found in the Judean Hill country is seen in the following features:

Cooking pots were of three types in the Middle Bronze Age: handmade, thick-walled cooking pots, curved-wall cooking pots, and an additional cooking pot shaped like a sliced-off ball with a broad opening. Various types of the first two kinds appear on page 251 (Vessels 5-9), but the third vessel is not to be found in the Judean Hills south of Bet-El, though it is common in sites north of Bet-El.

Jars may be divided into six groups, according to the shapes of their mouths. Four of these appear in various sites in the Judean hill country (on page 251: 1-4). Two other groups, one with a stepped edge and the other with an edge shaped like a shelf appear in Shiloh and in Shechem, but do not appear south of Bet-El.

Juglets (or **vials**) are small vessels apparently intended for the storing of precious fluids. Two main types familiar to us from this period are pear-shaped vials and vials with upright

sides, resembling cylinders. The cylindrical vials are characteristic of the end of the MBA, while the pear-shaped vials grow
steadily rarer. Studies carried out of the Judean Hill country
indicate that the cylindrical vials are relatively rare in the hill
settlements, but are found in graves. Cole claimed[430] that the
absence of cylindrical vials in a settlement site indicates that
the settlement had been destroyed before cylindrical vials were
manufactured. This explanation would reflect the situation in
the coastal plains, but it does not appear to have been valid in
the hill country settlements.

Cypriot Pottery and Colored Pottery

Towards the end of the Middle Bronze Age, a new ceramic
family appeared, known as "chocolate-on-white" because of its
characteristic decoration of brown stripes on the off-white body of
the vessel. This type of decoration on a vessel indicates the close of
the MBA. Also, vessels imported from Cyprus (Cypriot Pottery)
start to appear in various sites throughout the country, in strata
dated from the close of the MBA.

In the past, Kempinski[431] claimed that Cypriot pottery was
not found at all in the central hill country. However, the latest
findings indicate that while imported vessels and various kinds of
colored vessels (including "chocolate-on-white") are not common
in the central hills, the existence of a few potsherds of these types
in Shiloh negates his adamant statement. Some colored pottery has
also been found in Bet-El, but its nature is obscure.[432]

It seems that imported or colored vessels had not become
common in the Judean Hills even at the close of this period, a fact
which appears to confirm the relative isolation of the region.

Summary

The Bet-El region is the southern limit for the distribution of colored pottery and imported vessels, as well as for the
distribution of secondary types of cooking pots, various bowls,

and flasks. Furthermore, the cylindrical vials characteristic of the era are uncommon in the settlements in this region.

This finding matches the results of the petrographic tests of the Zimri Stream, Ma'ale Ha-Hamisha and Zova vessels carried out by Yuval Goren of the Antiquities Authority. These tests show that almost all these vessels belong to the *hawar*-Motza and dolomite sand group. In contrast, three separate petrographic groups (out of a total of seven vessels) were found in Shiloh, including one of the lowest Cretaceous layers of limited distribution, apparently originating from the Wadi Fari'a and Wadi Malikh region to the north-east of the site.[433]

The petrographic groups found at Shiloh are commonplace in various sites throughout the country beginning with the Chalcolithic Age. The fact that they are absent from the Judean hill country indicates that in this respect as well, the pottery industry managed with local, monolithic raw materials, unlike the hill country further to the north, the Hills of Menashe and Ephraim, where a broad spectrum of petrographic groups was found. If so, the geographical division which marked Bet-El as the northern boundary of the Judean Hills matches the distribution of various ceramic vessels. Bet-El served as an impassable border for certain pottery types. It may be concluded, then, that this geographical border was extremely significant in this respect.

The Political Status of the Judean Hills in light of Archaeological Findings

In recent years, the subject of the political set-up in the hill country in the Middle Bronze Age[434] has been discussed widely. However, in light of the new data, the question must be asked, does the data presented in this work put this subject in a new light?

We start the discussion with two major questions:

1) During the Middle Bronze Age, were the Judean Hills

subordinate to some external entity, such as Egypt, which was able to influence the settlement pattern and the internal balance of power, or were the settlement pattern and material culture the result of internal development?

2) What was the nature of the internal forces operating in the central hill country in general, and in the Judean Hills in particular?

To deal with these questions, let us look at the relevant archaeological and historical data.

Egypt and the Central Hill Country

We can learn from a number of sources about the involvement of Egypt in our region in the first half of the second millennium BCE:

a. Execration Texts from the period of the Middle Kingdom (19th century BCE), in which various sites in Israel are mentioned by name;

b. An inscription telling of a trip taken by Khusbakh, an Egyptian army officer, to "the land of Shechem" in the middle of the 19th century BCE; and

c. Egyptian artifacts found in excavations.

There are three alternative explanations regarding Egyptian involvement in Israel in the Middle Bronze Age:

1. Egyptian control extended throughout Israel;

2. the Egyptians controlled only certain areas, mainly in the coastal plain;

3. there was no Egyptian control over Israel at all, and the Egyptian artifacts merely indicate the existence of commercial ties.

Which of these is the most likely? We must subdivide our discussion of this subject into two separate periods: MBA I, which was contemporary, in the opinion of most scholars, with the period of the Middle Kingdom in Egypt, and MBA II-III, paralleling the Second Interim Period in Egypt. This subdivision is necessary because the difference in the settlement pattern between these two secondary periods is so great that it is not possible to treat the Middle Bronze Age as if it were a single, unchanging period of time.

Two relevant Egyptian sources originate in the period of the Middle Kingdom. No Egyptian source dealing with this region has come down to us from the Second Interim Period.

Middle Bronze Age I (The Period of the Middle Kingdom)

Evidence from the Judean Hills indicates that the region was only sparsely settled. Even in Jerusalem and Shechem, which were mentioned in the Egyptian sources, there is no evidence of significant settlement. In the central hill country, there are no Egyptian findings, except for a few scarabs.[435] It appears, then, that there was no significant Egyptian involvement in the central hill country during this period.

The position adopted by Nadav Ne'eman that the curses (in the Execration Texts) "are based on the assumption of Pharaoh's rule extending throughout the universe... There is accordingly no reason to seek out all the accursed places within the limits of actual Egyptian control"; whereas the journey of Khusbakh to the land of Shechem was apparently only a fleeting episode.[436] Daphna Ben Tor suggests that the 12th dynasty scarabs found in Israel were brought there at a later date, so that there is no evidence of an Egyptian presence in the Land of Canaan during MBA I.[437]

Middle Bronze Age II

A complete change took place in the settlement pattern in the Judean Hills in particular, and in the central hill country in general. There were a large number of settlements. Many scarabs were found in the central hill country, but no written evidence from Egypt has turned up at all.

While it is true that in the land of Israel no Egyptian pottery has been found from this period, except for a few alabaster vessels, many scarabs, dated by the excavators to the 13th to the

15th dynasties, have been found in various sites. The scarabs have been uncovered both in built-up sites and in graves, both in the Judean Hills and in regions further to the north.[438]

The number of scarabs found in the Judean Hills is without a doubt extremely impressive. Yet it is to be noted, that no "royal" scarabs appear in this long list (except for one scarab found in Shechem). On the other hand, royal scarabs have been unearthed in both the coastal and inland plains. The most recent findings, too, support the map of the distribution of royal Hyksos scarabs published by James Weinstein.[439]

The interpretation of Ben-Tor (*supra*) concerning the personal scarabs in Israel in the period of the Middle Kingdom also fits the situation in the hill country during the Second Interim Period in Egypt (1650-1550 BCE). In other words, the scarab findings reflect the adoption of Egyptian customs, but do not indicate Egyptian rule or deep involvement. Furthermore, the fact that Egyptian pottery or other artifacts have not been found at all in the Judean Hills strengthens the argument that the Egyptian presence in the hill country was minimal.

Late Bronze Age Egyptian Findings in the Hill Country

A comparison of the scarabs found in the hill country during MBA with the findings in the LBA indicates that Egypt was only minimally involved in the hill country during the MBA, but there was a much greater Egyptian presence during the LBA.

Despite the small number of LBA sites, the number of "royal" scarabs found in them is quite large.

- A scarab of Ramses II (13th century BCE) was found in Tel Hebron;[440] a scarab of the 19th Dynasty (the 13th century BCE) was found at Beth-Zur.[441]

- At Shechem, a scarab was found bearing the name of Ti, the wife of Amenhotep III (14th century BCE).[442]

- At Manahat, a scarab of Amenhotep III was unearthed.[443]

In addition to the "royal" scarabs, we must make mention of the alabaster vessels and the Egyptian potsherd found in stratum VI at Shiloh,[444] and the Egyptian findings discovered in Jerusalem including, among other things, an Egyptian stele fragment from the LBA.[445]

These findings support our knowledge of (at least partial) Egyptian involvement in the hill country, as reflected in the El-Amarna letters. It is, however, best to tread cautiously, as even royal scarabs do not point to Egyptian involvement or rule, for at Mount Ebal, a clearly Israelite site, two scarabs were found. One of these, bearing the name of Thutmose III, was made, according to Baruch Brandl, in the period of Ramses II.[446] No scholar claims there was an Egyptian presence at that site. This is true of Hebron and Beth-Zur, as well, where scarabs were discovered in a stratum dated from Iron Age I. In fact, most of the scarabs found in the hills were discovered in settlement strata from the Iron Age, rather than in collections dating from the LBA.

It seems reasonable that the scarabs came to be found in sites of marginal importance in the hill country, not as the result of the presence of an Egyptian potentate or of his officials. It is not likely that a ruler would scatter his seal about on all sides so that just anyone could make use of it. The scarabs served as amulets, and in the period of the Middle Kingdom, this phenomenon was uncommon. It is likely, therefore, that scarabs bearing the name of a king were less common, and that their value on the amulet market was high.

Conclusions

The large number of MBA scarabs in the hills indicates contacts with Egypt, though there is no clear evidence of the nature of these relations. The scarabs served as amulets, and scarabs bearing the names of kings were made long after the death of those kings, as well, whether as a sign of reverence for the king or because of the magical effects attributed to his name, for the kings of Egypt were considered to have super-human characteristics and the power to control natural phenomena. The king, often called "the good god," was believed to retain possession of his powers even after his death. The scarabs indicate that the hill country fell within the sphere of Egyptian cultural influence, but there is no evidence whatever that it was included in the area under the control of the Egyptian monarchy.

The Egyptologist Rephael Giv'on has commented, "In the period of the Middle Kingdom [Middle Bronze Age], there seems to have been a direct relationship between the administration and the scarabs bearing the name of the king. It is possible that only officials were able to carry royal seals... From the period of the 18th Dynasty [in Canaan, the LBA] on, the name of a king on a scarab lost all connection with the administration, so that every citizen could make for himself a seal with the king's name on it... As a result, no link is to be drawn between a scarab bearing the name of a king with the king ruling over the region where the artifact was found... This scarab could even have been goods serving as payment for the Canaanites in return for the agricultural produce they sent to Egypt."[447]

This conclusion matches additional data in this book, affirming that the hilly regions (in particular, the Judean Hills) were relatively isolated. We can say that the political and settlement pattern in the central hill country developed without any significant influence of external factors, while maintaining mutual relations with its surroundings.

The Internal Political System in the Central Hill Country

MBA II was one of the high points in the history of the community in the hill country. Because of a lack of historical sources, our analysis is based on three elements:

1. Archaeological finds dating from this period and from adjacent periods;

2. Historical sources from adjacent periods (MBA I and LBA II); and

3. The principle of "a lengthy period of time (Longue Dureé)".

Middle Bronze Age I

In this period, the permanent, unfortified settlements were abandoned, and the light population remaining in the region adopted a nomadic way of life. Archaeological research shows that at the end of the period (the 19th century BCE), small settlements like those at Shechem, Jerusalem and Hebron began to develop.

In the "Execration Texts" two places are mentioned by name, Shechem and Jerusalem, while the Khosbakh inscription tells of an Egyptian military campaign to "the land of Shechem." The fact that only these two sites are named indicates, in the opinion of a number of scholars, that the central hill country was divided into two large territorial units centered around Shechem in the north and Jerusalem in the south.[448]

The archaeological picture does indeed indicate that there was a certain amount of activity in Jerusalem and perhaps small settlements in Shechem and in Hebron, but it is difficult to assume that these small settlements controlled the entire central hill region.

Middle Bronze Age II

The wave of settlement that took place in the central hill country between the 18th and 16th centuries BCE was unprecedented in its scope. The settlement pattern that developed in the hill country was extremely varied, including fortified towns, various types of unfortified settlements, and a large nomadic population. These findings can be interpreted in more than one manner, and the political set-up in this period is viewed by scholars in two different ways.

One approach treats each fortified site as a city-state ruling over its environs, like the situation on the coastal plain in that period.[449] In other words, the central hill country was divided up among a number of city-states such as Shechem, Shiloh, Bet-El, Jerusalem, Hebron, and so on.

Though the arguments for this interpretation are indeed weighty, they do not come to grips with a central problem that arises from the excavations and surveys carried out in the Judean Hills and in the hill country of Ephraim. The area of the fortified sites that have been excavated, such as Hebron, Bet-Zur, Bet-El and Shiloh, is no greater than 30 dunams (Hebron: some 28 dunams; Bet-Zur: 8 to 12 dunams; Bet-El: 15 dunams; and Shiloh: 17 dunams.) Even if these sites were densely populated, the number of their inhabitants was no more than a few hundred. Furthermore, residential quarters were not found. The small area of the sites, together with the lack of residential quarters, make it impossible to view the fortified sites as city-states similar to the coastal plain and the valleys.

To find a solution to these problems, Israel Finkelstein raises another possibility,[450] based on the studies by M.B. Rowton in the mountainous regions of West Asia.[451] Finkelstein believes that some of the fortified sites were not city-states in the usual sense of the term, but rather outposts fortified by local warlords, who ruled over a mixed populace of nomads and a sedentary population (called Dimorphic Chiefdoms). These sites served as the domiciles of the ruler and the aristocracy, as storehouses for vital products, and as religious sites, more to show off the power of the chieftain than to provide for the defense of the principality.

Assuming that the historical sources from the 19th and 14th centuries BCE reflect this period as well, Finkelstein claims that the rulers of the mountain outposts enjoyed autonomy, but were subordinate to two large political entities: Shechem and Jerusalem, themselves mountain outposts as well.

Each region must be examined individually. If we adopt Finkelstein's approach, a small, fortified site without residential quarters was a local ruler's mountain outpost, while a larger site with residential quarters was a city-state, according to the pattern commonplace on the coastal plain. This approach solves many of the problems we have presented.

Nevertheless, the following questions must be posed:

- Are all the main sites in the hill country really fortified outposts?

- Can we demonstrate on the basis of archaeological research that Shechem and Jerusalem enjoyed a preferential status?

From the data presented in the present work, it would seem that Jerusalem does not meet the criterion for a mountain outpost, because its area is quite large.

We have already mentioned that recent excavators feel that the area of Jerusalem was about 60 dunams. According to the topographic logic of the line of the wall uncovered at a height of 670 meters above sea level, in the middle of the eastern slope in projection A and in area E, and on the basis of the distribution of finds in various parts of the site, this estimate seems reasonable. The giant towers uncovered in the excavations by Ronny Reich and Eli Shukrun, near the Gihon Spring which is located at the bottom of the eastern slope of the City of David, point to the possibility that the area of the city during the Middle Bronze Age was larger than previously thought, and may actually have occupied the entire slope.

It appears that Jerusalem was the largest town in the Judean Hills (over three times as large as the other sites), and only those sites in the north of the Hills of Menashe were of the same approximate size. Jerusalem was small in comparison with central sites in the lower parts of the country such as Tel-el-Ajul, Lachish, Megiddo and Hatzor (the area of each is over 100 dunams), yet larger than sites such as Tel Batash (40 dunams), Tel Bet-Mirsim (30 dunams), Bet-Shemesh in the low lands (40 dunams) and Bet-Shean (38 dunams).

The size of Jerusalem testifies to its preferential status.[452] To this, we may add the data already introduced in our discussion of the settlement pattern in the Judean Hills, i.e., that over half the built-up area in the Judean Hills is concentrated around Jerusalem.

In the Hills of Menashe, the situation is more complex because there is no one site prominently larger than all the others. While Shechem is spread out over an area of 40 to 50 dunams, despite the extensive excavations carried out on the site, no residential quarters have been uncovered.[453] Furthermore, additional sites of similar size or even larger were found in the Menashe Survey. At the same time, it seems that Shechem and its environs did enjoy a preferential status, since the sites are concentrated mainly in the Shechem Basin.

The End of Middle Bronze Culture, a New Look

The hundreds of settlements in the central hill country came to a violent end, signs of which are found in most of the sites located in the central hill country and in adjacent regions. These signs, of destruction and conflagration, indicate that the destruction encompassed wide swathes of Israel (including regions outside the central hill country and its immediate surroundings). Signs of violence have been found in Shechem, Shiloh, Bet-El, in Gibeon, Bet-Zur and in nearby areas, as in Tel Bet-Mirsim and Bet-Shemesh on the plains and Jericho in the southern part of the Jordan Valley.[454]

Egyptian historical sources provide a logical explanation for the causes of this destruction and for the time it took place. According to these records, the rise of the New Kingdom in the mid-16th century BCE, the conquest of Seruhen in the northwest Negev and the military campaigns of Thutmose III in the first half of the 15th century are the main, if not the only, causes of the destruction of the MBA settlements in Canaan.[455]

A contrasting opinion has been expressed, claiming that the historical records do not necessarily indicate that the systematic destruction of Canaanite towns were the result of the

Egyptian military campaigns.[456] In fact, the Thutmose list dealing with his military campaigns does not mention a single site
from the hill country. Furthermore, the results of the archaeological excavations and survey carried out in various sites in the
hill region and in Jericho provide grounds for a second opinion:
it appears that the hill country sites were not destroyed over a
short period of time, but rather over many years.

To be released from the "chains" of the traditional explanation of the Egyptian responsibility for the overall destruction
of the MBA culture requires providing alternate explanations
and dating for the conclusion of the period. Aharon Kempinski
proposed linking the destruction of the central hill sites with
the founding of the "Hyksos" center in the southern part of the
coastal plain and their abandoning of the hilly region.[457] This
would mean that the destruction of the sites in the hills began
in the days of the 15th dynasty, i.e., as far back as the 17th century
BCE.

In contrast, Piotr Bienkowski believes[458] that the destruction of the sites of this period resulted from a combination of
a number of factors including internal regional struggles, an
Egyptian military campaign, and an economic crisis. Adam Zertal proposes linking the destruction of some of the sites to the
drying-up of springs in the eastern part of the Hills of Menashe,[459] while Finkelstein believes that the destruction may be
due to the penetration of Hurrian and other northern elements
into Israel.[460]

This theory, developed by Nadav Na'aman, views the penetration of these northern elements as the main cause of the collapse of the Canaanite urban set-up. The new inhabitants slowly destroyed the settlement and trade arrangements in Canaan.
The campaign of Thutmose III took place at the end of a long
period of collapse and was carried out mainly in the coastal
plain, while the rest of the country fell without even fighting a
battle.[461]

Shlomo Bunimovits, too, claims that the split political

structure in the hill country and the hostile acts between the political factions there are the main reasons for the destruction of its sites. At the same time, he agrees that, "it is clear that the 'finishing touch' was administered to the old political order in Israel by Thutmose III."[462]

This multiplicity of proposals indicates that we actually have no notion of the causes that lead to the destruction of the MBA sites! The dates of this destruction are no more than speculation. Only one thing is agreed on, the period came to an end in violent destruction, just as the Early Bronze Age ended and as the Iron Age was to end at a later date.

This lack of agreement amongst the scholars necessitates a re-examination of conventional knowledge, particularly regarding the dating of the destruction of these sites. So long as this destruction was attributed to Thutmose III, we had a logical link between archaeological findings and an historical source; the moment this link was cut, there is no longer any need to date the destruction (or most of it) to this century. Furthermore, if we accept the middle of the 16th century BCE as the date of the destruction of the settlements of this period, a problem will arise regarding the 15th century BCE.

15th Century BCE, the Problematic Century

The opinions above are all based on the assumption that the destruction of the towns of the MBA took place no later than the 16th century BCE. Accepting this assumption raises many problems in connection with the 15th century. This period is described as a time when only a few small settlements existed, in contrast with the 14th century, when many settlements were rebuilt throughout the country.

This description is extremely problematic, since it does not match the Egyptian sources of the period, nor is it logical from a geographical-historical point of view.

An examination of the settlement situation throughout Judea and Samaria shows that in this period there was not even a single settlement south of the Jezreel Valley along the ridge of the central hill district.[463] This fact is surprising, because all archaeological periods are represented in the hill country, to one extent or another, except for this one. Is this "vacuum" reasonable? Is it possible that for over 100 years no settlements were established, and no nomads frequented the region?

The contradiction with Egyptian sources is even more prominent. A known source is the description of the Canaan campaign of Thutmose III, and the battle at Megiddo. His detailed description of the campaign notes some 70 settlements he passed on his way to the coastal plain. A central site noted in this campaign is Megiddo, which was a fortified settlement, that was besieged by Thutmose III for approximately seven months.[464]

This account does not fit in with the archaeological findings on two points:

- On the coastal plain in this period there were only a few settlements, a fact which does not match the 70 settlements noted by name in the description of Thutmose's campaign; and

- His description of the battle for Megiddo refers to a large, fortified city, whereas archaeological research reveals that the settlement dated to the period of Thutmose III (stratum IX) was small and unfortified.[465]

How can the description of the military campaign be reconciled with archaeological findings?

Moreover, the Egyptian sources show that the second half of the 15th century BCE was a period of instability. Amenhotep II embarked on three military campaigns, two of them in Syria and one in Israel.[466] The campaign to Israel focused mainly on the Sharon, Samaria, the Jezreel Valley and the Lower Galilee. This is the first time that an Egyptian source tells of an Egyptian king's military campaign that took place only in Israel (since scholars in Egypt use other chronologies, it is believed that the campaign took place in the second half of the 15th century BCE).

According to these sources, at this time in Israel there was a significant force that annoyed the Egyptian king. At the conclusion of the description of the campaign, this source gives a detailed list of various population groups numbering some 90,000 people that were taken as captives to Egypt.[467] While there are some who claim that this is actually a summing-up of all his military campaigns and not a description of the captives taken in Amenhotep II's final campaign only, it is clear that during the 15th century many were actually taken captive from Canaan to Egypt. Yet it appears that Amenhotep II did not succeed in putting down the unrest in Canaan. His successor, Thutmose IV, was compelled to carry out military campaigns, one of which was against Gezer on the inland plain. Captives were taken to Egypt on this campaign as well.

The picture we receive from the Egyptian sources is that Canaan was at this time a restless, unstable land of considerable population with a significant military force. This description, as noted above, contrasts starkly with the picture reflected by archaeological finds. These problems led to a re-examination of the argument that the MBA settlements had already been destroyed in the 16th century BCE.

The Destruction of Alalakh, and the End of the MBA

Fixing the 16th century BCE as the transition period between the Middle Bronze Age and the Late Bronze Age is based in the main on a combination of Babylonian sources, Hittite sources, astronomical observations, and archaeological finds.

On the basis of a list of observations made of the planet Venus in the days of Ammitsaduka, king of Babylon, known as "Ammitsaduka's Venus Table", and the chronological lists of various kings, astronomers and Assyriologists have drawn up timetables of the reigns of various kings and of events mentioned in Babylonian sources.[468] Hayim Tadmor notes that the astronomical data make numerous possibilities feasible, so the decision must be in accordance with an historical criterion independent of those figures. Another difficulty is that the original tablets recording the observations have not survived, and so we have only late copies available to us.

The archaeologists of Israel accept the approach known as "the middle chronology" which presumes that Babylon was destroyed at the onset of the 16th century BCE by the Hittite king, Murashili.[469] According to Hittite sources, the city of Alalakh in northern Syria was destroyed a few years earlier by the grandfather of Murashili, Khatushili I, and this destruction is found in archaeological stratum VII. The date of the destruction of Alalakh VII, in light of the Babylonian sources, is between 1620 and 1615 BCE.[470]

Stratum V at Alalakh is dated a few decades later than the destruction of stratum VII Alalakh, i.e., the middle of the 16th century. Unique vessels known as bichrome vessels[471] were discovered in this stratum. These vessels also were found in various sites in this Israel, including Megiddo stratum IX and Tel Ajul City II. This last was destroyed in a great fire. In the stratum of that fire, many bichrome vessels were found. Tel el-Ajul has been identified by Aharon Kempinski with the town of Seruhen, which was destroyed by Yahmose, the founder of the New Kingdom in Egypt in the middle of the 16th century BCE.[472]

Summary

Babylonian and Hittite sources enable us to date the destruction of Alalakh VII. Thus, we are able to date the destruction of Alalakh V as well. The existence of bichrome vessels in stratum V makes it possible to date various strata elsewhere as well.[473] Bichrome vessels have been found in many MBA destruction strata, so much so that the bichrome vessel has become the indicator of the end of MBA and the onset of LBA.[474] This fact fits the Egyptian sources dealing with the establishment of the New Kingdom and with the military campaigns of the early kings of the Egyptian 18th dynasty. The conclusion reached by scholars is that the destruction of the cities of the MBA occurred during the 16th century BCE.

The Problems with this Theory

The dates determined in this way have raised a number of problems, especially because they do not correspond with the dates of the Mycenean and Cypriote vessels found at Alalakh.

Leonard Woolley, who excavated Alalakh, points out in his excavation report that Mycenean vessels dating from the beginning of the 14th century BCE were found in the Nakam-pa palace in stratum IV, while according to the Babylonian chronology this stratum dates from the middle of the 15th century BCE.[475]

Other scholars who analyzed the ceramic findings in strata V-VII at Alalakh preferred later dates (known as "lower" ones). Marie-Henriette C. Gates chose to use the date 1575 BCE as the year of the destruction of stratum VII, and the year 1460 BCE as the date for Alalakh V on the basis of the Cypriote pottery found at the site.[476] William G. Dever prefers to date the destruction of stratum VII from 1550 BCE.[477] A similar conclusion is drawn by Thomas McClellan, who claims that the pottery of stratum VII resembles closely that of stratum V and that there is no great time gap between the two strata.[478] For our purposes, his conclusion is that stratum V should be dated from the middle of the 15th century BCE.

In light of the analysis of McClellan and Gates, Dever proposed ascribing the destruction of the Middle Bronze Age to Thutmose III and to adopt a new term to relate to the period between 1500 and 1450 BCE. He calls it MBIII/LBIA.[479] Like Dever, Manfred Bietak also claimed that there was a degree of uncertainty regarding the dating of various sites and that consequently he, too, suggests that there was a transition period between the 16th century and the middle of the 15th century BCE. He termed this period MCIIC/LBIA.[480]

It should be noted that these two scholars who disagree with one another on many topics do agree that it was only in the middle of the 15th century BCE that the transition period between the Middle and Late Bronze Ages comes to its end.

The analysis of the pottery finds at Alalakh does not match the Babylonian chronology, yet research still favors the Babylonian sources in comparison with the pottery analyses, and the accepted chronology remains unchanged.

The Approach of Gasche and his Colleagues

In 1998, a study was published, which altered the historical picture in Babylon. The archaeologists studying Babylon had been noticing for some time that there was a lack of coordination between the ceramic findings, which demonstrated a sequential development of pottery and the historical evidence indicating a settlement gap between the destruction of Middle Babylon (dated to the onset of the 16th century BCE) and the 14th century BCE beginning of renewed settlement in Babylon. As a result, a new study was carried out by various scholars in the fields of astronomy, Assyriology and archaeology and written about by Hermann Gasche and his colleagues.[481]

These scholars reached the conclusion that the destruction of Babylon by Murashili took place 90 years later than originally thought, i.e., in 1499 BCE. For our purposes, this emendation means that Alalakh VII was destroyed at the end of the 16th century BCE and not at the end of the 17th century, as had generally been assumed until now. It can thus be deduced that the destruction of stratum V dates from the middle of the 15th century BCE, just as the bichrome pottery dates from the 15th century. The amended chronology in Babylon matches the ceramic analyses carried out in the Alalakh excavations.[482] Despite this questioning of convention, and despite the significant change that has been adopted as a result in accepted chronology, the approach of Gasche and his colleagues has begun to seep into the literature dealing with this period in Babylon.[483]

The central question from our point of view is how this change can affect research in Israel. According to the amended Babylonian chronology, bichrome pottery can be dated no earlier than the 15th century BCE, thus fixing the end of the MBA at the second half of that century. Therefore, the fortified MBA settlements continued to exist all through the 15th century BCE (roughly the period of Joshua in Israelite history).

The Significance of the New Chronology

- •This chronology solves all the questions we posed at the beginning of the chapter. There was no settlement gap in the 15th century BCE in the Judean Hills or in Samaria, since the central MBA settlements in the hill country such as Shiloh, Shechem, Bet-El, Gibeon etc. continued to exist, just like the other settlements in the country, at least until the middle of the 15th century BCE.

- • The descriptions of the Egyptian campaigns that tell of the existence of many strong settlements in the country actually match the archaeological picture dating from the end of the MBA (for an estimate of the population of the country in the MBA, see above).

- •Stratum IX in unfortified Megiddo belongs to a later stage than the period of Thutmose III; Stratum X in Megiddo, which apparently was fortified, was the city conquered by Thutmose III.

This new chronology resolves four more puzzles, which have stumped scholars for many years.

The first concerns Megiddo. The traditional view, identifying stratum IX at Megiddo as the stratum destroyed by Thutmose III creates an unexplained gap between it and stratum VIII. The founding of the latter has been ascribed by recent excavators to the end of the 14th century BCE (according to David Ussishkin) or to the middle of that century (according to Israel Finkelstein).[484] It is unclear, then, what happened at Megiddo between the conquest of Thutmose III in the first half of the 15th century and the middle of the 14th century BCE. Should the period of unprepossessing stratum IX be extended from the 16th to the 14th centuries, as required by the traditional chronology? It is reasonable to assume that significant changes took place in the plan of the city, following the extended siege (seven months) of Thutmose III and these changes would be the result of renewed Egyptian rule of this central city. How is it possible, then, that this has never found expression in the findings at the site?

According to the proposed new chronology, stratum X is the stratum conquered by Thutmose III, while stratum IX was established only after the Egyptian conquest. This stratum lasted until the middle or even till the end of the 14th century BCE, as the most recent excavations at Megiddo have in fact shown.

The second puzzle is the problem of the archives at Taanakh. According to the head of the excavation, "There was no meaningful settlement here between the mid-15th century and the end of the 13th century BCE."[485] However, the excavation unearthed documents in cuneiform script that date approximately from the year 1450 BCE! From these documents, it may be concluded that Egypt was involved in what transpired in Megiddo and in Taanakh. Furthermore, there was a considerable military force equipped with chariots maintained there.[486] The dating of these documents does not conform to the decision of the excavator that there was no real settlement at this site. The later, amended chronology moves the destruction of Taanakh to the end of the 15th century, thus bringing the archives into accord with the existence of a developed settlement in the stratum dating from this period.

The third puzzle concerns Gezer, in the low lands. Egyptian sources tell of the Gezer campaign carried out by Thutmose IV, who reigned at the close of the 15th century BCE. These sources also say that captives were taken.[487] In the archaeological excavations directed by William G. Dever at the site, no settlement was found that could be ascribed to the 15th century BCE.[488] With the new dating approach, however, the period of the MBA settlement there lasted until the 15th century BCE, so it is indeed possible that Thutmose IV destroyed Gezer, and not his grandfather, Thutmose III.

Finally, the "low chronology" solves yet another major

problem in the archaeological study of Israel. For years, the question has been raised regarding the relationship between Hatzor and Mari. In the archives found at Mari, an important city that was located on the bank of the Euphrates in northern Syria, there is correspondence and other documents indicating well-developed relations between Mari and Hatzor in the Upper Galilee. From this correspondence, we learn that Hatzor was an important city that maintained commercial ties with Mari. Yet Mari was conquered and razed to the ground by Hammurabi, according to the accepted (middle) chronology, in the mid-18th century BCE. In other words, the letters date from a period preceding the destruction of Mari, i.e., the first half of the 18th century BCE. However, archaeological excavations reveal that the large city of Hatzor was built and fortified only at the onset of the 18th century *at the very earliest*, i.e., at the beginning of MBA II.[489] How could Hatzor have maintained such complex relations with Mari, including the dispatch of gold, silver, precious stones, (and even musicians)[490] at so initial a stage in the development of Hatzor?

Is it possible that the fortification of Hatzor took place at a somewhat earlier date? It is more likely that the chronology proposed by Gasche provides the solution to this problem. According to his approach, Hammurabi, the conqueror of Mari, lived decades later, i.e., at the turn of the 17th century (1696-1654 BCE). If this is indeed the case, Mari was destroyed during the 17th century BCE, at the time that Hatzor was already a large, important city. That it maintained strong economic ties with Mari is reasonable at this stage in its development.[491]

The new "low" chronology in Babylon, as advocated by Gasche and his colleagues, meshes well with the ceramic findings in Alalakh, with Egyptian sources regarding Israel, with the geographical logic of the central hill country of Israel and with the archaeological finds at Megiddo, Gezer, Taanakh and Hatzor.

Nevertheless, the archaeologists of Israel have not amended the relevant Israel data despite the changes made by the Assyriologists and astronomers who have studied the history of Babylon. This is a fact worthy of special notice. Since research in Israel has come up with no independent data enabling us to date the close of the Middle Bronze Age (at the present stage, Carbon-14 testing is not sufficiently conclusive in this matter), our data is based mainly on Babylonian chronology. One would expect that in the wake of the change in Babylonian chronology, a parallel change would have taken place in Israeli chronology. This has not occurred.[492]

Conclusions

The central chronological archaeological anchor demarcating the conclusion of the MBA is the existence or absence of bichrome pottery. The dating of this pottery depends on the analysis of Babylonian and Hittite sources. The study carried out by Gasche and his colleagues indicates that the Babylonian sources, the archaeology of Alalakh, as well as sources in Israel and Egypt can be collated, and that the end of the MBA should be dated some 100 years later than previously held.

However, even if we accept Gasche's new analysis, a question still remains regarding the "lifespan" of this pottery, which may have extended well beyond 100 years. It is quite possible that two different sites where bichrome pottery was found in the stratum marking their destruction, were actually destroyed at two different points in time, decades apart.

Moreover, the fact that no bichrome pottery has been found in the hill country sites raises a question, does its absence from those sites stem from their having been destroyed prior to the manufacture of the bichrome pottery characteristic of the period, or perhaps from the fact that this pottery never came into use in this region?

It would seem that the only solid facts remaining are the Egyptian sources dealing with the military campaigns of the kings of the 18th dynasty, which indicate that a series of conquests and exiles took place. If we accept these descriptions as reliable, then these conquests what transpired in their wake greatly influenced the settlement array in Israel.

All the above leads to the conclusion that although we have no solid evidence, it is more reliable to link the destruction of the MBA settlements to the campaigns of Amenhotep II and of Thutmose IV and to the numerous exiles carried out by these two kings.

It is by no means impossible that the weakening of the Canaanite cities served as a convenient prelude to the entrance into the country and the strengthening of the nomadic forces that appear in this period. These forces are mentioned many times in the El-Amarna documents which were composed several decades later, where they are called '*prw*. This population may well have been the Hebrews of the Book of Joshua.[493]

A Summary of the Archaeological Picture in the Middle Bronze Age

The Judean Hills are a closed, unified mountainous bloc. To the east and south of this bloc are dry areas, which come very close to the mountainous ridge. Even in the areas which are not particularly dry, agricultural lands are limited because of the rocky substratum. While movement over the mountain ridge is fairly convenient, the slopes to the east and to the west are steep.

Many scholars have considered geographical structure and climatic conditions as causes of the differences in material culture and in settlement patterns between the hill country and the plains, both regarding the overall dimensions of the phenomenon in the Mediterranean basin,[494] and regarding Israel.[495] The proximity of international roads that passed, naturally, through flat areas, and the existence of seaports led to the development of a culture open to external influences on the plains, which was in fact an integral part of the coastal culture throughout the Levant. In contrast, the mountainous topography made movement difficult and rendered it impossible to build large cities in the hill country like those in the plains and valleys. Difficulties in transportation to the Judean Hills generated a conservative material culture that absorbed innovations extremely slowly. This was best phrased by the French historian Fernand Braudel, "Urban civilization in the lower regions penetrated into the mountainous world incompletely and slowly. The hills resist historical changes together with the blessings and burdens they entail, or they accept them with reservations."[496]

Yet the central hill country itself is not uniform, and should be divided into smaller units. Mountainous areas crisscrossed by wide valleys providing greater accessibility and with more comfortable routes to the flatlands (the Hills of Menashe), as opposed to other, less accessible hilly regions which also have less comfortable geographical and climatic conditions (the Judean Hills).

The geographical boundaries are also significant from the point of view of culture and settlement. While the borders to the east, south, and west are quite clear geographically, the northern border of the Judean Hills, i.e., the northern part of the hills in the area of Bet-El, which is ambiguous from a geographical point of view, reflects a shift in cultural characteristics. This border was significant in later periods as well.[497]

The following is a summary of historical settlement patterns we have discussed in this book. This is based on an examination of 140 sites, approximately forty of which have already been excavated. The latter include the central sites of the region, unfortified settlements, and many gravesites.

Intermediate Bronze Age

After the destruction of the Early Bronze Age settlements, there began a process of resettlement throughout the Judean Hills, at sites that had not been settled earlier. The new array included unfortified settlements built on slopes adjoining fertile valleys as well as a widespread diffusion of a nomadic population, the traces of which are to be discerned in the hundreds of burial sites unearthed throughout the central hill country, especially in the Judean Hills. The large concentrations of burial sites were found mostly in semi-arid regions to the east and to the south, but large concentrations of graves were found also in the Gush Etzion region, in the northern part of the Hebron Hills and in Jabel Qa'qir to the west of Hebron, on the border of the raised lowlands. This style of burial is characteristic of the southern part of the central hill country (and of nearby Jericho), but is almost non-existent anywhere else in the country.

The Judean Hills are unique insofar as the pottery found there is concerned. William G., Dever[498] appreciated this fact, and defined the pottery of the hill country as a separate collection (CH). Signs of burnishing and of colored ornamentation, which began to develop in the plains are absent in the Judean Hills in this period as well, just as in the later periods.

The architecture of the settlements excavated in the Jerusalem area (the Refaim Valley and the Zimri Stream) is quite simple and resembles that of other parts of the country; its uniqueness rests in the fact that the structures are built to accommodate terraces or steps on a slope. The topographical structure dictated the building of rectangular structures along the contour lines of the hills, on the natural terraces on the slope.

From a study made of the unfortified settlements it seems that their inhabitants engaged in agriculture, mainly the growing of grains, and that their livestock included sheep, cattle, and pigs.

These economic branches underwent no substantial change in the Middle Bronze Age either, except for the fact that the ratio of cattle to sheep grew larger.

Even after the abandonment of the settlements of this period, at the close of the third millennium BCE or the start of the second millennium BCE, certain elements of this society continued to subsist throughout the Judean Hills in the Middle Bronze Age. This assumption is based on burial customs and on certain ceramic characteristics that continued to exist at the onset of the second millennium BCE.

Middle Bronze Age I

The severe crisis that befell the Judean Hills at the onset of the second millennium BCE is seen in the abandonment of most of the permanent settlements and in the nomadic population overwhelming the region.

An analysis of the findings from the graves to the north of the Hebron Hills and in the Gibeon area is indicative of a concentration of nomads in these regions. The findings point to new ceramic characteristics which have reached the hill country, originating in the pottery of the coastal plain. At the same time, traditional ceramic elements managed to survive. Burnishing, which is accepted as a clear indication of MBA I in the low-lying regions, is almost completely absent from the hill country.

Burial customs remained as they had been, contrary to the coastal plain, where new burial customs penetrated, such as burial in crates or in jars. Furthermore, the widespread process of urbanization that occurred on the plains and in the valleys in that period did not include the Judean Hills.

The small amount of pottery found in a few sites indicates the existence of only a few small settlements. It should be stressed that up until now no buildings have been found in the Judean Hills from this period. Only in the 18th century BCE did the MBA culture reach this area to any significant degree.

Middle Bronze Age II

A process of accelerated settlement began during the 18th and 17th centuries BCE, and both fortified and unfortified permanent settlements were built. A nomadic population co-existed with the population of the permanent settlements, apparently in symbiosis with it.

In the Jerusalem and Hebron Hills, the custom of burying in shaft-graves became less common, as it began to be customary to perform simple burials in the settlements or in close proximity to them. It seems that the changes in burial custom and the development of urbanization marked the penetration of a new population into the Judean Hills from the lower regions of the country.

The division of the Judean Hills into secondary units made it possible to identify differences in settlement pattern between the various regions. In the hill country of Bet-El, there were many small settlements around two major sites, Bet-El and Gibeon. In the Jerusalem Hills, a smaller number of settlements have been found, but their area was very large, and they seem to have been connected with Jerusalem, the largest city in the Judean Hill country. The broad valleys of the Refaim and Soreq Streams and the flowing springs led to the development of this pattern.

In the Hills of Hebron, there were fewer small villages spread along the roads, without any ties to the fortified cities of Bet-Zur and Hebron.

An analysis of the ceramic findings from the survey sites and from the excavation sites indicates that in the Bet-El Hills, the unfortified settlements began to be abandoned prior to the end of the period. At the very same time, large and small unfortified settlements were established in the hills of Jerusalem and of Hebron.

Regarding pottery, too, the Judean Hills display a number of unique regional characteristics (even when compared with the hill country further to the north). As in earlier periods, the pottery showed no signs of burnishing, nor was any imported or colored pottery found there. Petrographic tests indicate that the material the pottery was made from is local and uniform, unlike Shiloh (which is indeed not far from the Judean Hills, but is part of another region), where imported pottery and decorated vessels were found, and where vessels were made of numerous diverse materials. Moreover, we have seen that various types of local vessels found at Shiloh and Shechem were

Chronological Table of Excavated Settlements in the Central Hill Country

SITE	Inter-mediate Bronze Age	MBA I	MBA II	LBA (14th century)
SHECHEM	-	+	+ fortifications	+
TELL FAR'AH NORTH	-	- graves	+ fortifications	+
SHILOH	-	-	+ fortifications	only sherds
BET-EL	+	+	+ Fortifications	+
GIBEON	+ Graves	- graves	+ settlement and graves	- graves
JERUSALEM	+ Graves	graves	+ fortifications	graves and sherds
ZIMRI STREAM	+	-	+	-
REFAIM VALLEY	+	+ one grave	+	-
MANAHAT	+	-	+	+?
BET-ZUR	-	-	+ fortifications	+?? only sherds
HEBRON	-	+	+ fortifications	sherds and graves

(- Indicates no settlement found)

conspicuously absent from the sites in the Judean Hills. These characteristics point to the existence of local centers where the pottery was manufactured, as well as to the isolation of this region, even when compared to the hill country of Ephraim and Menashe.

This topographic structure affected the architecture in the settlements as well. The Middle Bronze Age is the first period in the history of Israel, during which widespread construction took place on hill slopes, rather than on summits or on rocky ridges. The slopes and natural terraces forced the people of the time to adapt their structures to the terrain, creating unique, large structures with multiple levels of flooring within them.

Many settlements belonging to this complex array have actually been excavated (see the table titled "Chronological Table of Excavated Settlements," which sums up the settlement process in the central hill country from the close of the third millennium until the last third of the second millennium BCE). Of the eleven settlements excavated, eight are in the Judean Hills and three are in Ephraim and Menashe. Eight of these are central sites, documented in historical sources.

In the six sites located in the hills of Bet-El and Jerusalem, activity began as early as the Intermediate Bronze Age; in contrast, Shechem and Hebron were founded in MBA I, while Tel Far'ah North, Shiloh and Bet-Zur were established only in the MBA II, i.e., in the 18th or 17th centuries BCE. The unfortified settlements in the hill country of Jerusalem, too, were founded in the 17th century BCE.

From the table, it appears that some activity transpired in the Late Bronze Age in eight sites, but to a somewhat limited degree compared to the early period. Not only does the comparison between MBA II and LBA II show a considerable quantitative different in the degree of settlement activity, it also indicates a substantial change with regard to the nature of the settlements, their size, and distribution.

CHAPTER

SUMMARY AND CONCLUSIONS

his book is based on three elements: the physical geography of the Judean highlands and the adjacent areas, archaeology and the Book of Books, the Bible. Each of these elements makes its unique contribution to the historical picture we have presented.

Geography

The Judean hill country is the highest inhabited region in western Israel. While the highest mountain peaks are not in this part of the country, as an entire geographical region it is undoubtedly the highest. Its high point is in Halhul in the highlands of Hebron, some 3,300 feet above sea level; Mount Ba'al Hatzor, in the hills of Beth-El, is 15 feet lower.

Rocky and cold with little agricultural land, this region has played a central role in this work. At the same time, the importance of the lowland with its soft, crumbly bedrock; of the dry Judean Desert dropping suddenly to the basin of the Dead Sea; of the Be'er-Sheva Valley; of the high and dry Negev plateau; and even of Samaria, crisscrossed with chasms, with its broad, fertile valleys, have not been overlooked.

We have indicated that the geographical structure of the Judean highlands is what led to the isolation of the hill country, and that its inhabitants, struggling against the trials of nature, did not tend to embrace innovations, changes, or passing fashions. The historical processes and the rapid changes taking place in the plains and along the sea coast were slower and more limited in the highlands, and especially in the hill country of Judea. Looking towards the Judean Hills from the western coastal area, from the more heavily populated region of the country, where the international coastal road passes by, one sees a wall. An almost impassable wall, except for a number of routes that wind their way through it.

This is the reason a number of regional battles took place along the roads leading to the Judean highlands, in both ancient and in modern times. The battle between Joshua bin-Nun and the five kings of the South was fought on the slope of Bet-Horon, linking the inland plain with the northern part of the Jerusalem Hills; David stopped the Philistine advance toward the hills of Hebron in his battle with Goliath in the Valley of the Elah; and Judah Maccabee struck at the Greek general Siron in the latter's attempt to climb the Bet-Horon slope. During the 1948 War of Independence, the Jordanians blocked the Israel Defense Forces, a little further west, in the Ayalon valley, cutting Jerusalem off from the coastal plain; while along the route to Jerusalem between Sha'ar Ha-Gai and Castel many serious battles took place between the Israeli Defense Forces and the Arab forces. From ancient times to the present day, there is a natural tendency to hold back when faced with the ascent from the coastal plain to the hilltops, since the attempt to do so involves risking many lives.

Anyone studying the history of this region must take into account the geographical and mental isolation of the hill country and its inhabitants, relative to the inhabitants of the lowlands. For instance, we have seen that while in the coastal plain urban culture had already begun to develop in the 20th century BCE, nomads continued to roam the highlands and continue their old way of life. It was only in the 18th century BCE that urbanization began to take place in the Judean Hills. The complex geographical and topographical conditions in the hills made it difficult to build large cities there. The massive earth ramparts characteristic of Middle Bronze Age sites in the lowlands and valleys are almost non-existent in the highlands, apparently because of the lack of appropriate soil in the hill country. The decorated and attractive pottery found on the plains, as well as the imported pottery from overseas, are less common in the hills than on the plains.

The differences between the highlands and lowlands were especially prominent during Iron Age I (the period of the Israelite settling in). The geographical division of the land produced a clear ethnic division between the Israelites in the hill country and the Canaanites, Philistines and other sea peoples on the plains. While an urban culture developed on the plains, made up of large, fortified cities with public buildings including Aegean-style temples, the people in the hills dwelt in small, unfortified settlements displaying uniform, local architecture. The pottery of the plains was decorated, variegated and influenced by Greek culture, while the pottery in the hill country was simple, had few adornments and showed minimal variation.

Can it be concluded from this that the hill population was culturally retarded relative to the population of the plains? No, for it was among these Israelites that alphabetic script advanced, where the people on the whole were literate. This script is what brought about the revolution in reading throughout the world because of its relative simplicity. Even if the inhabitants of the highlands seem to have been technologically inferior, culturally they were superior to their neighbors to the west. The fact is that the descendants of the Philistines adopted the Hebrew script and language, as seems clear from the 7th century BCE inscription found in Philistine Ekron.

In most parts of the world, the inhabitants of the plains are the standard-bearers of progress; this was true of Israel during much of its history. In the First Temple Period, however, a different and surprising situation developed. The inhabitants of the highlands accumulated economic, military, and cultural power, so that in time they took control of the plains and influenced them both materially and in matters of writing and language. Hebrew texts discovered in various sites on the coastal plain and in the Negev, as well as the finding of typical Judean pottery outside the borders of Judea, indicate the spreading of the highland culture to the plains. Contrary to all geographical rules, the largest city in Israel in this period was hilltop Jerusalem, itself divided from surrounding terrain by rifts and chasms and with "mountains all around it". The monotheistic faith that gained strength there burst out of the Judean hill country, crossing the geographical borders of Israel, to become the heritage of all peoples who share in Western or Islamic culture.

Archaeology

The history we have formulated of the Judean highlands is largely based on archaeological research that deals in rocks, bones, potsherds, and carbonized seeds. The experience of decades in this field has opened a previously unrecognized gateway enabling us to become familiar with human history. Archaeology has opened up a world of information that can contribute to our understanding of the difference between the hill country and the lowlands. It has taken note of settlement structure over the ages and has recorded the changes that took place in it.

Archaeology teaches us the type of houses in which human beings lived, as well as the building materials they used, the tools they employed, and the food they consumed. It informs us, too, of their burial customs and of the spiritual world their customs reflect. The unearthing of various sanctuaries and ritual artifacts add yet another stratum to our comprehension of their beliefs and their ways of life.

The description of the settlement patterns in various periods and the relationships between the fortified cities, the villages, and the "Hatzeirim Farms" results from intensive archaeological research that has gone on for many years.

At the same time, we have noted the limitations of archaeology. It is in great need of written sources to assist us in understanding silent archaeological finds.

The "Achilles heel" of the study of the past is the lack of clear separation between objective data and the interpretation provided by researchers. Interpretation stems from a broad knowledge of the field and the experience of many years. It also reflects the opinions of the interpreter. Researchers are tempted to "adjust" data to conform to their preconceived opinions. It is sometimes difficult to distinguish between an objective and relevant description and pure interpretation. Certainty and uncertainty are often interwoven and defy attempts to unravel them. Yet, it is incumbent upon us to try to achieve a reliable and accurate picture of the past.

Such an attempt has been made in this book: we have painted a picture of the past that differs to a considerable degree with previous archaeological literature. The main points are:

1. The nomadic culture of the Intermediate Bronze Age gradually came to an end in the hill country only in the 18th century BCE, unlike the lowlands where this period ended sometime in the 20th century BCE. We learn this from the study of the artifacts found in shaft-graves in the Judean hill country. This distinction is significant for the understanding of the connection between this period and the Pa-

triarchal Era, which apparently began in the transition period between the Intermediate Bronze Age and the Middle Bronze Age.

2. As a result of the impact of discoveries made in archaeological research with regard to the chronology of ancient Babylon, all the accepted dates should be "lowered" by some 90 years. This would require that the dates regarding Israel concerning the Middle Bronze Age also be lowered. This adjustment re-dates the end of the Middle Bronze Age to the close of the 15th century BCE. This correction resolves many problems in understanding the 15th century BCE, where there appeared to be contradictions between Egyptian sources and archaeological discoveries.

3. The onset of the Iron Age in the highlands should be dated to the beginning of the 14th century BCE, or perhaps a little earlier. This dating is based on a new analysis of the pottery found at various sites and the results of Carbon 14 testing at Tel Dan. The Late Bronze Age coincided with the first part of Iron Age I and was concentrated mainly on the plains and in the valleys.

4. The inhabitants of the highlands in Iron Age I were clearly different from the inhabitants of the plains. In contrast to the developed urban culture of the Canaanites and Philistines on the plains, the inhabitants of the hill country lived in small settlements, their architecture was simple, and no public buildings have been found. Their earthenware, too, was simple and there was no great variety in vessel types. Their highland agriculture was on terraces built on the slopes of the hills. The inhabitants of the hill country came from outside Israel, from east of the Jordan River, where settlements have been found with characteristics similar to those of the hill country to the west.

5. The early dating of the onset of Iron Age I and the later close of the Middle Bronze Age match very well the de-

scription of the conquest of Israel in the days of Joshua bin-Nun.

6. The descriptions of King Solomon's vast building projects are reflected by reliable elements in archaeological research, despite repeated attempts to undermine their historical reliability. The unambiguous chronological evidence based on the description of Shishak's military campaign and on the existence of single-age settlements in the Negev, together with the similarity of the pottery found at these sites and those of Hatzor, stratum X and of Megiddo, stratum V, which are ascribed to Solomon, leaves no room for doubt.

7. A combination of Biblical sources and archaeological findings indicates that the period of the Israelite Monarchy was an era of economic prosperity, when the state organized sophisticated settlement patterns and specialized economy. Also, the number of inhabitants of Israel was extremely large, greater than it had been in previous periods.

8. Contrary to geographical logic, which would rate Jerusalem low on the hierarchic settlement scale, by the close of the First Temple Period, Jerusalem had become the largest city in the country. The settlement density around Jerusalem at that time led to the establishment of an administrative region known in Hebrew as *S'vivot Yerushalayim*, (the Environs of Jerusalem) that served as the nucleus for the resettlement of the country in the period of the Return to Zion.

9. Hirbet Qeiyafa is a site located north of the Elah Valley, dominating the main route that passes from the southern coastal plain and the Shephelah to the Hebron Mountains and the Bet Shemesh-Lachish axis, two important cities in the monarchal period. Excavations carried out in 2007 and 2008 revealed a site of some 23 dunams fortified with a monumental wall some 700 m in circumference.[499] The wall

was built of massive stones that weighed about four tons. On the western part of the site, a gate was found with four chambers typical of the Iron Age. The pottery finds were characteristic of the tenth century BCE, and the Carbon-14 tests performed on olive pits were dated to the tenth century as well. Moreover, a potsherd was found bearing a five-line inscription written in ink in "proto-Canaanite" (Ancient Hebrew) script. As of now, the content of the inscription has not been deciphered. The excavator feels that the existence of a planned fortress on this location attests to the existence of a state-type entity that built up and reinforced the area. Where was the center of that kingdom located? Quite possibly in Jerusalem. Yossi Garfinkel, the excavator, feels that the results of the excavations at Hirbet Qeiyafa offer clear evidence that urbanization in Judah had begun as early as the tenth century BCE and that this attests to a ruling monarchial force that operated in the Shephelah region. This evidence also sits well with the results of the excavations at Tel Bet Shemesh located above the Sorek Valley. Uncovered there, too, were fortifications, a public structure, an underground water reservoir, and a structure that served as a workshop for processing iron. [500]

10. Until a few years ago, most inscriptions were dated to the end of the First Temple period. Some claimed that this was evidence that in the early days of the Israelite united monarchial period the knowledge of reading and writing was not widespread. In recent years, however, a number of ostraca (potsherds that served as a platform for writing) have been published that have been dated to the tenth and ninth centuries BCE. The ever-increasing number of inscriptions from this period demonstrates the spread of Hebrew alphabetic writing as early as the monarchal period and shows that literacy was shared by broad bands of the public. A review of the distribution of inscription locations in Israel shows that the spread of Ancient Hebrew script was ex-

tant through the entire country. Inscriptions such as these have been found in Kefar Veradim in Galilee, at Tel Rehov, and at Tel Amal in the Bet Shean Valley, at Tel Zayit in the Shephelah, at Bet Shemesh and Tel Batash in the northern Shephelah, at Tel Zafit on the border of the Shephalah and at the coastal plain. [502] As mentioned above, also at Hirbet Qeiyafa in the Elah Valley. To these we must add the Gezer Calendar discovered in the early twentieth century. Striking is the fact that at this stage most of the inscriptions have been found in the Shephelah. The written evidence demonstrates a literarily developed society that existed throughout the country as early as the united monarchal period (David and Solomon).

This research picture, based on data gathered in extended on-site studies, in which dozens of archaeologists took part and upon new studies made outside of Israel, has not been properly publicized in archaeological publications. This seemingly deliberate oversight undermines our faith in "pure" archaeological research, independent of personal foibles and prejudices!

Summary

Archeological evidence is continuously accumulating that informs us of the existence of a kingdom in Judah as early as the tenth century. Undoubtedly, the findings from Edom and the Shephelah cast new light on the historical information appearing in the Bible and form a solid basis for Biblical descriptions.

It seems that the archeological community in Israel is slowly returning to the old concept of the existence of a kingdom in the Land of Israel whose capital was Jerusalem as early as the tenth century. To be sure, there are a number of archeologists who cling to the opinion negating the existence of a united kingdom, but their number is declining.

The Bible

The probable reason you are holding this book at this moment is your interest in the Bible. Involvement in Biblical research undoubtedly stems from the profound and inexplicable connection we feel to its contents, its messages, and from our desire to understand it better. Our interest in the land of Israel as the Holy Land, a concept that is so central to the Bible, impels us to become familiar with its history, as well as its natural geography. Archaeological and geographical study has yielded greater knowledge.

The Bible breathes the breath of life into the silent relics uncovered by archaeologists. It links the past with the present and provides the future with significance.

The Bible is not a history book in the modern sense of the term; yet there is no doubt that one of its aims is to bring the reader into the arena in which Biblical events took place. The Bible text devotes considerable space to detailed descriptions of the geographical locations in which various events took place, it also adds further identification of ancient sites.

For instance, on occasion the Bible mentions the ancient name of a site, as well as its name in later times. A few examples: "the valley of Siddim, that is, the Dead Sea"; "the Spring of Mishpat, that is, Kadesh" (Gen 14); "the City of Four, that is, Hebron" (Gen 23:2).

The importance attributed by the Bible to the geography of Israel (in order that we understand events that took place in the past) must not be ignored. Furthermore, the books of the Prophets, in the main, are a product of Israel and its inhabitants; they reflect to a very high degree the attitudes and spiritual-cultural world of its Hebrew inhabitants.

Biblical heroes are not heroic figures, innocent of any misdeed or mistake, engaging day after day in heroic stunts and grandiose building projects. On the contrary, while the great people of the Israelite nation are certainly people of stature, they were also human beings, flesh and blood, displaying great virtues, but also at times revealing weaknesses and errors.

For example, the Book of Genesis deals with the failures and successes of the Patriarchs mostly with regard to family matters, and much less with wars and heroism. The Bible does not deal gently with the Patriarchs, with Moses or with David; they are not described as infallible. It is clear that they pay a heavy price for their failings (despite that Moshe is referred to in the Torah as "a man of G-d" and David is described as a "Servant of G-d"). The Bible succeeds in doing this without minimizing their unique importance and value in any way.

The candor described above indicates that the Bible is a book of truth, both in describing the lives of the Patriarchs and later leaders, and in its descriptions of the real world in which they were active.

Contrary to the attitude prevalent in the ivory tower of academia, which often casts doubt on the reliability of the Bible, we have adopted an approach that integrates archaeology and the Bible by viewing them as mutually supplementary. The Bible provides the silent findings with meaning, while the findings contribute to our comprehension of the geographical and historical background the Bible sometimes omits.

The people of the Biblical era possessed history books that helped them understand their past; these were :

- *Sefer Ha-Yashar,* "The Book of the Upright" (Jos. 10:13; II Sam. 18)

- *Sefer Divrei Shelomo,* "The Book of the Words of Solomon" (I Kings 11:41)

- *Sefer Divrei Yemei Malkhei Yehudah,* "The Book of Chronicles of the Kings of Judah" (II Kings 24:5)

- *Sefer Divrei Yemei Malkhei Yisrael,* "The Book of Chronicles of the Kings of Israel" (I Kings 14:19), and

- *Sefer Milhamot Ha-Shem,* "The Book of the Wars of G-d" (Num 21:14).

The Bible directs its readers to these volumes and quotes

certain sections from them. Since these books have been lost over the generations, we are unable to locate in them the details we lack for a more complete understanding. It is our hope that archaeology will serve as their substitute to some degree. Aided by the tools science has developed, and using the Book of Books as our guide, mankind will, as ever, strive to fulfill the injunction of Deuteronomy 32:7, "Remember the days of old; understand the years of many generations."

Appendix

Joshua bin-Nun and King Solomon
in Ancient Historical Sources

modern professional historians tend by their very nature to doubt statements made by earlier historians. This is the approach of the "new" historians to the work of their predecessors; this is also the approach taken by modern historians to the historians of the Roman and Byzantine periods.

It is indeed correct for a researcher to check and re-check his own work and the contemporary principles of his research field, yet there needs be a good, demonstrable reason to ignore or to negate an ancient historical source. In contrast to the opinion prevalent amongst modern scholars, it appears that we should adopt the approach accepted in the juridical world: that one is innocent so long as his guilt has not been proved. This is how one should regard the statements made by the historians of ancient times and accept them unless it is shown that they erred. In this appendix, I will quote statements made by historians of the Roman and Byzantine periods regarding two central figures of the Biblical period: Joshua bin-Nun and King Solomon; I will attempt to clarify whether or not reasons exist to question their validity.

Joshua bin-Nun

The Byzantine historian Procopius, who lived in the 6th century CE, tells us the following:[494]

"Since the historical narrative has brought us this far [i.e., up to the wars between Bellisarius, the Byzantine commander, and the Mauris (inhabitants of North Africa); Procopius served in Bellisarius's army in his African campaigns—Y.M.], we now have to relate the story of how the Mauri peoples came to Lybia and how they settled there.

"When the Hebrews came out of the land of Egypt and reached the border of Palestine, Moses—the wise man who had led them on their way—died, and his position as leader was inherited by Joshua bin-Nun. He brought the nation into the land and conquered it. In this war, he demonstrated superhuman courage. He defeated all the tribes, quickly conquered the towns, and was considered a person no one could best. At that time, the entire coastal strip from Sidon to the Egyptian border was known as Phoenicia. All the historians of the ancient days of Phoenicia agree that in the old days a single king ruled over all that country in which large tribes made their homes, such as the Girgashites and the Jebusites and other names listed in the history book of the Hebrews. Now when this people realized that there was no way they could resist the military commander opposing them, they left the country of their ancestors and went down to nearby Egypt, but could not find a good place to settle in there as Egypt had always been overpopulated. So they went on to

Lybia and settled there in many towns, and thus they conquered all of Lybia all the way to the Pillars of Hercules [the Straits of Gibraltar—Y.M.], where they live to this very day and speak in the Phoenician tongue. They even built a fortress for themselves in one of the cities of Numedia, where there is today a settlement called Tizgis. There, nearby the big spring, there stand two marble columns,[491] on which there are engraved in the Phoenician script Phoenician words which mean 'We are the people who retreated before the highwayman Joshua bin-Nun'."

This story is also found with minor variations in excerpts from the book written by a Christian historian known as Yohanan of Antiochia, as well as in the lexicon of Sueadas the Byzantine. They carry the following version of the inscription: "We are the Canaanites whom Joshua the highwayman pursued."

Yohanan Levi notes that Procopius and Yohanan of Antiochia are two independent sources and are in no way dependent upon one another, while Sueadas mixed the two sources and added material of his own.[492]

These sources fit in well with the Jerusalem Talmud that relates that "Joshua sent three letters to Israel before [the Israelites] entered the land: anyone desiring to leave, may leave; to surrender, may surrender; to wage war, may do so. The Girgashites, believing in God, left and traveled to Africa." (*Jerusalemi Talmud*, Sh'vi'it 6, 1)

Thus, the traditions of some of the Canaanite peoples moving to North Africa are found in three different sources of the same period, though the Jerusalem Talmud was earlier -- for it was completed around the year 400 CE, while the Christian sources are later. It is likely that the tradition of the Girgashite flight to Africa originated with the Talmudic sages, and since we are talking of a source later than the period of Joshua by over 1500 years, there is room to doubt the historical veracity of these sources. However, the testimony regarding the inscription that existed in Procopius's day is a solid datum that requires a good reason to be doubted.

Yohanan Levi attempts to reconstruct the story of the inscription:

"The Christian legend concerning the Canaanite origin of the African Phoenicians crystallized with the Christian mission to Africa: it is possible that African Christians—like Augustinus [a Church Father]—who heard the name 'Canaanite' mentioned by the Phoenician inhabitants of the place, found Phoenician letters engraved on an ancient slab near the spring supplying water to the Numeidic fortress Tizgis and understood it as an inscription by the Canaanites living there. The local tradition reached the ears of Procopius who took an interest in antiquities, for it is clear from his explanation that *he himself visited the site.*"[493]

Yohanan Levi thus claims that there was indeed an inscription in Phoenician letters, but it was read incorrectly. If we are really speaking of an ancient script which has gone out of use, such as Egyptian hieroglyphics, it is extremely likely that the inhabitants did not know how to read what was written. Yet since we are talking about an ancient Phoenician-Hebrew script, this argument is unreasonable, for in this period the relevant script in its various developments was definitely used in Israel and, according to Procopius, in North Africa as well.

The Samaritans in the Byzantine period were an important force that inhabited the northern part of Samaria and portions of the coastal plain. The script employed by the Samaritans was one version of the Phoenician script that they used in their Torah scrolls, on the mosaic floors of their synagogues, and on rings. Our Talmudic sages, also, engage in various questions regarding the halachic status of the ancient Hebrew script (Babylonian Talmud, Tractate Shabbat 115b; Megilla 8b). Thus the Hebrew script known to the sages as *ketav libbona'a*, i.e., a script from Lebanon which was Phoenicia, was familiar in this period.

Procopius, a native of Caesarea which adjoined the Samaritan region who, in Yohanan Levi's opinion, visited the place, would have been able to read that inscription easily.

One may argue that even if this really was the wording of the inscription, it was written at a later stage under the influence of traditions that reached the place upon the Christian penetration of North Africa and spread about the Bible stories, including the narrative of the conquest of Israel. This argument is possible, but its likelihood is low, for in that case a familiarity with the ancient Hebrew script would have been necessary in North Africa in the early centuries CE, as well as the ideological or economic motivation to carry out the project. The existence of such motivation is unlikely, for to a person growing up with the Bible, it would be extremely undignified to be considered a member of an accursed nation ("Cursed be Canaan; a servant of servants shall he be unto his brethren" as written in Genesis 9:25) – a nation that because of the sins of its ancestor was expelled from its land by divine decree.

There is no perceivable reason not to accept the inscription as authentic. It seems reasonable that it was inscribed by those who fled from their land for fear of the "highwayman" Joshua bin-Nun, viewing him as a negative element, contrary to the view of the Bible, desiring to preserve the memory of the circumstances under which they arrived at their new home.

Just as it is possible to cast doubt on any historical source, so too this historical source can be doubted, yet to do so one requires solid evidence of a kind as yet undiscovered.

King Solomon

King Solomon, too, is mentioned in documents external to the Bible dated to the Second Temple Period. Josephus Flavius adduces in his books *Against Apion* and *Antiquities of the Jews* sources from Tyre that tell of the existence of fascinating ties between Hiram, King of Tyre, and Solomon. He states:

"Now the people of Tyre have for many years held in their possession books compiled for the public benefit [that relate] to all the world-renowned deeds performed by them and by foreign nations. In these books, it is written that the Temple in Jerusalem was built by King Solomon one hundred and forty-three years and eight months before the people of Tyre founded Carthage... for Hiram, King of Tyre, used to favor Solomon our King in remembrance of his affection for his father [King David], and generously supervised the construction, together with Solomon, in order to enhance its magnificence... and in order to demonstrate that I have not invented out of thin air all this about the legends recorded by the people of Tyre, I shall bring in evidence *Dios*, a person reliable regarding the written history of Canaan... It is said that Solomon, the ruler of Jerusalem, sent riddles to Hiram and asked him to send him riddles in return... and in addition to this scribe I shall add *Menandaros*, an inhabitant of Epsos, who recorded the deeds of all the kings who ruled over the Greeks and the foreigners [barbarians], and made a point of learning history from the books of each and every nation. He spoke of the King of Tyre as well, and then reached the days of Hiram... He used to win occasionally in the riddles sent by Solomon, King of Jerusalem." (*Against Apion* I, 17; see the short equivalent in *Antiquities of the Jews* VIII, p. 282).

While these sources mention Solomon, they contain supplements not found in the Bible regarding the riddles Solomon sent to Hiram. Josephus Flavius brings in his books statements made by many historians that preceded him; thus, he is the only source for the statements of those historians. For example, he is the source for the reports of the Greek Manathon of Egyptian history, for those of Nicholaus of Damascus and of Barusos the Babylonian. There is no reason to doubt that he actually saw the writings of these historians, including the statements of those historians dealing with the history of Tyre. These historians link the construction of the Temple in Jerusalem with an extremely important historical event in Tyrian history, i.e., the founding of Carthage, the Phoenician colony in North Africa.

It should be emphasized that the historians Dios and Menandaros were not writing the history of the Israelites, but rather the history of Tyre, and it was Solomon's involvement in the history of Tyre that brought about his being mentioned in their books. This source cannot be integrated into the description of those minimalists who try to reduce the Kingdom of Solomon to the limits of the Judean Hills. One can, of course, doubt the reliability of any historical source, but in such a case we must, of course, doubt the reliability of the lists of Egyptian dynasties adduced by Manathon in that very same book, lists generally accepted today. The connection forged by the sources from Tyre between the building of the Temple and the establishment of Carthage, an accepted historical event, reinforces the likelihood of the source being reliable.

Here, too, of course, one can argue that the ancient Tyrian historians—in the wake of the Bible stories—invented a tale intended to establish Hiram of Tyre as the leading figure, but again such an argument requires solid proof, such as, for example, that the writers of the sources of Tyre, the period of their writing being unknown, were familiar with the Book of Kings or the Book of Chronicles. So long as such evidence is not forthcoming, the source must be accepted as reliable, at least in regard to the very existence of the wise king of Jerusalem and his ties with Hiram, King of Tyre. The historical framework we have constructed is not based on these sources, but they undoubtedly help to reinforce it.

ENDNOTES

Chapter 1

[1] In writing "the final stages of its formulation," I am not referring to the writers of the books of the Bible themselves, but rather to the decisions as to which books were to be canonized and which were to remain outside Holy Scripture. See, e.g., the debate of the Jewish sages over the books of Ezekiel, Proverbs, and Ecclesiastes (Babylonian Talmud, *Shabbat* 13b). For the question of the compilers of the books, see Babylonian Talmud, *Bava Batra* 14b.

[2] A critic of poetry and culture, Menahem Ben, stated in a newspaper interview, "A terrible thing happened to Israeli secular education, which is linked to the Bible and to Hebrew. Today children do not know how to read the Bible... This inept Bible instruction... has kept the children in Israel away from the Book of Books." He goes on to say, "Quite a few people have written of me that I am the best expert on poetry in the country, and as such an expert I can state that the Bible is of divine origin. No human being can write that way." Etti Elbaum, "Dyukan" *Makor Rishon*, 11 Tishrei 5765.

Things of this nature are said by other intellectuals as well, who are not considered part of the "religious sector." Thus, e.g., says the author, S. Yizhar: "When one engages overmuch in removing the innards, no complete animal remains." Tal Bashan, "The Generation of the Desert", Weekend Supplement, *Maariv*, 7 Shevat 5763, p. 52.

³ It is reasonable to assume that if there were other historians present at that time (and there probably were), they would have preferred to stress other events and to omit stories that the compilers of the Bible saw fit to expand on. History itself has been the judge: the Bible has survived and retained its vitality, while other writings (such as *Sefer HaYashar* and the Chronicles of the Kings of Judah, both mentioned in the Bible) have sunk into oblivion.

⁴ See the article by Zeev Herzog (in Hebrew) in *Al Atar* 7 August 2000 and S. Bunimovitz, "Cultural Exegesis and the Biblical Text: Biblical Archaeology in a Post Modern Context," *Kathedra* 100, 2001 27-46.

⁵ In recent years, it has become common to make use of carbon 14 tests to achieve precise dating. There are many problems with the reliability of these tests. See, e.g., the comparisons made between the findings of different laboratories relating to the very same samples taken from the same strata. Karmi and Bar-Yosef (Heb.), "Dating by means of Carbon 14," *Qadmoniot* 89-90 (1990/1), pp. 20-25.

⁶ Ruth Amiran (Heb.). The Ancient Pottery of Eretz Yisrael, Jerusalem 1971, p.80.

⁷ For a convenient presentation of this topic, see: Gabriel Barkai (Heb.), *An Introduction to the Archaeology of the Land of Israel*, (Tel Aviv: Open University, 1990/1), Unit 9, pp. 83-88.

⁸ From this source we learn that the town of Megiddo was a fortified city; furthermore it tells us: "The conquest of Megiddo was like the conquest of a thousand cities." Shmuel Yeivin (Heb.), "Thutmose III: The Annals (Year I)," *Journal of the Society for the Study of Eretz-Israel and its Antiquities* (1934/5), pp. 152-174.

⁹ See Rivka Gonen (Heb.), "The Urbanization of Canaan on the Eve of the Israelite Conquest of the Land," Millet: *Open University Studies in the History and Culture of the Land of Israel* I, (Tel Aviv: Open University, 1983).

¹⁰ Lawrence E. Stager, "Merneptah, Israel and Sea Peoples: New Light on an Old Relief," *Eretz Israel* 18 (1985), pp. 56-64; and see additional bibliography in the article by Singer, "Egyptians, Canaanites and Philistines in the period of the Conquest and of the Judges" in Nadav Na'aman, Israel Finkelstein, eds., *From Nomadism to Monarchy* (Heb.) (Jerusalem:Yad Yitzchak Ben-Zvi, 1990), pp. 352-353. In the excavations made by Stager in Ashkelon, no wall was found. See Stager's "Ashkelon" in Ephraim Stern, ed., *The New Encyclopedia of Archaeological Excavations in the Holy Land* (Jerusalem:Carta, 1991/2). The claim has been made by some that the Egyptian craftsmen carved out the

Canaanite cities in an abstract but standard fashion, so that no details can be learned of the city itself from its representation. For a discussion of this point, see Yigael Yadin, *The Art of Warfare in Biblical Lands*, (New York:McGraw-Hill, 1963), vol. 1, pp. 96-97, and see also Rudolf Naumann, *Architektur Kleinasiens*, (Tubingen:Wasmuth, 1971), p. 312, Fig. 421, who believes that one can learn of the details of the fortifications from these representations.

[11] See Gershon Galil (Heb.), "The Size and Political Status of the Canaanite Royal Cities in the 14th Century, B.C.E." *Cathedra* 84 (1996/7), pp. 7-52.

[12] The most recent archaeological excavations stressed this problem even more. See the debate on this point between Ussishkin and Finkelstein in: Israel Finkelstein, David Ussishkin and Baruch Halpern, eds., *Megiddo III: The 1992-1996 Seasons*, (Tel Aviv:Tel Aviv University, 2000), pp. 592-594. Despite the fact that both the archaeological findings based on Mycenaean ceramics and the carbon 14 tests show unambiguously that Stratum VIII at Megiddo cannot be earlier than the end of the 14th century BCE., Finkelstein moves up the dating of this stratum by some 50 years, to the middle of the 14th century, in order to adjust them to the historical evidence as reflected in the El-Amarna letters.

[13] See: Yitzhak Meitlis, "Culture of the Mountains and the Plains During the Second Millenium B.C.E." in Yaacov Eshel, ed., *Judea and Samaria Research Studies, Vol. 9* (College of Judea and Samaria, 2000), pp. 17-26.

[14] An interesting description expressing the fear of crossing over a hilly region (the 'Iron Stream' area between Megiddo and the coastal plain) appears in an Egyptian source called the "Anastasy Papyrus A," dating from the days of Ramses II (the 13th century BCE): "Behold the crossing is to be found in a channel two thousand cubits deep... the channel is dangerous, being full of robbers hiding amongst the undergrowth... their faces are fierce and their hearts – hard... Your route is full of ravines and rocks, without any footholds... you imagine the enemy is behind you and you begin to tremble." The Hebrew translation of the Egyptian sources can be found in Avraham Malamat, ed., *Sources for the History of Israel and of the Land in the Biblical Period* (Jerusalem: Hebrew University, 1984/5), p. 192. The 'Iron Stream was part of the international coastal road. It is thus easy to imagine the fear of traversing secondary roads. It is feasible that this fear is related to the words uttered by the servants of the king of Aram after their defeat in Samaria: "Their God is the god of the mountains." (I Kings 20:25)

[15] Archaeologists sometimes attempt to date the destruction of various sites on the basis of the absence of certain clay vessels at those sites. In light of the aforesaid argument, it is on occasion necessary to check whether the absence of a certain type of clay vessels from any site is not merely a function of the geographical location of the site, far from settlement centers, rather than the site having been destroyed prior to the manufacture of that type of clay vessel.

[16] Henri Pirenne, "What are Historians Trying to Do?" in Hans Meyerhoff, ed., *The Philosophy of History in Our Time* (Garden City, NY: Doubleday, 1959), pp. 87-99.

[17] Benny Morris, "Objective History," *Haaretz Weekly Supplement* (July 1, 1994), p. 40; with Oded Shermer, *Historical Scholarship and the Advance of the Critical Approach* (Ramat Gan:Bar-Ilan University, 2004), p. 117.

[18] Op. cit.

Chapter 2

[19] Albrecht Alt, "Die Landnahme der Israeliten in Palastina," *Reforationsprogramm der Universitat Leipzig* (1925) transl.*Essays in Old Testament History and Religion* (Oxford:Blackwell, 1966) pp. 135-169.

[20] Fernand Braudel, *On History* English trans.(Chicago:University of Chicago, 1982).

[21] Every rule, of course, has its exceptions, and this is true of this principle as well. We shall deal with this below.

[22] D. Nir, Geomonphology Of The Land Of Israel 1989 Jerusalem (Hebrew) Karmon and Shmueli, *Hebron – The Nature of a Hilltop Town*, (Heb.), (Tel Aviv, 1969/70); Karmon, *The Land of Israel–the Geography of the Country and its Regions* (Heb.), (Tel Aviv, 1982/3); Roth and Flexer, "The Rock Base in Judea and Samaria and its Exploitation by Man" (Heb.), in Shmueli, Grossman and Zeevi eds., *Judea and Samaria*, (Tel Aviv, 1976/7), pp. 3-13.

[23] The term "the Judean Hills" is the one used by geographers (below), as contrasted with "the Judean Hill", a term with historical significance that refers to the Hebron hills – the place of the Tribe of Judah.

[24] Yehuda Karmon "The Hills of Samaria – Physiographical Structure and Transportation Routes" (Heb.), in *The Land of Samaria* (Jerusalem, 1973/4), pp. 114-120; Dov Nir, *The Geomorphology of the Land of Israel* (Heb.), (Jerusalem, 1988/9).

[25] An anticline is a geological term used to denote a configuration of folded, stratified rocks that dips in two directions from a crest [from *The New Lexicon Webster's Dictionary of the English Language*, Encyclopedic Edition, (New York:Lexicon Publications, Inc., 1989), p. 39.]

Chapter 3

[26] James L. Kelso, "The Excavation of Bethel (1934-1960)," *AASOR* 39, 1968.

[27] James B. Pritchard, *The Bronze Age Cemetery at Gibeon*, (Philadelphia: University of Pennsylvania, University Museum 1963); Pritchard,, *Winery Defences and Soundings at Gibeon*, (Philadelphia: University of Pennsylvania, University Museum, 1964).

[28] William F. Albright, "Excavations and Results at Tel-el-Ful (Gibeah of Saul)", *AASOR* 4, 1924; Sinclair, "An Archaeological Study of Gibea (Tel-el-Ful), *AASOR* 34-35, pp. 1-52.

[29] Paul L. Lapp, "The Third Campaign at Tel-el-Ful. The Excavations of 1964", *AASOR* 45, 1978.

[30] Kathleen M. Kenyon, *Digging Up Jerusalem* (New York: Praeger,1974).

[31] Yigal Shiloh, "The Excavations in the City of David" (Heb.), *Qedem* 19, 1984, Jerusalem.

[32] Ronny Reich and Ei Shukroun, *Hadashot Archaeologiyot* 115, 2003, pp. 69-71.

[33] Yochanan Aharoni, *Excavations at Ramat Rahel, I, Seasons of 1959-1960* (Rome: Centro die Studi Semitici,1962) ; ibid., *Excavations at Ramat Rahel, II, Seasons of 1961-1962*, (Rome: Centro die Studi Semitici,1964).

[34] Gershon Edelstein; Ianir Milevski; Sara Aurant, "Villages, Terraces and Stone Mounds, Excavations at Manhat, Jerusalem 1987-1989," *IAA Reports* 3, 1998.

[35] Emanuel Eisenberg, "Nahal Rephaim – A Village from the Bronze Age to the Southwest of Jerusalem" (Heb.), *Qadmoniyot* 103-104 (1993-4), pp. 82-95.

[36] Yitzchak Meitlis, *The Judean Hill Country in the Middle Bronze Age*, Ph.D. thesis, (The University of Tel Aviv, 1997) (hereunder: Meitlis, 1997).

[37] Ovid R. Sellers, *The Citadel of Beth-Zur* (Philadelphia: Westminster Press,1933); ibid., "The 1957 Excavations at Beth Zur," *AASOR* 38, 1968.

[38] Hugues Vincent, "Une Funeraire Antique dans Louady et-Tin," *RB* 54 (1947), pp. 269-282.

[39] Robert H. Smith, *Excavations in the Cemeteryin Khirbet Kufin, Palestine* (London:Bernard Quaritch,1962).

[40] Rivka Gonen, "Excavations at Efrata: A Burial Ground from the Intermediate and Middle Bronze Ages," *IAA Reports*, (Jerusalem: Israel Antiquities Authority, 2001).

[41] Jeffrey R. Chadwick, *The Archaeology of Biblical Hebron in the Bronze and Iron Age: An Examination of the Discoveries of the American Expedition to Hebron*, Ph.D. Thesis, (University of Utah,1992).

[42] Avi Ofer, "The Excavation of Biblical Hebron" (Heb.), *Qadmoniyot* 22, 1989-90, pp. 88-93; ibid., *The Judean Hills in the Biblical Period* (Heb.), Ph.D. Thesis, (Tel Aviv University, 1993-4).

[43] Moshe Kochavi, *Judea, Samaria and Golan: An Archaeological Survey Made in 1968* (Heb.), (Jerusalem, Israel Antiquities Authority, 1972).

[44] Ofer (1993-4), *supra* n. 42.

[45] Yitzhak Meitlis, *Agricultural Settlement at the Close of the Iron Age in the Jerusalem Area* (Heb.), M.A. Dissertation (Jerusalem:Hebrew University, 1988-9), pp. 3-13.

[46] Yitzhak Magen and Israel Finkelstein, *An Archaeological Survey in Benjamin* (Heb.) (Jerusalem:Israel Antiquities Authority, 1993).

[47] See n. 36 there, pp. 100-129.

[48] Israel Finkelstein, "The Land of Ephraim Survey 1980-1987: Preliminary Report", *Tel-Aviv* 15-16 (1989), pp. 129-140.

[49] Adam Zertal, *Israelite Settlement in the Hills of Menashe* (Heb.), Ph.D. Thesis (University of Tel Aviv, 1985-6); ibid., *Hills of Menashe Survey I – The Depression of Shechem* (Leiden,Boston: Brill, 2004) (Heb.) (Haifa, 1992).

[50] Shlomo Bunimovitz, *The Land of Israel in the Late Bronze Age: A Test Case for Socio-Cultural Change in a Complex Society* (Heb.), Ph.D. Thesis (Tel Aviv University, 1989/90); ibid., "The Limits and Terminology of the Beginning of the Late Bronze Age" (Heb.), *Eretz-Israel* 23 (1991-2), pp. 21-25.

[51] Israel Finkelstein, "The Socio-Political Organization of the Central Hill Country in the Second Millennium B.C.E.", in Avraham Biran and Joseph Aviram, eds.., *Biblical Archaeology Today, 1990, Proceedings of the Second International Congress on Biblical Archaeology*, (Jerusalem:Israel Exploration Society, 1990), pp. 110-131.

Chapter 4

[52] William F. Albright, *The Archaeology of Palestine*, (Heb. edition), Tel Aviv (1965); hereunder: Albright 1965.

[53] Kathleen Kenyon, *We Have Uncovered Jericho* (Heb.), Tel-Aviv (1961).

[54] Nadav Na'aman, "The Story of 'The Conquest of the Land' in the Book of Joshua and in Historical Reality" in Nadav Na'aman & Israel Finkelstein, eds., *From Nomadism to Monarchy: Archaeological and Historical Aspects of Early Israel* (Heb.), (Jerusalem:Yad Izhak Ben-Zvi, Israel Exploration Society, 1990), pp. 288-289.

[55] See the Table summing up the settlement picture in the Appendix.

[56] Na'aman, "The Inheritance of the Sons of Simeon", *ZDPV* 96 (1980), pp. 132-152. It should further be noted that Biblical Be'er-Sheva should perhaps be identified with Tel Mashush, i.e. Khirbet el-Mashash (the ruin of the water-cisterns). This site is located some 12 kilometers to the east of Be'er-Sheva, on the bank of the Be'er-Sheva Brook. At this site, the remains have been found of an MBA settlement. For these excavations see: Aharon Kempinski *et al.*, "The Excavations at Tel Mashash – a Summing-up of the Three Excavation Seasons" (Heb.), *Eretz-Israel* XV (1980-81), pp. 154-180.

[57] Na'aman, op. cit.

[58] Israel Rosenson, "The Story of the past–Literature and History in the Bible – Contradiction or Complement?" (Heb.), *'Al Atar* VII (1999-2000), pp. 111-149.

[59] Na'aman, n. 54.

[60] Avi Ofer, "Biblical Judean Hill country – from a Nomadic Existence to a National Kingdom" (Heb.) in Na'aman and Finkelstein, eds., *From Nomadism to Monarchy*, pp. 205 ff.

⁶¹ Moshe Inbar and Nadav Na'aman, "An Account Tablet of Sheep from Ancient Hebron", *Tel Aviv* 13-14 (1986-1987), pp. 3-12.

⁶² Rosenson noted this phenomenon: "This book [i.e., Genesis – Y.M.] is not a book of writing, but rather of speech." He believes that this absence of writing reflects the nomadic culture of which the Patriarchs were a part, and that the language of the book is a nomadic one. For further elaboration, see Israel Rosenson, op. cit., (n. 58 *supra*), p. 146.

⁶³ *Supra*, note 61.

⁶⁴ It should be noted that the researcher Moshe Weinfeld noticed this and wrote in a somewhat obscure style: "In Jeremiah 32 there is a story of a purchase carried out by means of a written scroll, while in Genesis 23, the text does not mention any document at all, and we can deduce from this the antiquity of the circumstances reflected in this tradition." Moshe Weinfeld, *The Encyclopedia of the World of the Bible: the Book of Genesis* (1982), p. 147.

⁶⁵ Manfred R.Lehman, "Abraham's Purchase of the Machpela and Hittite Law", *BASOR 129*, (1953), pp. 15-18.

⁶⁶ Kenneth A. Kitchen, *On the Reliability of the Old Testament*, (Grand Rapids: W. B. Eerdmans, 2003), pp. 344-345.

⁶⁷ See the collection of arguments adduced by Na'aman, note 51. The arguments listed below are not those brought only by Na'aman, but since the subject is treated in a comprehensive, organized fashion in his article, we have decided to discuss the arguments there.

⁶⁸ Na'aman, *supra*.

⁶⁹ See Benjamin Mazar, "Heth", *Encyclopedia Miqra'it* (Heb.), Vol. III, col. 320-357, and Mazar's opinion as expressed there: "There is no basis for the argument that the tradition of Hittites in Hebron is a late one" (col. 356).

⁷⁰ Israel Finkelstein, *The Archaeology of the Period of Settlement and the Judges* (Heb.) (Tel Aviv: Israel Exploration Society, 1987), p. 196, and also Israel Finkelstein & Baruch Brandl, "A Group of Metal Objects from Shiloh", *The Israel Museum Journal* IV, pp. 17-26. See also *infra* Brandl (1993).

⁷¹ Finkelstein and Brandl, op. cit., p. 25. See also Na'aman's opinion based also on this finding as evidence for the penetration of northern groups into Canaan during the MBA. Nadav Na'aman, "The Hurrians and the End of the Middle Bronze Age in Palestine", *Levant* 26 (1994), pp. 175-187.

⁷² See Ruth Amiran, *The Ancient Pottery of Eretz-Israel* (Jerusalem, 1970-71), p. 133.

⁷³ Noemi Acreche, "Skeletal Remains from Efrata and Other Bronze Sites in Israel" in Rivka Gonen, *Excavations at Efrata: A Burial Ground from the Intermediate and Middle Bronze Ages*, IAA Reports (Jerusalem:Israel Antiquities Authority, 2001), pp. 95-109.

[74] Na'aman brings an example from the discovery of an Assyrian merchant colony that lived in a neighborhood of the city of Knish within the borders of Heth in the 17th century BCE. If not for the discovery of a written document, it would have been impossible to identify them as an ethnic group different from the other inhabitants. Na'aman (1990), p. 306.

[75] See Na'aman *supra*, note 71, for details of the content of these documents.

[76] See Loewenstamm, "Hivite", *Ensiklopedia Miqra'it* (Heb.) III (Jerusalem, 1964-5), pp. 45-47.

[77] Itamar Singer, "Egyptians, Canaanites and Philistines in the Periods of the Settlement and of the Judges", in Na'aman and Finkelstein eds., *From Nomadism to Monarchy*, pp. 352-353.

[78] See Rivka Gonen, *Burial in Canaan in the Late Bronze Age as a Basis for Archaeological Research and the Urban Population*, Doctoral dissertation at the Hebrew University of Jerusalem, pp. 231-238.

[79] An example of the repeated use of a single term to denote different population groups is seen in the term "Palestinian" which originates from the ancient Philistines. During the period of the British Mandate, the Jews of Israel were termed "Palestinians." Today the term is used only for the Arabs of Israel.

[80] Eliezer Oren, "New Insights in the Study of Interconnections in the Mediterranean World in the Middle Bronze Age", *Be'er-Sheva XV*, (2002), pp. 1-9.

[81] See Yehoshua Grintez, *The Unique Quality and Antiquity of the Book of Genesis* (Heb.) (Jerusalem 1982-3), p. 67.

[82] I find it incomprehensible that despite the data adduced herein, data which demonstrates the use of the camel as early as the onset of the second millennium, scholars such as Na'aman and Finkelstein continue to claim that no use was made of the camel prior to the close of the second millennium.

[83] See *supra* Albright (1965), p. 177.

[84] For the problem of dating Stratum VII, see above.

[85] See Lampert, "The Domesticated Camel in the Second Millennium", *BASOR* 160 (1960), pp. 42-45. See also Richard W. Bulliet, *The Camel and the Wheel* (London 1975), p. 64. It is interesting to note that Na'aman actually cites this source (Na'aman *supra*, n. 54 – in note no. 18), but conceals from the reader the fact that this source contradicts his own opinion.

[86] Ofer Bar-Yosef, "The Beginnings of Nomadic Societies in the Levant" (Heb.), in Shmuel Ahituv, ed., *Studies in the Archaeology of Nomads in the Negev and in Sinai* (Heb.) (Be'er-Sheva, 1957-8), pp. 7-25.

[87] Rudolph Cohen, *The Settlements in the Negev Highlands*, Ph.D. Dissertation at the Hebrew University in Jerusalem (1986), p. 303.

[88] See Bulliet, n. 85, p. 65.

[89] For more on the subject of various groups who viewed their nomadic lifestyle as the correct way to live, rather than as something forced upon them by circumstance, see the story of the children of Rechab (Jeremiah 35), and similarly the Nabateans at an early stage of their existence. See the description by Hieronymus adduced in Avraham Negev, *Lords of the Desert* (Heb.) (Jerusalem, 1983), pp. 25-27.

[90] See Amiran, note 72, p. 43.

[91] William G. Dever, "New Vistas on the EBIV (MBI) Horizon in Syria-Palestine", *BASOR 237* (1980), pp. 35-64.

[92] Yuval Goren, "The Southern Levant in the Early Bronze Age IV: the Petrographic Perspective", *BASOR 303* (1996), pp. 33-72.

[93] Nelson Glueck, *Rivers in the Desert: A History of the Negev* (Philadelphia: Jewish Publication Society of America, 1959), Hebrew edition: *Ka'afiqim ba-Negev* (Tel Aviv, 1970), pp. 58-76.

[94] Moshe Kochavi, *The Settlement Wave of the Middle Bronze (Canaanite) Age I in the Negev*, Ph.D. Dissertation at the Hebrew University in Jerusalem (1966-7), pp. 240-242.

[95] Note the statement made by the traditional commentator Ibn Ezra regarding the verse: *"And Abram passed through the land unto the place of Shechem"* (Gen. 12:6) – "Moses wrote it this way because Shechem did not exist in the days of Abraham." The phrase "the place of Shechem" seems, according to Ibn Ezra, to indicate that Abram reached the place where Shechem was to be built in the future.

[96] Yehoshua Grinetz, *The Origins of the Generations* (Heb.) (Tel Aviv, 1968-9), pp. 183-192.

[97] Yoel Bin Nun, 'The Hebrews and the Land of the Hebrews" (Heb.), *Megadim* 15 (1991-2), pp. 9126.

[98] The land of Shechem or the mountain of Shechem. Thus, e.g., Shechem is mentioned by name a number of times in an inscription found in the grave of an Egyptian military commander who led a campaign to "the mountain of Shechem" and also in the El-Amarna letters. See *supra*, Na'aman (1982), p. 141.

[99] For additional points indicating the early origin of the Book of Genesis, see: Grinetz *supra*, n. 81 and Kitchen *supra*, n. 66.

Chapter 5

[100] Archaeologists dispute to this day just when in the 13th century Hatzor was destroyed.

a) Hatzor: P. Beck & M. Kochavi, 'A Dated Assemblage of the Late 13th Century B.C.E. from the Egyptian Residency at Aphek' *Tel-Aviv 12, 1985*, pp. 29-42.

b) Lachish: D. Ussishkin, 'Levels VII and VI at Tel Lachish and the End of the Late Bronze Age in Canaan.' In J.N. Tubb (ed.), *Palestine in the Bronze and Iron Ages, Papers in Honor of Olga Tufnell,* London 1985, pp. 213-228.

[101] James L. Kelso, "The Excavation of Bethel (1934-1960)", *AASOR* 39 (1968).

[102] Gershon Edelstein, Janir Milevski and Sara Aurant, *Villages, Terraces and Stone Mounds, Excavations at Manhat, Jerusalem 1987-1989, IAA Reports III,* 1998.

[103] Moshe Kochavi, "Khirbet Rabud is D'vir" in Yochanan Aharoni, ed., *Excavations and Research* (Heb.), (Tel Aviv: Tel Aviv Instittute of Archaeology & Carta, 1973), pp. 49-76.

[104] Avi Ofer, "The Biblical Judean Hills from a Nomadic Life to a National Kingdom" in Nadav Na'aman & Israel Finkelstein, eds., *From Nomadism to Monarchy* (Jerusalem: Yad Izhak Ben-Zvi, Israel Exploration Society, 1990), pp. 115-214, illustration no. 3.

[105] Yitzhak Magen and Israel Finkelstein, *An Archaeological Survey of the Land of Binyamin* (Heb.) (Jerusalem:Israel Antiquities Authority, 1992-3), p. 25.

[106] Adam Zertal,"'In the Land of the Perizzites and the Rephaim' – Of Israelite Settlement in the Hills of Menashe" in Nadav Na'aman and Israel Finkelstein, eds., *From Nomadism to Monarchy,* pp. 53-100. See in particular p. 60.

[107] Magen and Finkelstein, note 1086 *supra.*

[108] Zertal, note 107.

[109] Moshe Kochavi, 'The History and Archaeology of Aphek-Antipatris: A Biblical City in the Sharon Plain', *BA* 44, pp. 75-86.

[110] See: M. Artzi, 'Nami, Land and Sea Project', *IEJ* 40 (1990), pp. 73-76.

[111] Adam Zertal, 'Cultic Site on Mount Ebal', *Tel Aviv* 13-14 (1986-1987), p. 137.

[112] Chester C. McCown, *Tel Nasbeh I, Archaeological and Historical Result,* (Berkeley:Palestine Institute of Pacific School of Religion, 1947), p. 180.

[113] Joseph C. Wampler, *Tel Nasbeh II, The Pottery,* Berkeley:,Palestine Institute of Pacific School of Religion, 1947).

[114] Amihai Mazar, 'Giloh: An Early Israelite Settlement Site Near Jerusalem', *IEJ* 31 (1981), pp. 1-36.

[115] Ovid R. Sellers, *The Citadel of Beth-Zur* (Philadelphia:Westminster Press,1933), p. 33, fig. 26; ibid., "The 1957 Excavations at Beth-Zur", *AASOR* 38 (1968), p. 36.

[116] See Stefansky, Segal & Karmi, "The 1993 Sounding at Tel Sasa: Excavation Report and Radiometric Dating", *Atiqot* XXVIII (1996), pp. 63-76.

[117] 18 Yochanan Aharoni, Volkmar Fritz & Aharon Kempinski, "Excavations at Tel Masos (Khirbet el-Meshash) -- Preliminary Report on the Second Season, 1974," *Tel Aviv* 2 (1975), pp. 97-124.

[118] Israel Finkelstein, *The Archaeology of the Period of the Settlement and the Judges* (Heb.) (Tel Aviv:Tel Aviv University, 1987), pp. 197-198. Finkelstein claimed that Aharoni's opinion was based on the fact that in the excavations carried out by the Danish expedition, no Late Bronze Age stratum was found at the site, and so he thought that the vessels from the LBA actually belonged to the stratum reflecting the Israelite settlement. This argument is unacceptable because in the Danish excavations a wall was found that was interpreted by the excavators as dating from the LBA, while only in the later Bar-Ilan excavation did it become clear that the wall was actually a Byzantine terrace (*ibid.*, p. 197). Thus, when the article by Aharoni and his colleagues was written, the prevalent opinion was that LBA architecture had been found on the site. Even in the excavations by the Bar-Ilan team, no real stratum dating from the LBA was found.

[119] Israel Finkelstein, ed., Shiloh: The Archaeology of a Biblical Site, (Tel Aviv:Tel Aviv University, 1993).

[120] Shlomo Bunimovitz and Israel Finkelstein, "Pottery" in I. Finkelstein, ed., *Shiloh*, pp. 81-196.

[121] Marie-Louise Buhl and Svend Holm-Nielsen, *Shiloh* (Copenhagen: National Museum of Denmark, 1969), pp. 34-35, 60.

[122] Amnon Ben-Tor and Yuval Portugali, "Tel Qiri – A Village in the Jezreel Valley. Report of the Archaeological Excavations 1975-1977", *Qedem* 24 (1984), pp. 257-258.

[123] Ibid.

[124] Ephraim Stern and Yitzhak Beit Arieh, "Excavations at Tel Kedesh (Tel Abu Qudeis)", *Tel Aviv* 6 (1979), pp. 138-145.

[125] To this must be added the findings from Tel el-Umayri across the Jordan River, on its eastern bank. There, too, a similar feature was discovered. Fortifications from the MBA and Iron Age I were found there, while from the LBA only sherds were discovered in waste dumps outside the settlement. This picture seems to fit in with that of the Jordan's western bank. Larry G.. Herr et al, *Madaba Plain Project: The 1992 Season at tel al-'Umayri and Subsequent Studies*, (Berrien Springs, MI:Andrews University, 2000), pp. 12-14.

[126] David Ilan, *Northeastern Israel in the Iron Age I: Cultural, Socioeconomic and Political Perspectives*, Ph.D. thesis, (Tel Aviv: University of Tel-Aviv, 1999), p. 141, plates 3, 12.

[127] Albert E. Glock, "Taanach" in E. Stern, ed., *The New Encyclopedia of Archaeological Excavations in the Holy Land*, vol. 4, (Jerusalem: Israel Exploration Society & Carta,1993), pp. 1428-1433.

[128] Zertal, "In the Land of the Perizzites…" p. 61. Ibid., n.106.

[129] Meitlis (1997), p. 154.

[130] Finkelstein, *The Archaeology of the Period of Settlement and the Judges*, p. 258.

[131] Ibid., p. 259.

[132] For the jar, see: Shlomo Bunimovitz and Israel Finkelstein, "Pottery" in work cited above, Finkelstein, ed., *Shilo*, p. 159.

[133] See Glass, Goren, Bunimovitz and Finkelstein, "Petrographic Analyses of Middle Bronze Age III, Late Bronze Age and Iron Age I Ceramic Assemblages" in Finkelstein, ed., *Shiloh*,, pp. 271-277.

[134] It seems that petrographic tests of the Einun vessels should be made. Such tests could support or disprove the source of these vessels.

[135] Yitzchak Meitlis, "The Highland Culture as against the Lowland Culture in the Second Millennium BCE" in Yaacov Eshel, ed., *Studies of Judea and Samaria: The Ninth Volume* (Ariel:Academic College of Judea and Samaria, 1999-2000), pp. 17-26.

[136] The direct connection between the Middle Bronze Age and the Iron Age requires that we assume that certain regions in the highlands, such as the Tubas Valley, were cut off from external influences for decades. It is difficult to accept such a claim, but it should be noted that studies carried out on the Egyptian scarabs in Israel show that royal scarabs of the 18th dynasty (the 16th and 15th centuries) have not been found in Samaria. Four scarabs were found in Gibeon and in Jerusalem, while in the coastal and inland plains some 200 scarabs have been found, most of Thutmose III. (I am indebted to Nir Lalkin for this information.) The lack of scarabs in the hill country, in contrast to their wide distribution in the lower parts of the country, is an indication of the region being indeed cut off.

[137] Adam Zertal, "The Pottery of 'Einun' – History, Significance and Future" (Heb.), *Studies of Judea and Samaria*, Vol. 14 (2002-3), p. 13.

[138] The collared-rim jar was especially widespread in the hill country of Judea and Samaria. In the Galilee, this type of jar was not in use, except for one extraordinary site – Tel Dan, at the northern tip of the Galilee, where a settlement stratum was found dating from the 13th century and the onset of the 12th century BCE. This site contained a large number of collared-rim jars. See Avraham Biran, *Dan – Twenty-five Years of Excavation at Tel-Dan*, (Tel Aviv, 1992), pp. 115-127. The excavator links this unique feature with the expedition of the Danites and their conquest of Layish (Judges 18).

[139] Finkelstein, ibid., n. 130, p. 249.

[140] See Zertal, *supra*, n. 38; Amihai Mazar, "A Ritual Site from the Period of the Judges in the Hills of Samaria" (Heb.), *Eretz Israel* 16, pp. 135-145. See also the paper by Gilmour who typifies the ritual sites in Israel by geographical region. G. H. Gilmour, *Levant in the Early Iron Age: An Analytical and Comparative Approach*, Thesis submitted to the University of Oxford, England, (1994).

[141] Moshe Kochavi, "Ostracon of the Period of the Judges from Izbet Sartah," *Tel Aviv* 4 (1977), pp. 1-13.

[142] For this, see Yochanan Aharoni, *The Archaeology of Eretz-Israel* (Heb.) (Jerusalem:Shikmonah, 1978), pp. 133-135.

[143] For more on the subject of the Hebrew script, see below.

[144] Near Khirbet Nisia, east of Ramallah (and close to the modern Israeli settlement of Pesagot), D. Livingstone excavated a burial site cut into the rock, which contained potsherds from the MBA as well as from Iron Age I. The state of preservation of this burial site was very poor. Potsherds and a few human bones, but especially hundreds of teeth, were found there. An examination of the teeth showed that dozens of human beings had been buried there.

[145] Baruch Rosen, "Economics and Survival in the Settlement Period" in Na'aman and Finkelstein eds., *From Nomads*, pp. 403-416. See also the summary of data from Canaanite and Philistine sites in Shlomo Bunimovitz and Zvi Lederman, "Six Seasons of Excavation at Tel Bet-Shemesh – a Town on the border of Judea" *Qadmoniyot* (Heb.) 113 (1996-7), pp. 22-37. For data concerning the bones in MBA sites, see Part IV.

[146] A list of references is adduced in Na'aman, ibid., n. 54, pp. 310-311.

[147] Ibid., p. 311.

[148] Shmuel Yeivin, "Asher'" in *Entsiklopedia Miqra'it* (Heb.), vol. 1 (Jerusalem, 1977-8), p. 783.

[149] George E. Mendenhall, "The Hebrew Conquest of Palestine", *BAR* 25 (1962), pp. 66-87.

[150] Finkelstein, ibid., n. 130, p. 318.

[151] Ibid., p. 304.

[152] Ibid., n. 90.

[153] Adam Zertal, *A Nation is Born* (Heb.), (Tel Aviv: 2000), p. 161.

[154] See Aharoni, n. 142.

[155] Moshe Kochavi, *Aphek-Antipatris: Five Thousand Years of History* (Heb.) (Tel Aviv:Tel Aviv University, 1989), p. 70.

[156] Various national groups attribute significance, and even sanctity, to the shape of their written characters. Thus, for example, the Chinese and Japanese will not give up their complex writing system, nor are they willing to adopt a simpler writing style.

[157] Israel Finkelstein, "The Israelite Settlement – the Sociological School and the Test of Archaeological Evidence" in Uriel Simon, ed., *Studies in Bible and its Interpretation II* (Heb.) (Ramat-Gan: Bar-Ilan University, 1985-6), pp. 175-186. It is to be noted that in a final note he wrote, "The writing of this article was completed at the end of 1983, and since then I have changed my mind in certain details."

[158] See Bunimovitz & Ledermann, op.cit. n. 145.

[159] It is to be noted that also in the excavations of the site known as "Tel Harasim," an LBA settlement was discovered, with bone findings similar to those at Bet-Shemesh. For this, see Shmuel Givon, *Judaean Shephela in the Late Bronze Age*, Ph.D Dissertation at Bar-Ilan University, Ramat-Gan (1998), p. 130.

[160] Israel Finkelstein, "The Settlement History of the Transjordanian Plateau in light of the results of Surveys", *Eretz-Israel* 25 (1995-6), pp. 244-251.

[161] Tom E. Levy *et al.*, "Reassessing the Chronology of Biblical Edom: New Excavations and C 14 dates from Khirbat en Nahas (Jordan)," *Antiquity* 78 (2004), pp. 863-876.

[162] Finkelstein, ibid., pp. 104-109; J. Maxwell Miller, "Moab in Iron Age I" in Nadav Na'aman and Israel Finkelstein, eds., *From Nomads*, pp. 242-256. See note 160.

[163] 166 Larry G. Herr *et al*, *Madaba Plain Project*, pp. 189-196.

[164] This is also the opinion of Adam Zertal, the researcher of northern Samaria, based on his studies of this region. For this see: Adam Zertal, "The Iron Age I Culture in the Hill-Country of Canaan – A Manassite Perspective" in Seymour Gitin, Amihai Mazar and Ephraim Stern, eds., *Mediterranean Peoples in Transition* (Jerusalem: Israel Exploration Society, 1998), pp. 238-250.

[165] An analogy can be drawn with the beginnings of the Muslim conquest of Israel, which is known to have come from the Arabian Desert. If we ignore historical sources, there is no clear archaeological evidence for this conquest. On the contrary, even after the Muslim conquest, the Byzantine-Christian churches managed to survive, and this is true of certain synagogues as well. The Dome of the Rock was based on an octagonal Byzantine church. On the basis of archaeological evidence alone, the Muslim conquest cannot be dated before the 8th century CE, decades after the date given in the history books.

[166] Albrecht Alt, *Essays on Old Testament History and Religion*, trans. from German by R.A. Wilson (Oxford: Blackwell, 1966), pp. 135-169.

[167] William F. Albright, "The Israelite Conquest of Canaan in the Light of Archaeology", *BASOR* 74 (1939), pp. 11-23; Yigael Yadin, "Is the Biblical Account of the Israelite Conquest of Canaan Historically Reliable?" *BAR* 7 (1982), pp. 16-23.

[168] Meitlis (1997), p. 53.

[169] It is interesting to note that near Gibeon, a Hivite city from the period of the Judges (according to the testimony of the Bible) rich burial sites were found from the Late Bronze Age, though at the site itself no settlement stratum was found from this period.

[170] Hayim Tadmor, "Chronology" in *Entsiklopedia Mikrait*, vol. 4 (Heb.) (Jerusalem, 1962), p. 300. We can also date the time of the building of Solomon's Temple using a combination of Shishak script (Egyptian) and the Bible.

[171] It is to be noted that this was the opinion of Aharoni as well. He expressed this view on a number of occasions, as did Anson F. Rainey in the new edition of *Carta's Atlas of the Biblical World*, (Jerusalem:Carta, 2006).

[172] William L. Moran, *The Amarna Letters* (Baltimore: Johns Hopkins University, 1992).

[173] Gershon Galil argues that the El-Amarna letters reflect the entire Late Bronze Age, though no proof of this exists. See Galil, "The Royal Canaanite Cities in the 14th century BCE: their size and status" (Heb.), *Kathedra* 84 (1997), p. 7.

[174] Nadav Na'aman, *The History of Eretz-Israel in Ancient Days* (Heb.) (Jerusalem, 1982), p. 219.

[175] EA = the El-Amarna letters.

[176] For further information on the Geshurites, see: Benjamin Mazar, "Geshur and Maacha", *Cities and Districts in Eretz-Israel* (Heb.) (Jerusalem, 1976), pp. 190-202, and also Yitzchak Meitlis, "The Central and Southern Golan", *'Al Atar* 4-5 (1998-9), pp. 16-18 and references there.

[177] Amihai Mazar, "The Relationship between Archaeology and Historical Research" in Lee Levine & Amihai Mazar, eds., *The Controversy over the Historical Validity of the Bible* (Heb.) (Jerusalem, 2001), p. 107. Mazar claims, nevertheless, that Taanakh, mentioned in the Book of Judges, did not exist as a Canaanite city at this time. However, Taanakh is a complex problem in archaeological research. According to the findings in excavations, Taanakh was destroyed in the 15th century BCE (Glock, 1992, above). In the El-Amarna letters from the 14th century BCE, however, Taanakh is mentioned as a city-state. In other words, a problem exists not only with the Book of Judges, but also with an historical source accepted by all as reliable. It should be noted that at the site letters were found from the second half of the 15th century as well, that were sent by the king of Egypt (apparently Amenhotep II) to the king of Taanakh. Excavation results show that at this time Taanakh was in ruins. It would appear that, in this case, the problem is with the archaeological excavation itself – or with the processing of the material.

[178] For a broad summary, see Na'aman, n. 174, pp. 233-241.

[179] Ibid., p. 240.

[180] Ibid., p. 239.

[181] Yochanan Aharoni, *Eretz-Israel in the Biblical Period, An Historical Geography* (Jerusalem, 1963), p. 154.

[182] A present-day analogy can be drawn. A researcher who studies the region we call today "Judea and Samaria" without any knowledge of the Six-Day War will not be able to point to any first wave of conquest of the entire region, followed by a gradual settlement process. The "archaeological" findings *in situ* simply indicate the establishment of mainly small Israeli settlements

near the major Arab population centers. As a rule, archaeology is unable to take note of short-lived events of construction and settlement. Thus, for example, archaeology is unable to put its finger on finds from the 52-year-long Babylonian period, except for the signs of the destruction of various settlements ascribed to the Babylonians. The connection between the signs of destruction and the Babylonians is based on historical and Biblical sources, rather than on archaeological findings. A further example is that of the Seljuk conquest of greater Israel at the end of the 11th century CE, which lasted 25 years. This conquest, like the others, has left no signs other than historical knowledge.

[183] Itamar Singer, "Egypt, Canaanites and Philistines in the Periods of the Settlement and the Judges" in Na'aman and Finkelstein, eds., *From Nomadism to Monarchy*, pp. 348-402. For the custom of the Bible to present historical events, see also I. Elitzur, "The Bible's View of History", in: Elitzur & Frisch, eds., *Israel and the Bible: Studies in Geography, History and Philosophy* (Heb.) (Ramat-Gan:Bar-Ilan Univ., 1999-2000), pp. 253-261.

[184] Op.cit. p. 360.

[185] An indication of the involvement of the people of Sidon in the history of the northern part of Israel can be found in the El-Amarna letters. In these letters (EA 148, 149), the king of Sidon is accused of raiding Tyre and conquering a town by the name of Uso, near Tyre. It is possible that in these events the Israelite inhabitants of northwest Galilee, too, were affected.

[186] A further indication of Egyptian activity in Israel up until the close of the 11th century BCE may be seen in the informative item concerning Benayahu ben Yehoyada, one of the warriors of David, who killed a spear-bearing Egyptian (II Sam. 23:21; I Chron. 11:23).

[187] Seymour Gitin, Trude Dothan and Joseph Naveh, "A Royal Dedication Inscription from Ekron", *Qadmoniyot* 113 (1996-7), pp. 38-43.

[188] Amihai Mazar, *An Introduction to the Archaeology of Eretz-Israel in the Biblical Period, Unit 8: Iron Age I*, (Tel Aviv: Everyman's University, 1990), p. 41.

[189] Op.cit., n. 143.

[190] Moshe Kochavi, ibid., n. 155. It is to be noted that the Yarkon served as a line of defense in two wars, the first – the war of King Yannai against Antiochus XII, and the second – World War I, where the Ottoman Turks succeeded in halting the British, who moved in from the south on the Yarkon line for a number of months.

[191] For this excavation and its findings, see Kochavi, *supra*, note 155.

[192] Bunimovitz and Lederman, n. 145.

[193] Nov has not been identified conclusively, though it was clearly near Jerusalem and actually overlooked it: "This very day shall he halt at Nov, shaking his hand at the mount of the daughter of Zion, the hill of Jerusalem." (Isa. 10:32)

[194] II Sam. 2:13

[195] Ofer, note 42, p. 202.

[196] For a broader discussion of this battle, see Yitzchak Meitlis, "'About the Giah' on the way 'of the wilderness of Gibeon'" (Heb.), *Al Atar 8-9* (2000-1), pp. 165-173.

[197] Nelson Glueck, *The Other Side of the Jordan* (New Haven: American Schools of Oriental Research, (1940), 50-88

[198] Thomas E. Levy and Mohummas Najjar, "Some Thoughts on Khirbat en-Nahas, Edom, Biblical History and Antropology-A Response to Israel Finkelstein. *Tel Aviv* 33, 3-17; ibid., "Edom and Copper: The Emergence of Ancient Israel's Rival," BAR 32 (July/August 2006): 24-35, 70; Neil G. Smith and Thomas E. Levy, "The Iron Age Pottery from Kirbat en-Nahas, Jordan: A Preliminary Study," BASOR 352 (2008): 41-91.

The reliability of Carbon-14 testing is occasionally questioned, but in this instance the dating had already been established by Nelson Glueck on the basis of the ceramics alone. Also, in our case there were numerous tests performed in different laboratories with all results indicating a similar result. The Egyptian artifacts described here fit in well with the other findings. I wish to thank Erez Ben-Yosef who kept me current on the results of the recent excavations.

[199] Thomas E. Levy et al., "High-precision radiocarbon dating and historical biblical archaeology in southern Jordan," *Proceedings of the National Academy of Science* 105 (2008): 16460-65

Chapter 6

[200] Cut and squared building stone.

[201] Arad is the exception to the rule. There, the reservoir cut into the fortress was filled by pumping from a well located outside the settlement and using manpower to transport the water.

[202] Benjamin Mazar, "Shishak's Campaign to Eretz-Israel", *Canaan and Israel: Historical Studies* (Heb.), (Jerusalem: 1973-4), pp. 234-244; Nadav Na'aman, "Shishak's Campaign to Eretz-Israel as reflected in Egyptian Inscriptions, the Bible and Archaeological Evidence" (Heb.), *Zion 53* (1997-8), pp. 247-276.

[203] Itamar Singer, "Egyptians, Canaanites and Philistines in the Period of the Hebrew Settlement and Judges" in Nadav Na'aman & Israel Finkelstein, eds., *From Nomadism to Monarchy* (Heb.), (Jerusalem: Yad Izhak Ben-Zvi, Israel Exploration Society, 1990), pp. 348-402

[204] In a royal inscription written by Shalmaneser III, we find a description of a large battle between the king of Assyria and a coalition of twelve kings from the region of Syria and Israel. In the inscription known as the "Monolith of Korah," there are details on the size of the coalition forces. In that same inscription, we find that Ahab had some 2000 chariots, the largest number of chariots of any of the 12 kings who participated in the battle.

[205] See Singer above, pp. 361-402.

[206] Israel Finkelstein, "The Archaeology of the United Monarchy: an Alternative View," *Levant XVIII* (1996), pp. 177-188; *ibid., Levant XXX* (1998), pp. 167-174; *ibid.*, "The Beginning of the State in Israel and in Judea" (Heb.), *Eretz-Israel XXVI* (1998-9), pp. 132-141 (below: Finkelstein, 1999).

[207] For an example of this, see: Yitzhak Meitlis, "On the Bible and Pottery and the Difference between Them" (Heb.), *Al Atar 7* (1999-2000), p. 97.

[208] Kenneth A. Kitchen adduces many detailed arguments against this theory in his new book *On the Reliability of the Old Testament*, (Grand Rapids: Wm. B. Eerdmans Publishing Co.,2005), pp. 139-156.

[209] Amihai Mazar, "Iron Age Chronology: A Reply to I. Finkelstein," *Levant XXIX* (1997), pp. 157-167; Amnon Ben Tor, "Hazor and the Archaeology of the 10th Century BCE," *LEJ* 48 (1998), pp. 1-37.

[210] Finkelstein (1999), *ibid.*, note 205.

[211] Fernand Braudel, *On History*, (English trans.) (Chicago: Chicago Univ. Press, 1980).

[212] Fernand Braudel, *The Mediterranean and Mediterranean World in the Age of Philip II*, (NY: Harper Collins, 1966), p. 38.

[213] Yitzchak Meitlis, "The Hill Culture as opposed to the Plain Culture in the Second Millenium BCE" (Heb.), *Studies of Judea and Samaria – the Ninth Collection* (1999-2000), pp. 17-26.

[214] Ephraim Stern, "Persian Rule (538-332 BCE)", in: I. Efal, ed.), *The History of Eretz-Israel, Vol. II: Israel and Judah in the Biblical Era* (Heb.), (Jerusalem, 1984), p. 291.

[215] Avraham Biran & Joseph Naveh, "An Aramaic Stele Fragment from Tel Dan", *IEJ* 43 (1993), pp. 81-98; *ibid.*, "The Tel Dan Inscription: A New Fragment," *IEJ* 45 (1995), pp. 1-18.

[216] S. Yefet, 'The Bible and History', in: Levine & Mazar, eds., *The Debate over the Historical Truth of the Bible* (Heb.), Jerusalem (2001), p. 85.

[217] Gabriel Barkai, 'Outlines of the Study of Jerusalem in the First Temple Period', *Landscape, Studies in Geography* (Heb.), *Ariel* 165-166, August 2004, p. 18.

[218] I Kings 9:15.

[219] The main road to Jerusalem in modern times – via Bab-el-Wad – was not an important route in earlier times. Fierce battles were waged over the road passing by Bet Horon (today called highway 443) in the days of Joshua, during the Hasmonean rebellion and during the Great Jewish Revolt against the Romans.

[220] Avi Ofer, "The Biblical Hills of Judea – from Nomadism to a National Kingdom" in Nadav Na'aman and Israel Finkelstein, eds., *From Nomadism to Monarchy* (Heb.), Jerusalem (1990), p. 202.

²²¹ Gabriel Barkay, "Jerusalem as a Leading City" in Shlomo Bunimovitz and Aryeh Kasher, eds., *Settlements, Population and Economy in Israel in Ancient Times* (Heb.), Tel Aviv (1988), pp. 124-125.

²²² See above, note 201.

²²³ David Eitam, "Fortifications in the Negev Highlands – Places of Settlement?" (Heb.), *Teva va'Aretz* 21 (3), 1978-9, pp. 124-131; Israel Finkelstein, "'The Fortifications' of the Negev Highlands – Sites of Settlement of the Desert Nomads" (Heb.), *Eretz-Israel* XVIII (1984-5), pp. 366-376.

²²⁴ Rudolph Cohen, 'The Israelite Fortifications in the Negev Highlands' (Heb.), *Qadmoniyot* XII/2-3 (1979), pp. 38-50.

²²⁵ Zeev Meshel, "Who Built the Israelite Fortifications on the Negev Highlands?" (Heb.), *Qatedra* 11 (1978-9), pp. 3-44; Meshel & Goren, "An 'Aharoni Fortification' next to Qesima – Another 'Israelite Fortification' in the Negev and the 'Fortification' Problem" (Heb.), *Eretz-Israel* XXIII (1991-2), pp. 196-223.

²²⁶ Yitzchak Meitlis, "The Central and South Golan in the Iron Age" (Heb.), *Al Atar* 4-5 (1998-9), pp. 11-40.

²²⁷ The campaign of Shishak can, of course, be dated some 100 years later, as required by those who hold with the "lower chronology." But doing so mandates a revision of Egyptian chronology.

²²⁸ Rudolph Cohen, "The Iron Age Fortresses in the Central Negev", *BASOR* 236 (1979), pp. 61-79.

²²⁹ Yohanan Aharoni et al., "The Ancient Desert Agriculture of the Negev", *I.E.J.* X (1960), pp. 97-103.

²³⁰ Zeev Meshel, "Horvat Ritema – An Iron Age Fortress in the Negev Highlands", *T.A.* 4 (1977), pp. 110-135. Regarding Tel Asdar see: Moshe Kochavi, "Tel Asdar" (Heb.), *Atikot* 5 (1968-9), pp. 14-48.

²³¹ Jane Cahill, "Jerusalem in David and Solomon's Time: Was It Really a Major City in the Tenth Century B.C.E.?", *BAR.* 30 (2004), pp. 20-31, 62-63; Amihai Mazar, "Jerusalem in the Tenth Century BCE: the Full Half of the Glass" (Heb.), in Avraham Faust and Eyal Baruch, eds., *New Developments in the Research of Jerusalem: the Tenth Collection*, (Ramat Gan: Bar-Ilan Univ., 2004-5), pp. 11-22.

²³² This is essentially a paraphrase of the statement by Nachmanides: "the holier the site, the more it is in ruins."

²³³ Eilat Mazar and Benjamin Mazar, "Excavations in the South of the Temple Mount", *Qedem* 29 (Jerusalem, 1989).

²³⁴ For opinions on the area of the kingdom of Jerusalem, see the summary in Yitzchak Meitlis, *The Judean Hills in the Middle Bronze Age* (Heb.), Ph.D. thesis, Tel-Aviv University, Tel-Aviv (1997-8), p. 177. See also Gershon Galil, "The Canaanite City-States in the 14th Century BCE: their size and political status", *Qatedra* 84 (1996-7) (Heb.), pp. 54-57. Also, see above.

[235] For these settlements, see Ephraim Stern, ed., *The New Encyclopedia of Archaeological Excavations* (Heb.), (Jerusalem: Israel Exploration Society, 1992), under the appropriate headings.

[236] For the archaeological findings of this period, see: A. Meyer, "Jerusalem before David: an archaeological survey from the close of the prehistoric period to the close of Iron Age I" (Heb.), in Shmuel Ahituv and Amihai Mazar, eds., *Sefer Yerushalayim: Tekufat HaMiqra* (1999-2000), pp. 33-66.

[237] A survey of the various opinions on this matter can be found in Israel Finkelstein & Neil Asher Silberman, "Archaeology and Bible at the onset of the Third Millenium: a View from the Center" (Heb.), in: *Qatedra* 100 (2000-2001), pp. 47-64.

[238] For the various suggestions regarding the location of the (H)aqra, see Yoram Tsafrir, "Concerning the Location of the Seleucid Haqra in Jerusalem" (Heb.), *Qatedra* 14 (1979-80), pp. 17-40; Meir Ben-Dov, "The Seleucid Haqra to the South of the Temple Mount" (Heb.), *Qatedra* 18 (1980-81), pp. 22-35; and Yehoshua Schwartz, "*B'r hqr, bwr hqr* and the Seleucid Haqra", *Qatedra* 37 (1985-6), pp. 3-16.

[239] B. Bar-Kochba, *The Wars of the Hasmoneans* (Heb.), Jerusalem (1980-81), pp. 315-329.

[240] A test case of this argument is the distribution of the finds from the Middle Bronze Age in Jerusalem. The MBA is represented impressively in the excavations conducted on the eastern slope of the City of David and near the Gihon. These excavations uncovered walls, towers and other structures. However, only a few potsherds have been found on the ridge itself. For the distribution of the finds from this period see Yitzchak Meitlis, "The Status of Jerusalem in MBA II in light of Archaeological Finds" (Heb.), *Judea and Samaria Studies – Proceedings of the Sixth Convention 1996*, College of Judea and Samaria (1997), pp. 11-16; Ronny Reich & Eli Shukroun, "Jerusalem, City of David", *Archaeological News* 112 (Heb.), 2000-1, pp. 102-104.

[241] For the reliability of Josephus Flavius regarding the descriptive data in his books, see Benjamin Mazar, "Joseph ben Mattithyahu – the Historian of Jerusalem" (Heb.), in Ahron Rapaport, ed., *Joseph ben Mattithyahu – the Historian of Eretz-Israel*, (Jerusalem, 1982-3), pp. 1-6; Magen Beroshi, "The Reliability of Joseph ben Mattithyahu – Descriptive Data in *The Jewish Wars* and its Sources" (Heb.), ibid., pp. 21-27. See also Ze'ev Safrai, "The Description of the Land of Israel in Josephus' Works", in: Louis H. Feldman and Gohei Hata, eds., *Josephus, the Bible and History*, (Leiden:EJ Brill,1989), pp. 295-324.

[242] See, e.g., the opinion of Bar Kochba, *supra* note 238.

[243] Yoram Tsafrir, "The Topography and Archaeology of Aelia Capitolina" (Heb.), in Yoram Tsafrir and Shemuel Safrai, eds., *The Jerusalem Book – the Roman and Byzantine Periods*, (Jerusalem, 1998-9), pp. 115-166.

²⁴⁴ See Shmuel Yeivin, "Ophel, Ha'Ophel", *Entsiklopedia Miqra'it* (Heb.) VI, pp. 320-321; Y. Pres, "Ophel, Zion and the City of David" (Heb.), in: Y. Pres, *Studies in Geography and Biblical Topography*, Jerusalem (1960-1), pp. 11-19.

²⁴⁵ F.L. Andersen & D.N. Freedman, *The Anchor Bible – Micah* (NY:Doubleday, 2000), p. 439.

²⁴⁶ Ibid., note 205.

²⁴⁷ Rudolph Cohen and Yigael Israel, "The Excavations at Ein Hatzeva – Biblical and Roman Tamar" (Heb.), *Qadmoniyot* 112 (1996-7), pp. 78-92.

²⁴⁸ Nadav Na'aman's reaction to the results of this excavation should be noted. It is an interesting example of how an historian attempts to distort the findings of an excavation without being familiar with the finds themselves. For this, see Nadav Na'aman, "Comments on the excavations at Ein-Hatzeva", *Qadmoniyot* 113 (1996-7), p. 60. See also the response of the excavators *ibid.*

²⁴⁹ Rudolph Cohen, "Kadesh-Barnea" (Heb.), *HaEntsiklopedia HaHadasha laHafirot Archaeologiyot beEretz-Israel* IV (1992), pp. 1351-1355.

²⁵⁰ Yochanan Aharoni, "Beer Sheba I, Excavations at Tel Be'er-Sheva, 1969-1971 Seasons", *Tel-Aviv* (1973); "Excavations at Tel Be'er-Sheva, 1973-1974", *Tel-Aviv* 2 (1975).

²⁵¹ Yitzhak Beit-Arieh, "Malhata, Tel", *HaEntsiklopedia Hahadasha lahafirot Archaeologiyot beEretz-Israel* (Heb.), Vol. III (1992), pp. 947-950.

²⁵² Eliezer Oren, "Shara', Tel", *HaEntsiklopedia Hahadasha lahafirot Archaeologiyot beEretz-Israel* (Heb.), Vol. IV (1992), pp. 1563-1570.

²⁵³ See Gottlieb Schumacher, *The Jaulan* (London: Scribner & Welford,1888), pp. 63-64. See also Bustenay Oded, *"Darb el-Haurana* – an Ancient Road", *Eretz-Israel* X (1970-1), pp. 191-197.

²⁵⁴ For details of the oil industry, see Yitzchak Meitlis, "The Oil Industry in the Iron Age," *Al-Atar* (2004-2005).

²⁵⁵ For further details and references, see Meitlis, op.cit.

²⁵⁶ Zif, too, appears on the list, but it is not clear whether this is Zif in the southern Hebron hill country or another Zif located on the plain. On the list of cities, Zif appears alongside Mareisha and Gat on the Shfelah (verse 8).

²⁵⁷ Ephraim Stern, "Azeka" (Heb.), *Ha-entsiklopedia Ha-hadasha Le-hafirot Archeologiyot b'Eretz-Israel, III* (1992), pp. 1165-1167.

²⁵⁸ David Ussishkin, "Lachish" (Heb.), *Ha-entsiklopedia Ha-hadasha Le-hafirot Archeologiyot b'Eretz-Israel III* (1992), pp. 858-859.

²⁵⁹ Nelson Glueck, "Kheleifeh, Tel-el," *Ha-entsiklopedia Ha-hadasha Le-hafirot Archeologiyot b'Eretz-Israel II* (1992), pp. 496-499.

²⁶⁰ Magen Broshi and Israel Finkelstein, "The Size of the Population of Eretz-Israel in the year 734 BCE" (Heb.), *Kathedra* 58 (1991), pp. 3-24.

[261] Magen Broshi, "The Number of Residents of Ancient Jerusalem" (Heb.), *Bein Hermon l'Sinai – Yad l'Amnon*, M. Broshi, ed., (Jerusalem: 1976-77), pp. 65-74.

[262] Yigal Shiloh, "The Number of Residents of Eretz-Israel in the Iron Age in light of a Sample Analysis of Urban Blueprints, Area and Population Density" (Heb.), *Eretz-Israel* XV (1980-81), pp. 274-288.

[263] Broshi and Finkelstein, *ibid.*, note 56.

[264] Gideon Bieger and David Grossman, "Population Density of a Traditional Village in Eretz-Israel" (Heb.), *Kathedra* (1991-92), pp. 108-121.

[265] Yehoshua Ben-Arieh, *A City Reflected by an Era, Jerusalem in the 19th Century* (Heb.), (Jerusalem: Yitzhak Ben-Zvi Institute, 1977), p. 318.

[266] Conrad Schick, "Studien Uber die Ein Wohnerzahl de Salten Jerusalem", *ZDPV IV*, 1881, p. 216.

[267] See the commentary by Avram Kahana to the Book of Nehemiah, and also M. S. Segal, *An Introduction to the Bible* (Heb.), Jerusalem 1977, p. 774.

[268] This is assuming that the size of the average family in this period was similar to that in the Ottoman period. See Natan Shur, "The Numerical Relationship between Houses of Fathers and the total number of people in the cities of Eretz-Israel in the Ottoman Period" (Heb.), *Kathedra XVII* (1980), 102-106.

[269] See Yoram Tsafrir, "The Walls of Jerusalem in the days of Nehemiah" (Heb.), *Kathedra IV* (1976-77), pp. 31-42.

[270] Thomas Chaplin, "Note on the Population of Jerusalem During the Siege of Titus", *Athenaeum*, 23/2 (London, 1878), pp. 255-256.

[271] Yizhar Hirschfeld, *The Residential Building in Eretz-Israel during the Roman-Byzantine Period* (Heb.), (Jerusalem, 1986-87).

[272] Chaplin, *ibid.* See note 269.

[273] Gideon Sojberg, *The Pre-Industrial City*, (New York: Free Press, 1965), p. 83.

[274] K. Davis, "The Role of Urbanization Development Process," *Rehovot Conference* (1971).

[275] Elisha Efrat, *Elements of Urban Geography* (Heb.), (Tel Aviv, 1979), pp. 57-65.

[276] Zeev Herzog, *The Archaeology of City: Urban Planning in Ancient Israel and its Social Implications*, Monograph Series (Tel Aviv: Institute of Archaeology, Yass Archaeological Press, Tel Aviv University, 1997) #13.

[277] Ephraim Stern, 'Crafts and Industry' in: Avraham Malamat, ed., *The History of the People of Israel, Period of the Monarchy, Culture and Society* (Heb.), (Jerusalem, 1981-2), pp. 169-190.

[278] Shilo, *ibid.*, note 60.

[279] Yehuda Dagan, *The Settlements in the Inland Judean Plain in the Second and First Milleniums BCE – A Test Case for Settlement Processes in a Given Region* (Heb.), Ph.D. Thesis, (Tel Aviv: Tel-Aviv University, 2001), Part II, pp. 18-32.

[280] Avshalom Shmueli, *The End of Nomadism* (Heb.), (Tel Aviv, 1980-81) p. 73.

[281] Gilmour in his work divided the sites of worship in the Land of Israel from the period of the Judges (Iron Age) on a regional basis. According to his division it is possible to see unique lines of distinction between the sites on the central mount in comparison to those in the Emek, in Beit Shean and in Paleshet. See: G.H. Gilmour, Levant in the early Iron Age, An Analytical and Comparative Approach. Thesis submitted to University of Oxford, England, 1995.

[282] A. Zertal, A Nation Born, The Altar at Mount Ebal and the beginning of Israel, Tel Aviv, 2000.

[283] A. Mazar. Site of worship from the Period of the Judges in the hills of Shomron; The Land of Israel, 16, Jerusalem, 1982. See pp. 135-144.

[284] Y. Yadin Hazor (The Shweich Lectures of the British Academy, 1970), London, 1972, pp. 132-134.

[285] On figurines called Pillar Figurines, typical of the Yehuda region. See R. Kletter. Between Archaeology and Theology: The Pillar Figurines from Judah and the Asherah, in A. Mazar (ed) Studies in Archaeology of the Iron Age in Israel and Jordan, Sheffield Academic Press, Great Britain, 2001, pp. 179-206.

[286] For detailed description, see Z. Meshel Kadmoniot 36, 1977. See pp. 119-124. Also from the above *Hurvat Teiman, New Encyclopedia of Archaeological Digs in the Land of Israel*, Vol. 4, 1992. See pp. 1577-1578.

E. Ayalon. The Iron Age II Pottery Assemblage from Hurvat Teiman (Kuntilet Ajrud) Tel Aviv 22/2. 1995 pp. 141-212.

[287] S. Achitov, Collection of Hebrew Inscriptions from First Temple period and the beginning of the Second Temple, Jerusalem, 1993.

[288] N. Avigad. *Inscription of the burial site of "Yehu who was in charge of the royal house"* Eretz Israel 3 (Book of Kesato) Jerusalem, 1954. See pp. 66-72.

[289] Y. Neveh, Hebrew inscriptions from the fortress Hashavyahu, Information about the investigation of Eretz Israel and its antiquities, 25, 1961. See pp. 119-128

[290] N.H. Tur Sinai, Lachish Letters (renewed edition by S. Achitov) Jerusalem, 1987. See p. 89; p. 174.

[291] Y. Aharoni, 'Excavations at Tel Be'er Sheva, 1973-1974.' Tel Aviv 2, 1975, pp. 146-168.

[292] Y. Aharoni, 'The Horned Altar of Be'er Sheva,' BA 37, 1974, pp. 2-6.

[293] ibid.

[294] A. Biran, Dan: 25 years of excavations in Dan. Tel Aviv, 1992. See pp. 188-189. (Heb.)

[295] Z. Herzog. Fortress Mount Arad. Tel Aviv 1997, See pp. 182-209. The Arad Temple; Herzog, 1997. (Heb.)

[296] R. Giveon, 'Egyptian Objects in Bronze and Faience,' in Y. Aharoni

(ed), Beer Sheba I, Excavations at Tel Be'er-Sheva, 1969-1971 Seasons, Tel Aviv, 1973, p. 54.

[297] ibid. Pl. 27,28.

[298] See Biran (as above, note 291) See p. 155.

[299] See M. Haran, Biblical Encyclopedia, Vol. 5 'Nachastan' 1978, pp. 826-827.

About the place of snakes in the Bible see: Y. Zakovitz, 'Temples, magic incantations and snakes.' In D. Kerem (ed) variety of opinions and points of view about the snake in the pardes. The Administration for Settlement Education, Aliyat Hanoar, 1998 pp. 25-37 (I thank Professor Israel Rosenson who drew my attention to this article).

[300] See R. Amiran, Ol Ilan, M. Saban, 'Canaanite Arad-City Gateway to the Desert' Israel Museum, Jerusalem, 1997. See pp. 98-101.

[301] On these ritual platforms and other parallels throughout the Middle East, see P. Beck 'Altar Platforms from Tanaakh.' For a clarification of the Iconographic tradition of instruments of worship found in the Land of Israel in Bronze Age I from N. Na'aman, Y. Finkelstein (editors) 'From Nomadism to Kingdom,' Jerusalem, 1990, pp. 417-446 (esp. 430). There are also references to other places.

[302] Aharoni (above, footnote 90) See note 290.

[303] Aharoni – Explained the finding of stone fragments in the wall attributed to stratum III by claiming that the stone was broken during the process of building the temple (see note 90, p 154). One should comment that it is possible to estimate the date of the destruction of the altar as corresponding to the time of the construction of the smooth slope of stratum III. There is no evidence that the altar was destroyed during the period of the building of stratum II. See note 290.

[304] According to the Mishne of Avoda Zorah it is possible to use stones of an altar designated for idol worship if most of the altar's stones were destroyed (Avoda Zorah, 53b).

[305] The appearance of figurines in stratum II on the site (see above, note 293) teaches us that the reform of worship by Chizkiyahu lasted only temporarily in Tel Sheva.

[306] Y. Aharoni - Inscription in Arad, Jerusalem 1976, Document 7. (Heb.)

[307] S.A> Loewenstamm, Document 7 from Arad Document. Evidence of Cessation of Work on New Moons, Beit Mikra, 21, 1976, pp. 330-332. (Heb.)

[308] The connection between the verses and the findings of the altar has already been discussed briefly by Z. Herzog 'The significance of the concept 'high place' in the light of archaeological findings,' Bet Mikra, 73, 1978. See pp. 177-182. (Heb.) It seems that Herzog changed his mind and accepted the opinion of Aharoni. See entry 'Beer Sheba' in *New Encyclopedia of Archaeological Digs in the Land of Israel*, Vol. 6, p. 140. There Herzog compares the temple in Arad to the altar in Beer Sheba.

[309] In this chapter I do not relate to sources which deal with the commandments to keep the Shabbat and Festivals, but rather how they are reflected in actuality in the days of the First Temple.

[310] Y. Naveh 'Hebrew Inscriptions from the Fortress of Hashavyahu.' See note 289. (Heb.)

[311] Y. Aharoni- Inscription in Arad, Jerusalem 1976, Document 7. (Heb.)

[312] For more extensive and detailed discussion see G. Barkai, 'Graves and Burial in Judea in the Biblical Period' from: A. Singer (ed.) 'Graves and Burial Customs in the Land of Israel in Antiquity,' Jerusalem, 1994, pp. 96-164. (Heb.)

[313] B. Oded, The World of the Bible, Chronicles II, Tel Aviv, 1995.

[314] A. Gorezladani, Administration Centers in the Iron Age in Nachal Tut. Days of study: 'Digs and Investigations in the Subject of the Central Region,' 2005. www.antiquities.org.il/article.

[315] See Y. Aharoni, Eretz Israel at the time of the Bible. Geographia Historical, Jerusalem 1987, page 144.

[316] Gabriel Barkai, "City of David," in *Studies on City of David and Jerusalem 3*, ed. Eyal Meron (2008), 44-58 [Hebrew]. Barkai offers this opinion as his, without noting that he heard it from me.

[317] Israel Finkelstein, "Jerusalem in the Persian (and Early Hellenistic) Period and the Wall of Nehemiah," JSOT 32 (2008), 501-20.

[318] Eilat Mazar, "Nehemiah's Wall," in *Studies on City of David and Jerusalem 3* ed. Eyal Meron (2008), 62-69 [Hebrew]

[319] Gabriel Barkai, "Another Look at Jerusalem in the Days of Nehemiah," in *Studies on City of David and Jerusalem 3*, ed. Eyal Meron (2008), 48-54 [Hebrew].

[320] Israel Finkelstein et al., "Has David's Palace in Jerusalem Been Found?" *Tel Aviv* 34, no. 2 (2007): 142-64

Chapter 7

[321] Gershon Edelstein; Ianir Milevski; Sara Aurant, "Villages, Terraces and Stone Mounds, Excavations at Manahat, Jerusalem 1987-1989," *IAA Reports* 3, 1998, n. 27.

[322] Cup-marks are small artificial depressions, which may have been used for grinding kernels of grain or for the manufacture of olive oil.

[323] Ibid., n. 36.

[324] See H. Smithline, "Khirbet Kishrun in Lower Galilee" (Heb.), in *Sugyot Archaeologiyot Nivharot, Sidrat Yemei Iyyun le-Hoqerim, Yom Ha-Iyyun Ha-Shelish,* (Jerusalem: Israel Antiquities Authority, February, 2001), p. 3.

[325] Kubiliyo Paran, "Social and Economic Aspects according to the Ein Hilu (Migdal Ha-Emek) Excavations" (Heb.), ibid., pp. 4-5..

[326] Rudolph Cohen, *Settlements in the Hills of the Negev* (Heb.), Ph.D. thesis, Hebrew University (Jerusalem:1986).

[327] James L. Kelso, "The Excavation of Bethel (1934-1960)," *AASOR* 39, 1968, pp. 22-23.

[328] Moshe Kochavi, "Khirbet Rabud is Biblical Dvir" (Heb.), in Yochanan Aharoni, ed., *Excavation and Study* (Heb.), (Tel-Aviv:1973), pp. 49-76.

[329] For details of the graves, see Meitlis (1997), pp. 141-151.

[330] See Ruth Amiran, *The Ancient Pottery of Eretz Israel* (Heb.) (Jerusalem:1971), p. 103.

[331] See Nadav Na'aman, *The History of the Land of Israel: the Ancient Periods* (Heb.) (Jerusalem:1982), p. 125.

[332] Yigael Yadin, *Qadmoniyot* 16 (1971-2), pp. 25-26.

[333] William G. Dever, "New Vistas on the EBIV(MBI) Horizon in Syria-Palestine", *BASOR* 237 (1980), pp. 35-64.

[334] Yuval Goren, "The Southern Levant in the Early Bronze Age IV: The Petrographic Perspective", *BASOR* 303 (1996), pp. 33-72.

[335] It can, of course, also be claimed that the potters — the makers of the ceramic vessels in the Judean Hills and on the eastern bank of the Jordan River — are the very same people who moved to the Negev highlands in order to sell their products. This is a reasonable interpretation, though the large number of vessels made in the Judean Hills, and especially across the Jordan River, makes it more likely that it was the people of the Negev themselves who moved from one place to another.

[336] Meitlis (1997), p. 160.

[337] This phenomenon was uncovered in the Etzion Bloc in the northern Hebron hills and in Khirbet Karmil in the southern Hebron hills.

[338] Yitzchak Meitlis, "Burial Formations – Indications of Different Ethnic Groups in the Judean Hills during the Middle Bronze Ages" in Yaacov Eshel, ed., *Judea and Samaria Research Studies, Proceedings of the Fifth Annual Meeting* (1995), pp. 23-26.

[339] Kathleen M. Kenyon, "Tombs of the Intermediate Early Bronze-Middle Bronze Age at Tel Ajul," *ADAJ* 3 (1956), pp. 41-56; William G. Dever, "The Beginning of the Middle Bronze Age in Syria Palestine" in Frank M. Cross et al. eds., *Magnalia Dei: The Mighty Acts of God* (New York: Doubleday & Co. 1976), pp. 3-38; *ibid.*, "From the End of the Early Bronze to the Beginning of the Middle Bronze" in: J. Amitai ed., *Biblical Archaeology Today: Proceedings of the International Congress on Biblical Archaeology* (Jerusalem: Israel Exploration Society, 1985), pp. 113-135; Pirhiyah Beck, "The Middle Bronze Age IIA Pottery from Aphek, 1972-1984: First Summary", *Tel Aviv* 12 (1985), pp. 181-203; Aharon Kempinski, *An Introduction to the Archaeology of the Israel in the Period of the Bible, Unit 6* (Heb.), (Tel Aviv: Everyman's University, 1988-9).

[340] Dever, *op. cit.*

[341] Patty Gerstenblith, "A Re-assessment of the Beginning of the Middle Bronze Age in Syria-Palestine", *BASOR* 237 (1980), pp. 65-84.

[342] Op. cit., n. 296, pp. 18, 21.

[343] Ruth Amiran, *The Early Pottery of Eretz-Israel* (Heb.), Jerusalem (1971), p. 1.

[344] Ruth Amiran, "The Pottery of the Middle Bronze Age I in Palestine", *IEJ* 10 (1960), pp. 204-225.

[345] Jonathan N. Tubb, "The MGAII Period in Palestine: Its Relationship with Syria and Origin", *Levant* 15 (1983), pp. 49-63.

[346] Amiran, ibid.

[347] Israel Finkelstein, "The Central Hill Country in the Intermediate Bronze Age", *IEJ* 41 (1991), pp. 19-45.

[348] It is possible that sections of a wall dating from this period were actually found in Hebron, as Jeffrey Chadwick claims (see *The Archaeology of Biblical Hebron in the Bronze and Iron Age: An Examination of the Discoveries of the American Expedition to Hebron*, Ph.D. Thesis, University of Utah,1992, though the findings are not all that unambiguous.

[349] Vessels characteristic of the northern coastal plain and the Jezreel Valley. These vessels are decorated and burnished, unlike the rest of the Intermediate Bronze Age pottery which has neither decorations nor burnishing.

[350] For this, see Meitlis, 1997, pp. 164-165.

[351] Ibid., p.165.

[352] William G. Dever, "MBA II Cemeteries at 'Ain es-Samiya and Sinjil", *BASOR* 217 (1975), pp. 23-36.

[353] One of the characteristics of the pottery of the Early and Intermediate Bronze Ages are jars with broad, flat horizontal handles reminiscent of shelves in a closet. Handles of this type no longer exist from the Middle Bronze Age on.

[354] The information regarding the Refaim Valley is adduced in the article by Eisenberg, n. 35, p. 94. For the data from Efrata and other sites see: Noemi

Acreche, "Skeletal Remains from Efrata and Other Bronze Sites in Israel", in Rivka Gonen, "Excavations at Efrata: A Burial Ground from the Intermediate and Middle Bronze Ages," *IAA Reports*, (Jerusalem: Israel Antiquities Authority, 2001), pp. 95-109.

[355] The subject of the changes in population composition is extremely significant for an understanding of the Patriarchal era.

[356] At Tel el-Hariri, not far from the Syrian-Iraqi border, the city of Mari was discovered. It was an important royal city and maintained contact with Babylon and with other kingdoms in Syria and in northern Israel. In the vast 300-room palace at Mari, an enormous archive containing some 25,000 documents was found. From those that have been deciphered, it is clear that multi-faceted relations existed between Hatzor and Mari. Mari supplied Hatzor with tin for the manufacture of bronze, a metal made of copper and tin.

[357] See James B. Pritchard, *The Bronze Age Cemetery at Gibeon*, (Philadelphia:University of Pennsylvania, University Museum 1963); Pritchard, *Winery Defences and Soundings at Gibeon*, (Philadelphia:University of Pennsylvania, University Museum, 1964).

[358] See Meitlis (1997), chapter 31.

[359] Patty Gerstenblith, *The Levant at the Beginning of the Middle Bronze Age*, Philadelphia: American Schools of Oriental Research; Winona Lake, IN: dist. by Eisenbrauns, 1983), p. 34.

[360] Stanslao Loffreda, "La tomba no. 4 del Bronzo Medio IIB a Betania", *LA* 34 (1984), pp. 357-370; Hugues Vincent, "Chronique", *RB* 23 (1914), pp. 438-441.

[361] Baruch Brandl and Benjamin Sass, "Forgotten Scarabs with Names of Officials from Canaan", *ZDPV* 101 (1984), pp. 111-113.

[362] R.A.S. Macalister and J. Duncan, "Excavations on the Hill of Ophel, Jerusalem 1923-1925", *APEF* IV (1926), pp. 175-176.

[363] Op. cit., pp.177-178.

[364] Kathleen M. Kenyon, *Digging Up Jerusalem* (London:Benn, 1974).

[365] Yigal Shiloh, *The Excavations in the City of David I (Qedem 19)*, Jerusalem (1984).

[366] See Ovid R. Sellers, *The Citadel of Beth-Zur* (Philadelphia: Westminster Press,1933); ibid., "The 1957 Excavations at Beth Zur," *AASOR* 38, 1968.

[367] See Shlomo Bunimovitz, *The Land of Israel in the Late Bronze Age: A Test Case for Socio-Cultural Change in a Complex Society* (Heb.), Ph.D. Thesis (Tel Aviv University, 1989/90); ibid., "The Limits and Terminology of the Beginning of the Late Bronze Age" (Heb.), *Eretz-Israel* 23 (1991-2), pp. 262-263.

[368] Benjamin Mazar, "Qiryat Arba' which is Hebron" (Heb.), *Towns and Districts in Erets-Israel*, Jerusalem (1975-6), p. 49.

[369] See Gonen, ibid. *Excavations at Efrata*. No pottery discussion, ceramic tables, or detailed sections of the various strata were added to this paper, which

is, consequently, at the level of a detailed first report, and there is no way to evaluate or discuss the conclusions drawn by the writer.

370 Ibid., Chadwick. See note 44, page 36.

371 See Meitlis (1997), Table 18: 11, 12, 13.

372 Moshe Anbar and Nadav Na'aman, "An Account Tablet of Sheep from Ancient Hebron", *Tel-Aviv* 13-14 (1986-7), pp. 3-12.

373 Israel Finkelstein, "Middle Bronze Age 'Fortifications': A Reflection of Social Organization and Political Formations", *Tel-Aviv* 19 (1992), pp. 201-220.

374 Yuval Peleg and Irina Eisenstadt, "The Late Bronze Age Tomb at Hebron (Tel Rumeideh)", in: Hananya Hizmi and Alon De-Groot (eds.), *Burial Caves and Sites in Judea and Samaria from the Bronze and Iron Age* (Jerusalem: Israel Antiquities Authority, 2004), pp. 231-259.

375 See, e.g., Israel Finkelstein, *The Archaeology of the Period of Conquest and Judges* (Heb.), (Tel-Aviv, 1986), p. 217. On the basis of this assumption, Finkelstein compares the process of conquest and settling the hill country in Iron Age I with the processes of conquest of Bedouin tribes at the outset of the 20th century (*ibid.*, pp. 223-228). See also the attempt of Bunimovits to compare the situation in the hill country in the Late Bronze Age to that in the Ottoman period in Shlomo Bunimovits, *The Israel in the Late Bronze Age: A Test Case for Social-Cultural Change in a Complex Society*, Ph. D. Thesis at Tel-Aviv University, p. 281.

376 Eliezer Oren, "Palaces and Mansions in the Middle and Late Bronze Ages" (Heb.) in: Hannah Katzenstein *et al.* (eds.), *Architecture in the Land of Israel in Antiquity*, (Jerusalem: Israel Exploration Society,1986-7), pp. 90-101, and also Aharon Kempinski, "Urbanization and Urban Planning in MBA II" (Heb.), *ibid.*, pp. 102-106.

377 Carol Kramer, *Village Ethno-archaeology: Implications of Ethnography for Archaeology*, (New York: Columbia Univ. Press, 1982), pp. 252-253.

378 Avshalom Shmueli, *Nomadic Settlement in the Jerusalem Area in the Twentieth Century* (Heb.), Ph.D. dissertation at the Hebrew University of Jerusalem (1973), p. 92.

379 Op. cit., p. 469.

380 Shmueli, "The Settlement of the Negev Bedouins as Part of the Bedouin Settlement Process in the Israel" (Heb.), in Avshalom Shmueli and Yehuda Gardos (eds.), *Eretz-Ha-Negev*, (Tel-Aviv, 1978-9), pp. 673-688.

381 David Amiran, David Shinar and Yosef Ben-David, "The Bedouin Settlements in the Beer Sheba Valley" (Heb.), in Shmueli and Gardos (eds.), *Eretz Ha- Negev*, p. 662.

382 Avraham Malamat, "'Hatzerim' in the Bible and in Mari" (Heb.), *Yediot ba-Haqirat Eretz-Israel va'Atikoteha* (xxvii) [1962-3], pp. 181-184.

[383] For this, see Yitzchak Meitlis, "The Agriculture of Farms around Jerusalem at the end of the First Temple Era" (Heb.), in Shimon Dar (ed.): *New Insights into the Study of Ancient Agriculture and Economy of Eretz-Israel* (Heb.), the Twelfth Congress (1992), Ramat-Gan, pp. 3-13. Op. cit., "Houses and Courtyards: Agricultural Systems from the First Temple Era" (Heb.), in: *Proceedings of the Eleventh World Congress for Jewish Studies* (Heb.) (1994), pp. 55-62.

[384] For the significance of this point as the background for the period of the Patriarchs, see Part I.

[385] Adam Zertal, *Israelite Settlement in the Menashe Hill Country* (Heb.), Ph.D. Thesis at Tel Aviv University (1985-86).

[386] Israel Finkelstein, "The Land of Ephraim Survey 1980-1987: Preliminary Report, *Tel-Aviv 15-16* (1988-1989)p. 123.

[387] Avi Ofer, *The Judean Hills in the Biblical Period* (Heb.), Ph.D. Thesis at Tel-Aviv University (1993-4), pp. 138-160.

[388] Meitlis, 1997. p.p. 100-128

[389] The built-up area estimate is based on the product of multiplying the average size class by the number of sites of that class.

[390] See Sites 86 and 139 in the List of Sites in my Ph.D. thesis, Meitlis 1997.

[391] For the built-up area estimate, see above.

[392] Adam Zertal, 1985-1986, note 11, p. 197.

[393] Moshe Kochavi, "The First Two Seasons of Excavations at Aphek-Antipatris," *Tel-Aviv 2* (1975), p. 30.

[394] Israel Finkelstein, "The Socio-Political Organization of the Central Hill Country in the Second Millennium BCE" in: Avraham Biran and Joseph Aviram (eds.), *Biblical Archaeology Today 1990. Proceedings of the Second International Congress on Biblical Archaeology* (Jerusalem: Jerusalem Exploration Society, 1993), pp. 110-131.

[395]. Michael Chisholm, *Rural Settlement and Land Use* (London: Hutchinson Univ. Library, 1962), p. 73.

[396]. Elisha Efrat, *The Elements of Urban Geography* (Heb.), (Tel Aviv:Ahiasaf, 1979), p. 77.

[397]. Israel Finkelstein, 1993.

[398]. M.B. Rowton, "Urban Autonomy in a Nomadic Environment", *JNES* 32 (1973), 201-215.

[399]. Yehuda Karmon and Avshalom Shmueli, *Hebron – the Profile of a Hill Country Town*, (Tel Aviv:Gomeh, 1969-70), pp. 23-32.

[400]. For the agriculture of the Bedouins in the Sanjak of Jerusalem in the Ottoman period, see Ehud Toledano, "The Sanjak of Jerusalem in the

16th Century – Rural Settlement and Demographic Trends" (Heb.), in Amnon Cohen, *Chapters in the History of Jerusalem at the Onset of the Ottoman Period* (Heb.) (Jerusalem:Yad Ben Tzvi,1979), p. 89.

[401.] Magen Broshi and Ram Gophna, "Eretz-Israel in MBA II: Settlements and Population", *Kathedra* 31 (1983-4), pp. 3-26.

[402.] The coefficient of 25 persons per dunam, as Broshi advocates, is quite reasonable in the settlements of this period (see Broshi and Gophna, 1983-84, ibid.), though one must not ignore the problematic nature of determining a uniform coefficient of population density for settlements of all kinds throughout the country. Gideon Bieger and David Grossman, "Population Density in the Traditional Villages of Eretz-Israel" (Heb.), *Kathedra* 63 (1991-2), pp. 108-121. Ram Gophna and Juval Portugaly, "Settlement and Demographic Processes in Israel's Coastal Plain from the Chalcolithic to the Middle Bronze Age", *BASOR* 269 (1988), pp. 11-28, and see also below with regard to the First Temple period.

[403.] Sites nos. 13, 20, 44, 45, 48, 50, 77, 83 and 85 in the List of Sites appearing in my doctoral thesis; Meitlis (1997).

[404.] Avshalom Shmueli, *The End of the Nomadic Era*, (Heb.) (Tel Aviv, 1981), p.73.

[405.] Eighty-five sites were actually counted in this survey, but since some of these were those in the northern Bet-El hills already considered, we have deducted 13 sites from the original number.

[406.] Israel Finkelstein, "The Land of Ephraim Survey 1980-1987: Preliminary Report", *Tel-Aviv* 15-16 (1988-89), pp. 117-183.

[407] The ways by which the areas of the Hills of Menashe settlement were estimated are similar to those we have used in this book. Adam Zertal, *The Israelite Settlement in the Hills of Menashe*, Ph. D. thesis at the University of Tel-Aviv, pp. 195-197.

[408] Israel Finkelstein, "The Central Hill Country in the Intermediate Bronze Age", *IEJ* 41 (1991), pp. 19-45.

[409] Adam Zertal, *The Menashe Hills Survey I – The Shechem Basin* (Haifa:Dept. of Defense and University of Haifa, 1992).

[410] Liora Kolska Horwitz, "Diachronic Changes in Rural Husbandry Practices in Bronze Age Settlements from the Refaim Valley, Israel", *PEQ* 120, pp. 44-54.

[411] Op.cit., p. 49.

[412] Avi Ofer, "The Biblical Judean Hills from Nomadic Life to National Kingdom" (Heb.), in Nadav Na'aman and Israel Finkelstein (eds.), *From Nomadism to Monarchy* (Jerusalem: Yad Izhak Ben-Zvi, Israel Exploration Society, 1990), p. 192.

[413] Shlomo Hellwing, Moshe Sade and Vered Kishon, "Faunal Remains" in Israel Finkelstein (ed.), *Shiloh: The Archaeology of a Biblical Site* (Tel Aviv: Institute of Archaeology of Tel Aviv Univ., 1993), pp. 309-349.

[414] The table is based on data from the sites in the Judean hill country and on Table 15.2 in Hellwing, Sade and Kishon (1993), see above. The figure there from Tel Masos is not included here, because it is based on only 8 bones. See Eitan Tchernov and Israel Derori, "Economic Patterns and Environmental Conditions at Hirbet el-Masas during the Early Iron Age", in Volkmar Fritz and Aharon Kempinski (eds.), *Ergebnisse der Ausgrabungen auf der Hirbet el-Mas^as (Tel Masos) 1972-1975* (Wiesbaden: O. Harrassowitz, 1983), pp. 215-221, pl. 1.

[415] Adam Zertal, "In the Land of the Perizzite and the Refa'im" – Of the Israelite Settlement in the Hills of Menashe, in: Nadav Na'aman and Israel Finkelstein (eds.), *From Nomadism to Monarchy*, p. 74.

[416] Elkana Billik and S.A. Loewenstamm, "Pig" (Heb.) in: *Entsiklopedia Miqra'it*, vol. 3, Jerusalem (1964-5), pp. 90-94.

[417] Baruch Rosen, "Economy and Survival in the Settlement Period" (Heb.), in: Nadav Na'aman and Israel Finkelstein (eds.), *From Nomadism to Monarchy*, pp. 403-416.

[418] Emanuel Eisenberg, "The Refaim Valley" (Heb.), *Hadashot Archaeologiyot* 95 (1990), pp. 55-61.

[419] Mordechai E. Kislev, "Food Remains", in Israel Finkelstein (ed.), *Shiloh*, pp. 354-361.

[420] Kathleen M. Kenyon, *We Have Uncovered Jericho*, (Heb.) (Tel Aviv, 1961), pp. 172, 177.

[421] Lawrence E. Stager, "The First Fruits of Civilization" in Jonathan N. Tubb (ed.), *Palestine in the Bronze and Iron Ages: Papers in Honour of Olga Tufnell* (London: London Institute of Archaeology, 1985), pp. 172-188; Amnon Ben-Tor, "The Trade Relations of Palestine in the Early Bronze Age", *Journal of the Economic and Social History of the Orient* 29 (1986), pp. 1-27; Israel Finkelstein and Ram Gophna, "Settlement, Demographic and Economic Patterns in the Highlands of Palestine in the Chalcolithic and Early Bronze Periods and the Beginning of Urbanism", *BASOR* 289 (1993), pp. 1-22.

[422] Shmuel Ahituv, "Economic Factors in the Egyptian Conquest of Canaan", *IEJ* 28 (1978), pp. 93-105.

[423] Clair Epstein, "Oil Production in the Golan Heights during the Chalcolithic Period", *Tel-Aviv* 20 (1993), pp. 133-143.

[424] For details, see Meitlis, 1997, p. 152.

[425] 107 Kathleen M. Kenyon, *Excavations at Jericho I* (London: British School of Archaeology in Jerusalem, 1960), p. 270.

⁴²⁶ Aharon Kempinski, *Palestine and Syria in the Final Stage of the Middle Bronze Age*, Ph.D. thesis presented to the Hebrew University in Jerusalem (1973-4), pp. 108-119.

⁴²⁷ Dan P. Cole, *Shechem I: The Middle Bronze IIB Pottery* (Ann Arbor, Mich: American Schools of Oriental Research, 1984).

⁴²⁸ William G. Dever (ed.), *Gezer IV* (Jerusalem: Nelson Glueck School of Biblical Archaeology, 1986).

⁴²⁹ Shlomo Bunimovitz and Israel Finkelstein, "Pottery" in Israel Finkelstein (ed.), *Shiloh*, pp. 81-196.

⁴³⁰ Op.cit., p. 71.

⁴³¹ Op.cit, note 48, p. 115.

⁴³² James L. Kelso, "The Excavation of Bethel (1934-1960)", *AASOR 39* (1968), pp. 57-58.

⁴³³ Yonatan Glass, Yuval Goren, Shlomo Bunimovitz and Israel Finkelstein, "Petrographic Analyses of Middle Bronze Age III, Late Bronze Age and Iron Age I Ceramic Assemblages" in Finkelstein (ed.), *Shiloh*, pp. 271-277.

⁴³⁴ Shlomo Bunimovitz, *The Israel in the Late Bronze Age; a Test Case for Socio-Cultural Change in a Complex Society* (in Heb.), Ph.D. Dissertation of Tel-Aviv University (1989-90); Nadav Na'aman, "The Borders of Canaanite Jerusalem in the Second Millennium BCE" (in Heb.), *Zion* 56 [4] (1990-91), pp. 361-380; Israel Finkelstein, "The Socio-Political Organization of the Central Hill Country in the Second Millennium BCE", in Avraham Biran and Joseph Aviram (eds.), *Biblical Archaeology Today – 1990, Proceedings of the Second International Congress on Biblical Archaeology* (Jerusalem: Israel Exploration Society, 1993), pp. 110-131.

⁴³⁵ Baruch Brandl and Benjamin Sass, "Forgotten Scarabs with Names of Officials from Canaan", *ZDPV* 101 (1984), pp. 111-113. In the graves excavated in Efrata, scarabs were found, but they date from the intermediate period between MBA I and MBA II.

⁴³⁶ See pp. 141 and 146 in Nadav Ne'eman, "Palestine in the Canaanite Period: the Middle Bronze and Late Bronze Ages (approximately 2000-1200 BCE)" in Yisrael Efal (ed.), *The History of the Israel, Volume One: The Ancient Periods* (Jerusalem:Keter & Yad Ben Tzvi, 1982), pp. 129-256. Below: Ne'eman (1982).

⁴³⁷ Daphna Ben-Tor, "The Historical Implications of Middle Kingdom Scarabs Found in Palestine Bearing Private Names and Titles of Officials", *BASOR* 294 (1994), pp. 7-23.

⁴³⁸ For a detailed list of the scarabs, see Meitlis (1997), pp. 174-175.

⁴³⁹ See Fig. 3 in: James M. Weinstein, "The Egyptian Empire in Palestine: A Reassessment", *BASOR 241* (1981), pp. 1-28.

[440] Jeffrey R. Chadwick, *The Archaeology of Biblical Hebron in the Bronze and Iron Ages: An Examination of the Discoveries of the American Expedition to Hebron*, Ph.D. Thesis, The University of Utah (1992), p. 185.

[441] Ovid R. Sellers, *The Citadel of Beth-Zur* (Philadelphia:Westminster Press, 1933), pp. 59-60, fig. 60:6-7, 51; "The 1957 Excavations at Beth-Zur", *AASOR* 38 (1968), pl: 6:50.

[442] G.Ernest Wright, *Shechem, The Biography of a Biblical City* (New York & Toronto: McGraw-Hill, 1965), fig. 65; Siegfried H. Horn, "Scarabs from Shechem", *JNES* 21 (1962), pp. 1-14.

[443] See Gershon Edelstein, Ianir Milevski and Sara Aurant, "Villages, Terraces and Stone Mounds, Excavations at Manahat, Jerusalem 1987-1989", *IAA Reports*, no. 3 (1998)

[444] See Baruch Brandl, "Clay, Bone, Metal and Stone Objects" in Israel Finkelstein (ed.), *Shiloh*, pp. 223-262, esp. pp. 230, 256.

[445] Gabriel Barkay, "An Egyptian Temple in Jerusalem from the Late Bronze Age?" (Heb.), *Eretz-Israel* 21 (1990-1), pp. 94-106.

[446] Baruch Brandl, "Two Scarabs and Trapezoidal Seals from Mt. Ebal", *Tel-Aviv* 13-14 (1986-1987), pp. 166-173.

[447] Rephael Giv'on, *Pharaoh's Footsteps in Canaan*, Tel-Aviv:Sifriat Hapoalim, 1984), p. 109.

[448] Benjamin Mazar, *Canaan and Israel* (Jerusalem:Mosad Bialik, 1973-4), pp. 25, 46.

[449] Adam Zertal, ibid., note 49, pp. 188-190, 197.

[450] Ibid., note 51.

[451] M.B. Rowton, "Urban Autonomy in a Nomadic Environment", *JNES* 32 (1973), pp. 201-215.

[452] The first to appreciate the status of a town in light of its relative size in its region was the geographer Mark Jefferson. See Mark Jefferson, "The Law of Primate City", *Geographic Review* 29 (1939), pp. 226-232. For the application of this geographical model in archaeology, see: Gary Johnson, "Aspects of Regional Analysis in Archaeology", *Annual Review of Anthropology* 6 (1977), pp. 496-501.

[453] G. Ernest Wright, *Shechem: The Biography of a Biblical City* (New York & Toronto: McGraw-Hill, 1965).

[454] For detailed references to these destructions, see Meitlis (1997), p. 180.

[455] Kathleen M. Kenyon, *Archaeology in the Holy Land* (London: . Benn, 1979), p. 194; James M. Weinstein, "The Egyptian Empire in Palestine: A Reassessment", *BASOR* 241 (1981), pp. 1-28; William G. Dever, "'Hyksos', Egyptian Destructions, and the End of the Palestinian Middle Bronze Age", *Levant* 22 (1990), pp. 75-82.

⁴⁵⁶ Donald B. Redford, "A Gate Inscription from Karnak and Egyptian Involvement in Western Asia during the Early 18th Dynasty", *JAOS* 99 (1979), pp. 270-287; James K. Hoffmeier, "Reconsidering Egypt's Part in the Termination of the Middle Bronze Age in Palestine", *Levant* 21 (1989), pp. 181-193; "Some Thoughts on William G. Dever's 'Hyksos, Egyptian Destructions, and the End of the Palestinian Middle Bronze Age'", *Levant* 22 (1990), pp. 83-89.

⁴⁵⁷ Aharon Kempinski, *Syrien und Palestina (Kanaan) in der letzten Phase der Mittelbronze IIB-Zeit (1650-1570 v.chr.)* (Wiesbaden: O. Harrassovitz, 1983).

⁴⁵⁸ Piotr Bienkowski, *Jericho in the Late Bronze Age* (Warminster, Wiltshire: Aris & Phillips, 1986).

⁴⁵⁹ Op.cit., note 49, pp. 183-184.

⁴⁶⁰ Op.cit., note 70, p. 309.

⁴⁶¹ Nadav Na'aman, "The Hurrians and the End of the Middle Bronze Age in Palestine", *Levant* 26 (1994), pp. 175-187.

⁴⁶² Op.cit., note 358.

⁴⁶³ See the Table in Meitlis (1997), p. 188. It should be noted that this table indicates that Shiloh was settled in the 15th century. In actual fact, only vessels were found on this site and no traces of a settlement have been found. The excavator believes there was a sanctuary at this site that served the inhabitants of the region. The pottery found there has been dated to the end of the 15th century and the beginning of the 14th century BCE. See the updated table below.

⁴⁶⁴ This source states that the town of Megiddo was a fortified city, and it also says that, "the conquest of *MKTY* (Megiddo) was like the conquest of a thousand towns." Shmuel Yeivin, "Thutmose III: The Annals (Year 1)" (in Hebrew), *Kovetz Ha-Hevra la-Haqirat Eretz-Yisrael va-Attiqoteha* (1934/5), pp. 152-174.

⁴⁶⁵ Rivka Gonen, "Urbanization in Canaan on the eve of the Conquest of the Land by the Israelites" (Heb.) (Tel Aviv: Millet: The Open University Studies in the History and Culture of Israel, 1983), pp. 25-38; and Aharon Kempinski, "Fortifications in the Middle and Late Bronze Ages" (Heb.) in Hannah Katzenstein *et al.* (eds.), *Architecture in the Land of Israel in Antiquity*, Jerusalem: Israel Exploration Society,1986/7), p. 115; Aharon Kempinski, *Megiddo, A Canaanite City-State and Israelite Royal Center* (Heb.) (Tel Aviv,1993), p. 61; Israel Finkelstein, David Ussishkin and Baruch Halpern (eds.), *Megiddo III: The 1992-1996 Seasons* (Tel Aviv: Tel Aviv Univ., 2000), pp. 592-594.

⁴⁶⁶ Nadav Na'aman (1982), pp. 188-190.

⁴⁶⁷ Yochanan Aharoni, *The Israel in the Biblical Period: an Historical Geography* (Heb.) (Tel Aviv, 1962/3), pp. 146-148.

⁴⁶⁸ For the complex calculations of Mesopotamian chronology, see Hayim Tadmor, "The Chronology of the Early East in the Second Millennium BCE" in

Benjamin Mazar (ed.), *The History of the Jewish People* (Heb.) (Jerusalem, 1981-2) pp. 40-61.

[469] There are three scientific chronological systems: high chronology, which puts the destruction of Babylon in the year 1651 BCE; low chronology, which puts it in the year 1531 BCE; and middle chronology, which puts at in 1595 BCE. This last is the system adopted by researchers of Israel because it fits best with data from Israel. The system employed by Kempinski and others is based on the middle chronology, though it should be noted that as far as data gleaned on the ground none of the chronologies is preferred decisively. See, in this connection, Tadmor, *supra*.

[470] Aharon Kempinski, *Eretz-Israel and Syria in the Final Stage of the Middle Bronze Age*, Ph.D. Dissertation, The Hebrew University in Jerusalem, 1973-4, p. 135.

[471] The bichrome vessels common at the end of the Middle Bronze Age, and especially at the onset of the Late Bronze Age I, are highly burnished flasks and cauldrons that are decorated in red and black. Animal life (especially birds and fish) was drawn on them. Some of these were of local manufacture, while others were made in Cyprus.

[472] It must be stressed that we do not know the lifespan of this bichrome pottery. Furthermore, it is possible that the bichrome pottery made its appearance in Israel before it appeared in Alalakh. Dever (*supra*) claims that the dating of the Cypriot pottery is not absolute in Cyprus either, and so it cannot be used as an indicator for chronological purposes.

[473.] William G. Dever, "The Chronology of Syria-Palestine in the Second Millennium BCE: A Review of Current Issues", *BASOR* 288 (1992), pp. 1-26; and see also Kempinski, ibid., n. 91.

[474.] A debate on principle is raging with regard to sites in the central hill country where bichrome vessels have not been found. In the opinion of Bunimovits, the lack of bichrome vessels indicates that these sites were destroyed prior to the development of the bichrome vessels (Bunimovits, 1990). In the opinion of the present author, the lack of such vessels is a regional matter, just as various imported vessels are not found in the hill country (Meitlis, 1997, *supra*).

[475] Leonard Woolley, *Alalakh* (London, society of Antiquaries, 1955), p. 370.

[476] Marie-Henriette Carre Gates, "Alalakh Levels VI and V, Chronological Reassessment", *Syro-Mesopotamian Studies*, Vol. 4/2 (Malibu, CA: Undena Publications, 1981).

[477] Dever, op.cit., n. 461, p. 14.

[478] Thomas L. McClellan, "The Chronology and Ceramic Assemblages of Alalakh" in Albert Leonard Jr. and Bruce Beyer Williams, *Studies in Ancient Civilization* (Chicago: Oriental institute of the University of Chicago, 1989).

[479] Dever, ibid.

[480] Manfred Bietak, "Relative and Absolute Chronology of the Middle Bronze Age: Comments on the Present State of Research" in M. Bietak (ed.), *The Middle Bronze Age in the Levant*, (Wien: Verlag der Osrerreichischen Akademie der Wssenschaften, 2002), p. 31.

[481] Hermann Gasche et al. *Dating the Fall of Babylon: a Reappraisal of Second Millennium Chronology* (Chicago: University of Ghent and the Oriental Institute of the University of Chicago, 1998), M.H.E. Series II, Memoir IV, ibid., *Akkadica 108* (1998)pp. 1.-5.

[482] A calculation similar to ours was also made by Soldt with regard to Alalakh, dating its destruction to the year 1460 BCE. See Wilfred H. van Soldt, "Syrian Chronology in the Old and Early Middle Babylonian Periods", *Akkadica 119-120* (2000), pp. 103-116.

[483] Gwendolyn Leick, *The Babylonians: An Introduction* (London and New York: Routledge, 2003), p. 43.

[484] For the disagreement between them, see Israel Finkelstein, David Ussishkin and Baruch Halpern (eds), *Megiddo III*, pp. 592-594.

[485] Albert E. Glock, "Taanach" in Ephraim Stern, ed., *The New Encyclopedia of Archaeological Excavations in the Holy Land*, Vol. 4 (Jerusalem: Israel Exploration Society & Carta, 1993), pp. 1428-1433.

[486] In one of these letters, the ruler of Taanakh is ordered (apparently by Amenhotep II) to put in an appearance at Megiddo with his chariots and his horses. Yochanan Aharoni (1963) deduced from this that, at the time, Taanakh was one of the more important cities in the Jezreel Valley.

[487] Na'aman (1982), p. 190.

[488] William G. Dever, "Gezer" in *The New Encyclopedia of Archaeological Excavations in Eretz-Israel* (Heb.), (Jerusalem, 1992), pp. 217-305.

[489] Yigal Yadin and Amnon Ben-Tor, "Hatzor" in *The New Encyclopedia* (Heb.), pp. 531-545.

[490] Avraham Malamat, "Musicians from Hatzor to Mari", *Qadmoniyot* 117 (Heb.), 1998-9, pp. 43-44. Malamat concludes from a letter found in Mari that there was an "Academy of Music" in Hatzor that was famed even at so considerable a distance.

[491] See also Amnon Ben-Tor, "Hazor and Chronology" in *In memory of Yigael Yadin Lectures presented at Symposium of the Twentieth Anniversary of his Death at* the Hebrew University of Jerusalem (Heb.) (Jerusalem: The Israel Exploration Society, 2004) pp. 13-27.

[492] It is worth noting that at the latest excavations in Lachish, a carbon-14 test dated grains of peas and pomegranates that were found in the palace ruins to the end of the Middle Bronze Age 1482- 1315 BCE. The date corresponds with the new dating method and the excavators point out that the date of the sample is a bit later than the accepted date. They also indicate that this is a short term

sample more valuable than tree trunks, where the date reflects the time that the tree was cut down and not the time of the destruction of the building. For this, see: Israel Carmi and David Ussishkin, "C-14 Dates" in D.Ussishkin, ed., *Renewed Archaeological Excavations at Lachish 1973-1994*, Vol. V, 2004, pp. 2508-2512. It is worth mentioning that carbon-14 tests of samples from Jericho show the dates as being early, too early even for the accepted method. It appears that it will be necessary to verify their accuracy.

[493] It should be noted that a similar chronological structure was already proposed by Bimson and Livingston. However, their arguments rested mainly on their desire to coordinate the books of the Bible with archaeological finds, rather than on solid archaeological or historical data. For this, see J.J. Bimson and D. Livingston, "Redating the Exodus", *B.A.R. Vol. XIII, no. 5* (1987), pp. 40-53, 66-68. See also J.J. Bimson, *Redating the Exodus and Conquest*. (Sheffield: Almond Press, 1991).

[494] Fernand Braudel, *The Mediterranean and Mediterranean World in the Age of Philip II* (New York:Harper, 1966).

[495] Robert B. Coote and Keith W. Whitelam, *The Emergence of Early Israel in Historical Perspective* (Sheffield: Almond Press, 1987); Israel Finkelstein, "Middle Bronze Age 'Fortifications': A Reflection of Social Organization and Political Formations", *Tel-Aviv* 19 (1992), pp. 201-220.

[496] Braudel (1966), note 493, p. 323.

[497] The cultural division between hill country and flatlands as a division between the plains adjoining the coastline and regions more remote from the sea, rather than mountainous regions, though the hilly terrain reinforces these differences. It should be noted that this feature is valid today as well. Thus, for instance, there is a difference in mindset between the inhabitants of metropolitan Tel Aviv and those of the Jerusalem area. It is indisputable that the relationship of the inhabitants of the Jerusalem area to religion is deeper and broader than that of the inhabitants of metropolitan Tel Aviv, which is identified as a clearly secular region. Many of the inhabitants of the Tel Aviv area feel no deep ties with the hill country in general, and with Jerusalem in particular. Despite the short distance between Tel Aviv and Jerusalem (less than an hour's travel), many inhabitants of metropolitan Tel Aviv do not usually visit Jerusalem. This is also true of the USA. The regions adjoining the eastern and western coastlines are considered more politically liberal (generally Democratic), while in the internal areas of the United States the inhabitants are more conservative and more religious, as, for example, in the Bible Belt (generally Republican).

[498] William G. Dever, "New Vistas on the EBIV (MBI) Horizon in Syria-Palestine", *BASOR* 237 (1980), pp. 35-64.

Chapter 8

[499] Yosef Garfinkel and Saar Ganor, "Horvat Qeiyafa-a Fortified City on the Philistia-Judah Border in the Early Iron II," in New Studies in the Archaeology of Jerusalem and its Region, Collected Papers, vol. 2, ed. D. Amit and G.D. Stiebel, G.D. (Jerusalem: Israel Antiquities Authority and the Hebrew University, 2008), 122-33 [Hebrew]; idem, "Excavations at Khirbet Qeiyafa and the End of the "Low Chronology" (35th Archeological Congress in Israel, April 2009), 4-5.

[500] Shlomo Bunimovitz and Zvi Lederman, "Jerusalem and Bet Shemesh: Between a Capital and Its Border," in New Studies on Jerusalem, vol 10, ed. Eyal Baruch and Avraham Faust (2004), 37-50 [Hebrew].

[501] For a group of references, see Aren M. Maeir et al. "A Late Iron Age I/early Iron Age IIA Old Canaanite Inscription from Tel es-Safi/Gath, Israel: Palaeography, Dating, and Historical-Cultural Significance," BASOR 351 (2008): 39-71.

Appendix

[502] This is based on the book by Dr. Yohanan Levi of the Hebrew University, *Olamot Nifgashim* (Worlds Meet), published by Mossad Bialik (1969), p. 60. See also: *Procopius*, with an English Translation by H.B. Dewing, Vol. II, *History of the Wars*, Books III and IV, London (1953), p. 289.

[503] Unlike Yohanan Levi, Dewing translates: "two columns made of white stone." This small difference is significant, for the use of marble – a metamorphic rock, according to geological terminology – was common from the Roman period on. This rock is of limited geographical distribution and is difficult to process. "A white rock" might well be simple chalk rock, the use of which was widespread as early as the Biblical period.

[504] Ibid., note 52.

[505] Ibid. p. 71.

INDEX